'For those of us who have to live with terrorism, when we leave home in the morning there is no guarantee that we will come back.' Thus Lakshman Kadirgamar, Sri Lanka's Foreign Minister in 1994–2001 and 2004–5, foreshadowed his own assassination in 2005. He was an astute and brave thinker and practitioner on many key issues in international politics. Long before 9/11 he warned Western democracies that they were too passive about the activities on their soil of foreign terrorist movements and their front organizations. He was a strong advocate of democracy and human rights, conducting the first-ever Amnesty International investigation into the problems of a particular country – Vietnam. He was uniquely effective in countering the propaganda campaigns of the separatist Tamil Tigers in his native Sri Lanka – the movement which ultimately took his life. This definitive work explores the continuing relevance of his ideas for the modern world. *Democracy, Sovereignty and Terror* presents Kadirgamar's distinctive voice in his major speeches. It also offers a convincing picture, by those who knew him, of a scholar-statesman who was both a realist and an idealist. He showed that these approaches can be combined in both thought and action.

DEMOCRACY, SOVEREIGNTY AND TERROR

LAKSHMAN KADIRGAMAR
ON THE FOUNDATIONS OF
INTERNATIONAL ORDER

Edited by
Sir Adam Roberts

I.B. TAURIS
LONDON · NEW YORK

Published in 2012 by I.B.Tauris & Co Ltd
6 Salem Road, London W2 4BU
175 Fifth Avenue, New York NY 10010
www.ibtauris.com

Distributed in the United States and Canada Exclusively by Palgrave Macmillan
175 Fifth Avenue, New York NY 10010

Copyright © 2012 the various contributors and Suganthie Kadirgamar

Copyright Editorial Selection and Preface © 2012 Adam Roberts

Copyright Individual Chapters © Peter Burleigh, Shaun Donnelly, Leonard Hoffmann, Karl Inderfurth, Suganthie Kadirgamar, Shivshankar Menon, Chris Patten, Nirupama Rao, Sinha Ratnatunga, Adam Roberts and Sarath Silva

The right of Adam Roberts to be identified as the editor of this work has been asserted by him in accordance with the Copyright, Designs and Patents Act 1988.

All rights reserved. Except for brief quotations in a review, this book, or any part thereof, may not be reproduced, stored in or introduced into a retrieval system, or transmitted, in any form or by any means, electronic, mechanical, photocopying, recording or otherwise, without the prior written permission of the publisher.

International Library of Political Studies 41

ISBN: 978 1 84885 307 2

A full CIP record for this book is available from the British Library
A full CIP record is available from the Library of Congress

Library of Congress Catalog Card Number: available

Printed and bound by CPI Group (UK) Ltd, Croydon, CR0 4YY

Contents

Foreword by Leonard Hoffmann	vii
Preface and Acknowledgements	xi
List of Illustrations	xv
List of Maps	xvi
List of Contributors	xvii

PART I: APPRAISALS

1. 'Dare the Deepening Tide': Lakshman Kadirgamar on the Revolution of our Times — 3
   Adam Roberts

2. Sketch of the Life of Lakshman Kadirgamar — 37
   Sarath N. Silva

3. Lakshman Kadirgamar: The Lawyer Turned Politician — 41
   Sinha Ratnatunga

4. A Duty of Service in an Age of Terror — 61
   Chris Patten

5. Reflections on a 'Citizen of the World' — 69
   Karl F. Inderfurth, A. Peter Burleigh and Shaun Donnelly

6. A True South Asian — 81
   Shivshankar Menon and Nirupama Rao

PART II: DOCUMENTS

1. Report to Amnesty International on my Visit to South Vietnam — 89
   Colombo, 1 January 1964

2. Why I Decided to Enter Politics — 107
   Colombo, July 1994

3. Human Rights and Armed Conflict — 111
   Kotelawala Defence Academy, 19 March 1996

4. The Global Impact of International Terrorism   121
   Chatham House, London, 15 April 1998

5. The Terrorism Challenge to Democracies   137
   *Potomac Institute for Policy Studies, Washington DC,
   13 September 2000*

6. Preventing the Recurrence of Harm
   to War-affected Children   151
   Winnipeg, 16 September 2000

7. Address to UN General Assembly   157
   New York, 18 September 2000

8. The Seven Sisters of South Asia: Where are they Going?   169
   *Tenth Lal Bahadur Shastri Memorial Lecture,
   New Delhi, 11 January 2003*

9. Flaws in the 2002 Ceasefire Agreement   193
   *Speech from the opposition, Parliament,
   Colombo, 8 May 2003*

10. Third World Democracy in Action:
    The Sri Lanka Experience   207
    Brookings Institution, Washington DC, 12 May 2004

11. The Peaceful Ascendancy of China:
    A South Asian Perspective   223
    *China Institute of International Studies,
    Beijing, 28 December 2004*

Notes   237
Index   255

Foreword

Lakshman Kadirgamar was a truly remarkable person whose achievements as a sportsman, international lawyer and statesman were all outstanding. I got to know him when we were both studying law at Oxford University. Coming from Ceylon and South Africa respectively, we had one unusual legal interest in common: the Roman–Dutch system of law, which had an odd after-life in our two countries even after it had been replaced in the Netherlands.

A word of explanation may be needed. The Dutch colonies of Ceylon and the Cape of Good Hope were occupied by the British early in the Napoleonic Wars, a few years before the Netherlands itself replaced its Roman–Dutch common law with a version of the Code Napoleon. The British rule that the laws of a conquered territory remain unchanged meant that the Roman–Dutch law survived, and continues to survive, in Sri Lanka and South Africa. It was this somewhat esoteric legal background, as well as our colonial origins, which Lakshman Kadirgamar and I shared when we came to Oxford in the mid-1950s. We met occasionally, although I saw rather more of his countryman Lalith Athulathmudali, who was reading, as I was, for a general degree in Jurisprudence, whereas Lakshman was engaged in the more solitary task of writing a thesis on the Roman–Dutch law of easements. He focused on the law of not only his native country, Ceylon, but also my native country, South Africa.

There was then a considerable gap until Lakshman as foreign minister, passing through London, picked up the acquaintanceship by occasionally asking me to a drink or dinner at the Sri Lanka High Commission. Our conversations were relaxed, between people with much in common, including Amnesty International. Lakshman had been the first person to have done an investigation into a country for Amnesty, which he did in South Vietnam 1963–4: the resulting report is reproduced in this book. At our meetings in London over 30 years later I knew that I was remote from the practical application of our liberal principles while Lakshman's were being daily tested by the hideous realities of terrorism in Sri Lanka.

It was only when I read the essays and speeches collected in this volume that I realized the full extent of Lakshman's talents and achievements. Quite apart from their content, they show that he was master of powerful English prose; clear, virile, succinct. The quotations from familiar literature are apt and often unacknowledged, paying the listener the compliment of assuming that no laboured attribution is required. (I particularly liked the reference to Thucydides Book 5 in his Shastri Memorial Lecture.) But the most impressive feature is of course their prescience and realism about terrorism: its international character and its effect upon an open democracy. On 18 September 2000 Lakshman said to the United Nations General Assembly:

> A democratic state, because of its openness, its laws, traditions and practices, and its commitment to tolerance and dissent, is especially vulnerable to the deployment of force against it by any group within its boundaries. An internal armed challenge to any state anywhere is a challenge to all states everywhere. Unless all states, democratic states in particular, agree to come to the aid of a state in such peril, democracy itself will be imperilled everywhere. Democracy will not survive.
>
> When the security and integrity of one state is threatened by an armed group within it, surely – especially in these contemporary times, with the Cold War far behind us – it behoves all other states to deny that armed group any encouragement, any succour, any safe haven. Today, for the prosecution of terrorist activities in one country, massive funds are raised with impunity in other countries, often through knowing or unknowing front organizations or other entities that now proliferate in many forms and in many countries – often, sadly, in the guise of charitable groups or groups ostensibly concerned with human rights or ethnic, cultural or social matters.

When Lakshman made this speech, he naturally had in mind the funds being raised for the Liberation Tigers of Tamil Eelam (LTTE) from the Tamil diaspora in North America and Europe. A year later came 9/11, funded with money raised largely in Saudi Arabia. Suddenly the United States and Europe had brought home to them the plain truth of what Lakshman had been saying. Draconian UN resolutions about the funding of terrorism were passed. Already in 1997, thanks largely to Lakshman's tireless advocacy, the United States had included the LTTE in a list of bodies designated as terrorist groups, thus assisting a process of limiting its sources of funds. Then in February 2001 the UK proscribed the LTTE and 20 other organizations. Other countries followed suit later – some only after Lakshman's assassination, though he had laid the groundwork earlier.

Often, at those international conferences in the 1990s, Lakshman must have thought himself a voice in the wilderness. And in the end, the inaction of the 'international community' in those years probably cost him his life. If governments had listened to Lakshman's consistent pleas earlier, and had curtailed the LTTE's fund-raising, the LTTE would not have been so strong and well armed; and recruitment of members to the terrorist organization would have been difficult. But at the same time his very effectiveness in getting the international community to wake up to LTTE activities added to the hazard of his position. He knew very well the risks he ran by his brave public stance, and he was prepared to pay the price, as he ultimately did in August 2005.

Lakshman achieved much for Sri Lanka, especially in winning respect for it during his time as foreign minister, and in getting the international community to act against the LTTE's international activities. We should all be grateful to Professor Roberts for producing this volume not just to keep his memory alive, but to give an account of Lakshman's coherent world view, a key part of which was his deeply serious attempt to indicate how terrorism could be tackled without undermining key principles of democracy, sovereignty, human rights and observance of the law of armed conflict.

Lord Hoffmann

Preface and Acknowledgements

I first came across Lakshman Kadirgamar in 1964. I was interested in the Buddhist-led campaign of civil resistance in South Vietnam in 1963 which had resulted in the deposition of the autocratic President Ngo Dinh Diem. While these events were unfolding, Kadirgamar, a young Sri Lankan lawyer widely respected for his abilities, had been asked to investigate the treatment of Buddhists in South Vietnam, becoming in the process the first person ever to conduct a formal investigation in a country on behalf of Amnesty International. I wanted to get hold of his report, so I wrote him a letter and with his help obtained a copy.

About four decades later, when I was Professor of International Relations at Oxford University and a Fellow of Balliol College, I discovered belatedly that Kadirgamar, by now Foreign Minister of Sri Lanka, was a former student of the college (1956–9) and, indeed, a former President of the Oxford Union. So our old correspondence was renewed. Shortly thereafter, in 2004, he was elected an Honorary Fellow of the College and came back to it on two occasions. I found him intelligent, interesting, hard-working and above all brave. He knew that, as the most prominent Tamil in the Sri Lankan government, he was a target of the separatist Tamil Tigers, and had clearly decided that if he was to be killed it would be with his head held high.

In March 2005, when I was visiting the region, I went to Sri Lanka at his invitation to give some lectures. My wife Prinkie and I saw him in action in Colombo with students, colleagues and at well-attended meetings, and we spent an evening with him and his wife Suganthie at their official residence. We also saw the extraordinary security measures to protect him from the inevitable. Hating to be so constrained, he would stop to chat when the security officials wanted to whisk him into the bullet-proof car. In August that year the security arrangements failed. A marksman, firing from a house overlooking his private residence, killed him after he came out of his open-air pool where he had been taking an evening swim.

We got on for some simple reasons. The most obvious is that we agreed about a lot beside the Buddhist campaign in South Vietnam. We shared an interest in international organizations: in both cases it was cautious, and was combined with a belief that the sovereign state is not about to disappear. We both recognized the virtues of democracy as a form of government, but were critical of spreading it at gunpoint. We had both written extensively about terrorism. On one occasion in my room in Balliol he asked me what the best analysis of suicide bombers was: when I dug out what I considered the most incisive study of that dismal topic, he could not wait to read it, and we went together to the college's copying room. I appreciated his enthusiasm for academic analysis – in my experience it was unusual among foreign ministers. I admired his principled opposition to bribery and corruption. But even more I liked his energy, wit, warmth and courage.

I conceived the idea for this book in the months following his assassination. It has no claims to being a biography, but it does offer a series of accounts of the man, his work and his ideas. I have prepared it because I found his work interesting and deserving of a wider audience. I was particularly intrigued by the way in which he combined consistent toughness against terrorism with a belief in respect for the sovereignty of states – a position very different from that of the US and UK in the 'war on terror' from 2001 onwards. Does Kadirgamar's position make sense? This book seeks to provide answers, but you must decide for yourself.

The first part of this book consists of appraisals by people who knew Kadirgamar and his work. He would not have wanted a hagiographical work. I have encouraged the contributors to be frank about his flaws and failures as well as his achievements. The contributors all knew him personally, and saw him from very different vantage points. The picture that emerges is, I believe, true to the man.

The documents, which form the main part of this book, comprise a small selection of his many speeches, lectures and reports. After inspecting a large number of them, mainly in Colombo, I chose those which best represented the various subjects in the politics and international relations of his time on which he had a distinctive contribution.

A word is needed about the sources for the texts of his speeches that I have used. I have not listed them separately for each document. In most cases there was more than one source for the same speech or statement: typically his original text (and sometimes more than one version of that), which I obtained from the Kadirgamar papers in Colombo; and a full transcript of what he said, often provided by the host organization. These materials show that he often made revisions, cuts and additions up to the last moment. I have generally accepted these changes, but where there was some gap, error or lack of clarity in the transcript I checked his original draft, using it as a basis for corrections.

I have edited the documents with a light touch, letting his words speak for themselves with the minimum of interruption. At the risk of allowing some overlap between documents, the only cuts I have made are of purely formal text such as his thanks to the chair, a few minor repetitions and his uses of such phrases as 'ladies and gentlemen'. I have followed the publishers' style rules in a range of minor matters, such as changing his lawyerly capital 'S' for 'State' into lower case, and shortening 'United Nations' to 'UN'.

All that I have added to the documents are (1) the prefatory notes indicating the context in which each speech was given; (2) the subheadings, to make the texts easier to navigate – only the 1964 Amnesty report had subheadings in the original; and (3) the endnotes, to provide information about people, parties, events and sources that might not be familiar to the reader. I take full responsibility for all these notes in the documents and for any errors in them: their wording is emphatically mine, not Lakshman's.

Where he quotes from a speech, treaty, article etc., I have generally been able to locate the source and provide an endnote reference to it. In a few cases I have made very minor corrections to the quotations in his text so that they conform to the original source of the quote: none of these significantly affects the meaning. As I was confident they would be when I embarked on this work, his references to facts, laws, court cases, writers and so on were accurate and well-sourced – which is remarkable from someone so busy in international public life.

******

In preparing this book I had significant help from many people. First and foremost I thank Lakshman's widow, Suganthie Kadirgamar. An experienced lawyer in her own right, she provided me with the texts of many of Lakshman's papers, she encouraged me to continue with the project and she dealt with my numerous queries. When I revisited Sri Lanka in 2006 she welcomed me to her home, let me look through an array of his papers, and introduced me to many of Lakshman's friends and colleagues.

I also thank the many other Sri Lankans who provided excellent guidance. It is invidious to name names, but perhaps I can be forgiven for giving particular thanks to two of that younger generation of diplomats for whom Lakshman ensured a high standard of professional training: Mahishini Colonné and Kulatilaka Lenagala, who worked closely with Kadirgamar in the Ministry of Foreign Affairs and are now Deputy High Commissioners of Sri Lanka in India and the UK respectively, provided prompt and thoughtful responses to my many queries. In addition, after enquiries elsewhere had failed, Sanjaya Colonné, Strategic Affairs Adviser to the Ministry of Defence, provided hard-to-obtain maps relating to the conflict in Sri Lanka.

Finally, I thank all those in the UK who assisted. At Oxford, Anna Sander, the Lonsdale Curator at Balliol College's newly-opened Historic Collections Centre, unearthed valuable material from Lakshman's time as a graduate student. The Oxfordshire Record Office, which holds the Oxford Union Society's archives, was notably helpful in digging out material about his time as President of the Union. The Bodleian Library in Oxford, and

British Library in London, came up trumps with exceptionally rare publications recording Lakshman's early achievements. At the British Academy, Kiare Ladner retyped some of the documents that I had only in paper form. My wife Prinkie helped crucially with proof-reading successive texts and transcripts: we had visited Sri Lanka together in March 2005 – the last time that either of us saw Lakshman. And at I.B.Tauris I thank particularly Iradj Bagherzade and Lester Crook, who were wonderfully consistent in their support for this project. Lester Crook's doctoral thesis at Birkbeck College, London, in 1969 was on 'The Colonial Office and political problems in Ceylon and Mauritius 1907–21': he knows more about Sri Lanka's history than I ever will.

Balliol College had an important place in Lakshman's stellar career and in his affections, so proceeds from this book will go to Balliol, with the aim of assisting students from Asia, and in particular South Asia, to study at Oxford.

AR, Oxford, June 2012

List of Illustrations

1. In hurdles race at Police Park, Colombo, 1948.
2. Running in the 110 m hurdles in Indian Inter-University Games, Bangalore, 1952.
3. Runners symbolizing unity of the peoples of Ceylon – at the Colombo Exhibition, 23 February 1952.
4. Oxford Union Standing Committee, Trinity Term 1958.
5. Result of the poll for the post of President of the Oxford Union, 28 November 1958.
6. Oxford Union Standing Committee, Hilary Term 1959.
7. Oxford Union order paper 22 October 1959, listing Kadirgamar as opposing the motion 'That Democracy is unsuitable for the underdeveloped Nations of the World'.
8. Kadirgamar on his appointment as foreign minister, 1994.
9. With Kofi Annan and Suganthie Kadirgamar, during the UN General Assembly session September/October 1997.
10. With US Secretary of State Madeleine Albright, New York, shortly before the US proscription of the LTTE on 2 October 1997.
11. With Nelson Mandela and Chandrika Kumaratunga, during the Commonwealth Heads of Government Meeting in Edinburgh, 24–27 October 1997.
12. With Hilary Clinton and Suganthie Kadirgamar, at the White House, Washington DC, 29 October 1997.
13. With Manmohan Singh, Prime Minister of India, New Delhi, May 2004.
14. With Chandrika Kumaratunga and Colin Powell, Colombo, 7 January 2005.
15. With Chris Patten at unveiling of Kadirgamar's portrait at the Oxford Union, 18 March 2005.
16. With Nirupama Rao, at his last official function, 12 August 2005, hours before his assassination.

List of Maps

1. Distribution of the ethnic groups in Sri Lanka, based on the 1981 census, p. xix.
2. Sri Lanka, province and district boundaries, p. xx.
3. Areas controlled by the LTTE following the Ceasefire Agreement of 22 February 2002, p. xxi.
4. Approximate areas controlled by the LTTE and the Government of Sri Lanka (GOSL) as of late 2005, p xxii.

List of Contributors

A. Peter Burleigh served twice in Sri Lanka, as US Ambassador from 1995 to 1997, and as a junior officer from 1968 to 1970. Though he retired from government diplomatic service in 2000, he was recalled to serve in 2011–12 as US Chargé d'Affaires in New Delhi.

Shaun Donnelly, a career diplomat for 36 years in the US Foreign Service, served as US Ambassador to Sri Lanka in 1997–2000. He was later Principal Deputy Assistant Secretary of State for Economic and Business Affairs and Assistant US Trade Representative (at the White House) for the Middle East and Europe. After retiring from the government, he was an executive at two large US business associations.

Leonard Hoffmann (Baron Hoffmann of Chedworth) was a Judge of the High Court of Justice, Chancery Division, in 1985–92, Lord Justice of Appeal, 1992–5, and Lord of Appeal in Ordinary, 1995–2009. From 1990 he served as unpaid director of the Amnesty International Charity Ltd – the charity wing of Amnesty. He has held a number of academic posts, and since 2009 has been Honorary Professor of Intellectual Property Law, Queen Mary, University of London.

Karl F. Inderfurth served as Assistant Secretary of State for South Asian Affairs from 1997 to 2001. He is currently Senior Advisor and Wadhwani Chair in US–India Policy Studies at the Center for Strategic and International Studies (CSIS) in Washington DC. Prior to his CSIS appointment, he was the John O. Rankin Professor of the Practice of International Affairs at George Washington University. From 1993 to 1997 he served as the US Representative for Special Political Affairs to the United Nations, with the rank of ambassador.

Shivshankar Menon has been National Security Adviser to the Prime Minister of India since January 2010. He had previously served as High Commissioner to Sri Lanka (1997–2000), to Pakistan (2003–6) and as Ambassador to Israel (1995–7) and China (2000–03). He was also Foreign Secretary (head of the Indian Foreign Service) in 2006–09.

Chris Patten (Baron Patten of Barnes) has been Chancellor of Oxford University since 2003. He has been Co-Chair of the International Crisis Group since 2004. He is also, since 2011, Chairman of the BBC Trust. He was

European Commissioner for External Relations, 2000–04. His books include *East and West* (Macmillan, London, 1998); *Not Quite the Diplomat: Home Truths About World Affairs* (Allen Lane, London, 2005); and *What Next? Surviving the 21st Century* (Allen Lane, London, 2008).

Nirupama Rao is India's ambassador to the USA. Having joined the Indian Foreign Service in 1973, she served as High Commissioner of India to Sri Lanka in 2004–06, and then as Ambassador to China in 2006–09. She was appointed Foreign Secretary (head of the Indian Foreign Service) on 1 August 2009. In 2001–02 she was the spokesperson of the Ministry of External Affairs at its headquarters in New Delhi. She has also served in the Indian embassies in Moscow and Washington DC. A collection of her poems, *Rain Rising*, was published in India in 2004.

Sinha Ratnatunga has been Editor of *The Sunday Times*, Colombo, since 1990. He is a director of the Sri Lanka Press Institute; the Sri Lanka College of Journalism; and the World Association of Newspapers and News Publishers (WAN-IFRA) based in Paris and Darmstadt. He is the author of *Politics of Terrorism: The Sri Lanka Experience* (International Fellowship for Social and Economic Development, Canberra, 1988). He is also an Attorney-at-Law with a special interest in intellectual property law.

Adam Roberts has been President of the British Academy since 2009. He is Emeritus Professor of International Relations, Oxford University; and Emeritus Fellow of Balliol College, Oxford. His books include *Nations in Arms: The Theory and Practice of Territorial Defence* (Chatto & Windus, London, 1976); and as joint editor, *The United Nations Security Council and War: The Evolution of Thought and Practice since 1945* (Oxford University Press, 2008).

Sarath N. Silva was Chief Justice of the Supreme Court of Sri Lanka from 1999 to 2009. He was first appointed to the Supreme Court in 1995. In 1996 he was appointed a President's Counsel. In 1996–9 he served as Attorney-General of Sri Lanka. His primary and secondary school education was at Trinity College, Kandy.

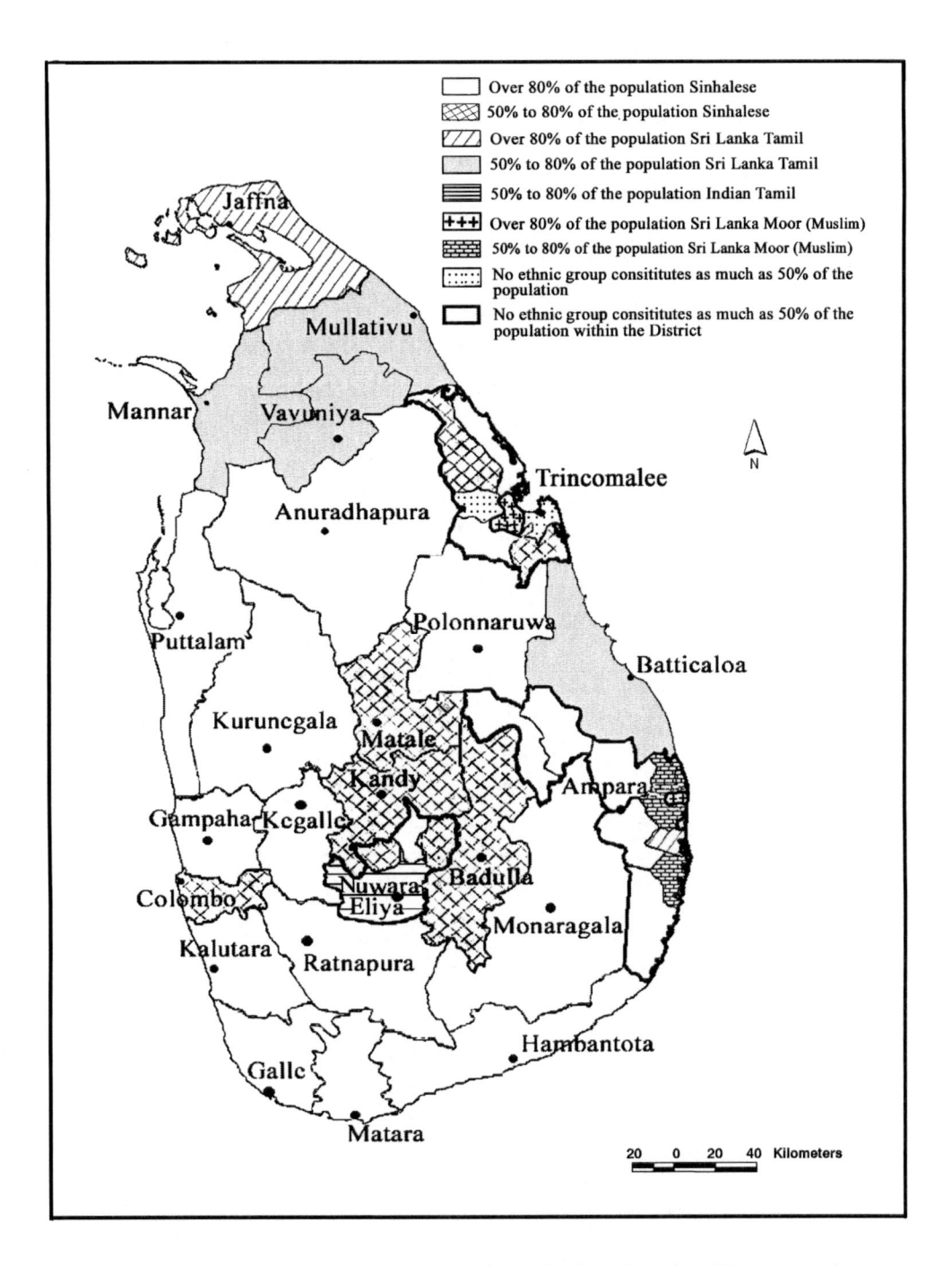

Map 1: Distribution of the ethnic groups in Sri Lanka, based on the 1981 census – the last to be conducted in all districts of the country. Significant changes since then are not reflected in this map. Prepared by the Department of Geography, University of Colombo.

Map 2: Sri Lanka, province and district boundaries. Prepared by the Survey Department of Sri Lanka.

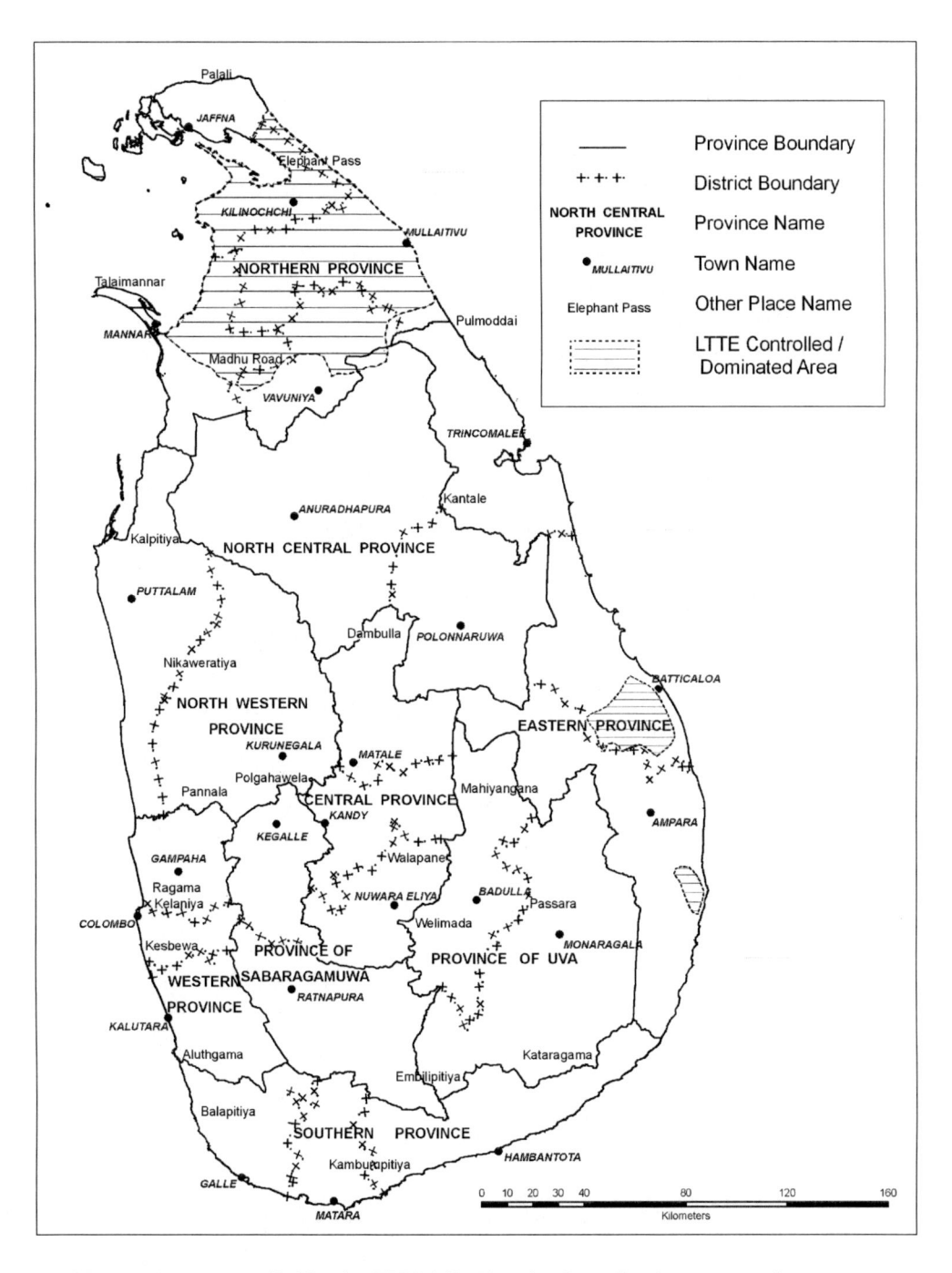

Map 3: Areas controlled by the LTTE following the Ceasefire Agreement of 22 February 2002. There were numerous breaches of the ceasefire. In May 2003 Kadirgamar criticised it strongly; and the government formally renounced it on 3 January 2008. Prepared by the Survey Department of Sri Lanka and adapted by the Ministry of Defence, Sri Lanka.

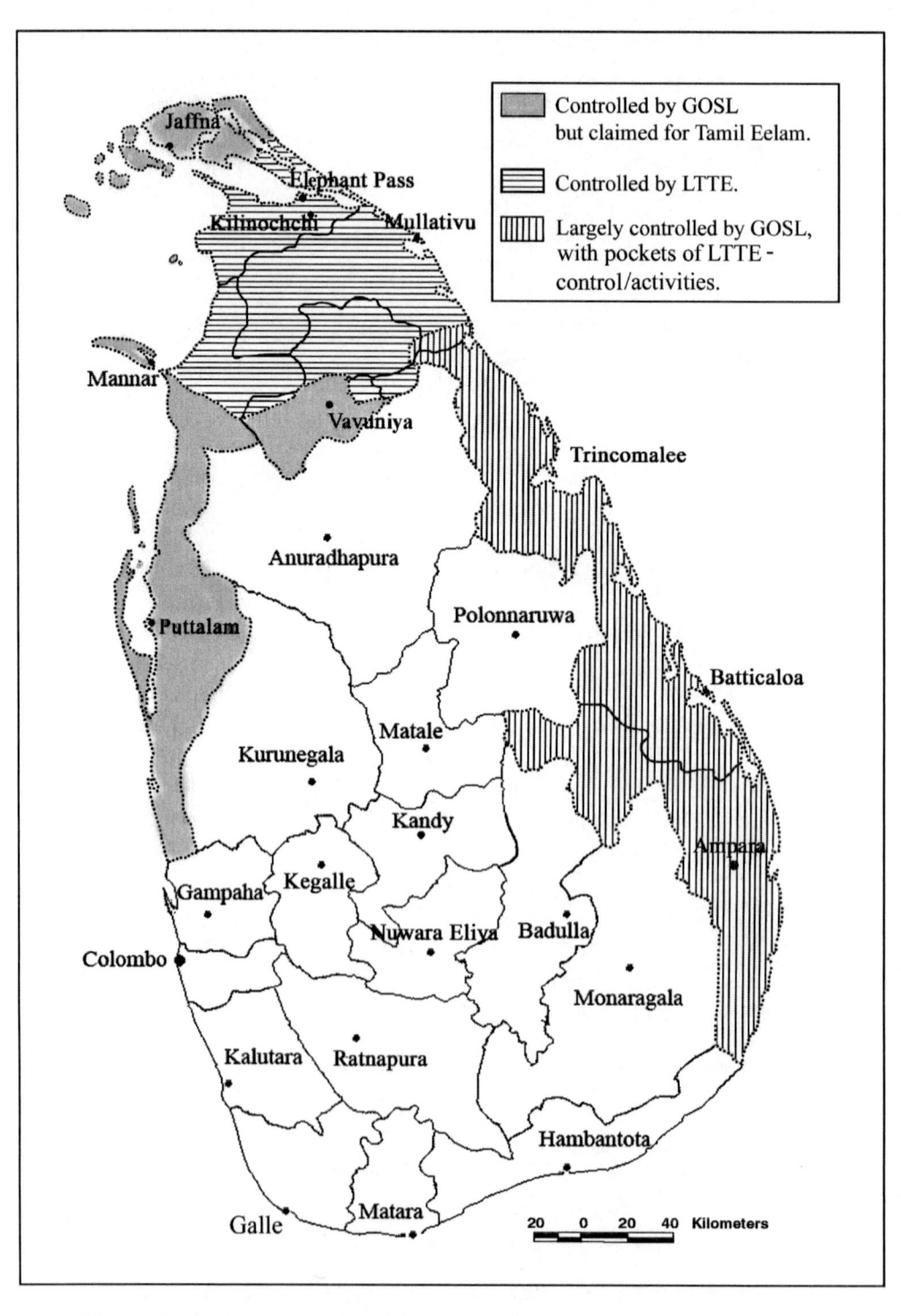

Map 4: Approximate areas controlled by the LTTE and the Government of Sri Lanka (GOSL) as of late 2005. Organizations supporting the creation of a Tamil state claimed all the areas shown in shading. Prepared by the Office of Strategic Affairs, Ministry of Defence, Sri Lanka.

PART I
Appraisals

CHAPTER 1

'Dare the Deepening Tide'
Lakshman Kadirgamar on the Revolution of our Times

Adam Roberts

The life of Lakshman Kadirgamar is symbolic of the great revolution of our times – the end of the old European colonial empires. Born in Ceylon under British colonial rule, he exemplified the hopes, the difficulties, the successes and the tragedies of the decolonization process. He had unusually clear views about the many difficult issues – both domestic and international – faced by post-colonial states: their changing constitutional arrangements, their economic development, the relations of their different communities, their vulnerability to corruption and political violence, their search for friends and allies, and their need for a strong framework of international norms and institutions.

Lakshman was just 15 years old when, on 4 February 1948, the state of Ceylon (since 1972, Sri Lanka) achieved its independence in a ceremony in Torrington Square, Colombo – subsequently renamed Independence Square. In the years that followed, as a brilliant athlete and as a representative of the country's Tamil minority, he took part in at least one prominent relay-running ceremony celebrating the country's independence and the unity of its peoples. Some accounts of this participation are probably myth.[1] However, the factual record is remarkable enough to need no embellishment. On 23 February 1952, the opening day of the Colombo Exhibition, Lakshman was one of four celebrated athletes who, at the final stage of four long relay runs from distant parts of Sri Lanka, carried respectively scrolls in Sinhala, Tamil, Arabic and English to four young ladies representing the major communities of the country.[2] This exhibition was closely tied to the ambitious economic development aims that had been proclaimed in 1950 in the Colombo Plan.[3] Lakshman's run was at once symbolic of his role as a Tamil, his commitment to inter-communal solidarity and his faith in the alluring prospect of an international wave of development of which his newly-independent country would be part. In short, this run by young athletes was a symbol of the hopes of a new and better post-colonial order.

Over half a century later, on 15 August 2005, it was again in Colombo, in Independence Square, that the assassinated minister was cremated. He was a victim of the political failures, communal divisions and systematic terrorism which he had consistently sought to tackle, showing extraordinary intellectual and physical courage as he did so. His journey from celebrations so symbolic of Sri Lanka's unity to a cremation so symbolic of its subsequent troubles is an exploration of the problems of the post-colonial age – not just those of his country and his times, but also those of our world and our times in the second decade of the twenty-first century.

Lakshman Kadirgamar is most widely remembered as a remarkably successful foreign minister of Sri Lanka in 1994–2001 and from 2004 until his assassination on 12 August 2005. He worked skilfully and steadfastly to achieve three inter-related objectives. The first was to secure good, even close, relations simultaneously with a range of countries that mattered deeply, if in very different ways, to Sri Lanka: these included China, India, Pakistan, Russia, the United Kingdom and the United States. The second was to engage Sri Lanka in support of international organizations and international norms: he was especially concerned to ensure that his country could stand tall in international fora, and could be clearly identified as supporting the rule of law, human rights and prohibition of the use of child soldiers. The third was securing the international isolation of the Liberation Tigers of Tamil Eelam (LTTE), usually known simply as the Tamil Tigers, with which the government of Sri Lanka had been in conflict since 1983. None of these three objectives was wholly new for Sri Lanka, and he never claimed that they were. However, in his periods of office the governments of which he was a member achieved more on all three fronts than their predecessors.

There is a strong tradition that 'the Head of Government in Sri Lanka has had his or her personal style and personal influence on foreign policy decision-making.'[4] Since the time of J. R. Jayewardene, Sri Lanka's first Executive President (1978–89), it has been the president, not the prime minister, who as head of government has the main executive authority.[5] Lakshman worked closely with Chandrika Kumaratunga, President of Sri Lanka from November 1994 to November 2005. However, as foreign minister he was more involved in actually making foreign policy than most of his predecessors had been; and in a difficult period for Sri Lanka, riven by internal conflict, he greatly improved the country's international position. On 12 August 2005 he was killed by the Tamil Tigers, as he was pretty sure he would be, but his achievements did not die with him. The diplomatic isolation of the Tamil Tigers, that he had worked so skilfully to achieve, helped to pave the way for their eventual, and controversy-ridden, military defeat in 2009.

On the central issue facing the government of Sri Lanka in his time and subsequently, he had a distinctive and clear view. He came to realize, more than many of his colleagues in Sri Lankan public life, that achieving peace with the Tamil Tigers was almost impossible. At the same time, he placed great emphasis on the need to wage the struggle in a manner acceptable to international opinion and consistent with the laws of war. And in the aftermath of the conflict he would certainly have worked to help achieve a magnanimous settlement taking into account the rights of minorities.

His was a remarkable record by any standard, and especially for a man who first became a member of parliament, and foreign minister, at the late age of 62, having previously had a very different career as a lawyer and as a senior official of the World Intellectual Property Organization (WIPO) in Geneva. The chapters in this book by people who knew him bear impressive witness to the extraordinary effectiveness of his public service from 1994 to 2005, and to the personal qualities and principles that were a key part of his achievement.

Yet this book is not written to bolster claims about Lakshman's success. This is not only for the obvious reason – that there were inevitably failures as well as successes – but also because, especially in politics, success is always a great deceiver. The events in which he was involved – deeply controversial anyway – may come to be viewed differently as times change and history moves on. Rather this book seeks to present Lakshman's thought as part of a coherent world-view that has strong claims on our attention today.

As foreign minister, he was deeply concerned with advancing a well thought-out view of that series of complex and often contradictory processes that constitute the international relations of our times. He attached great importance to his speeches on the subject, putting much personal work into their preparation. However, his work was not confined to his own speeches, nor to the usual duties of a foreign minister – extensive and intensive as these were. He felt that with its rich heritage Sri Lanka should give the world, as he put it, 'something more than just tea, tourism and terrorism'. He had extraordinarily wide interests, not least in the music, theatre and arts of both East and West. It was typical of him that he chaired a committee to assist in the preparation and publication of a stunning work about a fine Sri Lankan artist, Stanley Kirinde, spending much time coaxing potential donors and encouraging its author.[6] The book was launched in Colombo on 18 August 2005, just six days after Lakshman's assassination, amid many tributes to his role in the project.

He also made strenuous efforts to develop Sri Lankan expertise in international relations. He took steps to ensure that recruits for Sri Lanka's diplomatic service were chosen purely on merit, and he improved their training. His stint as foreign minister is considered a golden era, in which a previously disparate and ineffective group of diplomats was given punch and purpose – and were at last able to put up considerable resistance to LTTE propaganda work.

These efforts continued to the very end of his life. By a tragic irony, the day of Kadirgamar's assassination was also the day on which he fulfilled a long-held ambition by launching a new journal, *International Relations in a Globalising World*, of which he was editor-in-chief.[7] He had discussed the project with me at his official residence in Colombo earlier that year, inveigling me into writing an article for it. He told me how he saw the journal as central to his ambition to develop Sri Lanka's depth of expertise in world politics. In launching the journal at a ceremony in Colombo on 12 August 2005 he said: 'It is a great day of joy and achievement.' He indicated that the discipline of international relations had expanded to such levels that any conceivable topic had bearing on it. He said the journal was his dream and he decided to take a plunge into the deep end when some had raised doubts as to the viability of the project.[8] Within a few hours of this moment of joy and achievement he was assassinated. Although the LTTE issued a statement denying its involvement, it is widely believed that it was responsible.[9] As with many murders attributed to the LTTE, the investigators at the time were unable to capture the assassins, who were believed to have fled to LTTE-controlled areas. In 2008 six persons were indicted in connection with his killing. The first name on the list was Velupillai Prabhakaran, leader of the LTTE. He, along with three of the others indicted, was subsequently killed in the conflict. The two remaining indicted persons were held in custody and then tried in 2009–12 in connection with the assassination.

Twenty-first Century International Order

This chapter embarks upon, and the rest of the book continues, an exploration of Lakshman's understanding of international relations. As he was only too well aware, international order today rests on foundations which, while not wholly new, contain some new elements. The problems with which he grappled continuously as foreign minister were problems that are all too typical of the late twentieth and early twenty-first century. In particular:

1. It is conflict within states, not war between them, that poses the greatest problems in the everyday lives of millions of people, and in the conduct of international relations. Such conflict – which has taken many forms, from *coups d'état* to civil wars – is a reflection of difficulties inherent

in the process of creating, in the wake of empires of various kinds, states with legitimate governments, borders, constitutional arrangements and strategies for development. Ethnic and regional divisions within states often contribute to these difficulties.
2. Largely because of such difficulties, post-colonial states of the Third World have had to recognize that the threats faced by contemporary international society lie as much in their midst as they do in distant great powers and power blocks. In these circumstances the rhetoric of non-alignment, while by no means abandoned, is of reduced relevance.
3. Widespread unemployment and emigration exacerbate tendencies to view the state as illegitimate, and provide a basis for insurgencies and other challenges to the state. Diaspora communities sometimes become militantly opposed to the state from which they fled, thus contributing to its difficulties in establishing its legitimacy.
4. The capacity of outside powers to understand, and to take action regarding, conflicts within post-colonial states is distinctly limited, with ambitious attempts often resulting in humiliation.
5. Terrorism and the international struggle against it have become central preoccupations of many states. This has created new pressures for close cooperation between states. However, it has also raised difficult questions about whether, in pursuing the cause of countering terrorism, it is justifiable to invade and occupy sovereign states, and also to violate certain basic human rights, including freedom from torture.
6. The body of international law inherited from the last century is under pressure, and questions constantly arise about whether its fundamental rules, including the sovereignty of states, the laws of armed conflicts, and human rights rules, are capable of being implemented effectively today, especially in the context of internal conflicts and international terrorism.
7. Global international organizations, especially the United Nations, play a more important role in international politics than ever before, and are essential if global problems are to be tackled effectively. Yet their role is unavoidably limited, leaving a range of problems to be addressed at the level of individual states, or by other international bodies.
8. Regional groupings of states have sought to overcome some of the many problems – relating above all to economic issues and international security – resulting from the division of the world into sovereign states. Such groupings have made most progress in Europe, with the development of the European Union (EU), but are much less developed in other regions, including South Asia. Everywhere they have run into problems about the extent to which they can modify or even transcend the role of states.

9. Religions have a larger role in international politics than many advocates of secularism and modernization had anticipated: religious beliefs and organizations have been critically important in many positive developments, such as the civil resistance of the Buddhists in South Vietnam in 1963, as well as in exacerbating certain armed conflicts and terrorist campaigns.
10. New powers are emerging, raising the critical question of whether such a process can happen peacefully or must, as so often in the past, lead to war.
11. Multiparty democracy, the rule of law and respect for human rights are now the most widely accepted principles for the organization of human societies, yet they are far from being universally accepted or respected, and are hard to establish in some societies. Sometimes it is necessary for democratic states to have dealings, or even establish close relationships, with non-democratic regimes of various kinds.

In many speeches, especially in the years from 1994 to 2005, Kadirgamar addressed all of these enduring issues in international politics, and he did so in ways that were clear-sighted and articulate. Yet his position was not free of what critics would call contradictions, and others would more respectfully call creative tensions. He was a lifelong advocate of democracy, but at the same time consistently sought to maintain good relations with certain non-democratic states. He was a human rights advocate, and the first person in the world to conduct an Amnesty investigation in a country, but vigorously defended his own country despite many problems in its human rights record. He was a particularly strong and committed opponent of terrorism, but at the same time a critic of the idea that the cause of counter-terrorism justified military interventions in states and foreign occupations. He was a strong believer in the role of international organizations, but was concerned to keep the UN at arm's length from involvement in Sri Lanka's internal conflict. And he was a passionate believer in diplomatic solutions, but became the foremost critic of the 2002 Ceasefire Agreement – negotiated with Norwegian help, between the Sri Lanka government and the LTTE – because of specific flaws which he exposed forensically. The list could be extended, but its underlying core is clear: he embodied many of the apparent contradictions that any able and conscientious person must face when dealing with international politics. To put it all more simply, he was both an idealist and a realist, both a thinker and a man of action, and therefore much more interesting than those who can be tidily classified in only one of these categories.

All the chapters and documents in this book shed light on these key issues and on Kadirgamar's responses to them. In this introductory survey

I address four basic questions that arise from my knowledge of him and his work over a long period:

1. What were the personal beliefs and political convictions that sustained him in his career? And in particular, how did he see the role of religion and ethnic issues in public life?
2. How did his experience of school and university, in Sri Lanka and at Oxford, shape his world outlook?
3. How did his international calling evolve?
4. How coherent were his views on key issues in politics and international relations – about the role of democratic systems, the continuing validity of sovereignty, and the contributions of international law and organizations? And above all, how coherent was his view that terrorism had to be tackled within a framework of law? Or, put differently, is his amalgam of realism and idealism intellectually and politically defensible?

Inheritance: Religious and Ethnic Issues in Sri Lanka

Lakshman Kadirgamar was born in Colombo on 12 April 1932. The family, originally from the city of Jaffna, was Tamil – that is, part of the ethnic minority who inhabit many parts of Sri Lanka, especially the north. His forbears, like most Tamils, had been Hindus, but his grandfather had converted to Christianity, taking on the given name of Christian, and becoming the first Ceylonese Registrar-General of the Supreme Court. It was Christian Kadirgamar's son, Samuel, who established the family in Colombo, where he became the first President of the Law Society of Ceylon. He admired Mahatma Gandhi and presided over one of the many meetings attended by Gandhi during his visit to Ceylon in November 1927.[10] He married Edith Mather, whose father was a businessman. Lakshman was the youngest of their six children.

Religion

Sri Lanka has long experience of being multi-confessional. In the 1981 census – the last to be conducted in all 25 districts of the country – the population was about 15 million (today it is about 21 million). Of these, some 69 per cent of the population were Buddhists, 15 per cent were Hindu, 7 per cent Muslim and 7 per cent Christian.[11] Leaving on one side the question of whether Buddhism should be classified as a religion or a belief-system, Buddhists are in a clear majority.

While the Christian heritage was an important part of the Kadirgamar family life, Lakshman shared his father's respect for a range of religions and philosophies. In its application to Oxford on his behalf in 1958, the High

Commissioner for Ceylon identified Lakshman's religion as Anglican.[12] He himself, from his late teens onwards, did not generally categorize himself as a Christian. He had a close affinity to Buddhism that developed throughout his life. In 1999 Sri Lanka successfully proposed to the UN General Assembly that Vesak – the day which marks the birth, enlightenment and passing away of Lord Buddha – should be a day of observance at the UN.[13] As a colleague recalls, Kadirgamar's role 'from commencement to conclusion was of pivotal importance to all Sri Lankan endeavours, within and outside the UN over the preceding year and a half, to secure the adoption of the Vesak Resolution'.[14]

When Lakshman gave a lecture in Colombo in 1992 on the relevance of the Bible for our times, his impeccably scholarly approach revealed a remarkable mixture of scepticism and respect for all religions:

> Indeed, in my humble opinion it is precisely the tangled history of Christian doctrine, the mistaken arrogance of its claims, the circumstances of its propagation, that stand in the way of the Bible being seen and appreciated by all peoples, Christian, non-Christian, even atheist, for what it is; an immense treasure house of human experience; a vast repository of timeless wisdom; unparalleled, even by the Mahabharata, in its historic sweep; an anthology of prose and poetry of breathtaking beauty; and also in the Old Testament a down-to-earth, colourful mosaic of the daily lives of ordinary people (Jews, Romans, Egyptians, Babylonians, Syrians) and in the New Testament the story of a man who lived for only thirty years but whose teaching irrevocably set the course of history for two thousand years.[15]

He went on to indicate that the most difficult problems about the role of religion in a post-colonial society had to be addressed head on:

> Throughout history religion has divided man. It has set man against man. Abominable crimes have been committed in the name of religion. And, unfortunately, in the heyday of imperial conquest, Christianity was seen as, and often truly was, the juggernaut of religious fanaticism, persecution and repression. Painful though it is, the inglorious chapters in the saga of aggressive Christian expansion must be recalled because the eclipse of the Bible, its alienation from countless millions who profess other faiths, is due directly to the perception, deeply embedded in the psyche of once oppressed peoples, that the Bible was the motto of Empire, that it was used as the moral justification for the conversion of those peoples by force or seduction. It was thus an unwelcome, alien intrusion upon the ancient beliefs and cultures of those peoples.[16]

Kadirgamar's doubts about the dangerous certainties of some approaches to religion appear to have begun in his teens. In his 1992 lecture he referred to the time of Gandhi's assassination on 30 January 1948:

> I am also reminded of my own question, long ago, to a teacher of Christianity upon hearing the news that Mahatma Gandhi had been assassinated. My question was: Will not Gandhi go to Heaven? The answer was: No. He was a good man, but he was not a Christian. Even to my youthful mind there seemed to be a monstrous flaw in that reasoning.[17]

The central thrust of his 1992 lecture was that there are numerous common features in the parables and principles of the great belief-systems: Buddhism, Judaism, Christianity, Hinduism and Islam. Each is misrepresented, and its capacity for social good is diminished, if it is reduced to a dogmatic and exclusive core of rigid doctrine. One passage of his lecture, illustrating these points, prefigured the tragic events of 2005. He was discussing the teachings of Buddha:

> When a merchant who became his disciple proposed to return to his native town and preach to his people, the Buddha said 'The people of Sunaparanta are exceedingly violent; if they revile you, what will you do?' 'I will make no reply,' said the disciple. 'And if they strike you?' 'I will not strike in return.' 'And if they try to kill you?' 'Death', said the disciple, 'is no evil in itself. Many even desire it, to escape from the vanities of this life; but I shall take no steps either to hasten or delay the time of my departure.' The Buddha was satisfied, and the merchant departed.[18]

When Lakshman himself was assassinated, although his funeral in Colombo was held according to Buddhist rites, one of the speakers was the Anglican bishop of Colombo. This symbolizes the liberal and syncretistic approach towards which he had been moving ever since his schooldays. He combined a generally favourable view of religion with a disapproval of the dogmatism, exclusivism and quest for political dominance to which all great religions have been prone at one time or another, and from which Sri Lanka's Buddhists have not been immune.

Ethnicity

In Sri Lanka, as elsewhere, questions of ethnic identity are never simple. In the 1981 census, 73 per cent of the population were Sinhalese, 12 per cent were Sri Lankan Tamil, 5 per cent were Indian Tamil and 7 per cent were Sri Lankan Moors.[19] (Map 1 gives an impression of these groups' distribution.) None of these categories is sacrosanct. The distinction between 'Indian Tamils' and 'Sri Lankan Tamils' dates from the 1911 census. As the Sri Lankan historian Nira Wickramasinghe has pointed out, the categories placed on census forms in the colonial era tell one almost as much about the views and aspirations of the rulers as they do about the composition of the population.[20] Discussing the difficult period since the 1970s, which has been marked by the conflict with the LTTE, she particularly questions 'the very notion of a single Tamil ethnic identity'.[21]

How to handle the rights and status of minority populations – an ancient question in the theory and practice of politics – has not been answered particularly successfully in Sri Lanka. Both the Tamils and the Sinhalese can plausibly see themselves as threatened minorities – the Tamils because of their small proportion of the population of Sri Lanka, the Sinhalese because of their modest proportion if all Tamils, including in neighbouring India, are taken into account.

In Sri Lanka there has been a long history, both in the colonial era and subsequently, of seeking to achieve liberal progress without much respect for the ethnic divisions of the population concerned. Thus the 1833 Royal Commission's proposals, which had been influenced by the ideas of Jeremy Bentham and James Mill, resulted in 'a homogenising of the island's territory by the incorporation of all differences into a single society and space'.[22]

The homogenizing efforts continued in the post-independence era, and took many different forms. In the 1950s the question of the official language, or languages, of Sri Lanka became a key political issue, with the Sinhalese–Buddhist majority attracted by the idea of influence commensurate with their numbers. As de Silva has written: 'The linguistic nationalism of the mid-1950s was a popular movement, in contrast to the elitist constitutionalism of the early years after independence.'[23] Its outcome was the 1956 Official Language Act, which had made Sinhala the only official language of the state. Unsurprisingly, this was followed by much opposition, especially from Tamils who had good reason to fear a threat to their identity and a diminution of access to government jobs and political decision-making. It led to riots in June 1956 – 'the first serious occurrence of violence between communities since the Sinhala–Muslim riots of 1915' – and then to the May 1958 clashes between Sinhalese and Tamils that were 'the first major outbreak against Tamils and in many ways a point of no return'.[24]

Wickramasinghe has observed that 'in the 1970s the state was conceived as the supreme instrument for economic development and social progress in the socialist mould. Giving minorities special rights would have amounted to weakening state instrumentalism.'[25] This approach might be seen as having led logically to the formal title of the state as it is given in the 1978 Constitution, Article 1: 'The Democratic Socialist Republic of Sri Lanka' – a title which it has, against all the historical odds, maintained to this day. However, this title was in fact given by a right-of-centre government interested in shaking off its image as a capitalist party. Such are the vagaries of politics.

As a result of continuing troubles over the language issue, there were various modifications of the Official Language Act, some more convincing than others. They reached their illogical conclusion in the Constitution's current Article 22, as it was modified in 1987:

1. The Official Language of Sri Lanka shall be Sinhala.
2. Tamil shall also be an official language.
3. English shall be the link language.
4. Parliament shall by law provide for the implementation of the provisions of this Chapter.

Clearly this wording leaves everything to subsequent interpretation and implementation. The outcome was unsatisfactory. As Wickramasinghe puts it, 'the bilingualism that existed on paper was not effectively implemented.'[26] Progress has been slow in such matters as recruitment of Tamil officers to the police, and in implementing mandatory requirements for public servants to learn Tamil.

Where did Lakshman stand regarding ethnic issues in Sri Lanka? His ethnic identity as a Tamil was, like his identity as a Christian, more an acknowledged point of departure than an imprisoning category that excluded all others. Growing up in Colombo and Kandy, far from the Tamil heartlands in the north and east of the country, and attending schools where English was one of the languages of instruction, he was comfortable with multiple identities. He saw himself as first and foremost a Sri Lankan, who recognized the faults of his society but then sought to address them. In addition, he was from an early age an Anglophile and a member of an international English-speaking legal fraternity: as Chris Patten points out, he was very much at home in England.[27] Finally, he was a citizen of the world, whose professional work was almost all on a global stage, and who constantly sought to expand his understanding of the different worldviews and mind-sets that make international relations so interesting and problematic.

When Lakshman's political role was criticized, Sri Lanka's ethnic issues were never far from the surface. He was regularly condemned by the LTTE, which denounced him as a traitor to the Tamil cause. As Sinha Ratnatunga says, for them 'nothing could be as treacherous as a Tamil being dismissive of their armed struggle.'[28] Some Tamils not connected with the LTTE also had their criticisms. Resenting what they saw as their minority status in a predominantly Sinhala state, these people felt that he too easily absolved the majority of its record of discrimination and violence. In addition, it was sometimes said that, as an MP appointed to parliament from a 'national list', he never had to go out on the campaign trail to appeal directly to Tamil electors, and that he was not fluent in the Tamil language.

Throughout his career Lakshman was an open and principled critic of narrow ethnic exclusivity. He rejected the whole idea of a separate Tamil state. Furthermore, he rejected the use of terrorist methods, including a long series of assassinations, to achieve the separatist objective. He pointed out, with impeccable logic, that the Tamils are not arranged tidily, but are intermingled with Sinhalese, Muslims and others on the map of Sri Lanka – so the attempt to set up a separatist state by force is a threat to them as much as to the other communities. He believed that Sri Lanka had much to be proud of, including the fact that it had had universal suffrage – irrespective of race, ethnicity, language or gender – since 1931. Indeed, it had been the first Asian country to achieve this. It had done so following the work of a Special Commission on Constitutional Reform, chaired by the Earl of Donoughmore, which had been set up by the Colonial Office in London. The Commission's report, ahead of its time in many ways, has an ominous aspect. As one scholar has observed, it 'removed communal electorates from the Ceylon constitution, and so confronted the country with what many regard as a central problem of modern constitutional development in the Third World, *viz.* the relationship between the majority and minority communities within a colony or state bent upon national self-determination.'[29]

Lakshman was far from denying that there were serious problems in Sri Lankan public life. Although he did not speak out on fundamentals of the ethnic conflict as forcefully as some wished, he recognized – both at the time and subsequently – that one cause of the ethnic conflict in Sri Lanka had been the crude approach of past governments to state-building and to the language issue. He concluded that something akin to federalism was needed, but argued that the concept should be used with care because any solution had to be acceptable to the majority Sinhalese population. Thus he believed that a serious plan for devolution to the provinces, combined with safeguards against any kind of disintegration, was the best way to address the long-standing grievances of the Tamil population. (See Map 2, showing the nine provinces of Sri Lanka.)

He had a lively awareness that Sri Lanka faced a wide range of problems, by no means confined to the country's ethnic and religious divisions. He knew about the degree of corruption in public life, which he saw in a 1994 speech as corroding 'the very soul of our society'.[30] He was conscious that since independence in 1948 Sri Lanka had developed more slowly than many other newly-independent Asian countries. He knew the risks that the Sri Lankan armed forces, in pursuing the struggle against the LTTE, might (like any army facing an insurgency) come under pressure to violate some of the basic rules of the laws of war. He was painfully aware of the strength of feeling among the Tamil diaspora in favour of establishing a separate state of Tamil Eelam. He saw all these and more as matters that needed to be addressed, but remained fiercely critical of the view that the division of the island into two states on ethnic lines would contribute anything positive to the solution of such problems.

A Privileged and All-round Education

School and University in Sri Lanka

Lakshman had a privileged education of which he took full advantage. Its beginning was the result of tragedy: his mother's death. Shortly thereafter, from 1942 to 1950, he was a boarding pupil at Trinity College, Kandy. The town of Kandy is the historic capital of the last independent Kingdom of Sri Lanka. Trinity College, an elite independent boys' school, had been founded in 1872 by Anglican missionaries. He felt a lifelong debt of gratitude to the school: though established essentially for the Kandyan community, it embraced children from all the communities in all parts of the island.[31] The warmth of this welcome stayed with him and contributed to his belief in inter-communal co-operation in Sri Lanka.

The school's ethos influenced him deeply. A speech he made at a Trinity event in 2003 gives a vivid picture of the school and what it meant to him: an audio recording is available.[32] The school song – Henry Newbolt's 'The Best School of All' – epitomizes Newbolt's love of the public school ethos and of a certain idea of Englishness. While it is not the greatest English poem ever written, these lines convey the spirit that the school inculcates:

> And where's the wealth, I'm wondering,
> Could buy the cheers that roll,
> When the last charge goes thundering,
> Towards the twilight goal.[33]

The poem's invocation of honour, and of continuity in the face of inevitable death, is summed up in its appeal to 'dare the deepening tide' – not a bad description of Lakshman's later public role.

As Sarath Silva indicates in his short sketch of Kadirgamar's life, as a schoolboy Lakshman excelled at both work and sports.[34] He put himself heart and soul into school activities. He won awards for Ceylon history and also for English. In 1949 he also won the Ryde Gold Medal for the best all-round student, and in 1950 became head prefect. His sporting achievements, both at school and university, were remarkable. He represented the school in athletics, rugby and cricket (captaining the team in 1950). Then while at university he won the Indian inter-university 110 m hurdles title in 1951 and 1952; the all-Ceylon 110 m hurdles title, again in both 1951 and 1952; and he played cricket for the University of Ceylon, as he was later to do for Balliol College, Oxford.

After school, in academic terms he became less of an all-rounder and more a legal specialist. From 1950 to 1953 he read Law at the relatively new University of Ceylon (founded in 1942, and now called Peradeniya University), which is also in the Kandy area. Graduating from it with a first class LLB degree, and getting further legal training in Colombo, everything suggested that he was destined for a successful career as a lawyer.

Oxford University

His years at Oxford (1956–9) confirmed his abilities as a lawyer. His thesis, for which he was awarded the BLitt degree, was on a seemingly arcane legal topic, namely 'Strict liability in English and Roman-Dutch law'. Actually it deals with something quite down-to-earth – liability for the escape of sewage and water from domestic premises. It refers mainly to the case law on this in South Africa and Sri Lanka – two colonies in which the British colonial rulers had inherited the legal system of their Dutch predecessors. In these improbable colonial surroundings Roman–Dutch law survived the demise of the system in the Netherlands. Theses tell a lot about the skills and interests of their authors. In this case what comes across, powerfully, is Lakshman's clarity of mind; his precision of expression; and his deep interest in how, in colonial and post-colonial settings, the English common law had encroached on Roman–Dutch and other systems of law.[35] His supervisor at Oxford, Tony Honoré (who was to be Regius Professor of Civil Law at Oxford University, 1971–88), had a very high opinion of his abilities, admired him, and remained in contact with him.

While at Oxford he became a well-respected member of the Oxford Union Society – a student debating club with a difference. In one of his early performances there, he proposed the motion 'that the Churches have neither the strength nor the ability to deal with the problems of the twentieth century.'[36] Its debates are often a test of quick-wittedness as much as depth of knowledge, and Lakshman passed the test. In March 1958, in election for the Standing Committee, he came first of 20 candidates; in June 1958, in election for treasurer, he was top of the poll again, with more votes than the two rival candidates combined; and in November 1958, as the illustration shows, he easily won in the election for president.[37] In the same month he applied successfully to become a barrister of the Inner Temple in London.

When he took up the post of President of the Oxford Union for the Hilary (Spring) Term of 1959, he was not the first Sri Lankan to hold this title: the trail had been blazed exactly one year earlier by Lalith Athulathmudali (who, like Lakshman, was supervised by Tony Honoré). Tragically, both of them, having achieved prominence in the government and politics of Sri Lanka, would become victims of assassination. Indeed, Lakshman's political career there was to begin within months of his distinguished colleague's death in April 1993.[38]

Many of the issues that the Oxford Union debated were international, and Lakshman's skilful handling of them was a foretaste of things to come. As president, he organized a debate on France at which he succeeded in getting the attendance of former Prime Minister Pierre Mendès France by the simple device of turning up on his doorstep in Paris and catching him in his pyjamas.[39]

Perhaps the debate in which he participated that had the most long-lasting resonance was on the motion 'Democracy is unsuitable for developing nations.' One of the speakers was to be the Prime Minister of Ceylon, S. W. R. D. Bandaranaike, who had been Secretary and Treasurer of the

Oxford Union in 1923–4. In 1951 he had helped to found the Sri Lanka Freedom Party (SLFP), and he had been prime minister since 1956. In September 1959, one month before he was due to speak at the Oxford Union, he was assassinated in Colombo by a Buddhist monk in an act that came to be seen as the beginning of Sri Lanka's descent into political violence.[40] Lakshman – by now ex-President of the Union – stood in for Bandaranaike in the debate. In a speech of undisputed brilliance he vigorously defended democracy, helping to defeat the motion decisively, by 288 to 129 votes. As a report in a normally hyper-critical and satirical student magazine – precursor of the iconoclastic *Private Eye* – put it:

> His speech was beautifully delivered, factually sound, and, particularly when he talked about Bandaranaike and Ceylon, profoundly moving. He exposed the dangers of the alternatives to democracy – Communism and militant dictatorship – and said that the only answer to the enormous economic difficulties in this area was socialist planning. Listening to Kadirgamar was like drinking a vintage champagne after a third-rate meal. It was a flawless and fascinating oration.[41]

At school and then at his universities, Lakshman had gained knowledge and formidable skills: a striking capacity for hard work and clear thought; outstanding abilities as a communicator and leader; and a liberal and broad-minded acceptance of the different cultures of different societies, interestingly combined with a strong belief in democracy. He had a remarkable network of loyal and talented friends – from Trinity College Kandy, the University of Ceylon and Oxford – with whom he would be in close touch at many points in his professional life. He seemed destined for a career of high achievement, but it was not immediately obvious what form it would take. By one of the many ironies of his career, over 30 years later he would join the SLFP and ultimately he would suffer the same fate as its leader S. W. R. D. Bandaranaike, for whom he had stood in at that memorable Union debate in 1959.

International Calling

At first his calling did not appear to be especially international. After Oxford he returned to Sri Lanka and built up a law practice in the fields of commercial, industrial and administrative law. But his investigation of the situation in Vietnam in December 1963 for Amnesty showed a willingness to look to much wider horizons. It is possible that he entertained thoughts of a political career in this period, but visits to Jaffna revealed the emerging strength of Tamil nationalism – to which he was not prepared to pander. That was not the only storm-cloud. In 1971 the armed socialist uprising in the Southern and Central Provinces, led by the Janatha Vimukthi Peramuna (People's Liberation Front, generally known as JVP), and put down by the

Sri Lankan security forces with considerable loss of life, had a deep effect on Lakshman, for whom opposition to political violence was an intellectual starting point. However, the main factor influencing his decision to go abroad was the ceiling on income imposed by the government. He went, first to London in 1971/2, where he practised law, and then to Geneva.

Geneva

Geneva is where Lakshman's international career took off. In 1974–6 he worked as a consultant to the International Labour Organization (ILO), and then in 1976–88 he held senior positions at the World Intellectual Property Organization (WIPO) – both of them specialized agencies of the United Nations that sought to harmonize national policies on a wide range of practical issues. At WIPO Lakshman's expertise was recognized in 1983 with his appointment to the newly-created post of Director for Asia and the Pacific. This involved a major challenge, as intellectual property law in many Asian countries was either non-existent or arcane. The task was to help them to bring their intellectual property legislation and infrastructure into line with international standards. He recruited talented people from the countries concerned to assist him. He was exceptionally skilled in this pursuit of the cause of the global rule of law, helping to persuade some hitherto recalcitrant countries that they had much to gain by accepting international rules on such matters as patents, trade/service marks, industrial designs and copyright. For the flavour of this work, read Lakshman's graphic account of his trip to China in 1980 – preceded by an air crash, and followed by China's developing acceptance of an intellectual property system.[42] This was absorbing and effective international work. As Sinha Ratnatunga points out, although it did not lead to the promotion he might reasonably have anticipated, this international experience was a strong basis for what was to come for him in Sri Lanka.[43]

Transition to Foreign Minister

His occupation of the post of foreign minister, starting in August 1994, was marked by impressive achievements of which the chapters in this book are testimony. His international experience, especially in Geneva, ensured that he was already familiar with the different perspectives of the countries with which he would deal, and as a result he was able to make well-considered, independent and weighty contributions both to policy-making and to the understanding of international relations. He also had, as he had already shown at WIPO, a strong sense of purpose.

However, he was inevitably a controversial figure. Of the various criticisms that could be made of his ministerial role, perhaps the most fundamental, and also the most unfair, is that, while he greatly improved Sri Lanka's international standing, not enough was done to ensure that the country changed internally to reflect its improved image. When he became foreign minister, Lakshman was certainly well aware that there was much in Sri Lanka's record that could quite legitimately be questioned by international bodies. Earlier in 1994 a notably balanced report of the UN Human Rights Commission, addressing the problem of internally displaced persons, had indicated points of concern in Sri Lanka's record, but at the same time commended the country for its cooperation with the UN representative.[44] During and after Lakshman's periods as foreign minister, many reports by outside bodies presented evidence that, despite improvements, disappearances, arbitrary detention and torture had continued to be major problems in Sri Lanka;[45] that the general human rights situation was problematic;[46] and that the judiciary, operating within serious constraints, saw its independence weakened in the 1990s and in the first decade of this century.[47]

Such criticisms certainly confirm the difficulty of raising standards in public life. However, as they relate to Lakshman, they are wide of the mark in key respects. He was certainly no hireling: he had significant power within government because he added much-needed lustre, analytical power and sheer effectiveness. The criticism that he did not do enough to change Sri Lanka internally runs into some significant objections. In a system of cabinet government, there are limits to what one MP and foreign minister can achieve in areas outside his direct responsibility; and of course making reforms in the midst of a bitter ongoing conflict is inherently difficult. He did in fact achieve much in internal as well as international affairs; for example, by his strong support for the establishment of the Human Rights Commission of Sri Lanka (HRCSL).[48] Yet it is primarily on his contribution to international relations that he must be judged.

Contribution to International Relations

Lakshman's whole career, from student to foreign minister, raises many questions of general interest, transcending the individual case of Sri Lanka. Here I will focus on four.

1. Was his emphasis on the value of democratic systems of government soundly based and consistently upheld? Could it be squared with his strong defence of the sovereignty of states, and his opposition to doctrines justifying military interventions?
2. How coherent was his view that terrorism had to be tackled within a framework of law, both domestic and international?

3. In particular, was his emphasis on observing the laws of war justified in the special circumstances of the long-running conflict in Sri Lanka and the international campaign against terrorism?
4. Was his amalgam of realism and idealism intellectually and politically defensible, and what were the limits of his contribution?

Democracy and Sovereignty

Lakshman was as strong and consistent an advocate of democracy as any leading political figure in the Third World. His speech on this subject at the Oxford Union in 1959 had come from the heart. Throughout his career he continued to argue for multiparty democratic systems, mainly on the grounds expressed by Winston Churchill in the House of Commons in 1947:

> Many forms of government have been tried, and will be tried in this world of sin and woe. No one pretends that democracy is perfect or all-wise. Indeed, it has been said that democracy is the worst form of Government except all those other forms that have been tried from time to time.[49]

Lakshman was not complacent – he could hardly be – about the actual functioning of democracy, either generally or in his own country. He saw how in his lifetime Sri Lanka's long-established democratic system had failed to prevent the worrying growth of political violence, assassinations and then the uprisings of the JVP and LTTE. He would have understood many of the criticisms of his country's record.[50] The Sri Lankan constitution was hardly a rock of stability: since independence in 1948, it had undergone numerous fundamental changes, and in Lakshman's view more might be called for. In May 2004, in a major speech in the USA, he argued strongly that Sri Lanka's particular version of proportional representation needed radical reform in order to reduce its adverse effects, especially its tendency to lead to certain acts of violence. Yet he also celebrated the merits of Sri Lanka's constitutional arrangements: 'We have been free throughout our 56 years of any serious attempt to overthrow the democratic system.'[51] This was not a neo-Kantian argument that democracy is the solution to the problem of war, but a down-to-earth recognition that, if non-violent politics are to have any chance within a state, there has to be a constitutional right of the people to throw out their rulers from time to time – a right that has been exercised particularly often in Sri Lanka. As de Silva has written: 'On five consecutive occasions after 1956, the Sri Lankan electorate voted a government out of power, a record which no other post-colonial state can match.'[52]

Lakshman recognized frankly one particular weakness of democracies: their vulnerability to terrorism. He went so far as to say, in a lecture on terrorism in Colombo in 2001 in honour of an assassinated colleague:

'terrorism hardly, if ever, makes its presence felt in a dictatorship. If it did, retaliation would be swift and savage.'[53] In various lectures and speeches, including several in this book, he noted the terrorist-related troubles that some major democracies had undergone; the tendency of assassinations to be conducted during election campaigns, when politicians are most vulnerable; and the difficulty that the legal systems of democratic states had in adjusting their definitions of terrorist-related activity to encompass organizing and fund-raising in one country to support terrorist activity in another. His response to these problems was not to weaken his faith in democracy, but to urge democratic states to be at the same time tougher in responding to terrorist-related activities and more flexible in response to grievances whose existence facilitates the growth of terrorism.

His belief in toughness against terrorism had been evident for years. Indeed, long before 11 September 2001 he saw that this enhanced toughness needed to be international in scope. His belief in flexibility was no less central to his view of terrorism. This belief manifested itself, for example, in his work to cooperate with the JVP despite their previously extensive use of violence and indeed their record of commitment to revolution. The JVP's shift into electoral politics was not new: it can be said to have begun in the late 1970s. In 2003 and early 2004, when still in opposition, Lakshman was involved in giving leading figures in the JVP discreet advice that helped to reassure them of the benefits of entering the coalition with the SLFP. Thus he contributed in a modest way to the formation in January 2004 of the United People's Freedom Alliance (UPFA), a broad political grouping containing several parties, including the SLFP and the JVP. Following the UPFA's strong performance in the April 2004 parliamentary elections, a coalition government, headed by President Chandrika Kumaratunga and with Mahinda Rajapaksa as prime minister, came into office. Lakshman, foreign minister once again, continued the process of outreach to the JVP, which by now had four ministers in the cabinet. The path of the JVP's involvement in government was not smooth: the JVP withdrew from the UPFA and the government on 16 June 2005 in protest against the P-TOMS (Post-Tsunami Operational Management Structure) agreement that conceded some status to LTTE representatives – a protest with which Lakshman sympathized.[54] In September the JVP signed an electoral agreement with Prime Minister Rajapaksa to do away with P-TOMS and to preserve the unity of the Sri Lankan state. Rajapaksa then went on to win the presidency in the November 2005 elections. Subsequently, in April 2008, there was a split within the JVP party, with only a breakaway group continuing to support the government.

Lakshman's contribution in this chain of events was to help the JVP to get more entrenched in the democratic process, and to see the world in a less dogmatic way: he emphasized the need to work in the mainstream of politics, both domestic and international, including with India and the Western countries. This complex story is not free of those elements of moral and political ambiguity which always arise when flexibility is displayed in encouraging such movements to change their approach.

Lakshman's involvement in politics involved other elements of moral ambiguity. How did his pro-democratic principles square with the obvious need, of which as foreign minister he was daily aware, to collaborate closely with non-democracies as well? In 2004 he mentioned democracy and human rights in a major speech in Washington, DC, but not in his address in Beijing. Indeed, he said to his Chinese audience: 'In more recent times Sri Lanka has in a modest way been of assistance to China in international fora especially in the field of human rights where Sri Lanka, taking the view that China is being unfairly treated in certain quarters, has been her steadfast ally.'[55] Despite its Buddhist aspect, the problem of Tibet did not feature large in his statements. Similarly, on a visit to Myanmar (Burma) in 1996 he proposed a toast to his hosts, representing the military regime, when his own sympathies must have been with the democratically elected Aung San Suu Kyi, being kept under house arrest.[56] There are two arguments that can be made in defence of such statements and silences. The first is necessity: Burma and China are two important countries in the region, with many practical issues (for example, trade and maritime matters) to sort out between them – tasks that might be jeopardized by overtly seeking basic political change in the host country. The second is that, even if change is indeed sought, preaching is a poor way to achieve it – especially when the targets are post-colonial states, which are particularly allergic to anything that they see as latter-day colonial interference in their internal affairs. Lakshman believed there was a better chance of achieving change by example, and by the consequences that naturally flow from contact with the outside world, rather than by direct confrontation. These are not arguments to satisfy moral purists, and they are more convincing in some cases than in others.

Behind these two arguments lay a third consideration. A strong principle underlying much of Lakshman's thought was respect for the sovereignty of states. This principle is of course inherently difficult to square with belief in the universal value of democracy and human rights, but it was equally real in his mind, and was based on experience. Any society that has been through a period of colonial rule, as Sri Lanka had under successive waves of colonizers, is likely to be hyper-sensitive to pressure from outsiders. And if outsiders claim to speak in the name of democracy, human rights, and progress, that only reminds once-colonized peoples that earlier interveners in their societies, including the European colonialists of the nineteenth and twentieth centuries, also used such language as part of their pattern of dominance.

His emphasis on sovereignty was not just a lawyer's belief in the sanctity of the international legal principle that placed limits on the circumstances in which force could be used. It also reflected his own, and his country's, experience. Ceylon had faced difficulties in asserting its sovereignty after its independence in 1948. For seven years it had been denied admission to the UN. The Soviet Union had vetoed its membership on three occasions, claiming that it was too much in the shadow of British power – partly because it retained UK bases until the mid-1950s.

Sri Lanka's most important relationship – albeit one sometimes involving fears of subordination – is that with India. The contributions of Shivshankar Menon and Nirupama Rao in this volume give indications of how much Lakshman did to improve this relationship.[57] Already in the 1970s there had been concerns that Indian Prime Minister Indira Gandhi was seeking 'to weaken Sri Lanka deliberately as it turned away from a protectionist state socialism like India's to a free market economy and improved ties with the West.'[58] The fears of India acquired real substance in the 1980s, as the LTTE uprising gained momentum. Sri Lanka was concerned about the sanctuary and support given in India to militant Sri Lankan Tamil cadres.[59] India, for its part, indicated concern both about instability in its southern neighbour and the possibility that Sri Lanka might allow its ports to be used by the Chinese or US navies. In 1987 these problems came to a head when the Indian government called on Sri Lanka to halt its offensive against the LTTE. The main outcome of the crisis was the Indo–Sri Lanka Agreement to Establish Peace and Normalcy in Sri Lanka.[60] Intended primarily to end the conflict between the LTTE (not a party to the Accord) and the Sri Lankan government, it contained provisions reaffirming Sri Lanka's sovereignty, committing the Sri Lankan government to accept Tamil as an official language and to introduce constitutional reform, and placing obligations on India, Sri Lanka and the LTTE in such matters as amnesty, disarmament, verification and avoidance of military involvement of outside powers. In accord with its terms an Indian Peace Keeping Force (IPKF) intervened in the north and east of Sri Lanka in 1987–90. There were incidents between the peacekeepers and the LTTE. The Indian peacekeepers attempted to force the LTTE to comply with the disarmament provisions, and in the ensuing conflict about 1,200 Indian soldiers died.[61] The IPKF ended without its core mission being accomplished. According to Lakshman, this experience left the relationship with India 'absolutely in tatters', and he saw it as his first job as foreign minister to repair it.[62] The experience also indicated that in any future attempt to secure a negotiated end to the conflict in Sri Lanka, the LTTE would have to be directly involved.

Lakshman's view of sovereignty as a principle that was under threat was thus close to the oft-stated position on this matter of the Non-Aligned

Movement. Ceylon had been one of the movement's founding members, and featured prominently in all the major conferences (especially Bandung 1955 and Belgrade 1961) that brought the movement into existence. Indeed, it was at the time of the Asian Prime Ministers' Conference in Colombo on 2 May 1954 that the Prime Minister of India, Jawaharlal Nehru, had made a speech praising the five principles of coexistence – principles that played a key part in the emergence of what later came to be called the 'Non-Aligned Movement'.[63] While Ceylon valued the nascent movement, its participation in it was sometimes controversial. After it got rid of the British bases in the mid-1950s, the pendulum swung to the point where Ceylon had a thoroughly equivocal record on the Soviet intervention in Hungary in 1956, abstaining on almost all the key votes; and at times its form of non-alignment appeared to lean towards the Soviet side. Despite such episodes, and its subsequent involvements with various powers, Sri Lanka remained proud of its historic association with this movement.

Yet as foreign minister from 1994 onwards, Lakshman did not attach special importance to the Non-Aligned Movement. Partly this was because it was already of diminished relevance in a world that had ceased to be dominated by two poles of alignment – the two superpowers of the Cold War era. It was also because he regarded it as an instrument of limited utility due to its often shrill denunciatory tone, and its reluctance to recognize that post-colonial states were the source of many contemporary international problems. He attended some of its meetings, and did not try to withdraw from it, but he placed only limited reliance on it.

His defence of sovereignty was much more nuanced than that of the Non-Aligned Movement. He was well aware that the principle was not absolute, and did not trump all other considerations. Already in 1996 he said: 'every state has to be deeply conscious of the way in which it treats its own citizens if it wants to capture and preserve the respect of the international community and also ward off intervention in various forms legal, moral and ultimately even by force on the part of other states.'[64] It was five years later, in 2001, that the doctrine of 'Responsibility to Protect' was introduced.[65] Starting in the last decade of the twentieth century, and continuing into the twenty-first, some countries, especially the US, were developing interventionist doctrines and practices based on ideas of the universality of human rights, and also of the justifiability of military action to eliminate a possible future threat.

These developments posed a challenge to Lakshman. He had sympathy with US aims in some of its interventions, and sometimes perhaps with the means too. Unlike India and many other non-aligned states, he did not take part in the clamour against the North Atlantic Treaty Organisation (NATO)-led intervention in Kosovo in 1999, despite its lack of an explicit UN Security Council authorization. His non-condemnatory approach to the Kosovo action represented more than just an interest in cooperating with the Western democracies over the issue of terrorism: he also saw that for NATO to stand by while atrocities were committed would have been hugely problematic. By contrast, he was explicitly and publicly critical of the 2003 US-led invasion and occupation of Iraq.

In a lecture in New Delhi in August 2003, less than six months after the invasion of Iraq, he discussed at length some of the new or revived doctrines:

> I refer to the concept of the humanitarian war to prevent or punish genocide, ethnic cleansing and other heinous crimes, and the war to effect a regime change in order to liberate an oppressed people from dictatorship and install a democratic form of government. If such a war is waged with the approval of the Security Council, there would be no problem as to its legality. If, however, it were to be launched by a state that possesses the capacity to do so unilaterally or in alliance with other like-minded states, grave questions would arise as to its legality, moral validity and practicality. The war against Iraq brings these questions to the fore.[66]

Lakshman then carefully examined the strongest arguments for the invasion of Iraq, and more in sorrow than in anger he found them wanting. His mode of analysis – in this as well as other presentations – was unusual for a serving minister. He took into account legal, moral and practical dimensions of the problem. He was thoughtful, reasoned, scholarly and yet at the same time frank and robust. As this lecture showed, his was not a rigid or exclusively statist view of sovereignty. He recognized that states could quite legitimately be subject to scrutiny and even coercion from above, by international bodies including the UN. He also recognized that governments were subject to pressure from below: 'Modern peoples have the will to resist and the means to do so.'[67] Above all, this lecture epitomized his view that both the promotion of democratic values and the worldwide struggle against terrorism needed to be conducted in a manner that did not flagrantly violate the sovereignty of states and the UN Charter.

That conclusion, Lakshman would have been the first to concede, does not provide a simple answer for all problems. My personal guess is that, had Lakshman lived, he would have supported the US attack on Osama Bin Laden's residence in Abbottabad in May 2011. While understanding Pakistani concerns about sovereignty and lack of consultation, he would have been highly critical of Pakistan's long-standing failure to suppress terrorists operating in and from the country. He could accept that where a state had failed to carry out fundamental obligations, its immunity from attack as an independent sovereign state could sometimes be questioned. This recognition that statecraft requires fine balancing of sometimes countervailing legal principles, rather than the universal application of the non-intervention rule irrespective of circumstances, emanated from a deep respect for the law, and a recognition that its application has always involved intellectual complexity and moral hazard.

Addressing Terrorism within a Legal Framework

If there is one central message from Lakshman's speeches and actions, it is that the problem of terrorism has to be tackled within a legal framework; and that the struggle between terrorists and their adversaries is to a significant extent a struggle for legitimacy.[68] The way in which he pressed this argument was significant. Although he was a lawyer, he went far beyond merely calling for the observance of existing rules. He argued that law should be seen as part of a larger overall strategy for addressing terrorism; he proposed new rules, especially in the national laws of states, to address the problem; and while not opposed in principle to all agreements with terrorist movements, he was sceptical about them – as he showed in his powerful speech in the Sri Lanka parliament in May 2003 criticizing the 2002 Ceasefire Agreement with the LTTE.[69] (Map 3 shows the areas controlled by the government and the LTTE at the time of this agreement.) In sum, he advanced what he saw as a tough-minded and realistic strategy for addressing the terrorist threat. The key question is: does his strategy make sense?

He rightly saw that a critical aspect of terrorism in our times is its international dimension. Movements may operate in foreign countries to mobilize diaspora populations, raise funds, publicize their cause, obtain equipment, train their forces and even plan attacks. This capacity to operate internationally necessitated a twofold response. First, to build as strong an international coalition against terrorism as was possible – which to Lakshman meant operating within existing international law. Second, to get states to modify their existing national laws on terrorism – especially as these laws were often parochial, confining themselves to preventing terrorism on their own soil, not externally.

In his years as foreign minister he placed particular emphasis on the argument that democracies needed to co-operate in a common struggle against those planning and supporting terrorist action. If this is central to his approach, the first question that has to be faced is whether it is accurate, and useful, to label whole movements as 'terrorist'. Famously, in 1987 and 1988 the UK and US governments labelled the African National Congress of South Africa 'terrorist': this was a questionable branding even at the time, let alone in light of Nelson Mandela's later emergence as statesman. The ANC may have planned certain acts that could be labelled 'terrorist', but it was far from evident that the entire movement in all its branches and modes of activity merited this label. Lakshman always maintained that there were fundamental differences between the ANC's struggle against a policy of racial discrimination and that of LTTE for a separatist state. He repeatedly called the LTTE a terrorist organization, and worked hard and successfully to get other countries to take the same view. Was he right to do so? The consistent pattern of LTTE activities – suicide bombings, killing of civilians, use of child soldiers and so on – suggest that he had a serious case.

In these pages he presents an impressive argument for taking a strong line against the LTTE. His argument was at its most cogent and prophetic in his Chatham House speech of 15 April 1998. He addressed, with characteristic thoughtfulness, the perennially difficult question of the definition of terrorism. He also gave some extraordinarily well-informed indications of how UK law on terrorism was changing. He additionally offered sensible suggestions for further improvements, which were eventually taken up, as indicated in the endnotes that have been added here to the Chatham House speech. This is not to suggest that changes in UK law on terrorism were due directly to Kadirgamar's input, but rather to point out how alert Lakshman was to developments in the UK, and what a superb grasp he had of detail as well as of broad principles. It was in that Chatham House speech, delivered three years before the attacks of 11 September 2001, that he prophetically warned Western countries that they were turning a Nelsonian blind eye to terrorist movements operating in their midst.

It was partly because of his combination of a principled approach, clarity of exposition and grasp of detail that he contributed so much to the process of getting the LTTE classified as a terrorist organization. As Karl Inderfurth, Peter Burleigh and Shaun Donnelly amply confirm in their chapter, he played a key role in getting the US government to proscribe the LTTE in 1997.[70] He also had major input into the similar decision by the UK government in February 2001. He saw proscription largely in practical terms, as a critically important means of limiting the flow of funds and other forms of support from the Tamil diaspora.

The identification of the LTTE as a terrorist organization was due not only to Lakshman's efforts, impressive as they were: it also owed much to the ruthless and often self-defeating activities of the LTTE itself. Under the leadership of Velupillai Prabhakaran, assassinations were directed not only against individuals in Sri Lankan public life, but also against rivals in the separatist movement – and others. One of the worst excesses came in May 1991, when former Indian Prime Minister Rajiv Gandhi and 18 other people were killed by a female suicide bomber at an election rally near Madras. This led to the Indian proscription of the LTTE in 1992. Then in early 1995 the Indian government made a formal request to Sri Lanka for the extradition of Prabhakaran and two of his associates as prime suspects for the Gandhi killing. These events helped to turn international opinion against the LTTE.[71]

Lakshman's assassination in August 2005 led to another strong reaction against the LTTE. Less than a week later, as Wikileaks later revealed, a US diplomatic cable reported: 'EU missions in Colombo will recommend to Brussels that the EU designate the LTTE as a terrorist organization.'[72] The EU finally proscribed the LTTE on 17 May 2006.[73] Canada had already done so on 10 April 2006. It seemed that in death Lakshman completed the process, on which he had already embarked with notable success, of getting the LTTE proscribed in several key countries where funds had been raised from Tamil diasporas. All this was part of a broader process of isolating the LTTE internationally which he had done so much to advance. This process paved the way for their military defeat in May 2009. However, controversies about the proscription of the LTTE continued: for example, in a case in the Netherlands in 2011, a court indicated doubts about the proscription of the LTTE.[74] Also in 2011, a petition for deproscription was put on the agenda of the EU's General Court.[75]

There was an interesting logical inconsistency in Lakshman's successful campaign for proscription of the LTTE. He reluctantly accepted that in light of the probability of peace talks the proscription should not be implemented in Sri Lanka itself. The LTTE had been formally proscribed in Sri Lanka from 26 January 1998 until 4 September 2002, when the ban was lifted as a necessary preliminary to commencing peace talks with the LTTE in Thailand. Other governments reportedly assured Sri Lanka that their bans on LTTE would not be affected by a local deproscription.[76] (The Sri Lankan government re-introduced the proscription on 7 January 2009.)

Was Lakshman right to support the 2002 deproscription of the LTTE? His clear view was that it was important to try to negotiate an end to the conflict in Sri Lanka, and that Sri Lanka's ethnic problems required a political, indeed constitutional, solution: models of self-determination, autonomy, federalism and so on were up for discussion. In short, even while taking a tough line against a terrorist movement, he recognized that it was sometimes necessary to talk with it on specific issues, or at least demonstrate a preparedness to do so. He was under no illusion that the LTTE could be relied on to observe faithfully the provisions of a ceasefire, and was one of the leading critics of their poor record in that regard. On the other hand, he understood that talks might expose splits in the adversary's ranks, and also that a refusal to engage in serious negotiations would be damaging for the Sri Lankan government. This was a responsibility that only the Sri Lankan government could exercise. In short, Lakshman's position was illogical only if one starts from a dogmatic position that toughness in addressing the problem of terrorism is incompatible with flexibility in addressing the political issues involved. Lakshman was no dogmatist.

The Laws of War

The long-running conflict in Sri Lanka between the government and the Tamil Tigers was deeply etched on Lakshman's mind and informed his actions within and outside Sri Lanka. What is sometimes called the 'Eelam War' went through four main phases: 1983–7, 1990–95, 1995–2002 and (after his death) 2006–9. The first three phases ended in ceasefire agreements that failed to end the conflict. Lakshman's acute awareness of the larger political context of the struggle, as well as his legal professionalism, made him a particularly vocal advocate of observance of the laws of war, also called international humanitarian law. He made impressive speeches on this subject at military academies in Sri Lanka.[77] It is worth enquiring what his views might have been regarding the controversy-ridden final stages of the war, in 2006–9.

His position regarding the laws of war was not free of ambiguity. Under his watch, as under that of his predecessors and successors, Sri Lanka never became a party to the Geneva Protocols I and II additional to the 1949 Geneva Conventions, and dealing respectively with international and non-international armed conflict; nor to the 1998 Rome Statute of the International Criminal Court. Moreover, he declined to classify the armed conflict in Sri Lanka as either an international war or a civil war, referring to it instead as an internal conflict. In addition, he naturally recognized that the very existence of terrorists did not fit easily into the classification of belligerents in the Geneva Conventions, and that terrorist acts such as bombings of civilians are by their nature violations of the laws of war. At the same time he urged that in their struggle against a terrorist movement, the armed forces had to operate within a legal framework, one key part of which was observance of the laws of war. This was important for the armed forces' own cohesion, discipline and reputation; and it was also important if Sri Lanka was to minimize bitterness after the conflict, and to retain positive support from the community of states.

What does the last phase of the conflict in Sri Lanka, ending with the LTTE's defeat on 18 May 2009, tell us about the adequacy or otherwise of the approach that Lakshman had consistently taken up to his death in August 2005? (Map 4 indicates the approximate areas of control in late 2005.) He would have seen the necessity for battle, and would have been critical of some of the foreign advice being offered to Sri Lanka. When the military campaign gathered momentum in the early months of 2009, many governments, including the UK government, repeatedly advocated a ceasefire. This advocacy was badly received by the government of Sri Lanka and much public opinion there. This was partly because of a long-held Sri Lankan suspicion of international bodies proffering advice to make concessions to the LTTE. As Barbara Crossette had written in 2002: 'To many Sri Lankans, Tamils as well as Sinhalese, the advice from outsiders approached incomprehensible madness, and it left a residue of resentment, particularly toward international human rights groups, even though they have lately been far more critical of the rebels.'[78] A more immediate reason for refusing ceasefire calls was that the ongoing military campaign seemed at long last to offer a possibility of victory, and therefore of bringing an end to a hideous armed conflict that had lasted for 26 years. To judge by his record, Lakshman would have been an unwavering advocate of victory, and would have been against a ceasefire at that point.

Where it is much more likely that he would have had a significantly different approach from that of the Sri Lankan government is over implementation of the laws of war. The government repeatedly claimed to be observing the law. In 2008–9 it stated that it was implementing a policy of 'zero casualties to civilians';[79] and it announced 'No Fire Zones' (NFZs) in which civilians could gather.[80] At the same time there were some ominous developments, and a failure to communicate with the outside world. In September 2008, as the military campaign was developing rapidly, the government announced that it could no longer ensure the safety of international humanitarian personnel in the Vanni area in north-east Sri Lanka, and ordered them to leave.[81] It also actively discouraged international press reporting from the front lines. The government position exposed it to the obvious criticism that it was preventing the world from seeing certain actions that might be violations of the laws of war.

Subsequently there were numerous allegations that, in the final months of the conflict, Tamil civilians, including those who had fled to the NFZs, had been shelled and otherwise harmed by the Sri Lankan armed forces. The Sri Lankan government claimed that these allegations were simply part of a huge disinformation campaign waged by the LTTE and certain non-governmental organizations; and that the harm to civilians was mainly due to the LTTE or was unintended collateral damage by the advancing forces.

In April 2011 the *Report of the UN Secretary-General's Panel of Experts on Accountability in Sri Lanka* was published. Over 200 pages long, it concentrated mainly on the final period of the conflict, between September 2008 and May 2009. It stated:

> The Panel found credible allegations, which if proven, indicate that a wide range of serious violations of international humanitarian law and international human rights law was committed both by the Government of Sri Lanka and the LTTE, some of which would amount to war crimes and crimes against humanity.[82]

The Sri Lankan government, after receiving early information about this report, vociferously rejected its key conclusions.[83] On releasing the report on 25 April 2011, the UN said in a statement:

> The report was shared in its entirety with the Government of Sri Lanka on 12 April. The Secretary-General has indicated his willingness to publicize the Government's response alongside the report. This invitation was extended to the Sri Lankan Government throughout the week, including again on Saturday by the Secretary-General to the External Affairs Minister of Sri Lanka. The Government has not responded to this offer, which nonetheless still stands.
>
> The Secretary-General trusts that the Government of Sri Lanka will continue to respect the work of the United Nations and its agencies as well as its obligations to the safety of United Nations staff in Colombo. He regrets the inflammatory tone of some of the recent public statements emanating from Sri Lanka.[84]

The Sri Lankan government continued to denounce the report. However, it did not initially submit a detailed refutation of the allegations, and even, claiming that it had made 'adequate response', indicated that it would not do so.[85] In a statement at the UN Human Rights Council in May 2011 it accused the panel of bias, emphasized the successful rescue of many Tamil civilians, and urged that Sri Lanka's government-appointed Lessons Learnt and Reconciliation Commission (LLRC), which had been established in May 2010, should be given more time to do its work.[86]

The first full-length Sri Lankan official statement about the last phase of the conflict was in a 160-page report entitled *Humanitarian Operation: Factual Analysis*, published in July 2011. This was not presented as a response to the UN Panel and indeed makes no mention of it. Its purpose was indicated in its opening paragraph:

> This report sets forth the factual background and operational context of the Humanitarian Operation undertaken by the Government of Sri Lanka between July 2006 and May 2009 to free the country from the Liberation Tigers of Tamil Eelam (LTTE). An examination of these facts demonstrates why the Government of Sri Lanka engaged in a military strategy against the LTTE, why Security Forces used the level of force they did, and how at each stage in the operation Sri Lanka took extraordinary steps to respect and protect the lives of civilians.[87]

The slowness of Sri Lanka in responding to international criticism left it exposed. In September 2011 the UN Secretary-General sent the report of his Panel of Experts to the UN Human Rights Council in Geneva, stating pointedly: 'While the Secretary-General had given time to the government of Sri Lanka to respond to the report, the Government had declined to do so, and instead has produced its own reports on the situation in the north of Sri Lanka, which are being forwarded along with the Panel of Experts report.'[88]

In the event it was left to the Lessons Learnt and Reconciliation Commission, whose remit did not specifically refer to allegations of war crimes, to produce the first substantive response to some of the controversies about final stages of the war. Amnesty International, Human Rights Watch and

International Crisis Group all refused to testify to the LLRC because they considered it 'deeply flawed in structure and practice'.[89]

The LLRC's 400-page report, presented to the Sri Lanka parliament on 16 December 2011, contains extensive coverage of a wide range of issues that arose about the events of 2006–9. Its longest chapter is about international humanitarian law issues. It accepts that 'considerable civilian casualties had in fact occurred during the final phase of the conflict.'[90] It attributes much of the responsibility for this to the LTTE, not least for its use of the NFZs for military emplacements and operations, and its use of human shields.[91] In its conclusions, the LLRC does not completely exonerate the government side. On the one hand it states that 'the protection of the civilian population was given the highest priority' by the Sri Lankan armed forces. On the other hand, as regards specific instances of death or injury to civilians, it states:

> [T]he material nevertheless points towards possible implication of the Security Forces for the resulting death or injury to civilians, even though this may not have been with an intent to cause harm. In these circumstances the Commission stresses that there is a duty on the part of the State to ascertain more fully, the circumstances under which such incidents could have occurred, and if such investigations disclose wrongful conduct, to prosecute and punish the wrong doers. Consideration should also be given to providing appropriate redress to the next of kin of those killed and those injured as a humanitarian gesture that would help the victims to come to terms with personal tragedy, both in relation to the incidents referred to above and any other incidents which further investigations may reveal.[92]

Regarding controversies over the number of civilian casualties, the LLRC report called for 'a professionally designed household survey covering all affected families in all parts of the island to ascertain firsthand the scale and the circumstances of death and injury to civilians, as well as damage to property during the period of the conflict.'[93] This matter was already being officially addressed. On 24 November 2011 the Sri Lankan defence secretary, Gotabhaya Rajapaksa, announced that an official count of the number of civilians killed in the final stages of the war was close to completion. He added that the count so far showed that a very small number of civilians had died through military action; and he acknowledged that a small number of soldiers may have been responsible for some crimes. Questions were raised about how such a count was being conducted and how cause of death was being ascertained.[94]

The LLRC report was more thorough than some of the commission's early critics had expected. Although it placed much of the responsibility on the LTTE for locating military positions and personnel in the NFZs and close to hospitals, it did recognize that there had been a serious problem of civilian casualties, and it did call for further investigation of a number of key allegations.

International reaction to the LLRC report was mixed. In an instant response on the day the report was issued, Human Rights Watch in New York, while noting the LLRC's recognition that there had been extensive civilian casualties, said that the report 'disregards the worst abuses by government forces, rehashes longstanding recommendations, and fails to advance accountability for victims of Sri Lanka's civil armed conflict'.[95] On 19 December 2011, the US State Department, judiciously mixing praise and criticism, urged the Sri Lankan government 'not only to fulfil all of the recommendations of the report as it stands, but also to address those issues that the report did not cover'.[96] Three days after that, the International Crisis Group produced a measured assessment, mixing praise for the report's recognition of 'important events and grievances that have contributed to decades of political violence and civil war in Sri Lanka' with criticism of some of its shortcomings.[97] On 25 December the Indian government issued a statement noting the Sri Lankan government's assurance about implementation of the report's recommendations, and in particular calling for independent and credible investigation of alleged human rights violations.[98] On 22 March 2012 the UN Human Rights Council adopted a US-backed resolution noting that the report does not adequately address serious allegations of violations of international law, and calling on Sri Lanka to 'implement the constructive recommendations' in the LLRC report and 'to take all necessary additional steps to fulfil its relevant legal obligations ... to ensure justice, equity, accountability and reconciliation for all Sri Lankans.'[99]

The LLRC report and the debate it attracted show that questions remain about the manner in which the Sri Lankan government managed certain aspects of the final campaign of 2008–9 and the subsequent allegations relating to it. During the last months of the conflict, an approach which not only placed emphasis on the protection of civilians, but also permitted international verification of such protection, might have facilitated victory by encouraging even more defections than there were from the Tamil side. In the aftermath, greater respect for international institutions, and prompter and more coherent responses to accusations about these issues, might have reduced the spate of adverse international comment, which has continued to the present.

Lakshman, when foreign minister, always insisted that the relevant rules of the laws of war and human rights must be observed for reasons that were both moral and practical. Ever open to discussion on these issues, he was prepared to investigate, and respond to, criticisms made of Sri Lanka in international fora. He believed in handling such matters in an internationally acceptable manner, and gained support by so doing. Through his adroit management of Sri Lanka's diplomacy up to 2005 he provided a basis for the eventual defeat of the LTTE. Had he survived to play his part in the final phase in 2008–9 and thereafter it is likely that, as regards observance of the laws of war, he would have taken an approach distinct in certain respects from the course actually taken. He would have defended the government publicly – he was a loyal team player – but he would have pressed internally, and in all likelihood effectively, for a strategic and diplomatic policy less vulnerable to international opprobrium. Similar issues arise concerning the many post-2009 reports alleging that the Sri Lankan authorities were responsible for violations of minority rights and even torture.[100] His instinct would have been to react vigorously and to address these problems at their roots. In the aftermath of this long and bitter conflict, he would have pressed energetically for reconciliation; and for tackling the structural causes of Sri Lanka's conflicts, including through state reform.

A Special Amalgam of Realism and Idealism

Lakshman's approach to international affairs in general, and to terrorism in particular, contains some notably strong elements of realism: (1) a belief in the importance of sovereign states; (2) a recognition that power and interest are guiding factors in state behaviour, and that force may be essential to state survival in emergencies; (3) an interest in strategy as an enduring element of statecraft.

His approach also contains some equally strong elements of idealism, including: (1) a belief in democracy and in the rights of individuals; (2) an acceptance that law, both domestic and international, has a key role in protecting those rights and in limiting the worst excesses of the exercise of military power; (3) an appreciation of the role of international institutions, whether on the regional or global level. In short, he believed in a certain idea of progress, both as an actual achievement of human societies and as an aspiration for the future.

Such amalgams of realism and idealism are common enough in practitioners of international relations. What is striking about Lakshman's combination is the exceptionally clear way in which he articulated it, his willingness to take on the hardest problems and seek answers to them, and the practical spirit that imbued all his actions. His extraordinary work in persuading the US and UK governments to modify their views of terrorism in general and the LTTE in particular is ample evidence of how sheer skill and persuasiveness can affect diplomatic outcomes. His emphasis on the value of democracy, while being reluctant to act as a missionary for it, was a reasonable response to the world he faced as foreign minister, and is equally suited to the world today. Above all, his awareness that we live in a plural world – in which different societies are not about to adopt a single reach-me-down approach to democracy, development and international security – is a valuable antidote to the universalist claims which characterized Western attitudes to the post-Cold War world. He had the exceptional courage that was needed to immerse himself in that central challenge of our age – how deeply divided post-colonial societies can establish legitimate constitutional orders and stable relations with neighbours. He was not perfect, but he did have not only courage in full measure, but also a morally and politically coherent approach to some of the most difficult problems of our times.

'I did what I did and I have no regrets'

The last word should be Lakshman's own. In the question and answer session after his lecture at the Brookings Institution in Washington DC in May 2004, he gave one of many indications that he knew the fate that awaited him and could accept it with equanimity:

Q. Minister, you, in your earlier ...
The Honourable Minister: Incarnation? (laughter)
Q (continued) ... period in the office, you travelled around the world and lobbied for the LTTE to be included in the terrorist list. How much of an involvement are you thinking that you will play in the coming peace process? My feeling is that you know, you are not looked at favourably by the members of the Liberation Tigers. So you yourself may be an impediment to the progress of the peace process. So can you tell us, in what role you are going to be or how you are seeing your involvement will be?
A. I am only aware that the LTTE would prefer to see me dead. (laughter) You are right, and they might succeed. That doesn't bother me in the slightest. I did my duty as I saw it at the time. Because I was speaking, acting for the vast majority of the people of the country. The LTTE's behaviour at that time was atrocious. And I did what I did and I have no regrets whatsoever. If I have earned a death warrant from the LTTE, and I have, then, so be it. It doesn't frighten me in the slightest. Now on the practicality . . ., yes, if I am an impediment, I will certainly stand down. I will certainly make it very clear that I don't want to be an impediment when there is a much bigger cause than my self, because I am not looking for headlines or the flash bulbs or any of that kind at all. So it gives me no difficulty whatsoever to say categorically, and publicly, but first, to the Government, I will stand down, don't bother about me at all – and good luck to all of you.

CHAPTER 2

Sketch of the Life of Lakshman Kadirgamar

Sarath N. Silva

This essay is a revised version of the address by the Hon. Sarath Silva, Chief Justice of Sri Lanka. He was speaking at an event, or 'reference', in the Ceremonial Court of Sri Lanka's Supreme Court at Hulftsdorp, Colombo, on 4 August 2006 to commemorate the first anniversary of Kadirgamar's assassination on 12 August 2005.

*****

Lakshman Kadirgamar's father Samuel Kadirgamar was an eminent lawyer who served as the President of the Ceylon Law Society. Although his ancestors came from Jaffna, Lakshman was born in Colombo. He had his education at Trinity College, Kandy, where he excelled both in studies and in sports. He captained the cricket team, played rugger for the college and was a champion athlete. In the academic field, in addition to regular prizes, he won two coveted special prizes – the Nell History Prize and the Napier Clavering Prize. In 1949 he was awarded the prestigious Ryde Gold Medal for the best all-round student, and in his last year there, 1950, he was the Senior Prefect. Considering his unmatched achievements, from the perspective of a Trinitian, I would unhesitatingly say that he was the best of them all. His link with the alma mater continued: he was on the Board of Governors from 1996 to 2003, and also served a term as President of the Old Boys' Association, working actively to improve the facilities of the college.

He entered the University of Ceylon in the first batch of students of the Law Faculty, where too he continued his all-round excellence. He played cricket for the university, and in athletics won the Indian inter-university 110 m hurdles title in 1951 and 1952, and the All Ceylon title in the same event for those years. His academic excellence resulted in his being awarded an LLB Hons. degree by the University of Ceylon in 1953. In 1954 he completed his law education in Ceylon on being awarded a first class degree in the final examination for the admission of advocates. He entered the profession as an advocate in the year 1956 and soon left for further education at Balliol College in the University of Oxford, and there too continued his record of all-round excellence. In 1959, in recognition of his debating skills, he served as the elected president of the prestigious

Oxford Union. A few months before his death, the Oxford Union paid the highest tribute to him by unveiling his portrait.

In 1960 he was awarded BLitt degree at Oxford. Remarkably, in 1958 he had already entered the Bar as a barrister of the Inner Temple. In 1995, in recognition of the high eminence he achieved, he was made an Honorary Master of the Inner Temple.

He practised with great success as an advocate in Sri Lanka's courts – albeit intermittently in view of his extensive foreign assignments. He was a consultant of the International Labour Organization (ILO), Geneva, in 1974–76, and in 1976 took a permanent appointment at the World Intellectual Property Organization (WIPO), Geneva. He was instrumental in bringing about a codification of different legal regimes of copyrights, patents, trademarks and industrial designs, in a single code as the Code of Intellectual Property Law. He was the Director for Asia and the Pacific at the WIPO during the period 1983–88. He persuaded the then Minister of Trade, Lalith Athulathmudali, another product of Oxford, to adopt the model draft Code of Intellectual Property Law in Sri Lanka. In that sense he foreshadowed the current developments in the area of intellectual property law. He may be considered as the father of codification of law in this regard.

At the conclusion of his assignment with the WIPO in 1988 he had acquired such stature and international experience that could have easily fitted him to a high international position, but he chose to return to his motherland.

Immediately upon his return he took on several assignments to address the lawyers on the developments in the area of intellectual property law. He emerged as the leading counsel in that branch of the law and in 1991 took silk as a President's Counsel.

The watershed election in 1994 saw yet another change in his affairs. He was persuaded to be nominated as a National List candidate of the People's Alliance, and with the significant electoral triumph of that party he was appointed Minister of Foreign Affairs. All would agree that Her Excellency the President Chandrika Kumaratunga could not have made a better choice for the portfolio.

The international image of Sri Lanka was then at a very low ebb with a dismal record of human rights resulting from extra-judicial killings with brazen impunity. Kadirgamar set about the task with quiet unshaken courage and dedication. Drawing on the considerable influence he had in the international arena, and aided by a significant change in the human rights record within the country, he gradually improved the image of Sri Lanka.

He made use of his long tenure as the Minister of Foreign Affairs to go from one international forum to another and to grant interviews to leading TV stations of the world. Those of us who watched these TV interviews spent anxious moments when searching questions were put to him. But he was always adept in answering them. Being soft-spoken with immaculate pronunciation, clarity of exposition and logic of argument, he painstakingly retrieved the tarnished image of the motherland.

Thereafter, he gradually went on the offensive and exposed the double standards of some European countries that masked the true face of terrorism within this country; and he took the battle virtually single-handed to the enemy corner, relentlessly pressing for the imposition of sanctions on the terrorists. He was largely successful in this endeavour, and the sanctions imposed by the developed countries were in large measure the result of his sustained and skilful work.

Kadirgamar transcended the ethnic divide and was a nationalist to the core. He had a deep and abiding concern for the people of Jaffna, who may be described as the worst affected in the conflict that ravaged that part of the country for two decades. The burning of the Jaffna Library in 1981, and the subsequent setting off of bombs in 1985, had particularly affected the inhabitants of Jaffna and beyond. Kadirgamar identified the Jaffna Library, which was undoubtedly the richest literary heritage of the people of Jaffna, as a point where an immediate reconstruction effort should be started. In 1997 he was appointed co-chairman of the project to reconstruct the library. A little known fact, to which he deliberately avoided giving publicity, was that the entire reconstruction programme was monitored by a committee of the Ministry of Foreign Affairs. He first established an interim library in the building that had been previously used by the LTTE as its headquarters. Thereafter, he sent a team of officers to ascertain the views of the people of Jaffna, whether the old building which was destroyed should be reconstructed in that form or whether a new structure should be erected. The people opted for the reconstruction of the building at the original site on the same design. The actual reconstruction started in 1998 and continued till 2001. After the work was completed there was a change of government which resulted in no publicity being given to the fact that it was Kadirgamar who had painstakingly restored the building to its original grandeur. Throughout this period he made use of his extensive contacts in foreign countries and obtained books for the Jaffna library. These consignments of books were regularly sent to Jaffna to keep the process of re-establishment of the library on course. Thus he had a genuine patriotic concern to resolve the problem of the ethnic conflict, and to serve the Tamil people actively in the process of reconstruction.

This is the fourth reference we are making in respect of President's Counsel who have been cruelly assassinated by terrorist attacks. There were previously, references made to Hon. Lalith Athulathmudali, to Hon. Gamini Dissanayake and Dr Neelan Tiruchelvam. They were all legal luminaries with professional skills, who opted to serve the country in the political arena. Their capacity, skill and stature were such that they could have stood their own with the best in the world. We can say, on sad reflection, that the country has been deprived of the cream of eminent people of the highest ability.

It is strange that two of them are from the Sinhala community and two from the Tamil community, which fact detracts from any assumption that they were assassinated on the basis of an ethnic divide. More in the line of truth may be that these assassinations were cruelly revengeful acts to deny to this country men of excellence and to push the country into the dark abyss of death and destruction, where only the force of terror would prevail.

Kadirgamar was alive to the obvious danger he was courting through his national endeavour. An official of the foreign ministry who accompanied him wrote in an article that after making a most effective speech in Europe seeking sanctions on the terrorists, Kadirgamar had commented to him 'I have taken one more step towards the terrorist bullet.' Sadly, that prediction came to pass.

As a nation we owe a debt to this great statesman. In the Sinhala song that was composed and broadcast at his funeral, bringing tears to the eyes of many, it was poignantly stated that he 'was the world to us and that we stand indebted to him'.

Although he was a politician, he never lost his gentle way of life and qualities of compassion and kindness. The following passage in the final scene of Shakespeare's immortal play *Julius Caesar* aptly describes these attributes of Lakshman Kadirgamar:

> He only, on a general honest thought,
> And common good to all, made one of them.
> His life was gentle; and the elements
> So mix'd in him that Nature might stand up
> And say to all the world, This was a man!

The late Hon. Lakshman Kadirgamar had a vision for Sri Lanka. A vision of freedom from fear, of unity, reasonableness and truth. This vision is finely encompassed by the Nobel Laureate Rabindranath Tagore in the 35th verse of the collection entitled *Gitanjali*:

> Where the mind is without fear and the head is held high;
> Where knowledge is free;
> Where the world has not been broken up into fragments by narrow domestic walls;
> Where words come out from the depth of truth;
> Where tireless striving stretches its arms towards perfection;
> Where the clear stream of reason has not lost its way into the dreary desert sand of dead habit;
> Where the mind is led forward by thee into ever-widening thought and action –
> Into that heaven of freedom, my Father, let my country awake.

CHAPTER 3

Lakshman Kadirgamar
The Lawyer Turned Politician

Sinha Ratnatunga

Lakshman Kadirgamar returned to Sri Lanka in 1989 after a successful and effective stint since 1971 with UN agencies in Geneva. This service was principally with the World Intellectual Property Organization (WIPO), where he was Director for Asia and the Pacific from 1983 to 1988. He might have reasonably expected in due course to head the organization, but his calling to his roots for the 'last lap' of what was already an illustrious career may have played its part in his decision to leave. The best was yet to come.

He came back at a time when so many other professionals were contemplating leaving. The country was in total upheaval with two parallel insurgencies: one, by the minority Tamil youth of the Liberation Tigers of Tamil Eelam (LTTE);[1] the other, by majority Sinhalese youth of the Janatha Vimukthi Peramuna (JVP), or People's Liberation Front.[2] In the midst of the mayhem of 1989, with bomb explosions, curfews, transport strikes and gruesome killings on the streets, Kadirgamar resumed the law practice he had abandoned almost two decades earlier. I joined him to begin a law practice I had never started.

Not long after his return, the then Foreign Minister of Sri Lanka, Shahul Hameed, an old friend, asked him if he was happy with his present role. 'Yes,' replied Kadirgamar, and added for good measure, 'Let's say, I wouldn't trade it for another.'

Elections to the Bar Association of Sri Lanka were round the corner, and while chatting on a winter's night in England in 1992 he asked me if I thought Sri Lanka's lawyers would be prepared to vote for a minority Tamil like him as their president. His name had been bandied about as a non-political figure, capable of giving leadership to stand up to the somewhat authoritarian administration in the country at the time. The discussion expanded to politics in general, and the acceptance of 'a Tamil' in national politics, in particular. The seeds of entering public life in Sri Lanka were germinating in his mind.

Entry into Politics

Tumultuous events were taking place in Sri Lanka. President Ranasinghe Premadasa had become the head of state and of government. His increasingly autocratic rule saw an inevitable split in the powerful ruling party, the United National Party (UNP).[3] Premadasa had appointed Kadirgamar as a President's Counsel for his legal competence, but Kadirgamar found it perfectly in order to appear for the president's rival, Lalith Athulathmudali, an Oxford contemporary of Kadirgamar and one-time President of the Oxford Union like himself, who led a breakaway party. In April 1993 Athulathmudali was assassinated, and a week later President Premadasa himself was assassinated. In one week, the country's political structure had been shaken to its foundations.

When Athulathmudali was killed, Kadirgamar joined the Bar Association procession at the huge funeral rally in Colombo. Along with many others, he braved tear-gas shells fired by police riot squads to disperse the large gathering. Unable to make it to the cemetery in the resultant commotion, he returned home in a lawyer's car, dabbing his gassed eyes with a wet handkerchief. That gave him a taste of realpolitik in Sri Lanka.

Meanwhile, Kadirgamar was becoming increasingly disenchanted with the legal system: he found his arguments were not resonating with some of the judges in the lower courts who were not particularly attracted to the intricacies of the law. The die was therefore cast. Already knee-deep in the muddied peripheral politics of Sri Lanka, he was now wading through to the even murkier waters of active politics. He prepared a team of top criminal lawyers in the country to challenge a Scotland Yard report commissioned by the government that said Athulathmudali was killed by the LTTE. The innuendo in that challenge was clear: was he killed then by the government?

The UNP had by then been in office for over one and a half decades and its politicians were getting fat and stale. General (parliamentary) elections were called in July 1994, and Kadirgamar was ready, willing and able to plunge into the deep end of politics. He was reluctant to traipse along to party nomination boards seeking a ticket. So who was to invite him? And from which party?

In his chambers he would say things like, 'It's easy to turn the Foreign Ministry around,' which seemed presumptuous at the time. Here he was, not even an MP, let alone a government MP, a would-be first-timer in parliament in any event, imagining that the plum job of foreign minister could be given to a novice like him.

Then suddenly, everything began to fall into place. The ruling UNP, constricted as all parties that have ruled for long periods by the dead weight of their old stalwarts, had neither the time nor the inclination to look for new faces. On the other hand, there was a dearth of worthy sorts in the lacklustre opposition.

Ms Chandrika Bandaranaike-Kumaratunga had taken the reins of the main opposition, the Sri Lanka Freedom Party (SLFP)[4] from her ailing mother, the world's first woman prime minister, Sirimavo Bandaranaike. The daughter was a colourful new addition in the political firmament. She had played second fiddle to her late actor-husband for a while, and then gone into self-exile in London with her children after his assassination.[5] Armed with a smile and very little else, she was the rallying point for an electorate looking for an alternative to the fading incumbents.

Mother Bandaranaike, however, remained the party leader and was having treatment for a troublesome knee abroad when nominations for the general elections were called. The Sri Lankan electoral system is based on proportional representation and reserves a specific number of seats in parliament for candidates who are on what is called the 'National List' of their party. These places are allocated on the basis of the total number of votes a party receives at the general election. The National List is meant to accommodate intellectuals and others representing ethnic or unrepresented groups who have no particular constituencies to contest, or are not the contesting type but who are expected to make a worthwhile contribution to parliament. Each party must present their National List before an election. The daughter, acting for the matriarch of the party, proposed the name of a retired Chief Justice as a representative of the minority Tamils in Sri Lanka.

The judge had become the Governor of the Western Province after retirement and had come to know Ms Chandrika Kumaratunga during her brief stint as the chief minister of the province. But Mrs. Bandaranaike, on her return, was enraged on seeing his name on the list. 'Over my dead body,' she said. Her daughter had been thoroughly insensitive to the fact that the judge had sat on a Presidential Commission of Inquiry that recommended Mrs. Bandaranaike be stripped of her civic rights. This act, that effectively threw the Grand Old Lady into the political wilderness for a considerable period of time, was widely seen as part of a witch-hunt by the UNP after it came to power in 1977 to neutralize her as a political opponent.

Mrs. Bandaranaike still called the shots within her party, and the judge's name was promptly struck off. With the clock ticking for the closure of nominations, it was a scramble to find a suitable replacement. Aides began a frantic search for a minority Tamil. One of Mrs. Bandaranaike's siblings, Justice Barnes Ratwatte, a retired Supreme Court judge, suggested she ask Kadirgamar, who had studied at the same school – Trinity College, Kandy. Kadirgamar had been back in Sri Lanka for five years and was fairly well known beyond the narrow confines of legal circles. He had rekindled old acquaintances and made new friends, including diplomats in Colombo.

He wrote to the local newspapers on issues of current interest, was often invited to participate in professional seminars and was a sought-after guest speaker at formal society dinners. His family was well connected in the upper-crust circles in Colombo. Although his Queen's Counsel brother, Sam, was an election agent and lawyer for a former UNP prime minister, Lakshman was considered apolitical, as was another brother, Rajan, who was the island nation's one-time Navy Commander; they tilted if at all towards the UNP rather than the SLFP.

When the call came, it seemed as if destiny was calling. Like Mr Barkis in *David Copperfield*, Kadirgamar was willing. He hurriedly discussed the matter with some close friends, and consensus was reached the same night. He should agree to his name being placed on the National List of the SLFP on the guarantee that he be picked as one of the MPs after the elections. (You can have your name on the List and not be selected depending on the number of bonus seats the party is entitled to after the count.) The thinking was that at least he would be an opposition MP if the party lost the election.

During the campaign that was to follow, his brief was to appear on television time allocated to the party and speak in English. His theme – that he had received so much from society that it was time to give back – struck a chord in an otherwise brutally cynical electorate. As it turned out, the SLFP won the parliamentary election of 16 August 1994. Kadirgamar was made not only a Member of Parliament, but Foreign Minister of Sri Lanka. He had traded one calling for another, after all.

Foreign Minister, 1994–2001

After an election in Sri Lanka, curfews are traditionally imposed to curb political victimization. Kadirgamar's domestic staff had yet to return from voting in their respective villages. One of the first invitations he received as the new foreign minister was to the national day reception of Indonesia. He had to drive his own car. He had not got one yet from the government, nor did he have an official chauffeur; he had not even got his police guards. Not finding a parking space, he had to leave his car a fair distance from the reception venue and walk to it.

When you consider his 11-year roller-coaster career in politics what strikes one is the contrast in the casual way he came for that day's reception, in his first days of public life, and the manner in which he had to travel in the last days – in an armour-plated vehicle, surrounded by escort jeeps blaring their horns and a phalanx of army commandos armed to the teeth, waving motorists away.

Kadirgamar became a sensation with the majority Sinhalese community with his maiden speech to the new parliament:

Let it never be said, if it ever could have been said, that the Sinhala people are racists. They are not, Mr. Speaker. They are absolutely not, and I think this election has demonstrated that so handsomely, that that particular argument can be laid to rest forever.[6]

The SLFP campaigned on a platform of negotiating with the LTTE. Kadirgamar wanted to make an immediate statement about what he felt was the unfair blame the entire majority community, the Sinhalese, had received for dastardly acts in the 1983 race-riots which had targeted minority Tamils, and to a great extent had changed the course of the contemporary history of Sri Lanka. What was equally poignant was his call for bi-partisanship in political discourse. His was a refreshing breath of liberal air at the level of national politics.

In his maiden address to the UN General Assembly, he reiterated what he had said in his country's parliament: 'In my first speech one month ago in our newly elected Parliament, as a representative of the minority Tamil community, I made a statement that I shall now repeat here, in this supreme parliament of the peoples of the world.'[7] Sri Lanka's ambassador to the UN at the time had been troubled with the addition of these remarks to his minister's draft speech. He had, in fact, asked the minister if he really wanted them included, only to get a quick and firm reply in the affirmative.

These remarks got wide play in the local media again and Kadirgamar was hailed by the vast majority of the people of Sri Lanka, especially the Sinhalese, as a crusader for the respect and dignity they had yearned for since the self-inflicted madness of a few among them in the 1983 anti-Tamil pogrom.[8]

However, Kadirgamar soon incurred the wrath of the separatist guerrilla organization the LTTE. They saw him as a foreign minister of a 'Sinhala state' defending the Sinhalese. For them, nothing could be as treacherous as a Tamil being dismissive of their armed struggle. Soon he was branded a 'traitor' by many in his own community, even professionals and city dwellers who, like him, had lived with the Sinhalese, benefiting from universal free education, the franchise and employment opportunities. Some had an abiding grudge that they were treated as minorities and not as full-fledged Sri Lankans. They didn't blame the divisive politics of their own politicians for this, but rather the Sinhalese politicians who fuelled this division. And they refused to see Kadirgamar as a unifier of the two communities.

In local politics, Kadirgamar learnt his lessons early. The fresh idealism he brought with him was soon shattered by the bitter realities of politics and hard-nosed politicians. His early statements did not endear him to the dyed-in-wool politicians ingrained in a corrupt system. At a cabinet meeting, some of his colleagues chided him for making a public comment that corruption was rampant in the country – because the inference was that ministers were corrupt. The salvo came from senior politicians in the Sri Lankan body politic. In Kuala Lumpur where he had led a delegation of businessmen to explore joint venture opportunities, he spoke on the opening day about the downside of corruption in business. That evening word got to him, not from the Malaysians but from the Sri Lankan business elite, that they accepted corruption as part and parcel of doing business. He was politely told to drop the subject. Even years later, when he was established as a front-liner himself, he would rather not talk of issues such as corruption that would touch a raw nerve among his colleagues.

As early as 1995, only a year into public office, a senior police detective visited Kadirgamar by appointment to tell him he was on the LTTE 'hit list', and that his security needed to be 'beefed up'. Indeed, the LTTE had issued a 'fatwa'. The news shook Kadirgamar. That evening he remarked he would 'go up in smoke' – a reference to becoming a victim of a suicide-bomber, the LTTE's dreaded trademark. There was a tinge of apprehension mixed with sadness, and perhaps a second thought about what he had got himself into.

As time went by, he became accustomed to the security cordon around him: the dummy convoys, the air tickets under false names, informing foreign governments of the need for special security, and all that went with protecting a man who had become possibly the number one enemy of the LTTE. There was no turning back now.

Soon, the burden of not only combating the LTTE in the international arena, but even on the political and military canvas at home, fell on his broad shoulders. Unlike many others, he studied and analysed every statement made by the LTTE, as he would a lawyer's brief. He would make notes and draft responses. He would catch every nuance and every contradiction. He was quickly inducted into the National Security Council, the apex body prosecuting the 'war', and became an integral part of formulating national policy on 'the ethnic issue'. He would complain that these meetings were not professionally handled; that minutes were never kept so follow-up action was lacking. He asked that cakes, snacks and tea not be served during discussions – saying that the whiff of food was not conducive to serious thinking. He infused some gravitas into the war effort against a deadly enemy of the state.

He also kept a relentless pace travelling and briefing foreign decision-makers on the LTTE's activities. Sri Lanka's image had been badly tarnished by the riots of July 1983; further, an influx of Tamils to Western countries, where they became a well-organized diaspora and pressure group, had had its effects. To convince international opinion that there was another side to the story, that the Sinhalese people and the Sri Lankan state were not as bad as they had been portrayed, and that this was a question of terrorism and not liberation, was a tall order.

In his frequent visits to the West and to India it was not only the men in political office he would meet. Outside the gaze of the public, he entertained old friends by then in high places, and was, in turn, invited to their homes. With them he would discuss Sri Lanka's problem. They were all decision-makers, either in the political, judicial or bureaucratic arena; or legal luminaries who could advise him on knotty constitutional matters. Alexander Downer, Australian foreign minister of the time, admired the persistence with which Kadirgamar argued his country's case. He said that the Sri Lankan minister was 'like a dog with a bone – he wouldn't let go'. He also praised him for being 'ahead of his time' in confronting the scourge of global terrorism long before the events of 11 September 2001.[9]

Kadirgamar was quick to cement the bonds with the new friends he made by virtue of his office. The British politician Liam Fox, with whom he had interacted very closely in forging bi-partisanship in the fractured Sri Lanka polity, emphasizes the importance Kadirgamar placed on 'personal chemistry' in the conduct of official matters.[10] When US Secretary of State Colin Powell mentioned that he recalled a big tree – one of the biggest he had ever seen – on a visit as a serving military man to the President's House in Colombo, Kadirgamar got the Director of the Botanical Gardens to give him the history of that spreading Banyan tree, and had pictures taken and sent to Powell by diplomatic pouch. Such thoughtful gestures endeared him to the powerful men and women in world capitals, though they never got into the press. Such was the tenacity and finesse with which he pursued personal relations among public figures.

His years at Oxford, which he famously referred to as 'the icing on the cake' of his life ('though the cake was baked at home')[11] had given him the confidence to pat colleagues on the shoulder and not have any inferiority complex that he was the foreign minister of a relatively small country. He upheld the dignity of his office. At the UN, for instance, he would not be seen 'hanging around' for another foreign minister, however important a country he or she was from, for a scheduled meeting. Once when official confirmation of an appointment with his counterpart in Japan was still pending, he refused to leave Colombo, saying that a foreign minister must not leave his 'station' without a confirmed appointment. He would send a birthday bouquet to US Secretary of State Madeleine Albright while not hesitating to fire off a stern missive to her Assistant Secretary of State asking why a sovereign country like Sri Lanka was placed in the dock of the legislature of the US with questions of human rights violations.[12]

In early 2000, Kadirgamar, having become an indispensable persona in the decision-making process of his country, was faced with a sudden illness that shook the higher echelons of the government. Diagnosed with kidney failure, he required a transplant, and a young Buddhist monk was found as a compatible donor. In March that year both were flown to New Delhi where, at the well-known Apollo Hospital, a team of young US-trained Indian doctors performed successful surgery on the Sri Lankan minister.

While Kadirgamar was convalescing at the official residence of the Sri Lankan High Commissioner to India, all hell broke loose back home. In one of their biggest attacks, code-named 'Unceasing Waves', to wrest back control of the northern Jaffna peninsula from government hands, LTTE cadres made a successful incursion through Elephant Pass, the narrow gateway to their citadel from which they had been ousted in 1995.[13]

President Chandrika Kumaratunga was on one of her frequent visits to the United Kingdom at the time. The political leadership virtually fell on the Deputy Minister of Defence Anuruddha Ratwatte. Very soon, 40,000 Sri Lankan troops were trapped in the peninsula and an SOS went out to India to evacuate them.

Kadirgamar was commissioned into action from his bed or more to the point, jumped into action of his own volition. He sought the Indian government's help for a possible evacuation of the besieged soldiers. A bloodbath was imminent and a 1983-like backlash against the Tamils living in the rest of the island was a real possibility. India's military establishment, having suffered a bloodied nose during their foray in Sri Lanka as a peacekeeping force (1987–91) when 1,000 of their officers and men were killed by the LTTE, opted for a 'hands-off' policy. With the southern Indian state of Tamil Nadu politically pressuring New Delhi to remain uninvolved, they could only offer covert assistance. Kadirgamar turned to the Israeli Ambassador in New Delhi to make a request for urgent armaments; the quid pro quo was diplomatic recognition. Such a move could upset the local Muslim lobby so he convinced his Muslim cabinet colleagues on the telephone urging them not to jeopardize the lives of 40,000 soldiers.

Six countries – Israel, China, Pakistan, India, Ukraine and the Czech Republic – came to Sri Lanka's aid with military hardware and other help. Multi-barrel rocket launchers saved the day for the beleaguered soldiers, and the LTTE attack was eventually repulsed. The fall of Jaffna was averted. Such was Kadirgamar's unwavering commitment to his work. After a full recovery, he went back to his punishing schedule.

The 9/11, 2001 incident saw the West launch the 'global war on terror'. However much it was centred on the conflicts in the Middle East and Afghanistan, Kadirgamar exploited to the full the view that terrorism was a global problem. He had credibility because long before 9/11 he had warned Western countries of the seriousness of the terrorist problem, and had persuaded them to proscribe the LTTE as a terrorist organization. Already in 1997 the US had declared the LTTE an FTO (Foreign Terrorist Organization). It was Lalith Athulathmudali as Sri Lanka's then National Security Minister who had begun discussions with the Ronald Reagan administration in the mid-1980s to have the LTTE declared an FTO, but it was

Kadirgamar's dealings directly with Madeleine Albright that saw it to a close. In the first list of 1997, the LTTE was the only non-Middle Eastern, non-Islamic organization to be declared an FTO, even though it did not fit the criteria entirely as it had not attacked US citizens or interests. Kadirgamar was in the US at the time and Albright had asked him to wait an extra day for the announcement, which was on 8 October 1997. Then on 28 February 2001 the British government announced the proscription of the LTTE as a terrorist organization.[14] In Kadirgamar's own words, these proscriptions 'came as a shock' to the guerrillas. Kadirgamar was credited for almost single-handedly arguing the case against the LTTE. Consequently, his security was upped from the police task force to army commandos.

When Commonwealth Secretary-General Don McKinnon was in Colombo on the morning of 9/11, he and Kadirgamar argued on whether 'international terrorism' ought to be included in the declaration at the upcoming CHOGM (Commonwealth Heads of Government Meeting) in Australia. Kadirgamar insisted on it, but McKinnon had his reservations. It was evening in Colombo when New York's twin towers and the Pentagon were hit. The world turned upside down and the next day, McKinnon did a 180-degree turn himself. The *Sunday Times* in Colombo reported it thus:

> Barely 24 hours earlier, just hours before the attacks in New York and Washington, the same Mr. McKinnon, a former Foreign Minister of New Zealand, had asked senior Foreign Ministry officials, including Foreign Minister Lakshman Kadirgamar whether Sri Lanka insisted on having a reference to international terrorism in the final declaration of the Commonwealth Summit scheduled for Brisbane in October.
>
> When Foreign Minister Kadirgamar had emphatically said 'Yes' to Sri Lanka's insistence, Mr. McKinnon is reported to have made a face and nodded.[15]

By the early 2000s, the tables had been turned on the LTTE on the battlefield, and the guerrillas were facing difficulties. However, the Sri Lankan government was also on the back foot. The economy was haemorrhaging and had recorded an unprecedented zero growth rate. Inefficient fiscal management, and lack of direction and drive on the economic front, had resulted in an increased dependence on foreign donor countries, mainly from the West, who demanded a 'political solution' to the insurgency in return for the cash. The Sri Lankan government resented this intrusion but could not afford to reject the economic carrot dangled before them.

There were many foreign suitors – 16 countries in all – who offered to play broker in peace negotiations with the LTTE. In the period from December 1999 to February 2000 it became clear, mainly from various statements from President Kumaratunga and the Sri Lankan government, that the choice would be Norway.[16] Perhaps the Norwegians were chosen partly because they were the preferred choice of the LTTE as well.

They were to play a terribly controversial role. Initially it was Kadirgamar who was tasked to explain their entry into the conflict. He was at pains to point out that they were not 'mediators' or 'negotiators' but 'facilitators' of the peace process. For many it was a distinction without a difference. Kadirgamar was annoyed when the public and even the media loosely referred to them as mediators or negotiators and equally displeased with the prospect of now having to deal with a wider Nordic presence, as the Norwegians roped in their Scandinavian neighbours into ceasefire monitoring teams. This happened after the LTTE announced a unilateral ceasefire in late 2000 and early 2001, and then formalized a Ceasefire Agreement (CFA) with the government in February 2002 following sudden parliamentary elections held on 5 December 2001 that sent Kadirgamar and his party into opposition.

Opposition, 2001–4

From December 2001 to April 2004, Kadirgamar's party, the SLFP, was out of power, but its leader President Kumaratunga continued as the elected head of state and constitutional head of government. The UNP, the former opposition, was now in effective control of parliament. It ran the show and formed the cabinet. However, Kadirgamar was far from idle. He was still an MP, and he was intimately involved in a range of discussions and decisions regarding a renewed peace process with the LTTE initiated by the new government.

In January 2002, in a speech to parliament explaining the opposition's attitude to this CFA and the peace process, Kadirgamar made a confession. He admitted that when the Norwegian government first came on board as far back as in 1998 'I was very much a party to that decision.' He said that the government had reached the point where there would be no movement in the peace process without the help of an 'outside party'.[17]

There was considerable friction in the early days between President Kumaratunga who headed the People's Alliance (PA) and the newly elected UNP government under Prime Minister Ranil Wickremesinghe in a French-style cohabitation set-up. It was a carry-over of the bad blood that existed when the UNP was in opposition and had complained of shabby treatment by Kadirgamar's People's Alliance. Kadirgamar, who was retained as a National List MP, became the president's International Affairs Adviser. The president had wanted to retain the crucial Ministry of Defence, being already the Commander-in-Chief of the Armed Forces by virtue of her constitutional position as Head of State. The new premier nevertheless insisted that the defence portfolio should be for an MP from his party. Informal tripartite talks between the president, the prime minister and Kadirgamar were held, and it was Kadirgamar who persuaded the president to release the Ministry of Defence on the basis that the people's mandate was now with the prime minister's party.

On 22 February 2002, Prime Minister Wickremesinghe signed the formal CFA with the LTTE without a word to his own cabinet or the president. The CFA was brokered by the Norwegians, by then well entrenched in the peace process. The prime minister went to inform the president about the CFA (Kadirgamar had been called for the meeting). As they spoke they could hear the helicopter bringing back the signed document from the jungles where the LTTE was operating. It was a fait accompli and again Kadirgamar persuaded the president to allow the prime minister his way.

The next day, Kadirgamar's speech on the prime minister's statement in parliament displayed a high degree of bi-partisanship. He had come to be regarded as the conscience of his party on the LTTE question. Back in April 1997, he had tried to forge bi-partisanship between Sri Lanka's two main parties, the UNP and the SLFP, through the Liam Fox Agreement.[18] This was authored by the British Conservative Party politician, then the British Under-Secretary of State for Foreign and Commonwealth Affairs, who had been contacted largely due to the UK having succeeded in a major breakthrough in their protracted Northern Ireland issue. However, neither Sri Lankan party had been really interested in implementing the Liam Fox Agreement. Now in January 2002 Kadirgamar – while no doubt reserving for himself and his party the right to be critical of the CFA later – offered the opposition's support to the new prime minister in his attempt to pursue a peaceful negotiated settlement with the separatist LTTE – a move for which Prime Minister Wickremesinghe would later be crucified. Kadirgamar concluded his speech by saying:

> Mr. Speaker, what I wish to emphasize is this, that the Government can rest assured that the People's Alliance will extend to it on all matters concerned with starting the talks, moving the talks and helping them to progress rapidly and as sensibly as possible, its fullest co-operation. . . . I am saying what I am saying this morning with the full authority of President Kumaratunga and the Parliamentary Group of the People's Alliance.[19]

A year later, however, Kadirgamar fired the first salvo against the new government. He began by referring to his speech of 23 January 2002 where he had said his party reserved the right to criticize the CFA, and then went on to say: 'Sri Lanka is in danger of being reduced to a nominal sovereign state. Soon, Sri Lanka will be a sovereign shell: the major attributes of a sovereign state – the capacity to govern, to resolve justifiable issues, to enforce the law, to protect its citizens throughout the entirety of its territory are being drained away by stealth, fractured by assault, and worn down by attrition.'[20] He argued that the CFA was a structurally flawed document.

While there was a lot of truth in that point of view, the prime minister was hoping that the LTTE was being led into a corner – and to the negotiating table. The much-maligned premier privately said he was 'seducing' the guerrillas out of the jungle.[21] Later he received the two biggest 'compliments' from the two most important LTTE military leaders of the time. Velupillai Prabhakaran, the LTTE supremo called the CFA a 'trap' and gave that as the reason for calling a Tamil voter boycott in the North and East in the 2005 presidential elections.[22] (This boycott paved the way for Ranil Wickremesinghe's opponent Mahinda Rajapaksa to emerge victorious.) The other 'compliment' came from Prabhakaran's erstwhile deputy Vinayagamoorthy Muralitharan – alias 'Col. Karuna' who maintained that he fell out with Prabhakaran who called him a 'traitor to his race' for signing an agreement with the Sri Lankan government during peace talks in Oslo in 2003.[23] His breakaway from the LTTE in 2004 (just prior to the parliamentary elections of that year) was the beginning of the end of the LTTE's military machine, which was split in two never to fully recover. Wickremesinghe received no bouquets for triggering this split, only brickbats, an election defeat and the label 'traitor' from the majority Sinhalese.

Meanwhile ceasefire violations were mounting, and the Scandinavian-manned Monitoring Mission was proving thoroughly ineffective. The LTTE was making demands for the High Security Zones (areas close to military installations) in the North to be dismantled and for the people to be given back their lands; they wanted unhindered movement on the seas, while the Navy in the eastern port city of Trincomalee was being encircled by new LTTE camps which were within shelling distance. Prime Minister Wickremesinghe was stomaching all this towards the end-game – but the opposition was losing its patience, and it was good politics to say that a de facto separate state was in the making. Kadirgamar ended his May 2003 speech in the House saying; 'I have to say that the Opposition is of the view that we are moving inexorably towards the day when Sri Lanka will no longer be a sovereign state.'

Privately, Kadirgamar felt he could move away from Sri Lankan politics during the short time he was in the opposition. In about 1999 or 2000 he had pooh-poohed a suggestion that he become the next Commonwealth Secretary-General: although it was Asia's turn and there was a group of interested people in the UK who wanted him to throw his hat into the ring, Kadirgamar had refused, referring to the Commonwealth in private as an inconsequential body with no clout in international relations.

The post of UN Secretary-General would be coming up – Kofi Annan's second term being due to end in December 2006. The assumption was that the next Secretary-General needed to be from Asia. Diplomats known to Kadirgamar since his Geneva days implanted the idea in his head, and he was not averse to making the move. However, in the brief interlude when out of office, the question of the Commonwealth post was raised again. Since 2000 the post had been filled by Don McKinnon whose first term was due to end in 2004. On a trip to the UK, Kadirgamar was once again buttonholed by the same group with close ties to the Commonwealth and who were unhappy with the way the Commonwealth Secretariat was being managed. Kadirgamar took the bait and accepted the challenge this time, but being in opposition, he needed the support of the government of Sri Lanka to be nominated.

That was least of his problems. Prime Minister Ranil Wickremesinghe (who was administering the cohabitation government with a lame-duck president in office) readily gave his assent. In a last-minute frenzy, diplomats were despatched to South Africa where the vote was to be taken. The incumbent's camp played a deft card: Kadirgamar was portrayed as the candidate of the pro–Robert Mugabe (Zimbabwean President) lobby, which he was not. An influential section of the Commonwealth – UK, Canada, Australia – was alarmed. Kadirgamar did not go to South Africa to canvass. The Oxonian ethos of campaigning for high office without canvassing does not quite translate to international relations. In the election, held on 5 December 2003, he received a drubbing by 40 to 11. It was in any event the most number of votes a Sri Lankan has received in an international contest of this nature. Challenging the incumbent is neither conventional nor prudent, especially when the big boys rally against you. Kadirgamar remained in local politics and the experience made him rethink any consideration of the post of UN Secretary-General.

As the months passed, Kadirgamar voiced concerns that the peace process with the LTTE was compromising national security to a point of no return. After just over two and a half years (late 2003), President Kumaratunga, having had enough of cohabitation, took back the Ministry of Defence under the powers vested in her by the constitution (with the Supreme Court's *imprimatur*) which she kept for herself and the Ministry of Media (which she handed over to Kadirgamar). Then, flexing her muscle again as executive president, she proceeded to dissolve parliament in mid-term, early the next year. She called snap elections for 2 April 2004 with the Marxist-Nationalist JVP, a party she had once intensely disliked, in an alliance with her own party, the SLFP.

Foreign Minister again, 2004–5

The UNP was defeated at the April 2004 elections, and the SLFP–JVP coalition under President Kumaratunga came back into office. Wresting control of the new parliament, she could then appoint her own cabinet ministers. Kadirgamar was the automatic choice to resume charge of the Foreign Ministry. But he had by now become a seasoned politician who took a slightly more partisan view of politics. Indeed he began to harbour thoughts that would take him a step further than being the Minister of Foreign Affairs. He had not abandoned his bi-partisan approach but he had found it compatible to use the Ministry of Media, and the state media, as an arm of a political party – his party. He ignored his own guidelines that he had issued when he took over the ministry: these had provided for the state media to have a bi-partisan policy and balanced coverage of both the government and the opposition. He even justified the premature dissolution of parliament midway through its mandated six-year term by the use of one person's (the president's) powers arguing that the previous parliament, also mandated for six years (2000–06), had collapsed after only a year due to crossovers engineered by the UNP.

Such was Kadirgamar's increasing involvement in his party's political apparatus by now – he would address public rallies and speak a few words in the Sinhala language and pay courtesy calls on high-ranking Buddhist monks – that the president must have considered him an eminently suitable candidate to be her prime minister. Yet what should have been a joyous achievement for him turned out to be an occasion for monumental sadness.

President Kumaratunga had managed to give Kadirgamar the impression that she would have liked him to be her next prime minister. It was not merely the symbolic value of having a minority Tamil as the country's prime minister which would have been a giant leap in the context of Sri Lankan politics: he was the one person she could trust implicitly.

There had been in-depth consideration at the presidential palace to introduce a radical revision of the constitution to enable the president to become a member of parliament and thereby, potentially, a future prime minister at the conclusion of her maximum two terms, something like what, not much later, Vladimir Putin did in Russia.

What had been envisaged was for Kadirgamar to be appointed an interim prime minister for six months and for him to pilot the constitutional amendment through a constituent assembly. Once President Kumaratunga reverted to parliament (in the guise of abolishing the unpopular Executive Presidency) and became prime minister, Kadirgamar was to revert to his substantive role as foreign minister.

Jockeying for the premiership, however, had begun in earnest. Kadirgamar was hard done by political forces in the SLFP which drew on the support of senior members and influential Buddhist monks. Theirs was a distinctly anti-Tamil campaign to stultify Kadirgamar's chances. At the same time, ironically, others (also Sinhalese) argued that the peace process with the Tamil Tigers (LTTE) would be adversely affected because of the LTTE's opposition towards him.

While he was deeply anguished by these sentiments, what irked Kadirgamar most was a comment President Kumaratunga made to him the night after the election victory. She had told him, 'I suddenly realised that you were serious about the post of prime minister.'[24] That seemed incredible to Kadirgamar. All along, discussions were based on him becoming an interim prime minister and now it was met with feigned surprise by the president who was saying she didn't know that he was 'serious' about it. The man who had done so much for the Sinhalese and the party was being hung out to dry.

Kadirgamar put pen to paper the next morning and wrote a note to the president protesting about the poor treatment meted out to him. The gravamen of his complaint was not that he was overlooked but that the president had told him that she was embarrassed to know that he was interested in the job of PM. He felt that he had been made a loser in a race he never ran. The pain comes out in a passage where he recalls a poignant incident, when a friend of his late father had warned him: 'They will let you down.' The inference was clear. 'They' were the Sinhalese rulers. Kadirgamar had disagreed because he was for a united Sri Lanka and a pluralistic society. He was trustworthy and trusting. He asked the president: 'Was the old gentleman right?'[25]

He found the action of the JVP the one redeeming factor. The JVP, a party of nationalistic Sinhalese rural youth, had come to the defence of this Tamil gentleman. They condemned the SLFP's Tamil bogey and said that it was a phantom phobia in Sinhalese minds. He told the president that it was entirely her right to choose her prime minister and none should challenge that prerogative but that she should clear the air that he was disqualified for the post because he was a Tamil.

The JVP had even sent a strongly worded fax to the president urging her to appoint Kadirgamar as prime minister, but to no avail. A senior SLFP member from the south, Mahinda Rajapaksa had also staked his claim for the job of PM and got it. He went on to succeed President Kumaratunga as the President of the Republic.[26]

Something Kadirgamar came to know later was that a dollar millionaire businessman very close to the then president whom he had appeared against as a lawyer had also weighed in, in favour of Rajapaksa. Not for the love of Rajapaksa but because he knew that he would get no state patronage with Kadirgamar. This businessman had the backing of the president's brother Anura Bandaranaike, an MP, in this task. It was this lobbying that eventually was said to have tilted the president towards Rajapaksa, a decision she came to rue not long afterwards.

On Boxing Day (26 December) 2004, the tsunami devastated the island. Thousands lost their lives in the tidal waves. In the aftermath came a new opening for dialogue between the government and the rebels, as many Tamils living in the coastal areas of the North and East had died as had Sinhalese in the southern and south-western coast. A mass influx of aid followed from around the world.

There was a demand by the International Community that a mechanism be created by which this aid could flow directly to the LTTE-controlled areas of the North and East bypassing the usual government channels. Under pressure, the government established the P-TOMS (Post-Tsunami Operational Management Structure) mechanism which was to have some LTTE representation in it. The JVP, which had by then left the coalition government, accused the president of surrendering the country's sovereignty to the rebels. Kadirgamar supported the JVP's protest, though discreetly and behind closed doors.

This caused a further rupture in relations with President Kumaratunga who told Kadirgamar that a particular bishop had made critical comments about his opposition to including the LTTE in the aid distribution process, and that he should, for all intents and purposes, keep quiet on the issue.[27]

Thereafter, Kadirgamar's differences with President Kumaratunga intensified. The personal rapport that had developed between them over a decade – so much so that he could tell her to 'look presidential' before the cameras or to be punctual when meeting overseas guests, where they shared a bottle of wine and exchanged pleasantries both at home and on their many state visits abroad together – began to sour. Over the years he had offered her wise counsel and genuine advice that lesser politicians would not have ventured, not heeding the ramifications for himself, but all that mattered little.

What did grow was the unlikely relationship between Kadirgamar and the JVP. Although only the senior JVP leader Somawansa Amarasinghe could converse fluently in English, there was a great affinity between them. They respected him immensely, for his intellect, his nationalist stance and his ability to show them, with innate courtesy and kindness, the virtues of a wider worldview.

Meanwhile, with security threats heightening, he had to all but beg for additional protection from his own government. Letters written to the Ministry of Defence, which was under the president, were not replied to with any urgency, and when they were, it was usually in the negative. The LTTE knew that a presidential election was due either that year (2005), or the year after. Then the Chief Justice and the Supreme Court denied the president an additional year in office on the basis that she had, by virtue of having taken oath on a particular (earlier) date, forfeited that extra year she was hoping to have. It was time for the LTTE to somehow prevent Kadirgamar becoming the country's virtual choice for prime minister should his party win. In hindsight it might seem they had a two-pronged approach. First eliminate Kadirgamar, then allow his party's candidate to defeat Wickremesinghe, the main contender from the opposition.

Intelligence reports had advised him to curtail his movements drastically. He had sold his private residence and purchased a new one with sufficient garden space for a swimming pool so that he would not have to go to Army Headquarters for his exercise routine. One such report (which came from the Americans) shown to him indicated that the LTTE was planning to mount a frontal attack, to ambush his convoy when he was on the road in the month of August 2005. A week earlier some persons had been taken into custody for videoing in the vicinity of his official residence. Yet another ceasefire with the LTTE was 'on' and he was told by an old Tamil acquaintance who claimed to have links with the LTTE leadership that as long as he was foreign minister the guerrillas would not harm him for fear of incurring the wrath of the international community, whose support they still needed. Were these all smoke-screens?

On the fateful night of 12 August 2005 he was shot in the chest and mortally wounded by a sniper after he had come out of the pool at his private residence in Colombo. The assassin had, along with some others, been closeted in an unused bathroom on the upper floor of a nearby house overlooking his residence. They could have picked the date they wished for their heinous crime. All they required was for the target to walk into their telescopic sights. It had an almost Gandhian ring to it: a voice of moderation slain by fanatics.

The lapse in security was monumental, even inconceivable. The damage it caused the nation, irreparable. In the subsequent court inquiry, the relatively junior army officer placed in charge of Kadirgamar's security, under cross-examination, laid the blame for outer-perimeter security on the police. Just two constables from the local police station had been detailed for this task. But there was a guard tower manned by soldiers a grenade's throw away from that bathroom. One of Kadirgamar's nagging concerns all along had been that in the event of a threat to his life, members of his security team would have to sacrifice theirs. At least, he would have been happy they were spared that.

President Kumaratunga referred to her slain foreign minister as a 'hero of our time', but blamed 'political foes opposed to the peaceful transformation of conflict and who were determined to undermine attempts towards a negotiated political solution to the ethnic conflict' as responsible for his murder.[28] It was only later, after she was criticized for giving room for speculation and not having the spunk to name the LTTE as the killers, that she did so. The sniper and his accomplices got away with ease, and only the gardener who gave them the key and some others were brought to trial. LTTE leader Prabhakaran and his head of intelligence were indicted for conspiracy, but both were deleted from the list of accused by the state prosecutor on the basis that they were killed by the armed forces in 2009 in the final stages of the war, so could not be tried.

The Indian government sent a high-profile delegation for the funeral. The Norwegian facilitators were there in their black jackets by the bier, looking sheepish because they knew where the smoking gun was. Streams of people from all walks of life came to pay their respects. Many of them were ordinary Sinhalese and Muslims showing their gratitude to a Tamil who had refused to be classified on what he called 'tribal lines'. In the funeral procession that followed, there were only a few Tamils. Many of them were either angry with Kadirgamar's unifier role or afraid of the LTTE, or both. It was the Sinhalese-dominated JVP that put up posters and called their cadres to swell the ranks of mourners as his own party received no instructions to do so.

And so, Kadirgamar was consumed by the flames at a state funeral amidst the orations, the gun salutes and the sound of bugles, having made the supreme sacrifice for the country he so dearly loved.

His compatriots compared him in numerous eulogies to a Tamil national leader Sir Ponnambalam Ramanathan, whom the majority Sinhalese had picked at the turn of the twentieth century to represent them in their quest for independence from the British. Within a week, with the nation still numbed into mournful silence, his ashes were sprinkled where the waters meet in a town south of Colombo. He had played his chosen role in public life to near perfection, fulfilling his people's longing for a political leader who could rise above the cacophony, to be a statesman.

He was not without his faults, but they were well disguised. He had both the swagger and the substance; was gifted intellectually, but it was hard work, burning the midnight oil as it were, that made him very special. As a foreign minister he knew he would have to face hard-boiled foreign correspondents and give television interviews based on soundbytes. He trained himself by getting his old school friend, now an agro-economist, to ask him questions and time his answers, just as 50 years earlier he had clocked his timings on the athletics track before a meet. His command of the English language meant he was able to convey a particularly strong message, or defend a case with propriety, courtesy and gentle firmness. He had the ability to tread delicately when the occasion demanded it.

He had steered the Foreign Office in the right direction in the 11 years he was at its helm. He had professionalized the service by giving career officers their due quota vis-à-vis political appointees; inducted new recruits through a merit examination; got the veterans to impart their knowledge to the next generation through a diplomatic school; updated guidelines and minutes on such knotty administrative matters as marriages with foreign nationals and education of children. He had taken a hands-on approach to all of the nitty-gritty stuff in addition to overseeing the big picture where he would argue a state's obligations under international law or negotiate treaties on confiscation of terrorist funds.

What a pity Sri Lanka was saddled with this insurgency of global proportions – for had Kadirgamar been Minister of International Trade, for instance, what economic benefits his country could have reaped due to his contacts and indefatigable work ethic.

He had an abiding affection for the land of his forebears and his countrymen. He also had a deep-seated anxiety for the country. His long-time friend and colleague at the Bar, H. L. De Silva (who served a stint as Sri Lanka's Ambassador to the UN) said that 'he felt a passionate concern for many values which were part of our national ethos and its people, without any fanfare.' Alluding to his meteoric rise in politics, he said, 'He (Kadirgamar) turned out to be an instant success held in high esteem. He empathized amazingly with our troubles and in an authentic way with the vast body of people who considered themselves to be Sri Lankan in spirit, transcending such segmental divisions of race and religion, demonstrating by conduct and example a more holistic vision of the reality of things.'[29]

Right through his life, Kadirgamar refused to be bound by any stereotype. When as a young boy, his father offered him a choice of three schools and asked him which school he would like to attend, he chose, not the expected one all his elder brothers were attending, but one of which he knew nothing at the time. Asked much later why he did so, he replied: 'Just to be different.'[30] He did not fear to be different and this would explain the ease with which he could assimilate with political forces from a completely different social, religious and ethnic background. He would normally see the good side of most people, something that could irritate a journalist more accustomed to taking a critical view. He was a gentleman almost to a fault. A senior lawyer who liked him dearly once remarked that Kadirgamar was 'too nice' a person.

Cosmopolitan by nature, and blessed with amazing savoir vivre, the epicurean tastes he acquired while studying and working abroad, his intellectual and physical stamina and vast experience of men and matters made him a convivial host. An evening with him would last into the early hours of the following morning. Former Prime Minister Wickremesinghe put it well when he said that a dinner with him 'filled the stomach and also satisfied the mind'.[31]

How he would have welcomed the military defeat of the LTTE in May 2009. While he would have taken very seriously the subsequent controversies about some of the methods used, he would not have doubted that the aim of the military campaign had to be the complete ending of the LTTE's reign of terror. He gave his own life towards this end even though it is quite possible that his name could be forgotten in a list of heroes of our time.

The tone of his philosophy is marked by a framed wall hanging in his private office containing the oft-quoted lines from Shakespeare's *As You Like It*:

> All the world's a stage, and all the men and women merely players
> They have their exits and entrances.

That reflects in a nutshell his approach to public life. For his part, Lakshman Kadirgamar entered the world stage and exited – loving and serving his country, and beloved of his people. He showed that politics was not the exclusive preserve of the scoundrel. That noble men also have a role to play for the public good.

CHAPTER 4

A Duty of Service in an Age of Terror

Chris Patten

I first met Lakshman Kadirgamar at the UN General Assembly in 2000. He was there not only as Sri Lanka's experienced foreign minister but also as the chairman of representatives from the South Asian Association for Regional Cooperation (SAARC). I was in New York as the European Commissioner for External Relations.

Balliol College and the Idea of Public Service

In our waiting room in the bowels of the UN's skyscraper – a windowless, airless bunker, a little like a seminar room at a university – he was all old-world courtesy, speaking with the same sort of grave eloquence that the Indian foreign and finance minister Jaswant Singh deployed. And Lakshman was of course wearing a Balliol College tie. He obviously had other ties, too. Looking through photographs of him going about his public duties I could not spot the college tie, either in its striped or crested manifestation. But on almost every occasion that we met, the Balliol tie was in place, a statement I think of what we shared which was more than attendance at the same college. Remarkably, it was a photograph of him in his Balliol tie that was used in the Sri Lankan postage stamp issued in his honour in August 2006 – the first anniversary of his assassination.

Lakshman Kadirgamar once talked to me about Balliol's record of sending the young out to pursue a career in public service, and he clearly felt strongly the responsibilities that go with educational privilege. Reading his account of why he had left his career as a distinguished international lawyer for domestic politics is to be reminded that ideas about the duty of service are not pompous echoes of a bygone age.

The type of service for which Balliol men had often been prepared was running Britain's empire. Balliol's present-day historian of India, Professor Judith Brown, has calculated, for example, that between 1853 and independence in 1947 no fewer than 345 Balliol alumni of British and

European descent served the Raj, of whom 273 went into the Indian Civil Service; and in the same time-period 88 Indian students studied at Balliol, of whom 31 went into the ICS and 21 became lawyers.[1] Lakshman, like the Indian Prime Minister Manmohan Singh, would not have given any support to those who seek to defend or justify imperialism. But again like his distinguished fellow Oxford alumnus, he could point to some of its better relics: the English language, which he spoke and wrote so well, the rule of law, the institutions and values that comprise a liberal society. He was a patriotic Sri Lankan, who did not define his patriotism through criticism of the former colonial power and all its works. He was at home in Balliol's senior common room and the Oxford Union.

South Asian Regional Cooperation

For the meeting in New York in 2000 with the representatives of SAARC, an organization whose members represent a combined population of 1.5 billion people, I was deemed to be the most suitable spokesman for the European Union (EU). This reflected three things. First, SAARC was exactly the sort of organization of which Eurocrats heartily approved. Like the Andean Community or the Association of Southeast Asian Nations, SAARC was thought to be in some sense a pallid imitation of the economic and political integration which Europeans believed with some justification that they had practised more successfully than anyone else. This was the kind of regional cooperation which the EU should foster in its own image. Second, cooperation in SAARC had not, however, gone very far. Mutual suspicions, especially between India and Pakistan, and India's dominant weight in the region (similarly Brazil tended to unbalance the Mercosur countries of South America) had inhibited regional integration. So a meeting with SAARC was not a high priority for busy foreign ministers. I was accompanied at the meeting by a smattering of European ambassadors and officials. Third, the agenda was quite complicated and technical, dealing with issues that flew some way below ministerial radar screens. We were discussing issues like tariffs and deforestation, far distant from the preferred intellectual list of most foreign ministers. As a European Commissioner I often felt that it was ironic that matters such as these, on which the EU could make a real difference, were left to the Brussels cadre, whereas the 'blah-blah' that in the absence of hard power cut little ice with anyone outside Europe was the preserve of the foreign ministers of individual EU member states. Little has changed.

It was apparent at our SAARC meeting that Lakshman Kadirgamar's enthusiasm for the development of the organization considerably exceeded what it had by then achieved. He was right to be so positive, for reasons set out clearly in his Lal Bahadur Shastri Memorial Lecture in New Delhi in January 2003. He recognized that the refashioning of Europe after the twentieth century's terrible world wars, with two countries (France and Germany) that had fought each other three times in all in 70 years lashed together at the heart of the new integrationist project, was a model which for all its sub-continental turmoil and bloodshed South Asia was unlikely to follow with the same speed or political commitment. Yet he saw hope in the growing together across the region of businesses and professions, believed that for all their different national agendas the existence of SAARC had helped to defuse tensions between its members, and that practical social and economic programmes would in time promote prosperity, poverty alleviation, educational advance and environmental improvement. The challenge of water stress in the sub-continent would surely increase today his enthusiasm for regional cooperation. I am sure that Lakshman would have been delighted at the progress made in recent years in reducing tariff barriers and promoting free trade across South Asia.

Sri Lanka's Problem of Ethnic Division and Violence

Much of Lakshman Kadirgamar's life was shaped by the terrorism which ended it. Indeed, he made clear, when explaining his motives for entering politics, that resolving his country's ethnic problem, not just by military means but through the pursuit of a just and fair political solution, was a primary trigger for his sacrifice of a private life for public duty. As a Tamil, who believed in democracy, the rule of law and the integrity of the Sri Lankan state, he must have felt this particularly strongly. I know many Catholics in Northern Ireland who were moved by similar considerations, and who were also killed precisely because they eschewed the politics of tribal identity and asserted the primacy of civic idealism.

My own passing and partial knowledge of the ethnic division in Sri Lanka, my experiences in Northern Ireland where I served as a minister and later reorganized the police service as part of the Belfast Peace Agreement, and finally my concerns about the way Sri Lanka's civil emergency has apparently ended, have left me with opinions which Lakshman Kadirgamar would have understood but may not have shared for reasons rooted in his own life and knowledge.

I visited Sri Lanka three times as Britain's Development Minister from 1986 to 1989. We had a significant assistance programme there: among other projects we were building a large dam. But in 1989, Sri Lankan ministers suggested that I might like to visit Jaffna, the capital of the Northern Province. The name for this city in the Tamil dialect is 'the land of the harp player' but we know it better in recent years as the sad and battered heartland of the Liberation Tigers of Tamil Eelam (LTTE). Jaffna had been one of their strongholds from which they had been driven from time to time and from which they had themselves expelled many of the local Moslems. In 1987, the Indian Army, in the form of the Indian Peace Keeping Force (IPKF) had taken over Jaffna, and soon got involved in a full-scale conflict there with the LTTE. (This conflict was to lead directly to the assassination of Rajiv Gandhi in India in 1991 by a female LTTE suicide bomber.) In 1989 the Sri Lankan government asked me if I would visit the city and see what humanitarian and development assistance were required there. I was flown into the city in an Indian helicopter gunship and driven around the recently contested streets and buildings by a tall Indian brigadier in an open jeep. I could have wished for a rather less conspicuous tour of the city where the fighting had only just finished. One perception I took away with me was that the systematic destruction of facilities and equipment at the university did not suggest that much thought was being given to winning young Tamil hearts and minds. It was surely more than unhappy chance that had led to quite so many computer screens being smashed by rifle butts.

I did not go to Sri Lanka again until November 2003. The fighting between government and LTTE forces was still grinding on. There had been over a decade of terrorist atrocities since my previous visit. Children had been dragooned into the service of violence. Suicide bombers of both sexes and all ages had blown themselves and others to smithereens. The Tamil diaspora around the world had passed the tin to fund the LTTE struggle. The Sri Lankan Army had fought on. No political settlement had been found. But since 2000 Norway – with some encouragement from local politicians – had been patiently trying to broker a ceasefire, confidence-building measures and a political settlement.

The requirement for diplomatic patience was indeed considerable. The bi-partisan approach to finding a political and not just a military solution to the fighting frayed regularly at the edges, sometimes as a result of the ebb and flow of local political ambitions, sometimes under pressure from militant Buddhist activists, sometimes because of the serpentine manoeuvres and inflexibility of the LTTE's leader, Velupillai Prabhakaran. The Norwegian Foreign Ministry played its hand with considerable low-profile skill. There was little kudos in what was being done, valuable as it was, and few manifestations of international support. The existing United National Party government of Ranil Wickremesinghe was in favour of some show of political involvement by other governments in what Norway was trying to do, and the Norwegians themselves were equally enthusiastic about this. So the EU decided it would send me to Colombo to make clear that we were right behind the peace process. Prime Minister Wickremesinghe thought it would be helpful to go even further. He asked me to carry a message to the LTTE and its leader not only underlining European support for the peace talks but also making clear that the EU was totally opposed to any break-up of Sri Lanka as part of a settlement. We stood four-square behind the geographical integrity of the Sri Lankan state.

Since 2001, Wickremesinghe had been living politically in what the French call cohabitation with President Chandrika Kumaratunga of the Sri Lanka Freedom Party and the People's Alliance. It was a very uneasy political relationship. The prime minister and president were bitter foes, and the president engineered the ousting of her rival the following year.

The major cause of disagreement was over how to deal with the LTTE. How many political compromises should be made for a settlement? Would Prabhakaran accept any compromise short of the partition of the island? How long should peace talks be allowed to drag on? Were they simply a front behind which the LTTE could build up its financial and military resources? Should foreign intervention, however well-meaning, be encouraged or rejected? Mrs Kumaratunga's increasingly hard-line views were presumably affected by the assassination of friends by the LTTE and by the Tigers' unsuccessful attempt to kill her which had left her with one eye.

With political opposition growing to any visit by a foreigner to Prabhakaran on the grounds that it would seem to legitimize terrorism, I was clear that I would not make such a visit unless both the president and the prime minister supported it and unless I was taken to Prabhakaran's jungle head-quarters and hide-out in Kilinochchi in an army helicopter. I went to see the president to discuss this with her. Lakshman Kadirgamar was with her. He was her principal adviser on foreign and security issues, having left the foreign ministry after seven years in 2001 with the fall of the government in which he served and the election of Wickremesinghe's party. I am not sure how nervous Lakshman Kadirgamar was about such a visit, but he certainly offered the president moderately supportive advice to let it go ahead once I made clear what I was mandated to say to the terrorist leader. It helped perhaps that I had been obliged to deal with former terrorists in Northern Ireland, who had eventually given up violence for democratic politics. My brief was to make clear to the LTTE and its leader that the EU supported the Norwegian-brokered talks. However, I also wanted to stress that we were resolutely opposed to terrorist violence, the break-up of Sri Lanka, the barbaric treatment of Muslims in LTTE-controlled areas and the recruitment of child soldiers. On the understanding that this would be my message, allied to a call for a rapid and successful conclusion to the talks and to the promise of financial assistance from the EU for confidence-building measures, President Kumaratunga and Lakshman Kadirgamar agreed that I should go to Kilinochchi. They put an army helicopter at my disposal.

I have told the tale of this visit elsewhere.[2] I relayed the European messages to Prabhakaran and his leading political advisers at a curious meeting during which the terrorist leader himself said little. For a man who had ordered and organized so much violence, he was a remarkably humdrum fellow. The meeting clearly contained messages that he did not like, and it may well have served little if any purpose save to disabuse Prabhakaran of any misconceptions about European support. A year later the Wickremesinghe government fell, or was pushed out. Lakshman became foreign minister again, having been edged out of consideration for the prime minister's job, which went to Mahinda Rajapaksa.

The fighting resumed in 2005, and Lakshman was murdered in August of the same year. Rajapaksa captured the presidency in the November elections, partly because the LTTE terrorized many Tamils into abstaining from voting: in a tight contest they would have probably delivered victory, had they turned out to vote, for the more moderate Wickremesinghe. The usual extremist hostility to any moderate course of action produced, as ever, the sort of result sought, which, as is equally often the case, backfired on the LTTE. They were militarily defeated in 2009 amid well-sourced and justified criticisms of the lack of regard, during the final stages of the campaign, for the plight of innocent Tamil civilians. We must hope that the bloody conclusion to the conflict has not fertilized the roots of renewed future turbulence and terrorism. There is a need for generosity and magnanimity: President Rajapaksa has to demonstrate that he has these attributes.

What would Lakshman Kadirgamar have thought of the way in which the conflict ended and of the assault on civil liberties that accompanied and followed it? Early in his career, he had investigated the treatment of Buddhists in South Vietnam on behalf of the widely respected Amnesty International, which has recently produced outspoken reports on the systematic attack on civil liberties in Sri Lanka by the Rajapaksa government. Any attempt to answer these questions trespasses on the unknown; but it also raises some of the fundamental issues that have to be faced by any democrat who believes in the rule of law when dealing with terrorism.

Terrorism as an International Challenge

Lakshman Kadirgamar's definitions and descriptions of terrorism in his 1998 Chatham House lecture are close to my own and to those of most European democrats. A terrorist attack targets the whole of society and the 'democratic way of life'. Terrorism is directed indiscriminately at members of the public, aiming through the creation of fear to gain political objectives that would not be secured through democratic means. There is no moral equivalence between the suicide bomber who maims and slaughters and the proportionate response (though that begs many questions) of government. 'Terrorism is terrorism. Period.' This is an argument which all those who have contested terrorism have had to win to secure the necessary international cooperation essential to overcoming terrorist organizations that are so often funded by a global diaspora and its supporters, that purchase their weapons of civilian destruction abroad, and that use the artefacts of globalization – air transport, electronic cash transfers, containerization – to help wage their campaign. Fighting Irish terrorism, Britain had little success in persuading American politicians to prevent its funding by those of their own fellow citizens who sympathized with the IRA. The atrocities of 9/11 changed the US attitude to terrorism. Lakshman Kadirgamar spent much of his diplomatic energy and his formidable eloquence in attempting to persuade foreign governments to proscribe the LTTE in their own countries and stop the raising of funds for terrorism in Sri Lanka. He scorned the 'Nelsonian' attitude to terrorism of some countries. He was particularly active in supporting the drafting of the 1997 UN Convention for the Suppression of Terrorist Bombings. The respect he enjoyed internationally meant that his assassination nudged some foreign governments into taking a tougher line in prohibiting active support for the LTTE in their own countries.

International action is required to defeat the terrorists, but this is not the same as a military alliance in a war. The Bush administration's declaration of a war on terrorism – often defined in reductive terms as the struggle of good against evil – did not help to deal with what is a criminal activity, in which all forms of political, cultural and economic alienation may be mixed up with the readier availability today of the sorts of technology which can produce greater devastation than ever before and cause more widespread fear. Wars are usually fought within a very general set of international rules. They pitch armies of combatants against one another. They often involve acts of perhaps misguided but not dishonourable patriotism. Armies advance and retreat. There are surrenders and victories, reparations and political settlements. Wars are fought by personal nouns: France against Germany, Japan against China. The collective nouns against which 'wars' are fought – poverty, crime, terrorism – are simply the stuff of polemics. It dignifies Prabhakaran outrageously to talk of him as though he were the Duke of Wellington or Marshal Ney. Terrorism is a condition which has always been and will always be with us. It can be closed down in this or that place or country at this or that time. But we are not going to defeat it everywhere forever.

Fighting Terrorism, Maintaining the Rule of Law

Judgments become more difficult when you attempt to act decisively to combat terrorism without either compromising the standards of governance that distinguish a democratic government from terrorist groups or unintentionally exacerbating the political issues that frequently incubate terrorism. People talk easily about the importance of draining the swamps in which the terrorists breed. But it is always easier to do this once the terrorism abates, and it is more difficult to achieve it if the terrorists and their political representatives are politically inflexible. In Northern Ireland, the internment of Irish republicans without charge in the 1970s was a mistake that increased sympathy and support for the terrorist cause. The political concessions that helped to persuade terrorists later to lay down their arms were probably only possible once those terrorists had concluded that they would not win an armed struggle.

As a distinguished lawyer, Lakshman Kadirgamar would have been concerned about how the rule of law – domestically framed and also accepted through international treaties and countries – could be preserved while conducting an effective campaign against terrorism. Cicero argued that 'the safety of the people is the supreme law',[3] a point which would have been accepted without hesitation by President Bush and probably Prime Minister Blair. The latter, after all, argued on leaving office that it was 'a dangerous misjudgement' both 'misguided and wrong' to put upholding civil liberties before countering terrorism.[4] On the other hand, following the argument (often attributed to Benjamin Franklin) that 'he who would put security before liberty deserves neither', the most eminent British judge in recent years – Lord Bingham – has put a different view: 'We cannot commend our society to others by departing from the fundamental standards which make it worthy of commendation.'[5] Once you put the rule of law and its protection of civil liberties on one side, you find yourself on a very slippery slope. Moreover, you not only abandon the moral high ground in the fight against terrorism, you also complicate the pursuit of the political accommodations that are invariably necessary in order to win a stable and enduring peace. You may also find that the liberties you have trimmed or shredded to fight terrorists are sooner or later curtailed for other purposes that have purely political ends.

It would have been good in recent times to have had the views of Lakshman Kadirgamar on these complex and important questions. A Tamil and a fine lawyer with his early experience and advocacy of the protection of civil liberties and minority rights, he would have made a powerful contribution to this debate. I am not sure what he would have said about the circumstances in which the Rajapaksa government defeated the LTTE and about the events that have followed that military victory, well charted by Amnesty International and others and condemned by the EU. But I mourn the fact that terrorism wickedly silenced his voice.

CHAPTER 5

Reflections on a 'Citizen of the World'

Karl F. Inderfurth, A. Peter Burleigh and Shaun Donnelly

> I am first and foremost a citizen of Sri Lanka. I do not carry labels of race or religion or any other label. I would say quite simply that I have grown up with the philosophy that I am a citizen of the world. I do not subscribe to any particular philosophy; I have no fanaticism; I have no communalism. I believe that there should be a united Sri Lanka. I believe that all our peoples can live together, they did live together. I think they must in the future learn to live together after this trauma is over. We have four major religions in the country: Buddhism, Islam, Hinduism, and Christianity. All these religions exist very peacefully. They get on very well. I see no reason why the major races in the country, the Tamils and the Sinhalese, cannot again build a relationship of confidence and trust. That is my belief.
>
> *Lakshman Kadirgamar on Japanese National Television (NHK), September 2004*

Within a year of this statement, Foreign Minister Lakshman Kadirgamar would be dead, murdered by those driven by the very fanaticism he so opposed in words and in deeds throughout his life. However, these assassins could not kill the spirit that animated his life and that served as an example of the highest calling of public service, including to the three authors of this chapter.

We are American diplomats who had the privilege of working with Lakshman Kadirgamar during his years in office. Karl Inderfurth, who wrote the first contribution below, served in the US government as Assistant Secretary of State for South Asian Affairs in 1997–2001. Peter Burleigh and Shaun Donnelly, whose contributions follow, served as US ambassadors to Sri Lanka in 1995–7 and 1997–2000 respectively. Each of us had the opportunity to take the measure of this man, joining him in countless public settings and working with him behind closed doors. We never found him wanting. He was truly a 'citizen of the world'. We therefore offer in the three parts of this chapter our reflections on Lakshman Kadirgamar. These are drawn not from the lengthy documentary record compiled during his extraordinary career, but from our own impressionist recollections of a man who combined a mix of idealism with a tough realism that formed the basis of his approach to the challenges of his day.

Karl F. Inderfurth

My first opportunity to engage Lakshman Kadirgamar in his role as foreign minister came at a time of great diplomatic accomplishment for him, namely the designation by Washington of the Liberation Tigers of Tamil Eelam (LTTE) as a terrorist organization on 8 October 1997, just two months after I had taken office as Assistant Secretary.

Long before 11 September 2001, Lakshman had warned other countries, including the United States and many in Europe, about terrorism. He made it clear to all these countries that they could no longer turn a blind eye to terrorism as being somebody else's problem. Despite the frequency with which he warned about these threats, at first he received a rather limited response from other governments.

That changed in 1997 when Secretary of State Madeleine Albright placed the LTTE on the list of some 30 foreign militant groups under the 1996 US Anti-Terrorism Act.[1] That designation meant that US law enforcement agencies, including the Federal Bureau of Investigation (FBI), would move against any suspected violators of the ban on LTTE-related activities in the US, including fund-raising for the organization. Other governments would also be requested by the US to give due heed to this ban, and to take supportive measures in their own countries.

Lakshman was in Washington for the 8 October 1997 announcement, and was extremely gratified that the US – the 'sole superpower left', as he said at the time – had finally taken this step. He considered the action a significant breakthrough in his diplomatic efforts to bring LTTE terrorist acts to the attention of the world community. As he would later say in an interview: 'I think we are all now in this boat together, and little Sri Lanka, having blown the whistle some time ago, I hope we are going to get even more cooperation and collaboration from our friendly countries.'[2]

The US ban on the LTTE was a tribute to Lakshman's skills and perseverance as a diplomat, in service of his country's interests. It was also a reflection of his commitment to construct an international legal framework for addressing the scourge of terrorism which he saw as extending far beyond Sri Lanka's borders: hence the strong leadership he showed in supporting the 1997 UN Convention for the Suppression of Terrorist Bombings and the extraordinary role he would play with respect to addressing the question of child soldiers before it was widely recognized as a serious, widespread international concern. On a later visit to Washington, Lakshman and I would travel to the White House to discuss this with then-First Lady, Hillary Clinton. They shared a moral outrage about this abuse of children and a determination to press the international community to see it stopped.

As a postscript to Lakshman's deep satisfaction with the US ban, and his subsequent encouragement to other countries to follow America's lead, it is also important to note that he did not consider this an end in itself – only one further means to bring the bloody civil conflict in his country eventually to an end.

Soon after he returned to Colombo from Washington and the signing of the US declaration, Lakshman was asked if Sri Lanka would also ban the LTTE. He replied that this would be illogical. 'One has to weigh up the advantages against the disadvantages,' he said. 'There could be argument that if you ban the LTTE, you are sending a signal at this moment that you are shutting the door to the possibility of any kind of negotiations.' That is something Lakshman Kadirgamar would not do.

A second engagement with Lakshman that stands out in my mind involves the honour I had of representing the US at a banquet given in Colombo on 20 April 1998 to commemorate the 50th anniversary of the establishment of diplomatic relations between the US and Sri Lanka. His appreciation of the US role in Sri Lanka was in full display, demonstrating the remarkable extent to which a member of the Non-Aligned Movement could maintain such close and warm relations with the US.

Ever the student of history, Lakshman noted that our formal relations actually went back much further, indeed to 1850 when the US first established a Commercial Agency in Sri Lanka to service American shipping interests. However, the presence and contributions of individual Americans, he said, began earlier, with missionaries who came to Ceylon in 1810 to educate the people of the North in both English and their own Tamil language. He also referred to the arrival in 1880 of 'a remarkable man', Henry Steel Olcott, who 'came to Sri Lanka not in search of souls; not to convert, but to learn', and was 'a pioneering leader of the Buddhist and nationalist revival movement in Sri Lanka'.

Having said this, Lakshman did call attention (and rightfully so, I should add) to the fact that 'if there is a flaw in our relationship it is the relative infrequency of visits to Sri Lanka by distinguished Americans.' He combined this gentle chiding with his appreciative appraisal of the US political system – with words that were aimed at both his American guests in the audience and his fellow Sri Lankan citizens who were in attendance:

> We have noted with admiration how American society has striven to reconcile liberty and order, localism and centralization, the precepts of religion with the structures of government, political democracy and economic inequality – and all this without the traditional unifying force of a common religion, a royal house or a mono-ethnic society. . . . The basic principles of the famous Declaration of Independence are a continuing source of inspiration to all democratic countries. Among the most fundamental of all the different elements of democratic theory is the ideal of human freedom. American society is based on this noble and timeless ideal. Long may that foundation survive.

Lakshman Kadirgamar's deep commitment to democracy and the 'ideal of human freedom' brought him to Warsaw, Poland, in June 2000 to attend a ministerial conference entitled 'Towards a Community of Democracies'. I was part of the US delegation led by the principal organizer of the conference, US Secretary of State Madeleine Albright. It is this third engagement that I had with Lakshman that proved to be the most prophetic for events soon to come. As he had when we first met three years earlier, he called attention to the urgent need for democratic nations to join to confront the threats posed by terrorist groups around the world. If they do, he said, 'there will be no succour, no solace, no safe haven, no place to hide, no place to run for the terrorists of the world because all of us, the democratic states, will stand together and fight together.'

That fight continues today, but we no longer have the clear and resolute voice of Lakshman Kadirgamar to call attention to the dangers we face and the threats that we must confront. However, we can continue to draw upon his insights and wisdom on how to proceed in meeting these challenges. In my view, the most important insight can be found in an interview he gave in 1997 that focused on the tragic conflict in Sri Lanka, but has universal application today:

> [T]he ultimate, permanent, durable solution to this problem will not come from force of arms alone. It will not come from conquest or our vanquishing the LTTE. It has to come by acceptance of the people in their entirety, by the Sinhala and the Tamil people. That is a political settlement. And, a political settlement that is perceived by the communities, by the majority and the minorities, to be fair and just. It must be a settlement that is enshrined in law, and it must be enshrined in the hearts of people.[3]

Lakshman Kadirgamar himself deserves to be enshrined in the hearts of the Sri Lankan people, and of the international community, for his service and sacrifice, and for the values and principles he espoused. He was a 'citizen of the world'.

A. Peter Burleigh

During the entire period (1995–7) when I was the US Ambassador to Sri Lanka, Lakshman Kadirgamar was the Foreign Minister. In the normal course of official business, we met frequently in his office in the Foreign Ministry and we also regularly met socially, though Kadirgamar's ability to lead a normal life was severely restricted by the tight security which surrounded him at all times, day and night. As the senior Tamil in the government of the day, he was a well-documented target of the rebel LTTE, though this did not stop him from effectively planning and executing a successful international diplomacy and from serving as a key advisor to then President Chandrika Bandaranaike Kumaratunga.

Among his many professional accomplishments none was more of a source of pride to Lakshman than his status as a successful lawyer, President's Counsel (the equivalent of the British Queen's Counsel), and as an Honorary Master of the Inner Temple in London (which award ceremony occurred in 1995). Earlier, while he was at university, he was elected President of the Oxford Union – a remarkable achievement that reflected his exceptional debating skills. Before entering politics and diplomacy, Kadirgamar was a senior lawyer, sought out in his prestigious Chambers for the most difficult of cases, frequently involving complex and controversial commercial disputes, both among Sri Lankan businessmen and between international investors and their local sponsors. He was an expert on foreign investment and on the politically controversial taxation issues which related to it.

During the time of our deep diplomatic interactions, Kadirgamar was effectively focused on the international legal structures relating to terrorism and how to best shape them to benefit Sri Lankan government efforts to combat the revolt of some of its Tamil citizens, particularly those living in the extreme northern and eastern sectors of the country. (Sri Lanka has a larger Tamil population in the Central Hills and in the capital, Colombo, but these groups never joined the LTTE-led revolt in significant numbers.)

Already by 1995, it had become clear that the Sri Lankan Army and its other military services were not capable of defeating the rebels on their own, despite growing assistance and training in counter-insurgency from friendly countries, including the US, India, the UK and Israel. In that context, it became apparent to the Sri Lankan leadership that more international support was necessary, particularly to cut off the supply of finance and military arms which were flowing into areas of the island effectively controlled by the LTTE. The professional and financial success of the widely dispersed diaspora of Sri Lanka-born Tamils in Australia, Singapore, the UK and, increasingly, the US had become a major source of both voluntary and involuntary funding for the increasingly well-organized and well-financed rebels.

Lakshman Kadirgamar astutely assessed that both the US and its closest allies were increasingly concerned with the impact of international and domestic terrorism – and that they were struggling to create an international legal structure in which it would be possible to better cooperate, better pursue and prosecute, and better monitor the movement of arms, money and other support across national borders. For Sri Lanka, the challenge of getting key countries to ban the provision of services to the Tamil rebels had become essential.

After the LTTE planned and executed the assassination of former Indian Prime Minister Rajiv Gandhi in south India in May 1991, the Indian government moved from its previous policy of practical ambivalence towards the rebels, and in 1992 it effected a ban on them. This was of profound significance for the rebels who had become used to political, financial and logistical support from fellow Tamils in south India – and there was even an earlier history of Indian intelligence agencies' support for the rebels. Though enforcement of the ban was sometimes spotty, the easy cushion of support in the nearby country was at an end.

With India more effectively siding with the government after the Gandhi killing, Sri Lanka actively sought the assistance of other friendly countries – and this is where Lakshman Kadirgamar excelled. He was relentless and focused on the need to ban the LTTE as a terrorist organization and he pressed to stop the supply of money and arms from abroad. He worked on the bilateral front, through the United Nations and through the regional organization of South Asia, the South Asian Association for Regional Cooperation (SAARC) – all with a view to organizing a united international front against the LTTE. He also sought assistance from ASEAN, though Sri Lanka was not a member. This was important because after the Indian supply chain dried up in the early 1990s, Burma, Thailand and Malaysia-based individuals and front companies were set up by the Tigers to find black-market arms and get them shipped to northern Sri Lanka. Thus, in effect, a broad-ranging offensive against assistance for the LTTE was required.

It has often been observed that small countries have a difficult time asserting themselves internationally, but Sri Lanka, with the leadership of Chandrika Kumaratunga and Lakshman Kadirgamar, proved them wrong. Gradually, major countries became more focused on the threat from the LTTE. By the mid-1990s its record of killing civilians (both Tamil and Sinhalese), use of child soldiers, devotion to suicide bombing and assassination of a large number of senior Sri Lankan officials, including a president and many ministers and important politicians, was clear. In retrospect, though, the Gandhi assassination in 1991 was probably the event that crystallized international concern, as did the massive bombing of the Colombo financial centre in January 1996.

After the passage, in the US, of the 1996 Anti-Terrorism Act, Lakshman Kadirgamar saw his chance to press the US effectively to declare the LTTE a banned organization under the law, and to more effectively monitor, and stop, the financial assistance to the rebels which was flowing from the Tamil-American community. At the same time, more of that community began informing the US government of the kinds of intimidation and blackmail they were under as a result of LTTE pressures on their remaining family in northern and eastern Sri Lanka. His campaign, which he doggedly pursued, finally bore fruit when the US banned the LTTE in October 1997. Aside from the innate importance of this act by the 'one remaining superpower' as Kadirgamar called the US, an important signal was sent internationally that other governments should take similar actions. Most did.

After my posting in Sri Lanka, in 1997 (until 2000) I was assigned to the US Mission to the United Nations as one of our ambassadors. In that role, I saw Lakshman and his new wife, Suganthie, every September when they came for the UN General Assembly conclave. We had dinner each year, and occasionally met officially if there were issues concerning our two countries which were on the UN agenda.

During my tenure in Sri Lanka it was often asked why a man of Lakshman's ethnic background was willing to focus his substantial professional powers and abilities, and persuasiveness, on undermining the Tamil Tigers. I think the answer was simple: Lakshman was a highly educated and sophisticated Sri Lankan whose family, though their origins were in the Protestant Christian community of Jaffna, had also been based in Colombo for generations. He grew up in an English-speaking environment and had classmates and professional colleagues and friends of all communities, certainly including Sinhalese and Muslims as well as those of all of Sri Lanka's major religions. He identified as a Sri Lankan nationalist and not a Tamil first, though he was proud of his community's many accomplishments, particularly in the educational field and in the civil service. He often talked with awe of the large number of Ceylonese Tamils who, after being educated in mostly American missionary schools and colleges in Jaffna in the north and Batticaloa in the east, went, during colonial times, to Malaysia and are now an important part of both that country's and Singapore's educated elites.

Despite his sophistication and anglicized mannerisms, Lakshman Kadirgamar was always proud of his athletic records at Trinity College in Kandy. After a couple of scotches on the back veranda of his government-supplied ministerial residence, he would often wax nostalgic about those wonderful days, pre-conflict, of intense and proud competition on the cricket and rugby fields. He was an award-winning runner for the college. In those times, Sri Lanka was Ceylon, and Trinity College was the highly elite Anglican church-founded college in the hills. Its graduates were a mix of Sinhalese, Burghers, Tamils and Muslims. Their intimacy and inter-connectedness characterized Sri Lankan society for the generations up to the 1980s when identity by ethnicity, religion, even race, became more prevalent. This historic, and seemingly unstoppable, evolution of the island's society was deeply saddening to Lakshman Kadirgamar, because he sensed that it was a dead end as well as a recipe for conflict.

I last saw Lakshman in March 2004 when he was Chairman of the Bandaranaike Centre for International Studies (BCIS) in Colombo. He organized and invited speakers to a conference on South Asia and I was invited to speak on the US role in the region historically and currently.

During the conference, Lakshman, his wife and I were able to have one of those precious relaxed Sri Lankan evenings, on the veranda of their official residence. Reminiscences were rife but so was despair about the fate of the country if the conflict continued. It was while he was in the swimming pool at his private residence, which was near the official residence, that Lakshman Kadirgamar was assassinated by an LTTE sniper in 2005.

Writing now in 2010, it is clear to me that Lakshman would be deeply pleased that the immediate conflict is over and that the leadership of the LTTE has been eliminated. He would be one of those who would now be arguing that the government – and society in general – must urgently focus on recreating a feeling of 'Sri Lankanness' which transcends religion and ethnicity, though allowing all groups to prosper and be recognized as important components of the island's talented and creative people.

Shaun Donnelly

I was honoured to replace Peter Burleigh as the US Ambassador, arriving in Colombo in November 1997 and serving in that position for three years, until the summer of 2000. Throughout my three years in Sri Lanka, Lakshman Kadirgamar was Sri Lanka's Minister of Foreign Affairs. Like Ambassador Burleigh, I dealt frequently with Minister Kadirgamar on a range of important issues as well as, of course, seeing him regularly at diplomatic and social events.

Throughout our frequently intense dealings, Minister Kadirgamar was a consummate professional. He was a man of ideas, of strategies and of words. Words mattered to Lakshman and he used them with great care, precision and effect. He relished debate and was very, very good at it. It did not take me long to learn that Minister Kadirgamar had in his student days in the UK been President of the Oxford Union and a champion debater. I recall some spirited private discussions, or as we diplomats say 'full and frank exchanges', in the minister's office and over private dinners. There were no winners or losers in my discussions/debates with Lakshman: certainly he never lost, but I always emerged with a very clear understanding of his well-articulated positions.

Obviously the US and Sri Lanka enjoyed close, friendly relations throughout my time in Colombo but that is not to say there were no tough issues. Not surprisingly, my most important, most serious discussions with Lakshman Kadirgamar consistently dealt with the nexus of issues that have defined and bedevilled Sri Lanka for far too long – ethnicity, terrorism, human rights, constitutional reform and accountability. In my many private meetings with Minister Kadirgamar as we worked our way through some very difficult, very emotional and often heart-wrenching issues, he was a strong and effective advocate for his government and his country and for what he believed to be right. However tough those discussions might get, Lakshman Kadirgamar always treated me, and other American officials I took to meet him, with respect and understanding.

Lakshman Kadirgamar was a man of the law. Drawing on his impressive legal skills and his long experience inside and with the UN system, Lakshman was a master of international organizations and how they could be used to advance Sri Lanka's interests. On challenging issue after challenging issue, from 'child soldiers' to 'community of democracies', from 'terrorism finance' to 'women's rights', from the UN Committee on Human Right in Geneva to pushing the US Congress to place the LTTE on the US government's official list of terrorist organizations, Lakshman threw his full energy, intellect and creativity into advancing Sri Lanka's interests, and he often got real results.

Given the inability of anyone anywhere else in the Sri Lankan government to summon up the courage to deal with some very messy investment and commercial disputes, I often also found myself personally debating complicated business problems (expropriations, broken contracts and disputed contract awards) with the minister. I do not think Lakshman enjoyed those sessions or those issues any more than I did but he understood the need to resolve them and took on this duty when so many others around his government simply chose to ignore the festering problems. In these issues, as in every other issue I worked with Minister Kadirgamar, he was the consummate professional. And was he a tough negotiator! Fair, well prepared and tough. Together, somehow, we were able to find solutions for several of the most vexing, most politically toxic of these commercial disputes and, thus, were able to avoid potential damage to the overall bilateral relationship.

I was always struck by Lakshman Kadirgamar's incredible personal courage. Everyone in Colombo knew he was either number 2 or number 1 on the LTTE's 'hit list'. He and his family had to live with incredibly intrusive security protections, not just in Colombo but also on his numerous trips abroad. I never heard Lakshman complain of those security procedures, nor did I see him decide to forego an event or decline to take on an obligation. He just did his job, professionally and bravely, and absolutely refused to be intimidated by the forces of intolerance and evil.

I agree totally with Peter Burleigh that Lakshman saw himself first and foremost as a Sri Lankan. He was certainly proud of his Tamil heritage and his family's prominent history in and around Jaffna. However, Lakshman always saw himself and presented himself as a Sri Lankan and as a representative of an integrated, united, multi-ethnic Sri Lanka.

I personally witnessed Lakshman at his most passionate not in discussing LTTE atrocities or an urgent foreign assistance request, nor in defending the government operations of camps for internally displaced persons (IDPs), but rather in his personal remembrances of Jaffna and what Jaffna had long stood for – of the Jaffna Library and of the American missionary-founded Jaffna College and Uduvil School for Girls. Lakshman Kadirgamar had a deep sense of history – Sri Lankan history, world history and even US history – and how the issues we were working on at that time fitted into broader historical trends and principles.

Lakshman Kadirgamar had come into the foreign minister's job much more experienced and more comfortable in European and Asian issues, culture and politics than in those relating to other regions. Educated in Sri Lanka and the UK, a lawyer in the UK and Sri Lanka, a senior UN official based in Geneva and working on Asia, Lakshman really had only limited direct experience of America and Americans before he took on the foreign minister's role. Yet he worked hard to understand how the US administration and even the US Congress worked. US government and politics are very, very different from the Sri Lankan and British system he understood so well. Not a lot of very successful men well into their sixties would have studied so assiduously or worked so hard to figure out how to deal with this damn new strange breed – the Americans. However, Lakshman just knew it was something he needed to do, so he knuckled down and did it.

Lakshman plunged right in, travelling often to Washington and venturing out to meet and try to win over key American policy makers across the political and substantive spectrums. He knew he had a lot to learn about the US system and how to interact with it. He sought advice from me and others wherever he could find it. He learned how to deal with Washington and was, I believe, a good friend of the US and a very valued and respected interlocutor for top US officials.

Minister Kadirgamar understood the importance of symbolic events and using such events to make important political and public diplomacy points. I remember a couple of important public and semi-public events on which we personally worked together closely. Lakshman inspired my embassy and his ministry teams to work together to mark 'Fifty Years of US–Sri Lankan Diplomatic Relations' with a series of commemorative events, receptions and seminars, culminating in a large gala dinner Lakshman hosted at the Hilton when Assistant Secretary of State Karl Inderfurth visited Sri Lanka. One of my vivid memories was Lakshman showing good humour and pulling one of our commemorative US–Sri Lanka 'fifty-year T-shirts' over his impeccable Saville Row suit and grinning for the cameras. This was above and beyond the call of duty, and was certainly the only time I ever saw Lakshman Kadirgamar in a T-shirt!

It was also a real personal pleasure to work personally with Lakshman on a project to get from the Library of Congress in Washington, and present to him for the to-be-restored Jaffna Library, full sets of the microfilmed collection of the historic early Jaffna newspapers to replace those national treasures lost in a tragic fire which had wiped out Sri Lanka's only copies of that early documentation of Jaffna. Lakshman insisted on hosting a ceremony and formal dinner in the garden of his residence to mark the handover of the microfilm readers and the library of tapes. He invited the who's who of Sri Lankan government, business and society, as always from all ethnic groups, to that dinner and he spoke so eloquently about Jaffna's rich history, his dreams for its future and what it meant for all Sri Lankans. I could see, as could anyone attending that ceremony, that this was a real personal labour of love for Lakshman and a project he felt very important for all Sri Lankans. I was certainly proud that the US was uniquely positioned to be able to help in this very important area.

Finally, I want to add a word about Lakshman's partner throughout my time with him in Colombo, his wife Suganthie. Like Lakshman, Suganthie made incredible personal sacrifices when he stepped forward to serve his country in this challenging job. Suganthie, a prominent and widely respected attorney, gave up much of her career to support and travel with Lakshman. She faced the same terrorist threats and intrusive security regime as Lakshman. I never, ever heard her complain. She found time to be very active in the Colombo diplomatic scene and pushed to reinvigorate the diplomatic wives group. She introduced ambassadorial wives, including my wife Susan, to all aspects of Sri Lanka society, not just the easy tourist sites. She certainly did not do just 'sugar-coated' tourism. I recall Suganthie personally took Susan and a diplomatic women's group to the government's paediatric cancer hospital and other important, if not glamorous or always pleasant, social service projects. I always thought Suganthie was an unsung hero for the love and support she provided, and the deep sacrifices she made, to enable Lakshman do the very important work he had taken on for his country.

Lakshman Kadirgamar was and remains, in my view, a true Sri Lankan patriot, eschewing a lucrative legal practice leading to a comfortable and well-earned retirement to serve his country on the front lines at a critical time. I thought he served his country and its people very well and with incredible courage. Like so many other Sri Lankan patriots, he paid the ultimate price for that service. I consider myself fortunate to have had the chance to work with such an extraordinary man.

CHAPTER 6

A True South Asian

Shivshankar Menon and Nirupama Rao

The authors of the two parts of this chapter have both had distinguished careers in the Indian Foreign Service. In the first part, Shivshankar Menon assesses Kadirgamar's character and achievements mainly with reference to events during the period 1997–2000, when Menon was Indian High Commissioner in Sri Lanka. In the second part, Nirupama Rao, who was Indian High Commissioner in 2004–6, recollects her many meetings with him between 2001 and 12 August 2005 – the day on which he was assassinated. Both authors convey a deep admiration for Kadirgamar.

The similarities in the careers of the two authors are remarkable. Not only did both of them serve as Indian High Commissioner to Sri Lanka, but both subsequently became Ambassador to China. Both then became Foreign Secretary (head of the Indian Foreign Service). Both saw a great deal of Lakshman Kadirgamar, gaining direct experience of how he handled Sri Lanka's single most important, and historically often difficult, relationship: that with India. Both show an awareness of how much India–Sri Lanka relations had improved since earlier and more difficult times in the 1980s and early 1990s. Both were struck by his strong if sometimes optimistic emphasis on South Asian integration.

*****

Shivshankar Menon

Lakshman Kadirgamar excelled at whatever he turned his hand to. He could have chosen to be remembered as an athlete, a barrister in any of the most demanding legal systems of the world or an international civil servant of the first rank, who contributed to the development of a new jurisprudence and practice in intellectual property rights.

But what he really chose to be was a South Asian, a statesman who believed in the South Asian destiny without in any way compromising on what he saw as his duty as a Sri Lankan leader. He was one of the first to see that this was possible, that there was no contradiction between national loyalty and regional identity, and to make it so in his life and actions.

I distinctly remember the first time that I met Lakshman. Within a few hours of arriving in Colombo in August 1997 as India's High Commissioner I was sitting in the veranda of his house, surrounded by palm trees, moussanda and hibiscus. The introductions took no time at all, nor did the mundane business of settling in a new High Commissioner. Within minutes we were talking of the state of South Asia, of what it could be and what it was, and of how we could improve on the dissension and strife and poverty that worried us both. I was struck by the fact that the foreign minister of a country in the midst of a debilitating and long drawn out civil war was thinking beyond today's problems to see how to eliminate the causes of ethnic violence and poverty. Lakshman was convinced that only an economically integrated South Asia could be prosperous, that prosperity had to come to all of South Asia and that it had to be built on a common set of democratic political values.

If there was one weakness in Lakshman's vision for South Asia it was his belief, despite mounting experience to the contrary throughout the subcontinent, that justice and the right legal instruments could provide the basis for a resolution of problems. I remember hours on end spent discussing fine points of law in the Indo–Sri Lanka Agreement of 1987; as also his enthusiasm for the constitutional amendment scheme that he and President Chandrika Kumaratunga were working on to try to mainstream the Sri Lankan Tamils and end the ethnic conflict. But without that faith, and the hope it gave us all, where would we have been? Would we really have had the courage to soldier on in pursuit of ethnic peace in Sri Lanka and for a South Asia at peace with itself? I somehow doubt it.

I mentioned before that Lakshman lived his beliefs. For instance, when in 2000 it came to treating his serious kidney problem, Lakshman could have got the best treatment anywhere in the world. He chose to come to India, not just out of faith in Indian doctors, but because he told me the days when South Asia had to look elsewhere for its needs were gone.

Lakshman was a true South Asian. He believed in South Asia's future and its common destiny. Equally he held us in South Asia to a higher standard than ordinary politicians had done before his time. I had personal experience of several instances where Lakshman acted on these beliefs.

In late 1997 when we first considered formally proposing an India–Sri Lanka Free Trade Agreement, reactions in both capitals were similar. There was outright opposition and general scepticism about whether it was possible, desirable or politically practical. Lakshman was the first political leader and cabinet minister in Colombo who saw both the practical and the political utility of such an agreement. As the Sri Lankan economist and diplomat Lal Jayawardena and I tried to steer the agreement through its tortuous course between the wishes of the politicians, businessmen, bureaucrats and special interests in both countries, it was

Lakshman who was our pillar of strength, with clear advice on how to approach the task. The agreement was concluded in December 1998 and came into force in March 2000. His foresight was proven when the Sri Lankan economy was able to work its way through the protracted effects of the civil war in some part because of its access to the rapidly growing and diversifying Indian market. Today both countries are considering expanding the free trade arrangement to include services. It took courage on Lakshman's part to consider linking and opening the Sri Lankan economy to the much larger and more protectionist Indian economy. That he chose to do so was due in no small part because of his faith in South Asia as a whole.

It was also logical that he should be the one who pushed for the Colombo summit of the South Asian Association for Regional Cooperation (SAARC) in July 1998 to reinvigorate the long proposed but equally long dead negotiation for a South Asian Free Trade Agreement. The holding of the Summit itself was a triumph of Lakshman's hope over the harsh realities of South Asia's fractious politics. It was Pakistan's turn to hold the summit but for several reasons this was not acceptable to some of the others. Lakshman stepped in with an offer from Sri Lanka.

My most lasting memory of Lakshman as a South Asian was a magical weekend in May 1998 that we spent with our families in Anuradhapura, Sigiriya and Polonnaruwa, visiting the glorious remains of palaces and monasteries and universities and paintings from a time long past when South Asia was home to one of the most advanced civilizations on earth. After three days of undiluted joy in this wonderland for historians and archaeologists it suddenly struck me that in all Lakshman's erudition and pleasure in these places there was not a trace of chauvinism. Nor was there one mention of the ethnicity of those who had created these marvels. His sheer pleasure in the fact that human beings had achieved so much so early was contagious. In sharing his joy with us Lakshman was showing fellow South Asians what we had been, and therefore what we could be again. Nationality or ethnicity had nothing to do with it and did not even enter his thoughts.

If only we could all share, and act on, Lakshman's vision of South Asia.

Nirupama Rao

It was over a decade ago that I first met Lakshman Kadirgamar. In April 2001, as Foreign Minister of Sri Lanka, he was in Muscat, heading his country's delegation to a conference of the Indian Ocean Rim Association for Regional Cooperation. I remember being struck by the high seriousness of his speech at the conference and the eloquence of his words. Despite the ministerial aura, he was warm and friendly when I was introduced to him.

I met him next when I arrived in Sri Lanka in August 2004 to take up my assignment as India's High Commissioner to Colombo. The day after my arrival, I was in his office to present a copy of my credential papers, and to sit down to a discussion on bilateral relations between our two countries. Again, despite his pre-eminence and stature, he was welcoming and he spoke with me, with clarity and conviction, of his vision of India and Sri Lanka, and the ties that bind them. The next day, the photographs of our meeting made it to the front pages of the Sri Lankan dailies in English, Sinhala and Tamil.

For exactly one year after that, until his tragic assassination in August 2005, I met Lakshman Kadirgamar very frequently, in his study at his official residence in a leafy neighbourhood in beautiful Colombo, against a backdrop of many significant events, including the visit of the then President Chandrika Kumaratunga to India; the visit of our then Naval Chief, Arun Prakash, to Sri Lanka; the Indian Ocean tsunami of December 2004, and the deployment of Indian assistance to help the victims of this disaster along the coast of Sri Lanka, both south and north; the first blurred evidence of a possible existence of LTTE air assets; and many more such events. I deeply valued his insights and his analyses of emergent events, and our friendship. Although he was not associated with the world of poetry, he consented to release my book of poems, *Rain Rising*, in Sri Lanka in the summer of 2005. He was witty and irreverent, in a wonderfully good-natured and disarming manner, in his remarks on diplomats who are drawn to poetry, and I was proud to have him launch my book in his country.

Lakshman Kadirgamar spent many years at the helm of Sri Lanka's foreign ministry. During that time, he became not only a spokesman for his country's interests, but also an ardent advocate of South Asian regionalism and unity. He understood well the unique centrality of India to South Asia, and the 'unique character of the region that makes it an integer'.[1] Regionalism, to him, was the future. And, for India, his words and deeds were inspired by well-meaning friendship, and his grasp of the core meaning of a relationship of 'heart and mind', as our late Prime Minister Rajiv Gandhi once said of ties between India and Sri Lanka, or his understanding of the concept of the 'nearest neighbour' (the words are Mahatma Gandhi's). And, here, he probed the depths of this bilateral relationship with exceptional focus and intellectual honesty. He was frank in his assessments of the policies of both countries in regard to the factor of the internal armed conflict within Sri Lanka from the mid-1980s onwards. I know that his wish was that we should learn from that experience so that we could build a new chapter in our relations. He felt we were beginning to write that new chapter in the first decade of this new century, and that the definition of 'irreversible excellence' should apply to the India–Sri Lanka equation.

Minister Kadirgamar opposed terrorism fearlessly and resolutely. He was, at the same time, aware that the denouement of the internal conflict within his country was fast approaching and that it was necessary to dwell on the dispensation and scheme of things that would follow the end of the conflict. He was fully aware of the tragic history of minority–majority relations in Sri Lanka. He would, I am sure, have devoted himself to the cause of rehabilitation and to the meaningful reconciliation of the war-ravaged northern part of the country and its conflict-ravaged population with the rest of their countrymen and women in the post-conflict era. In the mind of Lakshman Kadirgamar, such a complex task would have evoked, I am sure, a passionate sense of commitment to finding a fair and reasonable solution to the ethnic question.

There is another issue on which Foreign Minister Kadirgamar spoke with a deep sense of belief and conviction. This was on the complexities of the management of a developing state – a multi-ethnic, multi-religious, post-colonial society. He was convinced, quite rightly, that the processes of globalization should not erode the integrity and wellbeing of the (nation) state. He wished to see a 'formative voice' for the developing world in the new development chapter for the twenty-first century. And, he also understood that there is 'no simplicity of circumstance, no uniformity in scenario, no easy solution' when it comes to internal armed conflict within states, especially those that are as complex as many in our region and in the rest of the developing world.

On that fateful Friday evening in August 2005, I became, by a twist of fate and circumstance, the last foreigner to see Lakshman Kadirgamar before his life was snuffed out by an assassin's bullet. He invited me to be chief guest at a function held to mark the release of a new journal on international affairs, *International Relations in a Globalising World*, being brought out by the Bandaranaike Centre for International Studies. I was to stand in for our former prime minister, I. K. Gujral, who could not travel to Colombo for the occasion. It was a timeless moment, that will stay etched in my memory forever. The function was brief, Mr Kadirgamar's words eloquent, as always, and full of empathy for India. We said our goodbyes with no knowledge that his killers were making final preparations for their ghastly act.

His death diminished us all.

PART II
Documents

DOCUMENT 1

Report to Amnesty International on my Visit to South Vietnam

Colombo, 1 January 1964

During the Cold War, Vietnam was one of several countries divided into two – one part Communist, the other anti-Communist. South Vietnam, officially known as the Republic of Vietnam, had since 1955 been under the rule of President Ngo Dinh Diem, a Catholic who had been strongly supported by the US. Beginning in the late 1950s, a communist guerrilla insurgency gained pace in South Vietnam; and in the early 1960s this 'Viet Cong' (Vietnamese Communist) insurgency, under the leadership of the National Liberation Front for South Vietnam and with the support of North Vietnam, resulted in the US becoming increasingly involved militarily in supporting the South Vietnamese government.

Meanwhile, President Diem and his family established a system of autocratic rule in South Vietnam. Elections regularly produced improbable majorities of around 99 per cent for the government. Various groups independent of the government were suppressed. Although well over half the population were Buddhists, as against the just under 10 per cent who were Catholic, there were numerous acts of discrimination against Buddhists that were well documented over several years. Then in May 1963 in the city of Hué the regime placed restrictions on the flying of Buddhist flags during Vesak – the anniversary of the birth of Buddha. This triggered a non-violent campaign between May and November 1963 which is described in this report. The campaign led to a stalemate between the regime and the majority population that was resolved only after a US-sponsored coup d'état on the night of 1–2 November 1963 by South Vietnamese army units resulted in the deaths of President Diem and members of his family.

Amnesty International had been founded in May 1961, the principal moving spirit being the British lawyer Peter Benenson. He had almost certainly met Kadirgamar in England – perhaps at Balliol College Oxford (where they both studied Law, but at different times) or in London (where they were both in legal practice). In about October 1963, while the Buddhist-led resistance campaign was still in full swing, Benenson commissioned Kadirgamar to go to South Vietnam to investigate the treatment of the Buddhists there.

This is believed to be the first ever report of an Amnesty International investigation into a crisis in a particular country. It is an early indication of Kadirgamar's interest in civil liberties questions in societies beyond those with which he was directly familiar, of his sympathy with Buddhists, and of his recognition of the difficulties of building a new political order in the wake of European colonialism. The report was based on a limited remit from Amnesty, and covers only the events of 1963. Although there are some hints, he does not here indicate directly his views on the US role or on the desirability of unification of the two Vietnams – eventually achieved in 1975.

*****

Since there is no consulate or embassy representing the government of South Vietnam in Ceylon, I made my first application for a visa to enter the country through the French embassy in Colombo about two weeks prior to the *coup d'état* which led to the overthrow of President Ngo Dinh Diem's government on 1 November 1963. No reply was received by the French embassy in Colombo to my request for a visa and I was advised by the French embassy authorities here that the silence of Diem's government was tantamount to a refusal to let me in. Even though the change of government and the consequent release by the military junta of all Diem's political prisoners had minimized the necessity for an Amnesty investigation, I decided that it would be worth going to South Vietnam to verify at first hand the reports of events in that country, some of which were of dubious origin, published especially in the propaganda journals of local extremist religious groups. Accordingly, I left for Singapore by air on 9 November, hoping to collect a visa from the Vietnamese consulate there. A series of lucky coincidences and fortuitous meetings with influential people helped me to secure the visa and also enabled me to make a number of useful contacts in Saigon. I spent ten days in South Vietnam, including two days in Hué, where the revolt against Diem's regime really began.

There were no restrictions at all on my personal movements during my stay in South Vietnam. Indeed, the new government gave me their fullest cooperation in the conduct of my investigation. The Associated Newspapers of Ceylon (the leading group of newspapers in Ceylon) gave me accreditation as a special correspondent and a letter of authority which also came in very useful as the Vietnamese press proved to be of great assistance to me.

Background of the Crisis

The cause of the explosion which toppled the Diem regime lies deep in the history of Vietnam. Discerning Buddhists and Catholics alike held the view that Diem was the legatee of a policy of discrimination against the Buddhists initiated by the French. The French recognized the corporate ownership of property belonging to the Church, whereas a similar privilege was not extended to Buddhist foundations. During the French occupation the

Buddhists were scarcely organized. Their ties were loose and there does not appear to have been any concerted pressure for the recognition of their religious rights. There was general agreement that Diem was a popular leader in the first few years of his rule after he came into power in 1954.[1] There was also general acknowledgement of the debt which the country owed to Diem for suppressing the Hoa Hao and Cao Dai sects which were the plague of the Vietnamese people in the early years after the country was partitioned. I detected considerable personal sympathy for Diem over the circumstances of his death but nothing at all for his brother Nhu and his wife.[2] Many expressed the view that Diem was a puppet in their hands. I was told by two people who met Diem shortly prior to the *coup d'état* – Fr Luan (Rector of the University of Hué) and a German Professor of Paediatrics at the same university – that in the last few months he was an object of pity, suspicious of everyone around him, except perhaps his brothers, hopelessly out of touch with the people, unwilling to recognize the possibility that the Vietnamese people would revolt against his rule which he passionately believed was benevolent and popular. He had become a prisoner in his palace. On the occasion of the last National Day celebrations prior to his fall the people were not allowed anywhere near the dais from which he took the salute at the march past of his troops. Roads were blocked and cordoned off in a wide perimeter and even those selected guests who attended the occasion by special invitation were not allowed to take their cameras, much to their regret as it proved to be the last occasion on which Diem appeared in public.

A Vietnamese army officer told me a story that may or may not be true but serves to illustrate the extent to which Diem had ceased to be in communication with his people. Apparently after the National Day celebrations he had given each of his palace servants a gift of 20 piastres with a homily on how lucky they were to be given such a large sum of money. Today a packet of cigarettes in Saigon costs 40 piastres and the price was higher just prior to the coup. I was told by a pressman who had accompanied Diem's entourage on a visit to a market in Saigon some months before the coup that Diem had inquired of a vendor the price of a kilo of vegetables. Confronted by the president and a vast array of security police the frightened woman replied that the cost was fifteen piastres. After the president and party had departed, the pressman asked the woman why she had said the price was fifteen piastres when the current market price was seventy piastres. She said that she did not dare to tell the president what the true price was. In his anxiety to preserve the regime, Diem, egged on by his diabolical brothers, saw in every protest against the harshness of his laws and the corruption of his administration a personal threat to himself and his family. He saw communists everywhere and his pathological fear of communist infiltration, cleverly manipulated by his brother Nhu, blinded him to the rottenness of his regime and his growing unpopularity.

A leading lay Buddhist in Hué told me that although Diem had appointed many Catholics to high positions in his administration, he felt that these appointments were made not with a view to favouring the Catholics but because Diem felt that for the preservation of his personal authority he needed supporters of whose personal loyalty and resistance to communism he could be assured. Otherwise, it would be difficult to explain how, of the 20 generals in the Vietnamese army 17 were Buddhists.[3] There is convincing evidence that in the rural areas of Vietnam, Catholics were given special privileges in respect of land settlements. Many of the refugees who came into South Vietnam from the North after the country was partitioned were led to the South by the local village priest, and in resettling them preference seems to have been given to Catholics and to those Buddhists who became Catholics. I was informed that certain restrictions were placed on worship in Buddhist temples, namely, that bells and gongs were not to be sounded and that communal prayer was not to be too loud. People who disobeyed these injunctions mysteriously disappeared especially in Central Vietnam. Buddhist soldiers who were seen too frequently at the pagodas were transferred to the front lines.

Thus the general consensus of opinion was that discontent was deep rooted, if not obvious, in Vietnam from about 1959. Saigon was riddled with spies and informers. The press was completely servile under rigid censorship. Numerous irksome restrictions on personal freedom like Madame Nhu's morality law, and the ban on meetings and demonstrations except under close supervision, aggravated a situation that was steadily worsening. Progress in the war against the Viet Cong was slow. It is axiomatic that a guerrilla war cannot be won by sheer force of arms; the active cooperation of the peasants who are really in the vanguard of the struggle against the Viet Cong is imperative. In the latter years of Diem's rule the only political alternative to communism in South Vietnam was the depressing prospect of the permanent hegemony of an autocratic family. The Buddhist crisis was the immediate cause of his downfall, although it was inevitable that sooner or later his end would have come. Diem's handling of the Buddhist affair was evidence of the degree to which he had become impervious to reason and isolated from the people. Trivial issues became national problems overnight. Pleas for tolerance and reforms made to him by his friends were ignored. A crisis that could easily have been averted and could certainly have been settled was allowed to grow until it consumed him. His motto was loyalty to himself at any cost. In the closing years of his life he had deluded himself into the belief that he personified the state, the people, the hopes and aspirations of the country. But nothing was further from the truth.

The City of Hué and its University

The Buddhist struggle began in Hué, the ancient capital of Vietnam, about 300 miles from Saigon by air. The road to Hué is dangerous. It is mainly used by the military forces as it passes through country which is very much the scene of war. Hué is a small city bisected by the famous River of Perfume which is the pride of its people. It has hardly been touched by the extravagances of civilization. There are no night clubs, only two cinemas, no taxis but it is now dominated by its university. The University of Hué was founded in 1957 and its first and present Rector is Father Cao Van Luan, a Vietnamese Catholic priest who was a close personal friend of Diem. When the university was established it was not expected to last for very long. It was considered by many to be a disastrous experiment – not it would seem for the reason that a Catholic priest would be the head of a university whose students were predominantly Buddhist but because it was thought that Vietnam could not afford a second university. But in the fifth year of its existence the number of students enrolled increased from 387 to 2488.

Long before the Buddhist crisis, Fr Luan wrote these prophetic words in the course of an appeal for funds for the university: 'It is the firm conviction of our staff and faculty that one day in the near future we shall say in all truth: "the University of Hué is successfully working for the fulfilment of its mission to educate the people of Central Vietnam in such a manner that they will be a positive asset to this young emerging nation and to the free world in general. This could not have been done without our faith in our own abilities, the surging strength of freedom and the warm encouragement and assistance of our friends throughout the world".' He could not have known how soon in the life of this young university its ideals would be so severely tested.

The Crisis

In April 1963, Archbishop Thuc celebrated the 25th anniversary of his ordination. The celebrations were on a grand scale and were financed by the state. Various flags including the Vatican flag were prominently displayed, and it appears that Decree No. 10 (passed by the French during the colonial regime) which regulated the conditions under which flags were to be flown on public occasions, was disregarded in the case of Archbishop Thuc's celebrations. No incident of any kind occurred during the celebrations but the Buddhists noted, and were naturally led to believe, that Decree No. 10 was now defunct.

Accordingly, when the Vesak celebrations (commemorating the birth of the Buddha) came round in May the Buddhists of Hué put up their decorations on the same lines as those displayed in the previous month for the Archbishop's anniversary. The Buddhist flag was flown in a prominent position along with the national flag of South Vietnam. On the day before Vesak the government ordered that the Buddhist flag be pulled down and cited Decree No. 10 in support of its decision. This naturally caused consternation among the Buddhists. For one thing it was a flagrant instance of discrimination, and for another the government waited till the day before Vesak to invoke this Decree.

On the morning of Vesak day a well-attended meeting was held at the Tu Dam pagoda in Hué. The meeting was addressed by leading monks of Hué who protested against the government's decision. I heard a tape recording of this meeting which was played back by the Vietnamese Professor of Literature at the University of Hué and it was clear beyond any doubt that the slogans adopted on that day demanded only the equality of all religions and the recognition of the Buddhist flag. Even under severe provocation there was no incitement to violence or abuse directed against any other religious faith. The traditional Vesak broadcast by the leading monk of the Tu Dam pagoda was to be made that night but shortly before the broadcast was to go on the air the government authorities refused permission. This was further provocation to the Buddhists of Hué. Later that evening they gathered in large numbers – estimated at about 20,000 – outside the radio station in Hué. Eye witnesses told me that there were no arms or weapons of any kind carried by this crowd who marched peacefully to the precincts of the radio station. The authorities were obviously alarmed, and troops and tanks were called up. The tanks opened fire. There were six explosions in all. Dr Quyen (Dean of the Faculty of Medicine at the University of Hué and Director of the Hué General Hospital) told me that two of the explosions were caused by cannon shells and three by rifle shots – the sixth explosion was mysterious, it was neither tank fire nor rifle shot. Eight people were killed. On 9 July 1963 the government published the following communiqué:

> According to the Coroner's statement and the findings of the Prosecutor's office it is concluded that all victims died of skull fractures and were wounded only on the upper parts of the body and not the lower parts. All bear the same marks as if caused by a shock wave of an explosion from a very powerful device which exploded violently about 80 to 100 centimetres above the ground. Therefore, the victims were killed by a Viet Cong plastic explosion (which the Vietnamese armed forces do not have) and not crushed by tanks or armoured cars as previously alleged. This fact was confirmed by Dr Quyen, Director of the Hué General Hospital, at a meeting with the Government delegate for the Central Delta and the Coroner on 2 July.

Opinion in Saigon at the time and even after the coup was that the government's version of the Vesak incident was false. Everybody believed that the name of the eminent and widely respected Dr Quyen had been falsely used to support the government's version. When I met Dr Quyen, I asked him about this incident, expecting him to confirm what I had been told in Saigon. But to my surprise he declared that the government's version was substantially true. He had personally examined the corpses at the General Hospital and was completely satisfied that the fatal injuries were caused by an explosion and not by tank or rifle fire. He kept saying to me, over and over again, how important and necessary it was to be absolutely objective in assessing the facts. He said that the government's propaganda on most of the burning issues of the day was a tissue of lies but on this occasion they had come out with the truth at least as to the cause of death, and he was emphatic on this point. But, of course, the government had imputed to Dr Quyen the conclusion that the victims were killed by Viet Cong terrorists. Dr Quyen declared that neither he nor any of the eye witnesses could possibly know from where the explosion had come or who threw the grenade. This part of the government's declaration is, therefore, false and Dr Quyen was also not certain whether any others had been killed by tank or rifle fire whose bodies had been whisked away from the scene without being taken to the hospital. I was very impressed by Dr Quyen's scrupulously fair and objective account of this incident. No praise can be too high for this great leader of men who even in the flush of victory for his people has maintained that integrity and obsession for the truth in all matters which has given to his leadership a supreme quality. (I refer more fully to my meeting with Dr Quyen at pp. 100–2.)

After the Hué incident events moved fast. On 9 May a 'heartfelt' letter was addressed by the Venerable Thich Tam Chau, Vice-Chairman of the General Association of Buddhists in Vietnam, to 'all superior monks, priests, and nuns and all Buddhists in Vietnam'. It was an appeal for the support of all Buddhists in the struggle 'to protect our just religion in an orderly, peaceful, non-violent manner'. It made no specific call for action other than telling Buddhists to be 'ready to march the road of martyrdom'. Numerous other letters and messages followed in quick succession. There was a letter from the League of Buddhist Students to student friends asserting that the struggle of the Buddhists is for 'freedom and equality' and asking for the support of all Vietnamese students. On 12 May, the Vietnam Buddhist Association published a communiqué announcing the determination of the Buddhists to achieve their Five Aspirations by peaceful means. It lists the slogans to be used and contains a copy of the telegram apparently sent throughout Vietnam announcing a period of mourning for Buddhists who died in the Hué incident. Not one of the slogans listed in this communiqué can be described in any way as aiming at the incitement of Buddhists to attack the followers of any other religious faith.

On 10 May a manifesto listing the Five Aspirations of the Hué Buddhists was published, signed by Chief Bonze Tuong Van and four administrative committee Chairmen from Central Vietnam. This manifesto was read at a meeting at the Tu Dam pagoda in Hué on the same day. The first part of the manifesto states the basic Buddhist position: 'we are with the government... have no enemies... fight only for religious equality... will use non-violent means of struggle... will not be "used" by any one.' The second part of the manifesto explains in detail the Five Aspirations which were as follows:

1. Let the government definitely abrogate the official telegram giving the order to bring down the religious emblem of Buddhism.
2. Let Buddhism benefit from the special status granted to Catholic missions and provided by Decree No. 10.
3. Let the government put an end to arrests and persecutions of the Buddhists.
4. Let the monks and the Buddhists faithful enjoy freedom of worship and the freedom to propagate their faith.
5. Let the government pay equitable compensation to the victims of the Hué incident and duly punish the instigators.

The third section of the manifesto is an appeal to the government to negotiate. A further statement was issued on 25 May stressing the patriotism of Buddhists in Vietnam both during the Viet Minh war and in the present struggle against the Viet Cong. This was followed by a manifesto issued by the monks of the Xa Loi pagoda in Saigon affirming their support of the Hué Buddhists and the Hué manifesto. On 8 June a joint statement was issued by Hué and Saigon Buddhists saying that a rumour is being spread that the Government of Viet Nam has agreed to the Five Aspirations, and denying that this is true. The statement was signed by the Venerable Thich Tam Chau. On 27 May an administrative notice under the signature of the Venerable Thich Tam Chau was issued to Buddhist pagodas throughout Vietnam containing instructions on fasting, conducting of memorial ceremonies for the victims of the Hué incident, etc.

Three other letters are especially significant at this stage: one was an open letter from the League of Buddhist Students of Hué to all Vietnamese describing what it calls 'the religious discrimination which has now reached the crucial stage in Hué' and 'the miserable lot of Buddhist believers in Vietnam'. It calls for support of Buddhists but makes no special appeal for action. The next is an open letter to Diem signed again by the Venerable Thich Tam Chau. It lists specific grievances (monks forced to sign pro-government statements, nuns arrested, etc.). It contains an anti-communist declaration and makes no specific call for action other than a general request that abuses be ended. The third is a communiqué signed by the Venerable Thich Thiem Khiet which states that 'the Buddhist Association of Vietnam is not aimed at overthrowing the government'.

The government finally agreed to negotiate on the five demands presented by the General Buddhist Association of Vietnam. On 16 June a conference was held at which government representatives and Buddhist leaders were present and a joint communiqué was issued which on the face of it concedes substantially the demands presented by the Buddhists. But the agreement was not implemented. Shortly after 16 June the Inter-Sect Committee charged, in an undated letter to the vice-president, that the government had failed to implement the joint agreement. Many other letters passed between the Buddhist leaders and the government, the details of which it is not possible to repeat here. Altogether, I examined 51 documents setting out the substance of the Buddhist complaint. To my mind what is significant in these statements is the reasoned, objective and completely fair treatment of a difficult subject by the Buddhist leaders under grave provocation.

To return to the incidents in Hué, early in June the students held a demonstration outside the residence of the Regional Delegate. It was a peaceful protest against the incident on Vesak Day. Three distinguished German professors of the medical faculty of the University of Hué were present on this occasion. The police used some form of gas to disperse the students and I was told that severe burns were caused to many of the students. Professors Wolff and Holterscheidt rendered medical aid to the students immediately after the attack. Shortly thereafter, Wolff and Holterscheidt were expelled from the country. At his own expense Wolff took off on a speaking and broadcasting tour of the United States, Japan and France, pleading the cause of the Buddhists of Vietnam. The return of these professors to the university is eagerly awaited by their students.

The Role of the Students – Instances of Torture

After the Vesak incident students were arrested by the hundreds. Many of them were tortured. Youngsters of 18 suffered along with the monks of the leading pagodas and distinguished citizens of Hué and Saigon. At the Xa Loi pagoda in Saigon I met the President of the Buddhist Students' Association of Vietnam – Tran Quang Thuan, a young lecturer at the University of Saigon. On 20 August – the night of the raids on the leading pagodas in Saigon and Hué – he was at home. When he heard of the attack he went into hiding, organizing cells, distributing literature and generally keeping alive the resistance of the students. For a month he succeeded in evading capture but on 20 September he was arrested, after a secret meeting with five other students, by Nhu's secret police, who were waiting in ambush. As they emerged from the house in which the meeting was held they were seized, put into a waiting car, blindfolded and taken away to prison. At first he was fairly well treated, but later he was subjected to electric shocks and the dreaded water treatment. Five times a day he was strapped to a table, a hose pipe was placed in his mouth and his body was pumped full of water until he lost consciousness; he was revived again and the process repeated. He was kept in solitary confinement for one month and twelve days. When he was released after the coup he was summoned by the Revolutionary Committee of Generals and asked to identify his torturers. He knew their names and identities but refused to disclose them to the Junta. When I told him that this was an incredible act of charity on his part he merely shrugged his shoulders and said that those who tortured him were carrying out a job which they were paid to do. He said revenge was purposeless, the past was past and now with freedom he did not see how revenge or rejoicing could help to undo what had gone before. He was a quiet young man, cultured, liked and respected by his friends. At first I did not know who he was but having spoken for a couple of hours to him and to many other students in the room who had suffered similar pain and humiliation I could see that whatever else this country may lack it has young men of outstanding quality to lead it one day.

As I was to find on many other occasions it was only after I had explained to the students that I had come from far away to investigate the causes of the Buddhist crisis and the events which led to the uprising that they began to speak, more I felt as a personal favour to a stranger who had a job to do, rather than with any sense of self-glorification. In order to satisfy myself that these stories of torture were true I had to ask some of the young students in the room to open their shirts to show me the bruises around the nipples where clips (rather like clothes pegs) had been attached for the purpose of administering shocks. The Vice-President of the Buddhist Students' Association of Vietnam, Ton-that Chuu, a young medical student, was arrested in Hué on 1 June. He was kept in solitary confinement for 24 days and frequently whipped to extract from him confessions implicating his friends. He told me the food was appalling. He was given two bowls of rice a day with a fish concoction that stank so high that he was unable to go near it, far less eat it. He was released later in June and subsequently rearrested on 28 August in Saigon after the raids on the pagodas. He too emphasized that the students participated in the struggle only for the cause of Buddhism. Now he looks forward to completing his interrupted medical studies when the University of Saigon reopens.

There were instances of Catholic and Protestant students being arrested when Buddhists were free. I recall in particular a group of three students in Hué – Tran Quang Long (Protestant), Truong Van Luong (Catholic), and Nguyen Ding Mau (Buddhist) – who joined in the student demonstration at Hué on 21 August. The object of the demonstration was to demand the return of Fr Luan, the Rector of their university. Of these three students the Protestant and Catholic were arrested, but not the Buddhist. All three of them declared that their struggle was against the Diem regime. They were patriots, not fanatics. I met a young Vietnamese woman, the wife of a Professor at Hué – Madame Van Dinh Hy who was herself the Principal of the Girls' High School at Hué and the mother of a 10-month-old daughter. She was arrested on 27 August – and what was her crime? She and her colleagues presented a petition to Diem requesting him to give relief to the Buddhists and urging him to prevent Madame Nhu from making irresponsible statements. The petition was dated 20 August. She was arrested and placed in a large dormitory with 900 men and women. She was not physically tortured but the food was impossible to eat and she did not see her husband or infant daughter for over two months. She told me that many of her girls were tortured by having fish sauce poured into their noses and ears. She was one of the persons who was allowed to meet the UN delegation. But she was unable to speak freely to them because she recognized among the crowd of persons present in the room where she was being interviewed by the UN delegation a number of secret police in plain clothes. In analysing for my benefit the causes of the Buddhist crisis she stated that the attack on the Buddhists was directed by Diem's family; it was not inspired by the Catholics or their Church and she said she bears no ill will whatever against the Catholic people. It was difficult to see her when she knew what I had come to find out. I had to wait for about half an hour until her husband persuaded her that it was her duty to tell me what she knew.

Both the President and Vice-President of the Buddhist Students' Association while in gaol were shown letters purporting to have been written by communists professing support for the Buddhist movement. They were asked to sign statements to the effect that the Buddhist movement was inspired by communist opponents of the regime. They were not satisfied with the authenticity of these documents produced by Nhu's secret police; fabrication would have been so easy. There may well have been secret communists among the students who sought to use the Buddhist agitation for their own purposes. Indeed in answer to a specific question which I put to General Minh, whether the persecution of the Buddhists was motivated by the Diem government's fear of communist infiltration in their ranks, the General replied at first that he was conducting an investigation into the matter but amplified his answer by stating that although 'the persecution was caused by Diem's fear of communist infiltration, to this new government there was no communist infiltration among the Buddhists during Diem's regime'.

General Minh and his team are shrewd professional soldiers now faced with the enormous task of reorganizing the civilian administration of the country, infusing new life and spirit into the people and finishing the long war of attrition against the Viet Cong. They have not lightly dismissed the former regime's charge but they, as well as their people, know very well that Diem was looking for an excuse to crush the revolt that threatened to topple his regime. When I asked General Minh whether he expected further trouble from the students, this was his reply: 'We are convinced that our students are patriots. They have expressed their readiness and will to collaborate with the new government and not to allow communist infiltration among their ranks.' There is no doubt that the new government is as popular with the students as with the rest of the people. The present mood in Vietnam is one of exultation. But it is too early yet to say whether the Revolutionary Committee will stand together as a team, and the trained observer of the political scene in Vietnam will not commit himself to a firm prediction on the structure of the new government. There is some uncertainty as to where, among the personnel of the Revolutionary Committee, real power lies.

From the religious angle the new government will certainly have the support of Buddhists and Catholics. The Venerable Thich Duc Nghiep, spokesman for the Inter-Sect Committee, expressed the deep gratitude of the Buddhist leaders to the Revolutionary Committee for liberating the country from the grip of Diem's family, and it is significant that when I asked General Minh what his government's attitude was towards the Buddhists and Catholics he replied 'equality for all religions', which was the dominant slogan of the Buddhist campaign.

Two Men who Played Leading Roles in the Buddhist Struggle

Finally, I want to speak of two men in Hué who contributed so much to the dignity, responsibility, and tone of the Buddhist campaign.

The first is Dr Le Khack Quyen MD, Professor of Medicine, Dean of the Faculty of Medicine at the University of Hué, editor of a Buddhist review and the person who could fairly be described as the leading lay Buddhist in Hué. I went to see this gentleman without an appointment as I was warned in Saigon that he avoided such meetings. I was fortunate to take him by surprise. This distinguished man lives in a quiet back street in Hué in the top storey of a dilapidated house. His tiny study was crammed with books spilling from the shelves and overflowing on to the floor. When I told him what my mission was he refused point blank to tell me anything about the past. The conversation opened in this way – he said he believed in tolerance against violence. He did not want to speak about the past. By dint of persuasion and pleading and emphasizing the fact that one of the primary objectives of my visit to Hué was to meet him and that time was short I succeeded finally in getting the doctor to talk. He began by explaining that after the coup, peace had been restored as far as the Buddhists were concerned and he told me in detail about a meeting held on 7 November at the Tu Dam pagoda which was attended by Buddhist monks and Catholic priests led by Fr Luan. The meeting which was in the nature of a thanksgiving was apparently very successful and was attended by over 150 people. He emphasized that the Buddhists were not interested in recriminations and reprisals. He told me that he and Fr Luan had sent teams of students to explain to the villagers in the countryside the tasks that lay before them now that freedom had been won. He confirmed that many Catholic priests who worked under Archbishop Thuc were strongly against the Diem regime. He explained that the Buddhists were weak and unorganized during the French regime and in the early years of Diem's rule, although at first Diem had given no cause for complaint from the Buddhists. Diem became unpopular after 1959 because he became despotic and the first organized opposition to Diem's regime came from the intellectuals of Vietnam. After the incident on Vesak Day the Buddhist movement became the focal point of opposition to Diem.

Still Dr Quyen would not speak of his own role as the leader and hero of the Buddhists of Hué. At the end of our conversation, as I was about to leave, yielding to a final plea to tell me what happened to him, he came out with these facts. He was arrested on 21 August and taken to prison in the shirt and trousers he was wearing at that time. He was placed in solitary confinement and did not have a change of clothing until he was liberated after the coup – two and a half months later. For 21 successive nights he was interrogated from dusk to dawn with a bright light shining in his face. He was not subjected to any of the other physical tortures which the ingenuity of Nhu's secret police had devised. But he could scarcely eat the food that was given to him. He dismissed all this lightly, almost apologetically, and when I was at the door bidding him farewell he said casually that after the coup he had been told by a high official in the Diem regime who was a personal friend of his that he had been sentenced to death without his knowledge and of course without a trial, and that the sentence was to have been carried out on 6 November, which means that if the coup had been delayed Dr Quyen would have been no more. I asked him whether he was not alarmed at the fate that would have overtaken him. Dr Quyen's reply is memorable. He scratched his head and said 'You know, if I had died I would not have known the crime for which I had given up my life.' That was all that troubled him, it was a problem unresolved, something that disturbed his tidy mind.

This interview with Dr Quyen was in the presence of a young editor of a leading Vietnamese newspaper, my friend and counsellor in Vietnam, who was meeting Dr Quyen for the first time. After we had walked down the rickety flight of stairs that led to his attic study and were at the outer door preparing to leave, I heard a clatter of footsteps. Dr Quyen came rushing after us and spoke to my friend in Vietnamese. He told him that under no condition must he mention his name in the Vietnamese Press. Dr Quyen imposed no conditions on me. Even if he had, I would have felt obliged to repeat the substance of this conversation for the edification of others outside Vietnam.

I was told two stories by his students which are also worthy of mention. Prior to 1945 during the French occupation an order had been issued that on the National Day, French flags were to be flown in every home. Dr Quyen refused to comply. The French police visited his home and forced him to comply under threat of dire punishment. Dr Quyen then took a broomstick, tied a small French flag to it and hoisted it on his gate post.

But the true measure of a man of his calibre can be gauged from the other story, which was told me by Au Ngoc Ho, Secretary-General of the University of Hué, a young American-educated Doctor of Geology. Two nights after the coup, a large crowd of students had surrounded the residence of Ngo Dinh Can, brother of Diem who was the Governor of the province of Hué. Rumours had been afloat that Can had been responsible for the murder of monks and nuns who had been imprisoned in the dungeons of his country palace. (Incidentally, up to the time of my departure no evidence had been uncovered by the new government to establish the truth of this rumour.) The army had thrown a cordon around Can's palace but the students were in an ugly mood and anything could have happened. Au Ngoc Ho told me that this was perhaps the only occasion, judging from the mood of the crowd, when serious Catholic–Buddhist clashes could have been caused. The students, many of whom had been tortured, thwarted by the army from seizing Can and sacking his palace, might have gone on the rampage in the City of Hué, and one ugly incident might well have sparked off a holocaust in the country. The young provost couldn't handle the situation, Fr Luan the well-loved Rector of the University of Hué was still in Saigon after he had been removed by Diem, and there was apparently nobody else on hand who could have calmed the inflamed crowd. Au Ngoc Ho telephoned Dr Quyen and asked him to come down immediately. The little doctor drove down to the scene and began to address the students. As he was spotted a burst of applause greeted him. Dr Quyen began to speak calmly and soberly. He made one telling point. He told the students that it was cowardly to attack a wretched man like Can after the coup. Personal and religious freedom had been restored to their country. Those who wanted to fight the regime should have fought it openly at the height of its power. I am told that the students dispersed quietly, perhaps ashamed of themselves, in the light of what Dr Quyen, who had suffered so much, had said.

The other outstanding man whom it was my privilege to meet is Fr Cao Van Luan, the Rector of the University of Hué. He was a close personal friend of Diem, and the foundation of the University of Hué was really a gesture by Diem to Fr Luan. In June after his return from a tour of the United States, Fr Luan went to see Diem. He told me he pleaded with Diem for many hours to reform his government and to accede to the just demands of the Buddhists. He was horrified to find that Diem was completely beyond persuasion. A few days after his return to Hué he was dismissed from his Rectorship, taken to Saigon and thereafter kept under house arrest. The students of Hué, who had come to love this man, came out in protest. Hundreds of them were arrested and gaoled. The academic staff of the University of Hué sent a mammoth petition to Diem asking for the release of Fr Luan. The Buddhist students of Hué will never forget that prior to his dismissal Fr Luan led them to pray at the Tu Dam pagoda in open defiance of Diem. When he returned to the university after the coup there was such a spontaneous demonstration of affection for him by a predominantly Buddhist university as had never been seen before.

Conclusion

I would not have been surprised to find nothing but bitterness and hatred between the Catholic and Buddhist peoples of South Vietnam. It would have been natural perhaps to find the desire for vengeance in the aftermath of liberation. But I found none of this. Everywhere there was reluctance to speak of the past – and not because the people had any fear of exposure or punishment in a country which has now been freed from the brutality of the Diem regime.

The press, after years of censorship, is at last free to publish what it likes, to express all its pent-up emotion. But I found that the press has deliberately eschewed sensationalism. While the pressmen will tell you that they have heard many salacious stories about the private life of Madame Nhu they have not the slightest interest in publishing them and there is a tacit understanding among the newspapers not to print pictures showing the cruelty of the Diem regime.

Young students freed again after months of imprisonment and torture might have been expected to run wild. But I found them quiet and sober, suddenly mature perhaps, and it was difficult to extract from them the details of atrocities perpetrated by the former regime. They kept saying that the past is best forgotten, that there is no point in dwelling on the misery of the last six months. They were concerned only with the future.

I met leading monks, professors, teachers, students, professional people, men and women, young and old and not one single person was keen to glory in his or her martyrdom. After a day or two I began to feel ashamed of my own inquisitiveness for details. I began to feel that a mere chronicle of events could never sufficiently reveal the true nature of the struggle of the Vietnamese people for their rights and liberties. I began to see that here was a human story unparalleled in my own experience and in many ways unique. The world has seen from time to time that ordinary men and women are capable of supreme heroism in times of war, that loyalty to each other and self-sacrifice are human qualities that are exhibited in unexpected quarters in times of crisis. But I venture to think that seldom if ever has a whole people shown such understanding and compassion in their hour of victory.

Political and religious extremists in Ceylon sought to create the impression that a religious war between the Buddhists and Catholics was fought in Vietnam. I did not find a shred of evidence to support this thesis. The ferment of political and religious movements in Asia today is such that I would not have been in the least surprised, indeed I expected, to find that the struggle of the Buddhist people of South Vietnam for their rights had been exploited for the achievement of ulterior purposes. But during the entirety of the campaign waged by the Buddhists there was never at any stage in any form whatsoever the manifestation of an intention to repress or persecute the adherents of any other religious faith. What appeared to me to be almost miraculous is that the mass of the people who were engaged in this struggle and who suffered for their cause were able always to define their goals with scrupulous objectivity. Their fight was against the Diem regime, against the personal autocracy of a powerful family. Their fight was for the elevation of the Buddhist faith, not the denigration of any other peoples or faiths. During the campaign for liberation not one anti-Catholic slogan was raised or published by the Buddhist leaders. I was not told, and I did not come to hear, of a single incident involving Buddhists and Catholics. The truth appears to be that the majority of the Catholic and Buddhist people stood together, united against tyranny, and that their respective leaders worked in harmony for the common cause. With the exception of Archbishop Thuc, the notorious brother of Diem, and his small coterie of followers who, judged by any standards would be a disgrace to their faith and their people, there were (to quote what General Minh told me) 'many gestures of sympathy from the Catholics towards the Buddhists. The messages of Pope Paul VI to the Vietnamese people and the two pastoral letters of the Archbishop of Saigon, Monsignor Nguyen Van Binh are the most important manifestations of their sympathy.'

The Venerable Thich Duc Nghiep of the Xa Loi pagoda, spokesman for the Inter-Sect Committee which was established during the campaign to co-ordinate the activities of the various Sects, told me: 'The Buddhist protest was against Diem's regime and family. There was no ill-feeling against our Catholic brothers. They showed sympathy with us.' The Venerable Nghiep spent 72 days in gaol. I was told by students that he had been severely tortured, but although I met him on two occasions and urged him to speak about the past, he steadfastly refused. He said in his flawless English that 'the last few months were a nightmare. It is past; there is no necessity to speak about it now.' As this incredible picture unfolded I asked myself often how it was that ordinary people with the failings and weaknesses and passions that all human beings are heir to could have behaved en masse in such a splendid manner.

The young Provost of the University of Hué gave me one answer. He said that in their hour of trial they were richly blessed with leaders both Buddhist and Catholic who were men of vision and tolerance, always concerned to offer to their followers by word and example the best advice and counsel in the interest of their cause and the unity of their country. The Venerable Thich Tam Chau – Chairman of the Inter-Sect Committee for the Defence of Buddhism in South Vietnam, the monk who along with the Venerable Thich Khiet and the Venerable Thich Tri Quang successfully led and organized the Buddhist revolt against Diem and paved the way for his downfall – has now retired to the peace and quiet of his tiny little room in a wing of the Xa Loi pagoda where he sleeps on a plank bed. He is a gentle man utterly devoid of vanity or arrogance, uncorrupted by the devotion which he has inspired among his followers. I had to see him twice with great difficulty because he shuns visitors and it was with the utmost reluctance that he finally consented to pose for a photograph. The monks of the Tu Dam pagoda in Hué and the Xa Loi pagoda and other pagodas in Saigon who were imprisoned and tortured for over two months had nothing but compassion and mercy for their tormentors. To all those heroic men and women, to Dr Quyen, Fr Luan and the many students who will forever remain anonymous, I would like to pay my own humble tribute. I feel that the memory of their achievements cannot be allowed to fade without it being brought to the notice of the world that men of such calibre and integrity are still amongst us. They have shown that once men and women unite across the divide of belief and allegiance no tyranny can survive.

DOCUMENT 2

Why I Decided to Enter Politics

Colombo, July 1994

In 1994, at the age of 62, Kadirgamar took the momentous step of entering Sri Lankan politics. He had been back in the country for six years following his departure from Geneva. In that period he had continued his legal practice in Colombo. He had also experienced many of the problems of Sri Lankan politics, and had witnessed or been aware of many violent incidents. He knew the risks only too well. His stance on involvement in public life in this period as well as subsequently is described in Sinha Ratnatunga's contribution in this volume.

The United National Party (UNP) had been in government since 1977. When parliamentary elections were scheduled for 16 August 1994, Kadirgamar agreed to be nominated for the People's Alliance (PA), a left-wing coalition formed in 1994 and led by Chandrika Kumaratunga, daughter of former Prime Minister Mrs Sirimavo Bandaranaike. The principal partner in the coalition was the Sri Lanka Freedom Party (SLFP). As one of the PA's candidates on its 'National List', Kadirgamar did not represent a particular constituency, but became a member of parliament thanks to the PA's overall performance in the elections and his high place on the PA list. Sri Lanka has a unicameral legislature with 225 members. In the elections, the PA won 105 seats – less than an absolute majority – but it quickly secured the support of certain other parties representing Muslim and Tamil communities and others. Mrs Kumaratunga was sworn in as Prime Minister on 19 August 1994, and Kadirgamar became Foreign Minister. Subsequently, Mrs Kumaratunga was successful in a presidential election, resigning the prime ministership and serving as President from 12 November 1994 to 19 November 2005.

In July 1994, as the parliamentary election process was getting under way, Kadirgamar made a statement on television about why he had decided to enter politics. Versions of this statement also appeared in Sri Lankan newspapers at the time. It had considerable effect, probably because of its forthright attack on corruption, its convincing emphasis on the idea of service to the country and its commitment to address Sri Lanka's 'grave ethnic question'.

*****

Many people have asked me why I decided to enter politics at this late stage in my life, and in particular, why I decided to join the PA. The first question is a difficult one. My answer is that at a time when in many areas of public life the country's affairs are at such a low ebb it is very important that everybody who might possibly be able to help in some small way to try to retrieve the situation into which we have descended should at least make that effort.

I have had a privileged life by birth, by education, by access to opportunities, and I have always felt that a time must come when you must give something back to the society in which you have grown up and from which you have taken so much. So-called educated people must not shirk responsibilities in public life. I have reached that stage in my life when, without being heroic about it, I feel I should participate more fully in public life.

I have also been asked whether and, if so, why I am prepared to give up my so-called independence and objectivity to enter partisan politics. I greatly value the independence which I have acquired over many decades of professional life. If you treat the democratic process as one of extreme and sustained confrontation and hostility to those of different persuasions, then there is little scope for independence and objectivity in politics. But we must reassert the value of independence and objectivity and make them important factors in political life. It is not a necessary requisite of membership of a political party that one must abandon independence and objectivity. In fact, it would be a great disservice to a party to have in it only people who are beholden to it for a living, for advancement, for preferment and who therefore relinquish their independence because they cannot afford to keep it. Independence based on reasoned positions, even in dissent, can only be healthy for a party and for society as a whole.

The next question is why the PA. The answer is very easy. First, we are witnessing today corruption on an unprecedented scale, corruption spread over the entire spectrum of public life, corruption in terms not merely of illicit financial gains, but corruption in the sense of the systematic undermining of the institutions of the state, an all-pervasive corruption which, combined as it is with a certain cynicism, corrodes the very soul of our society. We citizens have been obliged to contemplate in silent disgust and dismay the unparalleled plunder, pillage and waste of our resources by those on whom political power was unreservedly conferred by the people in 1977. Corruption, because it is brazenly flaunted in the face of the people, has a very deleterious effect on the morale of the young people of our country. They, like all of us were when we were young, are idealistic. They believe and hope, as we did, that there is a future for themselves and for our society, but they are witnessing and experiencing a complete negation of their legitimate hopes and aspirations. I believe that the PA gives some hope that the prevailing situation could be corrected. It is a hope that needs to be pursued and encouraged. I find myself wholly unable to explain, defend or condone the massive corruption that we are witnessing today.

Secondly, I believe that the PA holds out some hope, at least a modicum of hope, that there could be some movement towards the resolution of the grave ethnic question which confronts us. The ruling party today has no more to offer towards the resolution of this grave conflict than the constant reiteration of its belief that only a military answer can be given to the problem. I do not believe that is right or even feasible. I believe that with the PA a genuine effort will be made to achieve a just and fair solution to this problem acceptable to all. It will by no means be easy to obtain wide acceptance for such a solution. The PA does not, indeed cannot, when there are so many conflicting interests involved, guarantee that a solution of this nature can be found. What they do say, and what I believe, is that they will make a genuine effort.

I wish to address two other questions. One is this. There are uncommitted voters who are aware of, and are, equally with all their fellow citizens, revolted by the massive corruption that has taken over the country today. They do not like it. But they wonder, will the PA be any different. My answer to that concern is simple and direct. If you put the PA into power you do so on trust. You place power in their hands for a limited period of time. If they do not perform in power as they said, then they too in due time must be dismissed by the people. Sovereignty in this respect lies with the people not merely in theory; it must always lie with them in practice. Otherwise, the democratic process will be meaningless, and we must not allow it to become meaningless. Therefore, I say that there is nothing to be afraid of. We the people of the country are the final arbiters of the fate of any political party, however powerful it may be, and we must never be afraid to exercise that judgement.

Another question that I am asked is what the reaction of the business community should be to the PA. Now there too, in my way of thinking, the answer is simple. The business community of any country consists of hard-headed, pragmatic people. They want the ground rules to be laid out clearly, and applied fairly and equitably, and the private sector to be allowed to get on with their business with as little government interference as possible. Now the very business people who profess to be alarmed at the prospect of the PA coming to power are also often the very people who say that they too cannot any longer tolerate the corruption they are witnessing, and are called upon to participate in, unwillingly, under the present dispensation. Therefore, I say to the business community be pragmatic and down-to-earth. But do not put yourself beyond the pale. Do not put yourself against the wishes of the large majority of the people of the country. The business community cannot prosper, cannot thrive, in the context of an unjust, unfair, unbalanced society. Where inequity rules, business cannot thrive. It is an illusion that dictatorship, repression, suppression of dissent, the employment of state terror is good for business. That is wrong. It is dangerously wrong. It is much better for the business community to join with everybody else in the country to restore open, transparent government, to open the windows of our society so that a breath of fresh air, the wind of change, will blow through our land again.

DOCUMENT 3

Human Rights and Armed Conflict

Kotelawala Defence Academy, 19 March 1996

This speech is a strong exposition of the principle that human rights law, and also international humanitarian law (the law governing conduct in armed conflict), should be observed by the Sri Lankan government and armed forces even in the very difficult circumstances of the hostilities in Sri Lanka which had been in a particularly intense phase in the months before this speech was delivered.

The General Sir John Kotelawala Defence Academy, where Kadirgamar delivered this speech, was founded in 1980. Located at Rathmalana, near Colombo, it was instituted with the objective of educating men and women to be commissioned officers in the armed forces of Sri Lanka. (In 2007 it was renamed as the General Sir John Kotelawala Defence University.) Kadirgamar was speaking at the Academy's Convocation – the event at which degrees are awarded. This speech was no one-off: Kadirgamar later gave speeches with a similar strong message at other military institutions in Sri Lanka: for example, on 20 June 1998 and 20 February 2004.

In March 1996 Kadirgamar had been Foreign Minister of Sri Lanka for just under two years. Already it was clear that the major problem he faced was the struggle against the LTTE. It occupied much of his time as Foreign Minister – and he also knew already that his own life was under threat from the LTTE. The situation in Sri Lanka was the main focus of his speech. Four aspects of his remarks are noteworthy. (1) Long before the development of the idea of 'responsibility to protect', about which he was to have reservations, he recognized that states had to treat their own citizens decently if they were to ward off external intervention in its various forms. (2) He referred to the situation in his country, not as a 'civil war' (a term he consistently avoided in this connection) but as 'war within a state'. He always emphasized the extraordinary character of the struggle in Sri Lanka. (3) He particularly stressed the importance of observing the distinction between combatants and non-combatants. This issue was to be at the centre of controversies surrounding the actions of the LTTE (especially its use of 'human shields'), and of the Sri Lankan armed forces, in 2009 in the last months of the country's long-running conflict. (4) He was clearly very conscious of various accusations made against Sri Lanka in respect of human rights matters, and sought to deflect them by indicating the measures the government was taking to remedy the situation.

*****

International cooperation in solving international problems of an economic, social, cultural or humanitarian character is mandated in the terms of Article 1 of the Charter of the United Nations which also recognizes the promotion and encouragement of respect for human rights and fundamental freedoms as one of the principal objectives of the UN. Increasing international attention to the promotion and protection of human rights has brought about greater concern for the rights and the treatment of nationals within the territory of a sovereign state. It is argued that where the treatment of one's own nationals assumes such cruel forms as to constitute mass and flagrant violations of human rights on a scale which shocks the conscience of mankind, the matter ceases to be the sole concern of the state of nationality. This is a very important principle now universally accepted. No longer can a state say that human rights violations within its border are a matter entirely for that state alone; no longer can a state say that in matters concerning the violations of human rights within its borders citizens of other states, or other states themselves, have no right to voice concern. It follows that every state has to be deeply conscious of the way in which it treats its own citizens if it wants to capture and preserve the respect of the international community and also ward off intervention in various forms legal, moral and ultimately even by force on the part of other states.

Human Rights Measures

The increasing concern for the rights of the individual should be viewed and appreciated against the backdrop of a series of measures adopted both within and outside UN fora for the protection of human rights. The adoption of the Universal Declaration of Human Rights by the UN General Assembly on 10 December 1948, when the UN was still young, constituted a landmark in the universal recognition of human rights. The General Assembly proclaimed the Universal Declaration of Human Rights as 'a common standard of achievement for all peoples and all nations, to the end that every individual and every organ of society, keeping this Declaration constantly in mind, shall strive by teaching and education to promote respect for these rights and freedoms and by progressive measures, national and international, to secure their universal and effective recognition and observance, both among the peoples of Member States themselves and among the peoples of territories under their jurisdiction.'[1]

The Universal Declaration, however, was only a first step in the creation of an international legal framework for the promotion and protection of human rights. In other words, for breach of the Declaration no remedial action can be taken against the recalcitrant state. It was not a treaty of a legally binding character by which states would be obliged to give effect to fundamental human rights. It also lacked enforcement machinery; yet, it was a significant step forward in the evolutionary process of creating such a legal framework. Its importance lies in the fact that the international community of nations had made a moral commitment through the Declaration to respect human rights and fundamental freedoms.

The two International covenants – the International Covenant on Civil and Political Rights and the International Covenant on Economic, Social and Cultural Rights – which followed the adoption of the Universal Declaration, were adopted in response to the need to formulate legally binding instruments on human rights.

The common thread which binds these two important covenants is the theme of the 'indivisibility of human rights'. The General Assembly Resolution, which mandated the Economic and Social Council to engage in the initiative of formulating the two covenants, declared that 'the enjoyment of civic and political freedoms and of economic, social and cultural rights are interconnected and interdependent' and that 'when deprived of economic, social and cultural rights, man does not represent the human person whom the Universal Declaration regards as the ideal of the free man'.[2]

This pronouncement is an unequivocal expression of the indivisibility of human rights – that civil and political rights alone cannot be dealt with in a vacuum. The guaranteeing of economic, social and cultural rights, along with civil and political rights, is inextricably interlinked in the enjoyment of human rights and fundamental freedoms to the fullest.

The Universal Declaration of Human Rights and the two covenants constitute together, the core of the international legal framework for the promotion and protection of human rights. These principles were further reinforced and elaborated in the Declaration and Programme of Action on Human Rights adopted by the World Conference on Human Rights held in Vienna in 1993.[3] The central message of the World Conference on Human Rights was that rights should not only be enshrined in constitutions, international treaties and in other legal and administrative documents but more importantly be made realizable by every human being. Over 170 sovereign nations, members of the UN and some 7,000 participants including representatives from a variety of governmental, inter-governmental and non-governmental organizations agreed to a consensus that deliberate violations of human rights and fundamental freedoms cannot be justified under any circumstances even in a situation of grave national or international crisis. Professional men and women of the armed forces have the supreme duty of safeguarding the security and wellbeing of nations and their peoples. They therefore have a crucial and indeed an indispensable role to play particularly in time of conflict and war in protecting the human rights of the non-combatant civilians. This is a most important consideration. While it is universally recognized that the armed forces of a state have a duty to protect and assert the sovereignty of the state, to fight the battles of the state, they also have a duty to protect the human rights of non-combatant civilians. The line between combatants and non-combatants is clearly drawn in international law.

The efforts of the international community in the field of human rights have also been directed towards formulating legal instruments dealing with specific aspects of human rights. The results of these initiatives have been the formulation and adoption of the International Convention on the Elimination of All Forms of Racial Discrimination, the International Convention on the Suppression and Punishment of the Crime of Apartheid, the Convention against Torture, the Convention on the Prevention and Punishment of the Crime of Genocide, the Convention on the Rights of the Child, the Convention on Elimination of Discrimination against Women and the International Convention on the Protection of the Rights of Migrant Workers. These conventions constitute a collective response to a range of human rights concerns which have engaged the attention of the international community over a period of time.

International Humanitarian Law Applicable in Armed Conflict

I turn now to some basic principles of humanitarian law applicable in armed conflicts. The international legal norms which have emerged as international humanitarian law applicable in armed conflict is a body of law which for humanitarian reasons limits the right of parties to a conflict to use the methods and means of warfare of their choice and seeks to protect persons and property that may be affected by conflict. If war is inevitable, international humanitarian law attempts to humanize the conduct of hostilities. As was well stated by one writer on humanitarian law: 'The law of armed conflict is without doubt no substitute for peace. As the sparks of violence fly and passions flare, it does, however, constitute one last bulwark of sanity and human values, one final statement of human fellowship.'[4]

The early attempts to codify the principles of international humanitarian law commenced with the Geneva Convention signed in 1864. However, the legal achievement of historic importance was the adoption by the Diplomatic Conference of 1949 of the four Geneva Conventions, including the Geneva Convention relative to the Protection of Civilian Persons in Time of War.

The adoption of a set of rules for the protection of the civilian population in the conduct of hostilities represents a major step forward in the development of international humanitarian law. Article 3 common to the Geneva Conventions seeks to protect persons taking no active part in hostilities, i.e. civilians, by according humane treatment without any adverse distinction. Towards this end, the Geneva Conventions prohibit the commission of a series of acts at any time and in any place whatsoever with respect to civilian persons. These include violence to life and person, in particular, murder of all kinds; mutilation; cruel treatment and torture; taking of hostages; outrages upon personal dignity; in particular humiliating and degrading treatment and the passing of sentences and carrying out of executions without previous judgement pronounced by a regularly constituted court.[5]

The international legal framework for the protection of civilians in armed conflict received further impetus in 1977 with the adoption of the two Additional Protocols I and II dealing with international armed conflict and non-international armed conflict respectively.[6] The reason for supplementing the existing rules of international humanitarian law was the emergence of new types of conflict often involving guerrilla warfare and the use of sophisticated and indiscriminate weapons which hardly make a distinction between a combatant and non-combatant. The recourse to guerrilla warfare by irregular armed groups often compelled civilians to accept combatants in their midst who thus became vulnerable in conflict situations. They often became subjects of forced displacement by such groups and were used by them for the achievement of military objectives.

The legal regime of the Geneva Conventions reiterates the principle that the civilian population and individual civilians shall enjoy general protection against the danger arising from military operations. Those safeguards cover protection of objects indispensable to the survival of the civilian population, protection of works and installations containing dangerous forces, protection of cultural objects and places of worship and prohibition of forced movement of civilians as part of military strategy.

These principles, given their underlying humanitarian content, are so fundamental that they have received the general acceptance of the international community and have acquired an existence of their own as principles of general humanitarian law quite independent of their treaty character. That is to say, even if a state does not have specific legislation covering these matters the state will be held accountable by the international community for violations of the kind which are prohibited by this body of humanitarian law. The rationale is that if armed conflict is inevitable, the right of the party to the conflict to choose methods or means of warfare is not unlimited and all persons who do not take a direct part in hostilities should be protected and treated humanely. In other words, no state can say, with any hope of acceptance by the international community, that the state alone will decide how it is going to fight a war, what weapons it will use, what military means it will pursue.

Sri Lanka's Record

Sri Lanka is fully conscious of and committed to ensuring humane treatment of civilian personnel in our armed conflict situations. The statement of the representative of the UN Secretary-General on internally displaced persons in his report to the UN Human Rights Commission underlines this fact in the clearest possible terms:

> Sri Lanka presents the unusual situation of a central Government providing relief aid to persons under the control of the main opposition group. In a world replete with examples of Governments and rebel groups using food as a weapon against civilian populations, the situation in Sri Lanka is one that deserves closer attention if not more publicity as an important precedent.[7]

This refers to a fact which is not sufficiently well known internationally, that Sri Lanka has for many years been feeding and tending our own civilians in the North and East, although they are largely under the control of the enemy fighting the state. That is the remarkable precedent that is referred to in the statement of the UN Secretary-General. It is something we can be justifiably proud of. The clear distinction between armed groups engaged in conflict and the civilians who are virtually hostages of these groups must always be maintained. This has been the underlying rationale of the rehabilitation efforts of the government during the ongoing conflict in the North and the East. The recently concluded 'Operation Riviresa' stands out as a signal precedent.[8] Our forces maintained throughout the operation this important distinction between the enemy and the civilian. The forces displayed a high degree of care by giving advance warning to civilians and taking precautions to avoid destruction of objects of religious and cultural value, despite the ploys used by the terrorist group to make use of such places for attacks on the forces, inviting possible retaliatory attacks by the forces. Similar protection was given to protected zones such as hospitals during these operations.

Thus our forces have in these recent operations demonstrated a remarkable degree of care in adopting, to the maximum extent possible, measures for the protection of the civilian population and thereby ensuring the highest respect for the principles of humanitarian law. It is this element of care and understanding for the civilian population that is the hallmark of a well-disciplined force and which distinguishes its actions from the wanton acts of sheer brutality of terrorist groups to whom civilians are mere pawns considered 'legitimate targets' in their campaign of unbridled terror. The Sri Lankan armed forces are fully aware of the fact that a war waged wantonly and won by recourse to ruthless means most certainly results in a lost peace or a fragile peace so heavily compromised that it carries within it the bitter seeds of future war.

It is also heartening to note that our forces are engaged in a continuing process of instructing their members on upholding norms of international humanitarian law in all military activities through various courses and seminars conducted for commanding officers as well as junior officers, and through them the soldiers who are battling on the forward defence lines. The Kotelawala Defence Academy could perform an invaluable role in facilitating the widest possible dissemination of international humanitarian law. It is a matter of considerable satisfaction that the UN guidelines which are aimed at promoting wider appreciation and adherence at the national level to principles of humanitarian law in armed conflict have been widely disseminated in all languages among our forces.

The government also took a series of measures aimed at the humane treatment of persons arrested in conflict situations. We have gained much international credit for that. The Human Rights Task Force (HRTF) which has been established under the emergency regulations has a vital task to perform in this area. Her Excellency the President took the initiative to issue directives under the HRTF regulations which were designed to ensure the humane treatment of persons arrested and to guarantee their fundamental rights. Under these directives a person making any arrest or detention under the Emergency Regulations, or Prevention of Terrorism Act (PTA), is required to issue to the next of kin an arrest receipt acknowledging the fact of arrest.[9] The name and the rank of the arresting officer, the time and date of arrest and the place which the person was detained are also required to be specified. Every officer making an arrest or order of detention is also required 'forthwith and in any case not later than forty eight hours from the time of such arrest or detention' to inform either the HRTF or a Regional coordinator of the HRTF or any person especially authorized by the HRTF, of such arrest or detention and the place at which the person is being held in custody or detention.

These provisions are designed to eliminate extra judicial executions, disappearances, torture and arbitrary arrests. Sri Lanka ratified the UN Convention against Torture and enacted the Convention against Torture Act in November 1994 with enhanced penalties which would strengthen the legal safeguards against the practice of torture.[10]

The UN has identified Sri Lanka as one of those countries in the Asian region which is taking decisive measures to establish national institutions for the promotion and protection of human rights. One of the most important legislative measures being taken by the government is now before parliament and will be debated on the 22nd of this month; that is, the establishment of a National Human Rights Commission – another milestone in our effort to establish a permanent and stable human rights regime in our country. The bill provides for the establishment of a Commission with an effective and independent mandate with investigative and remedial powers. The Functions of the Commission are wide-ranging and would include monitoring functions in respect of executive and administrative practices and procedures, investigative functions to inquire into complaints regarding infringement or imminent infringement of fundamental rights and to provide for their resolution by mediation and conciliation. The Commission would also be vested with advisory and other functions which would empower the Commission to make recommendations to the government to ensure that national laws and administrative practices are in accordance with international human rights norms and standards. The proposed legislation contains several innovative features. It could investigate an allegation of an infringement or imminent infringement of fundamental rights by either executive or administrative action or those violations of human rights committed by any person which would be tantamount to an act of terrorism under our law. This latter element brings to the surface the question whether individuals or groups could be permitted to evade responsibility for massive violations of human rights often brutally targeting innocent civilians through indiscriminate attacks as we have recently seen. Could these groups be considered to be outside the pale of the norms of conduct set out by international humanitarian law? This is an issue which is being widely discussed in international fora and we have thought it fit that the Commission should also be mandated to go into such grave violations of human rights by private individuals and groups resorting to shock, intimidation and terror as a means of achieving their narrow political objectives. The Commission is also empowered to entertain complaints of violations of human rights not only by individuals but also by groups or those acting on behalf of affected persons. This provision would enable public interest groups such as non-governmental organizations to invoke the machinery provided under this law.[11]

The proposed constitutional reforms also seek to enhance the national legal framework for the protection of human rights by bringing the fundamental rights provisions of the Constitution into line with those of the International Covenant on Civil and Political Rights, in particular by the inclusion of the right to life, liberty and security of person. It is also proposed that existing rights under criminal law, such as those guaranteeing freedom from arbitrary arrest, detention and punishment would be transformed into constitutional guarantees through their incorporation into the Constitution.

My final plea is this. In times of war within a state of the kind that we are experiencing now, and have been for a decade or more, strains on the armed services are very considerable. I understand these strains – to fight effectively, to fight a ruthless enemy, to fight an enemy that is difficult to find, to fight an enemy who is inextricably mixed up with a civilian population, to fight an enemy in a battle that is not frontal. All these are complex and difficult questions that the armed services have to face on a day-to-day basis on the battle-front. But in addition the armed forces have to make an effort – an almost superhuman effort – to observe the distinction – the difficult line – between combatants and non-combatants. We are fighting not merely to vanquish an enemy, we are fighting ultimately to build a lasting peace in our country that can only come about by welding the communities together, not driving them apart, by seeing to it that the war does not leave permanent scars on the psyche of its innocent victims. When the day comes, and I believe it will come, for the armed forces to lay down their arms because they have done their duty and won their battles, the peace that is going to be constructed basically by civilians will be rendered possible only if the armed forces have seen to it that in fighting the war they also respected and had regard for and wherever possible looked after, cared for and tended the civilians who in those difficult times were geographically on the side of the enemy. That is a difficult task but a task profoundly worthy of your best attention, your unflinching attention at all times, bearing in mind the supreme responsibility you have not only for seeing to it that the country remains whole, but that the country ultimately remains united.

1. Schoolboy athlete at the dawn of Ceylon's independence: Lakshman Kadirgamar (nearest to the camera) in a hurdles race at Police Park, Colombo, 1948.

2. Student champion: Lakshman Kadirgamar running the 110 m hurdles in Indian Inter-University Games at Bangalore in 1952. He won this event two years in succession.

3. Ceremony symbolizing unity of the four major communities of Ceylon. At the end of a relay run from all over the country, Lakshman Kadirgamar, 3rd from the camera in the left-hand row, is about to hand over his scroll to a young Tamil woman at the opening of the Colombo Exhibition, 23 February 1952.

4. Oxford Union Standing Committee, Trinity Term 1958. Both the Sri Lankans in this picture – Lakshman Kadirgamar (back row on left) and Lalith Athulathmudali (front row on right) – were to become victims of assassination. The committee also includes Kenneth Baker (back row, left of centre) and Tony Crosland (front row, right of centre).

The following is the result of the Poll for PRESIDENT held on Friday, November 28th, 1958.

	1st Count	2nd Count transfer	RESULT	
Lakshman Kadirgamar Balliol, Treasurer.	308	61	369	elected.
Tony Newton Trinity Ex-Librarian	165			
Andrew Rowe Merton Librarian.	200	53	253	

November 28th, 1958.   Ex-President.

5. Triumph at the hustings. Result of the poll for the post of President of the Oxford Union, 28 November 1958.

6. Oxford Union Standing Committee, Hilary Term 1959. Kadirgamar, as President, is seated centre. The committee also includes Dennis Potter and Peter Jay (back row, 2nd and 4th from left) and Brian Walden (front row, 2nd from left).

OXFORD UNION SOCIETY

Thursday, October 22nd, 1959, at 8.15 p.m.

Visit of

MR. LAKSHMAN KADIRGAMAR

Question for Debate

"That Democracy is unsuitable for the underdeveloped Nations of the World."

Proposed by Mr. HILLIER WISE, St. Catherine's

Opposed by Mr. STANLEY HENIG, Corpus Christi

Mr. PHILLIP WHITEHEAD, Exeter, will speak third

Mr. WILLIAM MYERS, Lincoln, will speak fourth

Mr. PETER CLYNE, University, will speak fifth

Mr. LAKSHMAN KADIRGAMAR, Balliol, Ex-President, will speak sixth

Teller for the Ayes	Teller for the Noes
Mr. JOHN CARTER, St. Peter's Hall	Mr. RICHARD WOOLLETT, Merton

October 19th, 1959
St. Catherine's

JOSEPH TRATTNER
President

7. Oxford Union order paper 22 October 1959, listing Kadirgamar as opposing the motion 'That Democracy is unsuitable for the underdeveloped Nations of the World'.

8. National flag, Oxford tie. Kadirgamar with Balliol College tie and Sri Lankan flag, in Colombo in 1994, on his appointment as foreign minister.

9. With UN Secretary-General Kofi Annan and Suganthie Kadirgamar, during the UN General Assembly session September/October 1997 at a reception hosted by Lakshman for his international colleagues.

10. With US Secretary of State Madeleine Albright, shaking hands over dinner table, in a hotel in New York, shortly before the US proscription of the LTTE on 2 October 1997.

11. With Nelson Mandela and Chandrika Kumaratunga, during the Commonwealth Heads of Government Meeting in Edinburgh, 24–27 October 1997.

12. With First Lady Hilary Clinton and Suganthie Kadirgamar, at the White House, Washington DC, 29 October 1997.

13. Oxford graduates together. With Manmohan Singh, Prime Minister of India, New Delhi, May 2004.

14. With Chandrika Kumaratunga and Colin Powell, Colombo, 7 January 2005, during Powell's one-day post-Tsunami visit to Colombo.

15. With Chris Patten, Chancellor of Oxford University, at unveiling of Kadirgamar's portrait, Oxford Union, 18 March 2005.

16. The last picture. Foreign Minister Lakshman Kadirgamar at the Bandaranaike Memorial International Conference Hall on 12 August 2005, just hours before his assassination. He presented the first issue of *International Relations in a Globalising World*, the journal of the Bandaranaike Centre for International Studies, to Indian High Commissioner Nirupama Rao. Kadirgamar, President of the BCIS, personally edited the journal.

DOCUMENT 4

The Global Impact of International Terrorism

Chatham House, London, 15 April 1998

This address was by no means Kadirgamar's first on the problem of international terrorism, but it was his most thorough exposition on the topic to date, the most challenging, and arguably the most influential. Speaking as foreign minister, he memorably warned his British colleagues and friends of the dangers of allowing the LTTE (Tamil Tigers) to operate freely in Western cities, especially London. The plain language of the speech is especially notable when it is remembered that Kadirgamar had already known, since 1995, that he was on the LTTE 'hit list'.

Issued three years before 9/11, his warning about the complacency of Western countries on this issue came in due course to be seen as prophetic. That a foreign minister from a non-aligned country should reproach London, and other Western capitals, for being too lax with regard to a terrorist movement was an interesting reversal of normal roles. There were, of course, precedents for it: in the nineteenth century many foreign rulers complained that London tolerated the presence of émigré movements that, though not directly a threat to Britain, were certainly viewed as a threat by the governments of their own countries.

Kadirgamar had a strong reason to make the speech when he did. Its timing was impeccable and its message chimed with other pressures for changes in UK policy. Only a few months earlier, in October 1997, the State Department had included the LTTE in its list of terrorist organizations. Kadirgamar was hoping to get the British government to move in a similar direction, as indeed it eventually did two years later. In the Terrorism Act 2000 there were changes in the UK definition of terrorism which were very much along the lines he had indicated in this speech. In addition, in a written statement to the House of Commons on 28 February 2001 the UK Home Secretary, Jack Straw, announced that the LTTE was one of 21 organizations being added to the list of proscribed organizations under the Terrorism Act 2000. This address at Chatham House was certainly not the sole cause of these changes, but it does illustrate how informed Kadirgamar was about the direction in which events were moving, how clear he was about his objectives, and how articulate and skilful he was in pursuing them. The endnotes include some examples of how his speech preceded change along the lines he had indicated.

The meeting was held under the joint auspices of the Royal Institute of International Affairs (Chatham House) and the International Foundation of Sri Lankans.

It was chaired by John Field, former UK High Commissioner in Sri Lanka. It included a Q & A session which is also reproduced here.

*****

Terrorism is by no means a new phenomenon. It has been with us from the dawn of recorded history. Every country in the world, every civilization has at some time in its history suffered the cruelty, the agony of terrorism. But what is new today, or what has been new over the last 30 years, is that terrorism has acquired an international dimension that has brought with it new concepts of terror, new and more sophisticated methods of dealing out terror. The past three decades have seen the marriage of high technology and sophisticated banking with terror. That development is new, it is sinister, it is immensely frightening, particularly to those who are presently the victims of terror. But the implications of this new dimension must be taken very seriously even by those who are living today in secure countries.

International terrorism means quite simply terrorism which is supported in one form or another from outside the country where the terrorist act occurs. There is a narrow definition of international terrorism that refers only to state-sponsored terrorism. This evening I will be dealing with terrorism in all its manifestations, whether state-sponsored or sponsored by sub-units of states or indeed by individuals.

One asks oneself the question why is terrorist crime so abhorrent. For one thing it is clear that in the last few years, in particular, a number of societies have suffered from terrorism and have been very frightened by what has happened to them and to others. They have been shocked and revolted. The World Trade Centre bombing[1] in New York a few years ago and the Oklahoma bombing[2] a few years ago caused only 174 deaths, but the ripples, the shock waves of those two events were felt far and wide in the US. Twenty deaths in one incident is certainly more sensational, more news worthy than 20 separate incidents with one death in each incident. That is understandable. But in the US 15,000 deaths a year are caused by shooting and that is not a matter of particular alarm.

Another aspect of the impact of terrorism is that it is something which happens indiscriminately. It is something that happens in a mindless kind of way. But, on the other hand, even burglary does not occur in the context of a relationship between perpetrator and victim. It is also in a sense a mindless crime.

There is something else about terrorism that causes so much shock and revulsion. A terrorist act is seen as an attack on society as a whole, on democratic institutions, on the democratic way of life. A terrorist attack is an act of war against society.

Definitions of Terrorism

Much time has been spent in recent years in national legislatures and at international fora on working out a definition of terrorism. The definition of terrorism is something that is beset with many difficulties, indeed it is a veritable semantic minefield. But I think we are now approaching the stage in the evolution of an international response to terrorism where states are coming to focus much more sharply on a working definition, to produce a definition that may not be absolutely perfect, legally and philosophically, but is a good practical, working definition based on common sense.

The following elements I think are relevant. Terrorist violence is typically directed towards members of the public or a section of the public, indiscriminately or at random – the bomb in the market place, the bomb in a city centre. But often terrorism is selective and purposive – an attack on worshippers in a temple, on tourists visiting some cultural site many thousands of miles away from home. Terrorism can also be aimed at a single individual – the assassination of a political figure. Secondly, terrorism frequently involves the use of lethal force and is capable, therefore, of causing extensive damage to property and heavy casualties to the civilian population. Thirdly, terrorism creates fear among the public which is precisely what is intended and designed to do. Fourthly, its purpose is to secure political or ideological objectives by violence or threat, and therefore it aims to subvert the democratic process. Fifthly, the terrorist act is often committed by well-trained, well-equipped, highly motivated, more than adequately financed individuals acting on behalf of organizations, often overseas.

In the United Kingdom there is a definition of terrorism. It is to be found in section 20 of the UK Prevention of Terrorism Act. This was, in my opinion, a useful working definition but it has been found now to be too narrow. The definition is as follows: 'The use of violence for political ends, and includes any use of violence for the purpose of putting the public or any section of the public in fear.'[3]

In recent years, in the UK there have been many prestigious inquiries conducted into the scope and purpose of legislation covering terrorism. The most recent one was chaired by Lord Berwick. His report was submitted to the House of Commons in September 1996.[4] In the course of a comprehensive study of the subject, he proposed a wider definition based on the working definition of terrorism which is used by the US Federal Bureau of Investigation (FBI). This definition, in my opinion, is acceptable. But there is room for some further qualification and refinement, filtering perhaps, to catch some of the nuances of the various manifestations of terrorism that we are now becoming more familiar with. Lord Berwick's definition, with the few additional words that I propose, reads as follows:

Lord Berwick suggested 'the use of serious violence against persons or property'. My addition is the 'or the use of or the threat to use any means to disrupt vital computer installations or communications'. I would add those words because we have already reached the stage when interference with computer installations and electronic communications of various kinds is a focus of terrorist activity. The definition would go on 'to intimidate or coerce a government, the public or any section of the public, in order to promote political, social, ideological, religious or philosophical objectives'.[5] I would expand the definition in that way to bring in objectives of terrorism which are wider than the merely political.

Two Approaches: *Nelsonian Blind Eye* v. *Enlightened Self-interest*

There are, as I have discerned it, two basic approaches to terrorism that are adopted by states. The first is what I call the 'Nelsonian' approach, turning a blind eye! Many states which are not directly affected by acts of terrorism on their own soil, but which are aware that terrorist acts are committed on the territory of other states and that there are links between the terrorists in the other state and in their own state, adopt a policy of studied indifference – 'what's happening is happening somewhere else; those terrorists are their terrorists; they are not our terrorists, thank heaven for that; we will wait and see.'

Sri Lanka has been the victim of that approach for a long time. Sri Lanka is one of four or five countries which by any reckoning are the most seriously afflicted by terrorism. The others which might fall into that category are perhaps Peru, Algeria and Egypt. But certainly, unarguably, Sri Lanka is one of them.

I have had it said to me in the course of discussions which I have had on behalf of my government with other governments, all friendly governments: 'We are very sorry that Sri Lanka is undergoing terrorism of this kind, we wish we could do something to help you, unfortunately there is nothing we can do because we do not have laws in place that enable us to do anything about terrorism in your country.'

And when I say that the terrorism in my country is financed to a very large extent by the activities of a certain organization in the country where I am discussing this question, I am met with the answer: 'Well, we don't have much evidence; if you can find the evidence we might be able to do something about it,' to which my reply has been: 'How can I possibly find evidence of preparations which are taking place in your country to commit terrorist activities in my country which is thousands of miles away from your country?'

This has gone on for many years. There have been many occasions when – after a terrorist attack in Sri Lanka, in a city, in a temple, in a mosque, on a railway train, in a business centre, in a school – numerous messages of condolence, sympathy and succour arrive, and I have often said to myself, 'well it is good to know at least that our friends remember us on these sad occasions'. But as the messages have gone on and on one finds that the senders, all friendly countries, begin to run out of adjectives, these condolence messages become routine, repetitive and hollow. It is a question of 'horror', 'shock', 'outrage' – and then the cycle is repeated all over again the next time a bomb goes off.

Well, so it has gone on, and I have had to accept two kinds of limitations in this area. One, it is true that many countries do not have legislation which is tailor-made, or capable of being adapted, to cover a situation where terrorist activity is sought to be countered. But I also know very well that where there is a will there is a way, where there is political will to do something about terrorism in some other state, a way is found, a way has been found and I know the ways that have been found.

There is another limitation which is timeless. It will always be with us. It is the limitation of being small, relatively weak and relatively lacking in what is called 'political clout'. When you are in that position what you get from your friends is sympathy, commiseration and condolence, not much more.

Some years ago, a few years ago, the situation began to change very dramatically on the international scene: the World Trade Centre bomb went off in New York in 1993, and the Oklahoma bomb went off in 1995. That bomb as you well know was a fertilizer bomb. It was not one of those deadly Semtex or RDX type of bombs. There was a nerve gas attack in the Tokyo subway.[6] There were bombs in Manchester and Paris. There was an attack on a US army camp in Dhahran.[7] There were suicide bombings in Israel. Suddenly, the international community, an expression that is used to describe the group of nations which is affluent and influential, came vividly alive. In rapid succession, high level meetings were held in Lyon in France at the summit level, and in Paris shortly thereafter, and in great haste the international community began to put together a package of proposals to combat terrorism at the international level.[8]

The message was very clear. When one's own national interests are seriously affected the realization comes home very quickly that terrorism cannot be fought alone by individual countries, it can only be fought effectively by countries standing together, working together and expressing a common political will to tackle a problem that is capable of menacing everybody.

This approach, the second that I have discerned, I describe as the approach of enlightened self-interest. Enlightened self-interest, in the last two or three years, having galvanized the international community into action, led with amazing speed to the adoption by the United Nations General Assembly of the Convention for the Suppression of Terrorist Bombings.[9]

Usually, UN conventions take years of discussion and argument before they mature and become ripe for enactment. This particular convention was adopted in two sittings of the General Assembly in 1996 and 1997. It was opened for signature on 12 January 1998. On my instructions, Sri Lanka was the first country to sign it, which it did on the morning of 12 January 1998.[10]

The UN Convention I have just referred to is a very significant development in the campaign against terrorism. The resolution put to the General Assembly and adopted unanimously addressed the question of terrorist groups taking advantage of the openness and vulnerability of public facilities, and the need for the international community to cooperate in protecting and securing public buildings and utilities as well as transport and information systems. It recognized the increasingly widespread nature of terrorist attacks using bombs, explosives or other incendiary or lethal devices.

The Convention creates a legal regime of universal jurisdiction and requires states to take steps to establish jurisdiction over the offences created under the Convention. It provides for an 'extradite or prosecute' regime with a view to ensuring that the terrorist offenders do not enjoy safe haven in any part of the world.

The offences under the Convention are to be treated as non-political offences so that the so-called political motivation would not preclude the extradition of terrorist offenders to stand trial and to bring them to justice.

What this means is simply this: it will no longer be open to an organization that uses terror for the purpose of advancing its own political objectives to plead that it is a national liberation organization and not a terrorist organization. Under the new definition adopted by the UN nobody will be able to take the plea that terrorism can be used legitimately in pursuit of political objectives which are considered to be of the nature of a liberation struggle or something of that kind. Terrorism is terrorism. Period.

Another important aspect of this Convention is that it obliges the state parties to cooperate in the prevention of offences related to terrorist bombings. These preventive measures require states to prohibit illegal activities of groups and organizations, in particular fund-raising activities by such groups in one state for the perpetration of terrorist bombings in another state.

It is vital that all those states who signed this Convention, and it is certain that at least 25 or 30 states will sign it in the first instance, should get to work with speed, with all speed, to bring domestic legislation into force in their respective countries. Otherwise all the work that has gone into the formulation of this important Convention would have been in vain.

Another critical issue which is of particular concern to all countries who are affected by terrorism was addressed by the Convention, and that was the question of depriving terrorists of their sources of finance. In particular, the Convention explores the means of tracking and freezing assets used by terrorist groups. For the first time, it has now been recognized internationally that front organizations, some ostensibly with charitable, social or cultural goals, could be used by terrorists as a cover for their fund-raising activities. It is recognized that the state concerned must take measures to look behind the front to see what the purpose of the funding which is being handled by that organization really is.

LTTE in Western Capitals

As the Minister of Foreign Affairs of Sri Lanka it would be idle for me to pretend that my interest in the subject on which I am speaking this evening in London is merely academic. It is obvious that I speak with a particular terrorist group very much in mind. The Liberation Tigers of Tamil Eelam, the LTTE, has been engaged in terrorism for at least 15 years. The terrorist activities which they have carried out in my country range all the way from attacks on human beings, on children, on priests, on economic targets – the Central Bank of the country, the World Trade Centre in Colombo – to an attack on the most sacred Buddhist shrine in the world – the Temple of the Tooth in Kandy.[11]

It is well known that the LTTE is able to sustain such terrorist activities by virtue of the continued flow of funds to their coffers through which they are able to procure illicit arms, explosives, weapons, including missiles. The flow of such funds to the LTTE is sustained through their own offices or front organizations operating publicly in a number of Western capitals. The LTTE maintains their so-called International Secretariat at No. 211 Catherine Road in London, and several front organizations operate in this great city which raise and transmit funds which go towards the purchase of weapons and explosives.

The Times of London, in its issue of 23 October 1997, in an article headed 'British Tamils fund war in Sri Lanka', reported the raising of sterling £250,000 a month by the LTTE from Tamil nationals living in Britain.[12] According to this report, the LTTE's worldwide income is believed to be about sterling £1.25 million per month, some of which goes to humanitarian causes but most of which funds its sophisticated war machine. *The Times* of London is not a hysterical newspaper.

Recently one has become aware of the use by the LTTE of electronic or wire communication systems or networks to carry out criminal acts.

The LTTE has actively engaged itself in using international information networks such as the Internet for their fund-raising activities to perpetrate acts of terrorism in Sri Lanka. Appeals have been made through the Internet bulletins which are designed to appeal to the humanitarian sentiments of the donor communities but in reality they are aimed at raising funds for LTTE activities. In these bulletins the LTTE has been specifically listed as one of the organizations to which funds could be channelled for, I quote, 'humanitarian purposes'. These bulletins appeal for donations to be made to LTTE-related organizations based in Western capitals rather than to recognized international humanitarian organizations such as the International Committee of the Red Cross and reputed NGOs based in Sri Lanka. Thus the humanitarian façade is only a convenient cover for the perpetration of terrible crimes by the terrorists.

An appeal for money for the LTTE made through freenet.carleton of Carleton University of Canada openly acknowledged that this particular fund-raising is for the purchase of missiles for the LTTE. I have seen that particular advertisement.

Furthermore, the LTTE has also made attempts at interfering with and disrupting email communication systems of the Sri Lanka government agencies through technical sabotage.

Another development which requires the immediate attention of the international community is the resort by the LTTE through its overseas offices to issuing direct threats to international maritime navigation, as evidenced particularly by the threat issued from its London-based International Secretariat at 211 Catherine Road.

The LTTE does not confine its activities to the mere issue of such threats. It has also demonstrated its policy of unlawfully interfering with international maritime navigation by attacking vessels, in the territorial waters of Sri Lanka. Such attacks have caused violence to persons on board, damage to vessels and cargo and danger to the safety of navigation.

In carrying out these acts the LTTE is deliberately targeting the movement of civilians and foodstuff being transported for distribution among the people in the Northern Province of Sri Lanka. Their offices in these Western capitals continue to be the nerve centres for the perpetration of these activities in Sri Lanka.

International cooperation as envisaged in the UN resolution and declaration[13] has therefore become vital to set in motion regulatory controls on the abuse of electronic mail or wire communication systems and networks, recognizing that terrorist groups are now openly abusing Internet facilities for criminal activities with impunity.

Another important issue on which the UN Convention has focused is the abuse of refugee status. There is a clear linkage between fund-raising activities of terrorist groups in foreign countries and the trafficking of asylum seekers into those countries. The presence of a substantial population of asylum seekers on foreign soil greatly facilitates the generation of funds through extortion.

Apart from supporting the perpetration of terrorist activities in Sri Lanka, the abuse of asylum and trafficking of persons also facilitates the displacement of people both internally and externally. The so-called refugees are known to have exploited and abused the welfare system generously provided for them by the host country. It represents a gross distortion of a system of protection that was provided with purely humanitarian considerations as its objective.

The UN declaration makes it clear that the convention relating to the status of refugees does not provide a basis for the protection of perpetrators of terrorism.[14] In other words, under the new UN Convention it would not be open to persons who claim the status of refugees to seek protection if they are found to be guilty of assisting or conspiring in the commission of acts of terrorism.

Measures for the UK to Take

I wish to make some proposals with regard to legal measures that could be taken, indeed, in my respectful opinion, should be taken by the UK to combat LTTE terrorist activities.

First, measures should be taken to introduce the necessary domestic legislation to give effect to international legal obligations undertaken in the field of the suppression of terrorism. In particular legislation should be introduced to give effect to obligations under the Convention for the Suppression of Terrorist Bombings which was passed by the General Assembly last December. Legislative and other measures should also be introduced to deal with the abuse of the Internet communication facilities.

Secondly, measures should be taken to reform the law relating to conspiracy in the UK. It is well known that there is a lacuna in the criminal law of the UK dealing with the crime of conspiracy. At the moment it is not a criminal offence to conspire within the UK to commit or abet the commission of a terrorist act outside the country. The most recent survey of antiterrorism legislation conducted in the UK, that is the Committee headed by Lord Berwick, came clearly to the conclusion that 'the most significant additional measure which the Government can take is to amend the law of conspiracy so as to facilitate the prosecution of those who conspire here to commit terrorist acts abroad'. The report went on to say: 'It may take a prosecution or two before this measure takes full effect but it should then serve as a demonstration, both to those involved and to the international community, of the Government's determination to make the UK as difficult and uncomfortable a place as possible for supporters of terrorism overseas.'[15] I urge that this particular recommendation of Lord Berwick's report be implemented with the least possible delay.

Thirdly, the very important question of terrorist fund-raising. The existing legislation in the UK has provision in the Prevention of Terrorism Act for curbing fund-raising activities of foreign terrorist organizations. This provision is circumscribed by certain limitations. It applies only to a certain number of designated countries, 24 in number, which means it does not apply to countries which are not designated under the Act, and Sri Lanka is one such country which is not designated under the Act. Lord Berwick therefore proposes that there should be a significant extension of the powers conferred on the authorities in the UK to curb fund-raising activities indulged in by terrorist organizations.

I will quote from Lord Berwick's report. He says:

> [A] better approach ... would be to introduce new powers based on proscription which ... should extend to international as well as domestic terrorism. The approach would be similar to that recently adopted in the USA ... But it would differ from the US power to designate an organisation as a terrorist organisation in that it would not be necessary to demonstrate that the terrorist activity threatened the UK's national security or the security of United Kingdom nationals abroad.[16]

Lord Berwick's suggestion is that proscription powers should extend to foreign terrorist organizations operating or seeking support in the UK. Once an organization has been proscribed provisions equivalent to Sections 2 and 10 of the existing Prevention of Terrorist Act would come into force making it an offence to be a member of the organization or to give or receive funds for its benefit. An application could then be made to restrain the organization's assets pending proceedings leading to forfeiture. The report goes on to say:

> This approach overcomes the principal difficulty inherent in proceeding under the other terrorist finance provisions, of establishing a link between the funds and particular terrorist acts. The Secretary of State would decide, on information and intelligence provided to him, that the organisation was a terrorist organisation and liable to proscription. The order would obviously need to take effect immediately, but should, perhaps, be subject to review by a specially appointed advisory committee. It would then be for the organisation to appeal against the decision by way of judicial review if it wished to do so.[17]

I wish to say that the mandate under which Lord Berwick conducted his inquiry required him to assume that there would be a lasting peace in Northern Ireland. In other words he was asked to proceed with his inquiry on the assumption that there would be lasting peace in Northern Ireland. He was required to look into the various legislative measures that would be required to combat terrorism in the future in the UK.

And his report, I venture to suggest, is very interesting because he proceeds precisely on the basis of the assumption that he was required to proceed on, that is removing the Northern Ireland situation from the scene, as it were. All the suggestions he made for curbing fund-raising, for proscription, the definition of terrorism and so on, were measures which he suggests should be adopted in the UK in a peacetime situation. He says on this point in his report:

> In my view there should continue to be a power to proscribe terrorist organisations as at present. It should not be limited to Irish terrorism. It should be extended to include international as well as domestic terrorism. The purpose of proscription will be twofold. First, it will furnish a conclusive presumption that an organisation which is for the time being proscribed is a terrorist organisation. This will facilitate the burden of proof in terrorist cases. Secondly, proscription will be the starting point for the creation of a number of fundraising and other offences, especially fundraising for terrorism overseas. ... This is the purpose of designation in the US Terrorism Prevention Act. Proscription is another word for the same thing, and will serve the same purpose.[18]

Lord Berwick had no doubt at all in his mind that the power to proscribe terrorist organizations was an essential tool or weapon in the legislative armoury that the UK should be equipped with to combat terrorism.

Anti-money laundering legislation is another area in which legislation should be introduced. Such legislation would give greater powers to carry out financial investigations and to provide courts with the necessary authority to impose sanctions to deter terrorist financing and to seize funds which are used for terrorist-related purposes. As the law presently stands in the UK, it is an offence to raise funds to support terrorism abroad only if the act of terrorism itself is triable in the UK. As I suggested a moment ago, and indeed as Lord Berwick has suggested, the proposed conspiracy law reform should take care of that particular lacuna in the law that was discovered when investigations were being conducted into the common law basis of the law of criminal conspiracy.

Fourthly, legislation should be introduced to prevent the abuse of asylum as envisaged in the UN Declaration. In fact, the abuse of asylum proposal was indeed a UK initiative taken in connection with the preparatory work for the UN Declaration. As I said, the object of legislation on that particular point is to prevent the grant of refugee status to an asylum seeker seeking refugee status if he had been engaged in terrorist activities; and the status once granted is not to be used for the purpose of preparing or organizing terrorist acts intended to be committed against other states or their citizens.

Fifthly, the need to enter into bilateral treaties covering matters such as extradition and the confiscation of terrorist funds. There is increasing recognition in international treaty practice relating to extradition that the political offences exception should not apply in respect of terrorist crimes, so that as I mentioned a moment ago, the so-called political motivation should not preclude the extradition of a terrorist offender to stand trial. Agreements for the confiscation of terrorist funds provide a comprehensive legal regime for mutual legal assistance among states and that is an avenue that could be explored to strengthen the efforts that are being made by countries working on a concerted basis to prevent terrorists from accumulating funds in one country for the purpose of financing terrorist activities in another.

I have suggested a few practical measures that could be taken by the UK because I happen to be addressing this subject here at Chatham House tonight. These are measures that will have to be taken sooner, I hope, rather than later by all those countries who profess to be concerned with combating terrorism at the international level. The UN Convention requires that such domestic legislation be brought into force.

With regard to the UK, I close with this simple observation. The UK and Sri Lanka have been friends for a very long time indeed. The relationship was forged in the colonial era. It was a relationship which subsisted for over 150 years. Sri Lanka and the UK parted company, in the legal sense, in 1948. This year, indeed, is the 50th anniversary year of Sri Lanka's independence. But our two countries parted company as friends. The struggle for independence was bloodless. We have remained friends, staunch friends, close friends for 50 years. I have no doubt that the relationship will continue as strongly in the future.

That is why I would be failing in my duty if I did not tell you this evening that the question of the role of the LTTE, unarguably the most effective, ruthless, terrorist organization that we have seen this century, its role in the UK in relation to Sri Lanka, is one that gives my people, our people, very great pain of mind. I cannot tell you how deeply grieved and sad the Sri Lankan people have been in recent years when they have seen, as bomb after bomb has gone off in our cities killing, maiming, hundreds, thousands of people, a response from the UK that has been far less positive than we would expect from a close and valued friend.

How galling it is to our people, I must tell you, to see, the day after a bomb goes off, a flurry of brave communications issuing from 211 Catherine Road in London. I do not say for one moment that what happens there at 211 Catherine Road or elsewhere is something which the government of the UK, past or present, connives at or condones. But I do say that there is a degree of passivity in its reaction to the role that this terrorist organization plays in this country that causes very great distress to the Sri Lankan people.

It is difficult for them to understand, indeed it is very difficult for me to understand, why it is not possible, and why means cannot be found, to at least make it clear to this terrorist organization that its presence in this country in all its multifaceted manifestations is unwelcome. One has not seen that happening.

What we ask is not much. If the laws are deficient, and I accept the fact that there are deficiencies in the laws of the UK, for the simple reason that those laws were not enacted at a time when all aspects of terrorist activities could be foreseen; if the laws are deficient the laws can be suitably adjusted because one is dealing here with immense human suffering. That suffering is far away in a friendly country, while the terrorist organization is firmly and comfortably established in the UK, acting as though it can do what it likes with impunity.

I am confident that in the near future, I hope in the very near future, the government of the UK will adopt such legislative measures as are necessary to honour the international treaty obligations that it has undertaken by virtue of the newly adopted UN Convention for the Suppression of Terrorist Bombings.[19] I am also confident that the government of the UK will find the political will to implement those measures once they are enacted. I am confident that once that is done we will begin to see the end of the flow of funds which go to purchase the deadly weapons that are killing, maiming and mutilating the innocent people of Sri Lanka. I thank you very much.

Question and Answer Session

Q. What precautions have we taken in Sri Lanka against biological terrorism and chemical terrorism?
A. For reasons of security I cannot tell you precisely what measures have been taken. All I can say is that we have given close consideration to all aspects of the possible forms of terrorism that we might encounter.
Q. You have very eloquently put across all the reasons why the UK should act as quickly as possible to try and support your government in combating terrorism. You are confident and hopeful, but we in the UK are not that hopeful, that the UK government is going to take any action that quickly. There are Members of Parliament like Mr Jeremy Corbyn and others who are so sympathetic to the cause of the Tamil Tigers. There are so many others who are sympathetic on the superficial values. Could I appeal to you and ask you, Mr Minister, what confidence have you got and what guarantees have you got from the UK to suggest that they would take immediate action and what more do you want, your government want, to convince the UK to act quickly and urgently?
A. I am confident that the government of the UK will honour the international treaty obligations that it has recently undertaken. I do not have the slightest reason to doubt that the government of the UK, a responsible government of great stature, will not honour the obligations that it has to honour under those treaties. I don't look for guarantees, because

my best guarantee is the record of the UK in international fora for many, many decades.

Q. How closely is the British High Commission in Sri Lanka working together with the Sri Lankan government to clamp down on bogus asylum seekers who form part of the fund-raising machinery in the UK? Most of them come from the south and not from the war zone. There is a lot the British High Commission in Sri Lanka can do to help us. Secondly, this refers to the NGOs. From my experience of local, Sri Lankan organizations, we have come across considerable contributions made from them on behalf of the refugees, some of whom are bogus refugees who come for the same purpose, and they are actually spreading a lot of propaganda which is damaging the image of Sri Lanka. They are distorting a lot of things. I think that is an area that you need to look into as well, because they do play a very considerable part as humanitarian groups.

A. I doubt if the British High Commission in Sri Lanka – and John Field will correct me if I am wrong on this – can do very much to curb the exodus of bogus asylum seekers from the country. The asylum seekers usually find a way out of the country in the hands of very sophisticated, able, cunning, undetectable organizations that operate these illegal rackets. And the British High Commission, I would have thought, would be pretty helpless in joining the hunt for illegal immigrants leaving Sri Lanka. Efforts are now being made by a number of countries to which these illegal immigrants go, to see that they are intercepted as quickly as possible on route. We are getting numerous requests, almost by the week, from various countries to take people back because they have been intercepted in the most far-flung areas of the world. Recently there was a request for us to take some hundreds of people back, who had been intercepted in Senegal. It is a question really of governmental authorities matching their wits against these very 'competent' racketeers. As often happens in real life, the racketeers tend to be a step or two ahead.

Q. You rightly and eloquently described the situation in the UK regarding fund-raising. There is one aspect which I would like to request you to bring to the attention of the British people. The British taxpayer and the British ratepayer are not aware that a lot of the local councils, specially in London, are contributing hundreds of thousands of pounds every year to front organizations of the LTTE. They go under the guise of Tamil women's associations, and other Tamil associations, and this is done without the British ratepayer knowing this. I would inform the minister that there is a role for the mission here to highlight these things to the local people here and they themselves will then take up the matter with their local councillors or the MPs. And the other matter I would like to ask is what we read recently, that President Clinton is prepared to bring up measures for the arrest and trial of Pol Pot of Cambodia. Could not you in your foreign travels make sure that a similar request is made for the arrest of Prabhakaran and his group and to bring them before an international court of justice because of the crimes they have committed against humanity?

A. On your first point, I have no doubt that the High Commissioner for Sri Lanka will take note of it. With regard to the Pol Pot point, all I can say is that Mr Prabhakaran is now the number one convicted assassin of Rajiv Gandhi, late Prime Minister of India. He is very much a wanted man in India. He is very much a wanted man in Sri Lanka. The question is how does one manage to get hold of this wanted man. If President Clinton is able to do that with Pol Pot, then we might consider asking President Clinton whether he could lend his good offices to doing the same thing for us.

Q. We are profusely thankful to you for taking all the risks and performing your job very successfully. We are all aware that Tony Blair has just brought peace to Northern Ireland and we hope that you could convince him that there is a similar case and could he intervene and bring about a settlement which we would greatly appreciate. . . .

A. Like every right-thinking Sri Lankan, I hope, wish, long for the day when peace will return to our land. But those of us who have to run a government and contend with the various problems know very well that peace is not easy to find. It is a hard, long road with many complexities strewn on it. As for Rt. Hon. Tony Blair, he has just accomplished a very considerable achievement. We are all hoping that the agreement will stick. It is too early to say whether it will or not. But I think it would be cruelty in the extreme to inflict on the Rt. Hon. Tony Blair an invitation to grapple with our problem as well.

DOCUMENT 5

The Terrorism Challenge to Democracies

Potomac Institute for Policy Studies,
Washington DC, 13 September 2000

This lecture was given by Kadirgamar at a time when the conflict in Sri Lanka had imposed heavy costs on the country, which badly needed outside support. It was delivered at a time – one year before the 9/11 attacks – when it was not easy to get US institutions to focus on terrorism as a threat that might involve US society directly. As foreign minister, he sought concrete assistance in such matters as a tightening of US laws to make fund-raising for terrorist campaigns abroad more difficult.

The Potomac Institute, at which this lecture was given, focuses on policy research in science, technology and national security issues. In 1998 it established the International Center for Terrorism Studies, directed by Professor Yonah Alexander. He and the Center's Senior Adviser, Professor Edgar H. Brenner, are mentioned in the lecture.

In the following years Kadirgamar gave several further lectures on the subject of terrorism. Perhaps the most important was the Memorial Oration delivered in Colombo on 20 June 2001 on the first anniversary of an event mentioned in the present lecture – the assassination of C.V. Guneratne, Minister of Industrial Development.

*****

First, allow me to say that it is indeed for me a great privilege and honour to be here today. I must confess that I did not, until a few months ago, know of the existence of this distinguished Institute. I am happy that our ambassador in the United States made contact with your institute and that we have over the last month exchanged correspondence. I can tell you frankly and sincerely that this discovery means a great deal to me and to the Government of Sri Lanka – the fact that there is a group of this kind, consisting of distinguished persons, focusing on the important and troublesome question of terrorism. I can tell you that it gives us much solace to know that you exist, and that you work on matters concerning terrorism in depth. When one is far away, as far away as we are in Sri Lanka from a think tank of this kind in Washington, and one didn't even know it existed, one feels lonely. One feels that in this terrible battle that is being fought against terrorism there is nobody who really understands it, nobody who can help with an insight, a thought, a discovery, with some piece of research. It is a lonely position to be in, I can tell you. That is why I am so particularly glad not only that we found you but that I am able to be here this afternoon. I hope we are going to establish from now on a link between Sri Lanka and your institute.

Scope and Complexity of Terrorist Activities

Terrorism, as Professor Alexander rightly observed, is not a new phenomenon by any means. It has been with us since the dawn of time. But what is new in the last decade or two is the enormous range and scope and complexity of the terrorist activities that are taking place on a global scale. When one considers the fact that the spread of terrorism today is greatly assisted by the means available to disseminate information rapidly, by the complexities of the banking system and in various other ways one begins to realize that the reach of terrorism today is truly global. It is only in the last few years that this awareness of the global reach of terrorism has begun to surface. That is a new development.

I can tell you from my own personal experience that in the early years of my tenure as the Foreign Minister of Sri Lanka – I have held that office for six years – I went to a number of foreign offices, particularly in the West, to plead our case not only for raising awareness of what is happening in my own country but for help of some kind, practical help. Why practical help? Because much of the terrorism that we in Sri Lanka encounter today is funded, most unfortunately, by people living in the West, particularly by the expatriate Tamil-speaking people who left Sri Lanka, some of them perhaps 15 years ago. I do not for one moment say that every one of them supports terrorism – most certainly and categorically they do not. Indeed the vast majority of the Tamil-speaking people who live abroad – more than half a million – in various countries but largely in the West, are moderate, reasonable and peaceful. The funding comes from, I would say, a relatively small minority. The answer I used to get from foreign offices in this part of the world and in Europe was that they had no laws to deal with terrorism, especially the funding of terrorism. I was told: 'This is a new phenomenon. Our legal system does not provide for combating international terrorism. We have old penal laws.' In the United Kingdom, for instance, there was a lacuna in their criminal law, even to the extent that it was not a criminal offence to conspire in the UK to commit an offence abroad. That was a plain and simple lacuna in the law. It was set right recently.[1] But that was the kind of problem we encountered in those years. We would get sympathy and expressions of concern and when the terrible bombings occurred in Sri Lanka we would get condolences from the leaders of various countries, but no practical help.

New Legal Foundations for the Struggle Against Terrorism

Now, what has happened in the last couple of years is that there has been a spate of bombings in the West. You will all recall the Oklahoma bombing, the Twin Towers, bombings in Paris, in Manchester when the IRA was still active, in Saudi Arabia, gas attacks in Japan and so on, and all these terrorist acts came together, more or less. These events wonderfully concentrated the minds of those who ought to have been thinking about such problems much earlier. As a result, about three or four years ago, there was a meeting held in Lyon in France, attended by heads of state and heads of government, which went into the question of the urgent necessity for action to combat international terrorism.[2] A declaration came out from Paris shortly after that summit meeting which spelt out the basic principles. Then in the UN drafting work began on two conventions which would provide the foundation on which the fight against terrorism would be conducted. The first was the Convention on the Suppression of Terrorist Bombings which was passed by the UN General Assembly in one session in 1998, quite a record for the adoption of a UN Convention. The second convention came shortly thereafter in 1999. That was the UN Convention on the Suppression of Financing for Terrorist Purposes, on a French initiative.[3] There is a third convention now being considered by the General Assembly; it is a comprehensive, umbrella-type convention on terrorism introduced by India.[4]

Therefore, in the last three years large strides have been taken, as far as the international jurisprudence on this subject is concerned. For instance, earlier there were no useful definitions of terrorism. There are now. Where the implications of terrorism had not been spelt out earlier, they have been now. Sri Lanka was, literally, the first country to sign the Convention on the Suppression of Terrorist Bombings, and the second country to sign the other one on the Suppression of Terrorist Financing.[5] A number of countries have signed both conventions. Signatories are obligated to introduce national laws to match these conventions. The UK, for instance, has just done that. In July this year they enacted a law – the Terrorism Act, 2000. It is a very comprehensive piece of legislation. It faithfully mirrors the requirements of both conventions. It contains provision for the proscription of terrorist organizations. It defines a terrorist organization. It deals with fund-raising and with front organizations which are difficult to penetrate because they look innocent. It is, undoubtedly, a very comprehensive law. At last this law is in place in the UK. The next question is going to be its implementation, and for that you need political will and commitment.

I must say that when three years ago, the US government declared the organization known as the Liberation Tigers of Tamil Eelam (the LTTE or the Tamil Tigers) a terrorist organization that declaration was a milestone along the path that all of us have to take to deal with the problem of terrorism.[6] It was an event of considerable significance. After the first two-year period expired the declaration was renewed for a further two-year period. We are now in the third year of that declaration and I can tell you that the declaration gave us in Sri Lanka considerable heart because we felt that at last something was being done by an influential country like the US in the battle against terrorism.

My first point at this stage is that there is a universal regime now building up of legislation on terrorism. There are a number of old enactments dealing with the safety of navigation, aircraft hijacking, hostage taking and so on. Those have been around in the international community for a long time. The two new conventions I referred to earlier add considerable weight to the existing corpus of legislation. The third convention now under consideration by the UN will complete that corpus of international legislation. That is a very encouraging development.

Definition of Terrorism

On the question of the definition of terrorism, I must say that I am not greatly enamoured of attempts to hammer out definitions because they normally end up in arid, futile, semantic disputes about words. A lot of time can be wasted on definitions. If the political will and commitment is there a definition can be a useful tool in the implementation of international legislation.

Let us look at an early attempt to define terrorism. It was in the SAARC region. SAARC is the South Asian Association for Regional Cooperation which consists of the seven countries of South Asia – Bangladesh, Bhutan, India, Maldives, Nepal, Pakistan and Sri Lanka – together encompassing some one and a quarter billion people. This association was founded about 15 years ago, and in 1987 it adopted a Regional Convention on the Suppression of Terrorism which contained a definition of terrorism. Article 1 of the Convention says that 'murder, manslaughter, assault causing bodily harm, kidnapping, hostage-taking and offences relating to firearms, weapons, explosives and dangerous substances when used as a means to perpetrate indiscriminate violence involving death or serious bodily injury' is a terrorist act.[7] To my mind the significance of that early attempt to define terrorism was the identification of indiscriminate violence as the hallmark of a terrorist act. Those of us who live our daily lives under the threat of terrorism know exactly what that means. It was a brave attempt in 1987 to try to get a useable definition of terrorism. The UN Convention on the Suppression of Terrorist Bombings of 1998 has a comprehensive definition of terrorism. The point I would emphasize is this. Each state party shall adopt such measures as may be necessary, including where appropriate domestic legislation, to ensure that criminal acts within the scope of the Convention (the criminal acts are defined), in particular where they are intended or calculated to provoke or strike terror in the general public, or in a group of persons, or in a particular person, are under no circumstances justifiable by considerations of a political, philosophical, ideological, racial, ethnic, religious or other similar nature and are punished by penalties consistent with the grave nature. Thus, there are two important points in the UN Convention. One is that the terrorist act provokes a state of terror among the general public or among a group of people or in an individual. The second is the removal of the possibility of arguing that a terrorist act can be justified on political, philosophical, ideological, racial and ethnic grounds and so on. There we are left with a clear statement which is very important in the fight against terrorism, that when a terrorist act is committed there is absolutely no argument available in the international community, and assuming the existence of corresponding domestic legislation, on the grounds that the end justified the means, that terrorism is a legitimate weapon in pursuit of political, philosophical, ideological, racial and ethnic considerations. That argument has been decisively rejected. And in fact some courts recently, in the US and Canada, have actually dealt with that point. It is one of the arguments used when people are prosecuted, that the organization concerned is a national liberation organization and not a terrorist organization. The Canadian courts recently found no difficulty in holding that whatever the object of the organization is, if some of the methods used are of a terroristic nature then the organization falls within the framework of the law.

Canadian and US Cases

In that connection I would like to invite your attention to two passages from recent judgements of a Canadian Court and the US Court of Appeal in California. In Canada a prosecution was launched against a man for fund-raising for the LTTE. Canada has no law on terrorism at the moment. Canada is working on a law, but it hasn't yet come out. Canada will soon have a law, I am sure, because Canada is very concerned with this problem. What they did was that they brought a prosecution under the immigration law, on the ground that a person who engages in terrorist activities is an undesirable alien and had to be deported. The court came to this finding. I quote:

> It is true that there are no allegations of criminal activity against the appellant, nor allegations that he engaged in terrorism in Sri Lanka or was involved directly in the procurement and supply of weapons for the LTTE. However, activities which are undertaken in support of and in furtherance of terrorist activities constitute reprehensible conduct outside the protection offered by the

Charter [that is the Canadian legislation]. In my view, those who freely choose to raise funds used to sustain terrorist organizations bear the same guilt and responsibility as those who actually carry out the terrorist acts. Persons who raise funds for the purchase of weapons, which they know will be used to kill civilians, are as blameworthy as those who actually pull the triggers. Clearly, freedom of association and expression are rights accorded to those who seek political goals. But those rights do not enure to the benefit of those who seek to achieve political goals through means which undermine the very freedoms and values which the Charter seeks to support. Contrary to the argument advanced by the appellant's Counsel, the values underlying section 2 of the Charter, such as the pursuit of 'truth', 'social participation in the community' or 'individual fulfilment', simply do not come into play in the present case.[8]

This case is presently before the Supreme Court of Canada.[9]

The judgement of the US Court of Appeal, California, is also very instructive. Here, two organizations, the PKK[10] and the LTTE, sought to overthrow the US Antiterrorism and Effective Death Penalty Act of 1996 on the ground of constitutional invalidity. Both organizations argued that the provision of material support to these organizations would be directed to aid friendly, non-violent, humanitarian and political activities of the designated organizations. The prohibition of such support, it was argued, would infringe their right to association under the First Amendment. The Court rejected that argument and the Court emphasized that what the Antiterrorism Act prohibits is the act of giving material support and that there is no constitutional right to facilitate terrorism by giving terrorists the weapons and explosives with which to carry out their deadly mission. The Court further stated: 'material support given to a terrorist organization can be used to promote the organization's unlawful activities, regardless of donor intent. Once the support is given, the donor has no control over how it is used.'[11]

In its judgment the court reiterated the US Congressional finding that 'foreign organizations that engage in terrorist activity are so tainted by their criminal conduct that any contribution so such an organization facilitates that conduct.'[12] The court continued:

> [T]errorist organizations do not maintain open books. Therefore, when someone makes a donation to them, there is no way to tell how the donation is used.... Even contributions earmarked for peaceful purposes can be used to give aid to the families of those killed while carrying out terrorist acts, thus making the decision to engage in terrorism more attractive. More fundamentally, money is fungible; giving support intended to aid an organization's peaceful activities frees up resources that can be used for terrorist acts.[13]

Effects of Terrorism on Democracy in Sri Lanka

Let me turn now to the question of how terrorism affects democracy in Sri Lanka. Many of you probably know that democracy began to put down roots in Sri Lanka well over a century ago, long before the British left that part of the world. Indeed, when they were getting ready to leave they began to experiment with democracy in Sri Lanka, formerly called Ceylon, and the reason might well have been that the education system in Sri Lanka was well known in that part of the world to be very advanced. Much credit must go to the British because they established schools in various parts of Sri Lanka, particularly in the North, well over 150 years ago. Some of those schools are still very active, very much alive. And many of those schools were started by religious orders, by Christian priests. There was a very substantial input from the US, from the Boston area. People went out there and founded schools and the beginnings of a university. I believe the British felt that Sri Lanka could be trusted with a limited measure of democracy to start with. Early in the twentieth century we found them establishing small legislative councils and municipal councils. The right to vote was given to the so-called educated class. Step by step these councils were enlarged until a landmark event occurred in 1931. Universal adult franchise came to Sri Lanka. That means that about 70 years ago women had the vote in Sri Lanka.

When you consider the fact that in some countries it was only 20 or 25 years ago that women received the right to vote, when you look back on it, it is an event of considerable political significance. Ever since, Sri Lanka has been voting continuously with no interruptions at all. We had a Parliament established with independence in 1948. The multiparty system that goes with democracy began as far back as 1930. There are a large number of parties in Sri Lanka, but as in other countries, like the UK and the US, we had two major parties emerging quite early, similar to the Republicans and Democrats, the British Conservatives and Labour.[14] We had two major parties on the political scene and there were many others as well.

There are three countries in the world where democracy is not only vibrant, it is probably rampant, it is so vigorous that it often goes out of control. Those three countries make a very strange category of countries. One of them shouldn't really belong to that group at all. But it does. They are the US, India and Sri Lanka. Why do I say that? Because in all three countries, democracy and democratic conduct and behaviour are in the lifeblood of the people. The press, for instance, in all three countries, is no respecter of persons. That is one of the great hallmarks of a truly democratic society. The press gets into trouble from time to time. I am very happy to see here my old friend of 50 years, a former Sri Lankan Ambassador to the US. He might or might not agree with some of the things I say. And the other thing is that the voting habit is so deeply ingrained in our people that nobody can take the vote away from them. We have had no *coup d'état* in 50 years of independence, just one or two abortive ones which did not take off the ground at all. There is no climate for a *coup d'état*; the people would simply not allow it. The fact is that Sri Lanka's voter turnout is one of the highest in the world. Every one of our elections brings out at least 80 per cent of the vote, 70 per cent is considered low. Sometimes it tops 90 per cent. That is because our rate of literacy is high, it is in the region of 90 per cent. So, given all that, I would firmly say that a fair description of Sri Lanka is that it is an active, practising democracy. That is the position.

But today we are a democracy under siege, gravely under siege because of terrorism. And what does terrorism do to democracy? Let me take you through some of the details of terrorism. I would put it like this. When you have a situation of conflict in a country, particularly when you are dealing with terrorism, you have to have certain types of special legislation that do not belong within the legislative framework of a democracy in a normal situation. One such item of legislation is called the Prevention of Terrorism Act.[15] Many countries have this. It is an Act that confers on the authorities power to apprehend and place in custody a person who might be suspected of being involved in a terrorist act. It is a kind of preventive custody. The period of custody is limited and if the state cannot bring charges against the person within a stipulated period of time he has to be released. That piece of legislation is on the Statute Book and I am afraid it has to remain there until such time as our conflict is resolved. It is a necessary weapon in the armoury of the security force. But it is an erosion of democracy, there is no doubt about that.

Secondly in a conflict situation the physical aspect of terrorism is very pronounced. In our major cities we have security check points at various places and this means that the ordinary citizens are put to inconvenience, at the least, and sometimes they have to go through harassment which in peaceful times would not occur. Some people have to be body-searched, vehicles have to be searched, and so on, and that kind of situation is an obvious restriction on freedom of movement.

Thirdly, unfortunately, but perhaps inevitably, certain restrictions on media freedom begin to emerge. The question of censorship becomes important. The tendency is for governments facing a conflict situation to clamp down an unnecessarily heavy censorship, where the bounds of censorship go beyond actual necessity. This kind of situation is not only irksome to the press and to the ordinary citizen but it is clearly an erosion of the freedom of the press. Fortunately the highest court in our country, our Supreme Court, has often struck down legislation on censorship which in its view violated the fundamental right to freedom of expression enshrined in our Constitution. Quite recently it struck down a censorship law passed by this government on the grounds that it was too broad and unwarranted even in a situation of terrorism. The Court confined the application of censorship to the censoring of war news.[16] War news came into the picture because it was found that some irresponsible journalists, a few – we do have a few irresponsible journalists – used war news as a way of whipping up hysteria. Often it was hysteria directed against the government of the day. And that can have a very debilitating effect on the morale of the armed forces. We had examples of that, and so war news, as the Supreme Court has directed, will be under censorship for some time to come. There again it is an erosion of democracy. It may be justified up to a point, but it is an erosion.

Then I come to the major question of interference with the normal electoral process that we have been used to. We are used to completely open election campaigns where all the candidates go about freely and canvass. They go in cars, they go on foot, they hold public meetings. We don't have the same kind of electronic reporting that you have. We cannot afford it. So it is very necessary that candidates should be able to get about and meet their voters. Now terrorism brings a very serious constraint on free movement.

The record of the LTTE in our country has been sharply focused on assassinating our political leaders during election time. Consider what they have done for a moment. They assassinated Prime Minister Rajiv Gandhi of India when he was attending an election meeting. That is the point of time, and that is the kind of venue, at which a democratic politician is most vulnerable. Not all the security forces in the world can protect him, because he is out there to meet the people. He is not going to be able to meet the people and press flesh, if he is completely surrounded by security guards. So he has to take the risk. Rajiv Gandhi paid for it with his life. Then they assassinated President Premadasa of Sri Lanka when he was getting ready to address a May Day rally and was organizing his supporters, standing in a jeep, with people all around him. Again a highly vulnerable situation in a democratic society. Then last December the present President of Sri Lanka, President Kumaratunga, while addressing her final election rally, was bombed. Everybody knows that she escaped with her life only by a miracle. There is absolutely no other way of describing it. Had she been standing fully upright beside her Mercedes Benz bullet-proof car, if her head was a few inches higher than the roof of the car, she would have gone. As it happened she was bending down to speak to a *Time* reporter and, therefore, her head was not fully above the roof of the car. A piece of shrapnel hit her in the right eye and she has lost the use of that eye. I was due to accompany her to that meeting but I was not well that day and I didn't go. Had I gone to the meeting I would, at the end of the meeting, have gone to the other side of the car in order to sit next to her, and on that side five men were blown up. So this is the kind of thing that happens when you have to live with terrorism daily. Recently the LTTE assassinated one of our ministers, a peaceful man, the Minister of Industrial Development who was leading a peaceful march in the city, some months ago. It was a suicide bomber who went up to him in the street and offered him the traditional sheaf of betel leaves and then blew himself up and blew up the Minister and his wife.[17] They have killed a number of our political leaders. The Leader of the Opposition in 1994 when addressing his final election rally was blown up by a claymore bomb, by a suicide bomber.[18] The story doesn't end there. It goes on and on. The list is interminable. The LTTE has walked into a mosque and sprayed bullets into hundreds of innocent Muslims at prayer. Then they bombed the Central Bank, again causing hundreds of deaths, all civilians, entirely civilians, not a single soldier. They have attacked one or two hotels. They have bombed a commuter train taking people back home after work, again all civilians. They attacked the famous Temple of the Tooth in the city of Kandy in the hills of Sri Lanka, probably the most sacred Buddhist shrine in the world. There again it was an absolute miracle that the Tooth Relic itself which was inside the Temple was not destroyed. All the walls around the Temple were cracked and blasted. It was a mindless attack. When one talks of indiscriminate bombing these are the examples I place before you. The list goes on and on. It is a very depressing list, something we have to live with. And now that there is a general election coming shortly they will strike again. We all know that. They know that democracy is very vulnerable at that time. So this is one of the severe constraints on democracy that we have to live with.

Now I come to something else. Because of this artificial, unnatural state of affairs in which we live, trying to cope with terrorism within a democratic framework, one tends to get human rights violations on the part of the security forces. They are under severe pressure, and every now and then they tend to over react and do something which in normal, peaceful times would never happen. Therefore, for the government of the day it is a constant battle to see that the security forces are educated, drilled, trained and disciplined to the extent that they fully understand that, on the one hand, they have to fight the terrorists and, on the other hand, they have to protect the civilians. I can say proudly that over the last six years our record in this respect has improved enormously. It is not perfect by any means but it has improved. That again is a constraint, a problem that arises directly out of terrorism.

Now I must say a word about the culture of violence that has grown up in Sri Lanka. That is a very great pity indeed because up to about 30 years ago Sri Lanka was a developing country with disparities in wealth, social and political dogmas of all kinds, including Marxism, but we had a free democratic society. Every philosophy was allowed to flourish. The level of violence was hardly anything to bother about. But today with a terrorist problem to contend with there is a spillover into other walks of life. All kinds of people have guns and bombs. Criminals have a field day because they are able to get hold of weapons which otherwise would not be accessible to them. This is one of the most regrettable and unfortunate consequences of terrorism on our society. A perfectly peaceful country has now become a country where there is violence all around us. Violence is manifest not only at election time but at all times. It also makes our politics confrontational – very confrontational. So those are some of the problems that arise from the impact of terrorism on a democratic society.

International Aspects of Terrorism

Now I wish to say a word about the international aspects of terrorism. As I said at the opening of my address this afternoon what is new in the world today is the fact that terrorism can be exported from one country to another using all the advanced technology, electronic and otherwise that is available in the world today. And this is for all of us a very, very dangerous situation. I am sure Professor Alexander and Professor Brenner, and all of you who work here, are fully aware of that, and I think that is why you are particularly concerned about the international aspects of terrorism. There are grave dangers for everybody and it is absolutely no good for any country to say it is not our problem; thank heaven, it is somebody else's problem. You can't say that anymore; even in your own national self-interest you can't say that. Leave selfishness aside. National interests are basically selfish, everybody recognizes that. I am not arguing against that proposition. It is eminently a matter of one's own self-interest for all of us to be alert and aware that these things are happening, and that the terrorist who was sitting on somebody else's doorstep yesterday could be on our doorstep tomorrow. There are no boundaries anymore. It is very easy to have access to countries. Boundaries have been eroded to the point of extinction.

So, therefore, it behoves the international community to be very, very concerned about the export of terrorism, and when one speaks about that then naturally one speaks about fund-raising. In our case fund-raising is taking place in the affluent countries. That is because there is a large expatriate community of Tamil-speaking people living in these countries, well over a half million who by and large are doing well. They are able, if they wish, to fund terrorist activities in Sri Lanka. Millions of dollars a month are raised in Australia, Canada, Europe, the UK and the US. Certainly, there is enough money available to buy light arms, and enough to buy missiles. Today missiles are cheap. There is a glut of missiles in the market because arms are available in so many parts of the world. If you have the money you can buy the arms. It is not a problem at all. A large amount of money is coming from countries which have no business with the terrorist activities or the politics of another country. The laws relative to asylum and fundamental rights, in a climate of free expression, are susceptible to abuse. Terrorists soon become masters at spotting the loopholes in the law and organizing themselves in such a way that they can steer clear of the law. These are the problems that have to be seriously addressed in international forums.

I would venture to suggest one or two practical things that countries can do now with the enactment of new laws based on the new UN Conventions. New laws will come in many countries, within the next five years. Details will be spelt out about fund-raising and front organizations. What we have to do is to get together, all of us, and use our national intelligence services with a high degree of cooperation with international services such as Interpol. Bilaterally countries should get together and exchange information and contribute what they can in that way to the general common effort. That is very important, to keep at least in step with, if not one step ahead of, the terrorist organizations of the world which are expert at finding ways around legislation.

There is another matter I wish to mention. In the democratic countries we are getting groups of people of the same foreign ethnicity who are able to contribute a bloc of votes to a candidate standing for election to congress or parliament. This to a politician is a very tempting prospect. A politician who knows that he has a few thousand votes in his pocket assured from a certain ethnic community is vulnerable to pressure. I can tell you with absolute certainty that this is happening. It is happening in Canada, in the UK, in the US and in Australia, to give you just four examples. And how does one deal with that? You need great discipline on the part of the politician. He must be able to say: alright, I will accept the funds you raise for my campaign, but I am afraid I can't go as far as supporting your terrorist cause. How many politicians will have the courage to do that? But we have to work on that because that is one of the ways in which terrorist groups will begin to get round the people who legislate in these matters and impose the law. That is something we have to think about seriously.

I would also say that the media has a very important role to play. I think it is only the media that is able, if it wishes, to focus a strong spotlight on the murky activities that go on usually underground, unnoticed by most civilians. When that happens it has a very salutary effect because it shocks the conscience of the ordinary man who doesn't know all this. The ordinary man living in an average democratic society, in an affluent society, is perfectly comfortable, he is not bothered with terrorism itself, his daily life is not ruined by terrorism.

But for us who have to live with terrorism when we leave home in the morning there is no guarantee that we will come back, at the end of the day, absolutely none whatsoever; not even a bullet-proof car will protect you from a suicide bomber, because a suicide bomber when he or she detonates the bomb is able to generate something like 8000 centigrade of heat which will melt a bullet-proof car. An ordinary person living in the West does not have to face all that. If the press is able to spotlight some of these things it will at least open eyes and stir the conscience, and that could have a salutary effect on the authorities who have to deal with this problem.

The work this Institute is doing, and proposes to do, could be very valuable indeed to open the eyes of the people to the implications of what is going on in the world around us. And finally, I would say, there is no substitute for continuous dialogue in the international community on these issues. It is an issue that is now in the open. The Declaration of the Millennium Summit has a strong paragraph on this question of internal conflicts and terrorism.[19] It is something the world community is mindful of. The Security Council passed a resolution in October 1999 focusing sharply on terrorism and spelling out the various steps that have to be taken.[20] Much of what I have said today, and much of what this Institute is working on, is in that area. The problem is recognized. But we must keep engaged. Sometimes such problems surface, they attract a lot of attention and then other priorities come on centre stage and these problems tend to get forgotten.

Child Soldiers

Finally, I would be failing in my duty if I didn't tell you something about child soldiers. Professor Alexander mentioned that. The use of child soldiers in Sri Lanka by the Tamil Tigers is absolutely distressing. It is terrible. We have a lot of evidence. We find little bodies on the battlefield with guns which are as tall as the child carrying it. Some of these guns are so light today. All that is required is that a child be able to carry a gun. And worse, we find a cyanide capsule round the neck of the child. Their instructions are to bite on the cyanide capsule to avoid capture. But the children are increasingly not doing that. They are conscripted forcibly from schools, from parents, and are put through some kind of rudimentary training. Then they are thrown into battle. Often they are in the vanguard of the older soldiers. They are sent into battle against barbed wire fences because they are able to crawl through them. Some of them are actually strapped with explosives, so there is no escape at all for them. If they succeed in getting away and coming over to the armed forces, we have a couple of hundred of them now, we are trying our best to rehabilitate them. We need money for that kind of programme. Well, I am going to ask you: if your conscience is troubled then help us to do something concrete to rehabilitate these youngsters. One day peace will come and these little children who escaped with their lives are going to be walking time bombs. They are scarred psychologically. They are ruined. They have lost their childhood completely. Some of them are conscripted at the age of 7. We found recently a girl of 7. There are many in the age group of 12 to 15.

The UN produced a report in 1996 by Graça Machel, wife of President Mandela – an excellent piece of work which I came across in 1997.[21] In my 1997 address to the UN General Assembly, I devoted half of it to the problem of child soldiers. At just about that time the UN Secretary-General appointed a Special Representative for Children in Armed Conflict.[22] I invited him to come to Sri Lanka in 1998 and we sent him up in to the jungle. He met some of the Tiger people and they gave him a whole lot of assurances; the first one being that they would not recruit children under the age of 17 and that they would not deploy children in battle under the age of 18. Needless to say they have not given these assurances the slightest bit of attention. Two months ago that Special Representative denounced the LTTE in a television interview. He said that 'the assurances given to me were absolutely worthless; nothing has happened'. And two months ago, UNICEF also came out finally and made a strong statement saying that numerous parents were reporting to them the loss of their children to conscription by the LTTE. This is going on all the time. The *New York Times* article that you referred to, Professor Alexander, is relevant. Newspaper people have gone to see these children. It is a most horrifying story. I cannot imagine something more cynical, cruel, barbarous and ruthless. These are your own people after all. This is what the LTTE is doing to its own people. It looks as though they are systematically wanting to eliminate a whole generation of young people or to make them robotic. How can one stand aside and see this happening?

There is a conference being held at Winnipeg in two days time hosted by the Canadian government on the whole question of children in armed conflict. Attention will be focused on child soldiers. There is going to be a world conference next year on the same subject. Well, attention is being paid to this subject now but we have to move from words to deeds. And my simple proposition is this. Any country that has in its midst any terrorist organization which is found to be using child soldiers must not tolerate that organization to the slightest extent. If the terrorist organization has an office it must be closed down. If it is using funds for fuelling a war, it must be told that the funds are going to kill these innocent children. There cannot be any compromise in regard to that sort of thing in the face of human tragedy of that dimension.

DOCUMENT 6

Preventing the Recurrence of Harm to War-affected Children

Winnipeg, 16 September 2000

This statement was made at a workshop on preventing the recurrence of harm to war-affected children, part of the International Conference on War-Affected Children held at Winnipeg, Canada, on 10–17 September 2000. Organized by the Canadian International Development Agency, the conference reviewed developments relating to the protection of children in armed conflict since the 1996 study by Graça Machel, Impact of Armed Conflict on Children. The final two days of the conference consisted of a ministerial-level meeting of approximately 800 delegates and observers, with participation of representatives from 132 governments, including 45 ministers. Kadirgamar also spoke on child soldiers at a session of the conference on 17 September, making some pointed comments at the LTTE's use of child soldiers; and on the following day he was to raise this issue in his address to the UN General Assembly (see pp. 162 and 165–7).

Kadirgamar had a long record of opposition to the use of child soldiers. For example, his speech to the UN General Assembly on 3 October 1997, strongly praising Graça Machel's 1996 report, had largely concentrated on this issue. As he mentions here, Sri Lanka had ratified the Convention on the Rights of the Child (CRC) in 1991. It had also been involved in drawing up the Optional Protocol to that Convention, on Involvement of Children in Armed Conflict, specifying that children under the age of 18 should not take part in hostilities: this had been adopted by the UN General Assembly on 25 May 2000, and Sri Lanka had ratified it on 8 September 2000 – just eight days before Kadirgamar spoke at this conference.

*****

War-affected children could be categorized as those recruited forcibly, or belonging to displaced families who are directly exposed to violence, and also the children of armed forces personnel killed or wounded in action.

In Sri Lanka at least 60 per cent of LTTE fighters (the Tamil Tigers) are below the age of 18 years. The LTTE cadres captured in combat have revealed that at least 40 per cent of their fighting cadre consists of girls and boys ranging from the ages of 9 to 18 years. Of the more than 100,000 internally displaced children in my country, thousands have either lost one or both parents as a result of this conflict. Hundreds are without limbs due to explosions caused by mines and artillery fire. Children are trained to kill and are eventually killed. These child soldiers are manipulated to mirror the barbarity of terrorism. Children are trained in all activities involved in war except leadership positions. What is the fate of these innocent children? If they survive they will be either permanently disabled or unemployed due to the deprivation of formal education. It is our obligation to ensure that these children are not therefore made social outcasts and to prevent them being subjected to more harm.

Range of Measures to Help Scarred Children

How can these scarred children be integrated into civil society? It is imperative to take all possible measures to rehabilitate them. First, we have to address the root causes for the outbreak of violence and the disintegration of society. To promote sustainable human development and the protection of human rights there are three key elements: democratization, good governance and a functional civil society. Preventive strategies have to respond to the economic crises and environmental degradation of conflict-ridden countries. Civil society should build upon the local traditions of conflict resolution and prevention. Civil society organizations should – at national, regional and subregional level – establish mechanisms to ensure a due process of accountability for those who have violated the rights of women and children in conflict situations.

The family is the most important social, economic and cultural institution in society. The role of women and the concept of family in promoting education for peace and reconciliation have to be strengthened. The diverse roles played by a woman as a mother, community leader, activist, professional, widow and bread-winner, should be carefully woven into any plan for promoting peace and resistance to violence.

Education is an important building block in the integration of war-affected children into civil society. Educational approaches, either formal or informal, in promoting reconciliation and harmony are an important strategy. The 'militia' itself should be mobilized for this purpose. The military should be the extended arm of society to protect civilians and promote conflict resolution. They need to be trained in human rights and humanitarian law, which would enable them to function objectively and not allow hatred to filter into war-traumatized children. On the part of children, they should be educated through schooling, vocational training and peer group activities on war-related dangers. Appropriate health measures for physical and psychosocial recovery must be put in place. These educational activities should be related to the child's own culture, tradition, religion and social context. Religious leaders could play a very significant and productive role in ensuring the prevention of harm to children through war.

Peace education for children and adults is another important issue. This process should enlighten society on the existing legislation protecting the rights of children and also create structures in society to enforce them. It should promote dialogue, healing and reconciliation. Parents and youth should also play an active part in structuring these educational programmes. Vocational and life skills should be shown to be a better alternative for youth than rejoining armed groups. Financial support has to be extended to enable them to support projects of their own to make a living.

Vocational training facilities should identify and develop human capabilities for a productive and satisfying working life. These courses should be carefully planned on the basis of assessments of needs, training and education in basic skills and knowledge. This should flow from a realistic evaluation of the level of existing human resources and future employment prospects and obstacles. In Sri Lanka, the educational curriculum has taken these factors into consideration and has introduced skill training for children at an early stage of life in order to enhance their inherent talents and capabilities. These training programmes should also comprise numerate literacy and elementary management skills, which are basic requirements for employment, and should also encompass civic education.

Media support is indispensable, and should be put to better use, in creating awareness among the population. It should be used as a tool for education and value formation among children and youth, in a bid to force violators of children's rights into wider political dialogue. The media should focus on children, particularly, with reference to their manipulation for political ends and achieving the maniacal ambitions of terror groups.

Expatriate communities living in western countries could be most influential, due to their affluence. The media could facilitate a campaign to educate these communities on the reality of situations and to expose the perpetrators of crimes against children and their long-term implications on childhood destroyed.

The true road to recovery for these war-affected children would only begin when peace dawns in the theatres of conflict. It has to be realized that there is an absolute obligation on every government, every society to prevent the involvement of children in armed conflict. This realization would rejuvenate a sense of personal responsibility and respect for human life. The crucial factor is the sanctity of human life. For sanctity to be achieved a delicate balance of ethical, moral, legal and political accountability between civil society and the political leadership has to be established.

The concept of human security must emerge against all odds, over and above military security. Every responsible nation should pledge to reduce the volume of arms trade, and military spending, channelling such expenditure towards human security and development. Countries must stop providing safe haven to front organizations of armed groups in conflict, in order to dry up the flow of funds to illegal war chests, allowing vulnerable children to survive. We must not deprive them of their basic needs, and more so their right to life. Their needs and aspirations cut across all other doctrines in life. Children themselves are a unifying force cutting across all barriers, and they generate compassion among all people. It is, therefore, easy to mobilize nationally and globally for the sake of children.

Developments in Sri Lanka

In Sri Lanka we have formulated a National Plan of Action in careful consultation with experts in this field. A four-pronged strategy has been carefully crafted to provide for the welfare of disturbed children. One priority is their security. Rehabilitation centres have to be equipped with trauma experts, teachers and other consultants for counselling and therapy for former child soldiers. Structural improvements are being made to identified centres, serving as transit facilities for traumatized children before they are sent for vocational training in specific skills. We are concentrating on enhancing the capacity of technical centres, creating an environment for youth to rehabilitate and integrate into civil society positively. In shelters for the internally displaced, vocational training facilities are being arranged, to ensure that they are constructively engaged, as a measure to prevent them from getting involved in violence.

We have embarked on a series of programmes to prevent children from being lured into armed conflict. Whilst creating awareness of 'child rights', we have concentrated on implementing compulsory education legislation and providing the basic amenities for children and their families in welfare camps. In Sri Lanka we have found that much of the recruitment of child soldiers by the LTTE is done in schools. Schools and their immediate surroundings have been demarcated as 'zones of peace' with the teaching staff being charged with not allowing recruitment to take place.

A Presidential Task Force on Human Disaster Management has been established to organize psychosocial support for traumatized children and help families affected by terrorism and violence. Of the seven subcommittees formed, one deals with issues peculiar to war, handling its most intricate realities with respect to widows, orphans, wives and children of disabled persons, women in vulnerable areas and internally displaced families. The subcommittee on psychological issues concentrates on pre-impact and post-impact issues, seeking to minimize the effects of sustained psychological trauma.

Our final goal is to prevent further recruitment of children by this terrorist group. Focal points are being established to receive confidential information on the LTTE's recruitment drive. We have established mechanisms to relocate and protect children who are targeted for recruitment. A protection framework for children in welfare camps has also been set up for the prevention of their recruitment. Even in the conflict-ridden areas state-run free health and educational services are provided.

For ending the perpetuation of violence on children, we have to take legitimate judicial action by strengthening the domestic and international laws in bringing the perpetrators of war crimes to justice. Sri Lanka ratified the Convention on the Rights of the Child (CRC) in 1991. Based on this convention we have adopted the Children's Charter in 1992.[1] Additionally, the Human Rights Commission of Sri Lanka monitors compliance with the Charter. The National Child Protection Authority also plays a supporting role.[2] Sri Lanka was actively involved in developing consensus for the adoption of the Optional Protocol to the CRC on Children in Armed Conflict. We have ratified this protocol. Our proposed new constitution has strengthened the existing laws and introduced stronger provisions, directly derived from the CRC.

Ways Forward

Whilst all these mechanisms are in place the time has come to address our minds to terror groups, who have managed to evade the law in the pursuit of their senseless ambitions, causing immense human suffering. In the long term, the democratic states of the world need to take strong, punitive and coercive action against such non-state actors, operating on their soil directly or indirectly. The Committee on the Rights of the Child, in its capacity as the treaty body monitoring compliance with the CRC and the Optional Protocol, must stand firm against terrorism and urge the international community to ban these terrorist organizations.[3]

Children have a right to be participants in mapping out their own future. They have a right to their own beliefs and to utter them. They should be an integral part of the programmes and strategies of governments directed towards their care. They rely on us in all their innocence to give them a hand for a better tomorrow. We as delegates representing independent entities of the international community have met, discussed and concluded hundreds of international conferences in the past. Yet have we been unable to combat the growing menaces that threaten peace at every level and jeopardize the young? We shall therefore pledge this afternoon not to confine this august assembly to just another gathering. Every word spoken today needs to be urgently translated into action. Peace would be the ultimate objective of all our endeavours.

DOCUMENT 7

Address to UN General Assembly

New York, 18 September 2000

Foreign Minister Kadirgamar addressed the UN General Assembly on many occasions, including on 26 September 1994 and every year thereafter to 2001. As Chandrika Kumaratunga said in a speech to the General Assembly on 17 September 2005, just a month after Kadirgamar was assassinated, and two months before the end of her six-year term as President of Sri Lanka: 'For eleven long years Mr. Kadirgamar, from this very podium warned this Assembly about the threat posed by terrorism to the democratic way of life, not only in Sri Lanka, but across the globe.'

The speech reproduced here, given on 18 September 2000, is noteworthy for its assertion of the continued importance of the principle of sovereignty; its frank recognition that the main form of conflict is now internal, not international; and its strong concluding plea to address the problem of child soldiers. Above all the speech movingly addressed the subject of terrorism and the international networks that sustain it, both in Sri Lanka and more generally. In this it foreshadowed the events surrounding the 11 September 2001 attacks on the US. It was with some justification that Kadirgamar was to quote verbatim some significant parts of this speech when, on 2 October 2001, he took part in the UN General Assembly's debate on terrorism following the 9/11 attacks.

John De Saram, Sri Lanka's Permanent Representative to the UN in 1998–2002, recollects in a May 2011 message: 'It was his habit to continue working on speeches, statements, etc. to the UN after his arrival in New York. Recollections of the special intensity of our work together at the "Millennium Assembly and Summit of the United Nations" in September 2000 often still resurface, poignantly, in my thoughts. Some days after the conclusion of the Millennium Summit, addressing the General Assembly's regular annual plenary debate, he delivered, on 18 September 2000, what I believe was his finest speech ever to a UN body.'

*****

The Millennium Summit is over. I fervently hope that its dreams and hopes for a better world will never fade from the hearts and minds of all mankind. The President of Sri Lanka, Her Excellency Chandrika Bandaranaike Kumaratunga, unable to attend the summit, conveyed, through a message I had the honour to read to the summit, her hopes and her vision for the future of humanity. Her words were:

Peace among all States and peace among all peoples within States so that all, and not only some, may in safety, without fear, in dignity without humiliation, in good health, and in material and spiritual well-being enjoy the wonders of life on this miracle we call the planet Earth.[1]

Therefore, the President of Sri Lanka spoke, with emphasis, of the necessity of protecting and preserving, for the future, those minimal, and most fundamental, certainties, that the member states of the United Nations have been able to establish – in particular, to preserve what was and continues to be the organization's very foundation: the entity we know as the state. She pointed out that it was here in the General Assembly that representatives of governments, of peoples and of states gather together under a Charter that assures states of their sovereign equality, their political independence and their territorial integrity. These are the fundamentals of the UN system.

And that is as it should be. States are the principal organizational entities into which the peoples of this planet have gathered. The principal, over-all organizational edifice of the international community is the inter-states system. For the entity we know as the state, there is no substitute. If states weaken, so will this organization. If states are diminished, so will this organization be diminished.

Thus, it was the plea of the President of Sri Lanka that everything possible be done to protect and preserve, and not to decry or endeavour to erode, the stability and the well-being of the entity we know as the state, for whose sovereignty, territorial integrity and political independence the Charter gave us its assurance.

Human Rights, Sovereignty, and the Pressures of Globalization

Before proceeding any further I should make it clear – in view of recent statements on the part of speakers of obvious goodwill and intention, but with whose fundamental premises I fundamentally differ – that those who assert the necessity of continued reaffirmation of the sovereignty of the state in terms of the Charter must not be regarded – I repeat must not be regarded – as having in any way diminished their commitment to the importance of universal adherence to human rights and all that is required for the dignity of the individual. Sri Lanka is deeply committed to the promotion and protection of the human rights of its own people and of all peoples everywhere.

There is, however, a substantial body of opinion, within which Sri Lanka includes itself, which is of the view that the way to proceed in the matter of human rights and the dignity of the individual is properly through continued and close cooperation between all states, while respecting the sovereignty of each. The way of multilateralism or globalization, which appear expressly or by implication to overlook or diminish the sovereignty of states have often had disastrous consequences. With that initial clarification and a reminder that human rights are for the observance not only of states, but non-state entities as well, I shall proceed with the remainder of my address.

We must bear in mind that the entities we know as states are national and international corporate entities of enormous complexity, differing in so many respects from corporate entities of the private sector and, of course, differing as well from those innumerable entities, in their thousands now, to which we refer, broadly and benignly, but somewhat simplistically, as civil society.

If the management of a developed state with more than adequate resources at its command is a complex undertaking, how much more complex would be the management of a developing state without such resources and such infrastructures. Then there are those developing states such as Sri Lanka, with their multi-ethnic, multi-religious societies where the legacies of centuries of a colonial past take more than one generation to erase.

Aside from the pressures inherent in the very nature and history of a state, let us not forget the additional external pressures a state is subject to – economic, social and political, legitimate and illegitimate, civil and uncivil, and often criminal – that the age of information and its consequences have brought in their wake. These are external pressures that raise troubling uncertainties for many states, and for developing states in particular, that are without the blessings of abundant resources and advanced infrastructures. These are uncertainties that strain the structures of states and could come close to threatening their very existence.

Where the processes of globalization are exploited to their advantage by the irresponsible or the illegitimate or the criminal, one is reminded of the report from the Secretariat received by this Assembly three years ago:

> Government authority and civil society are increasingly threatened by transnational networks of crime, narcotics, money-laundering and terrorism. Access by underworld groups to sophisticated information technologies and weaponry as well as to the various instrumentalities through which the global market economy functions are vastly increasing the potential power and influence of these groups, posing a threat to law and order and to legitimate economic and political institutions.[2]

Of course, where there is the use of internal armed force against a state, as in my country, the complexities within a state compound themselves many times over; and we know that the use of armed force against a state is the greatest threat of all to its preservation and well-being. This is particularly so in democracies, whose very openness makes them most vulnerable; and Sri Lanka is a democracy of long-standing and unwavering commitment to democratic fundamentals.

The Challenge of Internal Armed Conflicts

Peace *among* states, the primary purpose of the Charter, has to a large extent been achieved; if not in fact in every case, at least in general, and in terms of generally observed rules of international law, under and pursuant to Charter provisions that proscribe the use of armed force by one state against another state, except in self-defence or as authorized by the Security Council.

Yet when we turn to peace *within* states, and the use of armed force against a state internally, we see an entirely different, and an often confusing and frustrating, picture. Each armed conflict is unique; each a creature of its own history; the nature of each determined by its own surroundings. There is no simplicity of circumstance, no uniformity in scenario, no easy solution. Internal armed conflicts come in many different forms.

The relatively clear-cut format of a UN response to inter-state armed conflicts – where, following a cessation of hostilities recorded in international agreement by representatives of warring states, the UN intervenes to monitor a truce and keep the peace – seems, for internal armed conflicts, inadequate or inapplicable.

The Charter does not prescribe how this organization should proceed, in cases of internal armed conflicts, except for the wise admonition in Article 2, paragraph 7: 'Nothing contained in the present Charter shall authorize the United Nations to intervene in matters which are essentially within the domestic jurisdiction of any state . . .'

In view of the varieties, complexities and intricacies of internal armed conflicts, this organization appears to be without the necessary structure, the knowledge, the expertise, the experience, the resources, and often – it would seem – without the necessary collective will.

To suggest that the UN should intervene in internal armed conflicts across the board – a suggestion made, on occasion, by persons of obvious goodwill but with little knowledge of local circumstances – is wishful thinking of the most simplistic kind, and incorrect in the extreme.

A proposition of such a nature ignores the fundamental premise, indeed the truism, articulated so impressively to the Millennium Summit by the Head of State of Algeria, President Bouteflika, in his forceful summation of the deliberations of round table four, that a democracy, offering to all its peoples the fundamental necessities of peaceful all-inclusive political processes, simply cannot tolerate armed defiance of the democratically expressed will of the populace of the state, which an armed terroristic attack on a democratic state so obviously constitutes.[3]

At a more practical level, where would this organization – woefully under-financed for fulfilment of its development objectives, for which billions around this world expectantly await – obtain the further resources for such far-flung interventions in internal domestic crises?

Charter provisions and UN practice affirm that a state may act in individual or collective self-defence should there be an armed attack across its frontiers. Yet against massive internal armed attack, the abilities of most states, or at least the abilities of most developing states, to react with equivalent armed force in self-defence, or in enforcement of the law of the land, or in the maintenance of law and order, are very limited. Traditional police services are inadequate in design, in training, in equipment and in experience. Few states have ready, and affordable, access to the necessary information or intelligence. Few states are able to maintain military infrastructures effective against heavily armed guerrilla-type onslaughts and the horrors of terror.

Armed Groups and Fund-raising: Sri Lanka's Experience

Such has been the experience of my country. Sri Lanka has for many years had within its territory an armed conflict that has complicated the lives of the entire population of the country. It is a conflict of an extraordinary nature. A very small group of armed fighters and supporters – numbering less than 15,000 persons in total – schooled in and totally devoted to violence; rejecting the processes of peaceful society and participatory governance; achieving, through the practice of systematic terror, national and international notoriety; rebuffing all overtures for settlement of such problems as they may have through dialogue – continues, in defiance of law and order, in rebellion against the state to fight for the establishment of a separate, monolingual, mono-ethnic state in our territory.

A democratic state, because of its openness, its laws, traditions and practices, and its commitment to tolerance and dissent, is especially vulnerable to the deployment of force against it by any group within its boundaries. An internal armed challenge to any state anywhere is a challenge to all states everywhere. Unless all states, democratic states in particular, agree to come to the aid of a state in such peril, democracy itself will be imperilled everywhere. Democracy will not survive.

When the security and integrity of one state is threatened by an armed group within it, surely – especially in these contemporary times, with the Cold War far behind us – it behoves all other states to deny that armed group any encouragement, any succour, any safe haven. Today, for the prosecution of terrorist activities in one country, massive funds are raised with impunity in other countries, often through knowing or unknowing front organizations or other entities that now proliferate in many forms and in many countries – often, sadly, in the guise of charitable groups or groups ostensibly concerned with human rights or ethnic, cultural or social matters.

The magnitude of the collection of funds abroad for terrorist purposes, and the extensiveness of the reach of the international networks developed for the purpose, boggle the mind. Their receipts seem to exceed the receipts of many transnational conglomerates – and all free of tax. Revenues come, of course, from the customary illegal trade in drugs, arms or other merchandise, including the smuggling of humans.

Yet there also exists a far more abundant and seemingly limitless reservoir of funds – namely, expatriates of similar ethnicity settled abroad. As the Western media has reported over the last few years from time to time, collections from expatriates abroad for the armed group, known as the Tamil Tigers, which is battling the government of Sri Lanka, are staggering in their magnitude: for example, US$ 400,000 a month from one country; US$ 600,000 a month from another; US$ 2.7 million a month from yet another; and large additional funds from expatriates in still other countries.

In 1998 an excellent study was published on 'Financial Havens, Banking Secrecy and Money-Laundering'. It was a study commissioned, to experts in the field, by the UN Office of Drug Control and Crime Prevention.[4] In order to implement adequately the provisions of the recently adopted International Convention for the Suppression of the Financing of Terrorism, a study of a similar nature by UN bodies on the collection of external funds for massive, continuous internal armed rebellion against a state, such as occurs in Sri Lanka, becomes especially necessary when the armed group battling a state is in blatant violation of human rights and humanitarian norms and standards – including those relating to children and children in armed conflict – that this organization so correctly and so diligently espouses as the minimal contemporary requirements in human society.

I proposed such a study at the fourth round table of the Millennium Summit, and that proposal was endorsed by our chairman, President Bouteflika of Algeria, in his summation to the General Assembly of the proceedings of our round table.[5] I urge that favourable consideration be given to that proposal by the international community.

As the years go by, and the armed conflict fuelled by such massive funds from abroad continues within a state, paradoxically, international perceptions seem to blur, not only among those in civil society, who are often uninformed, but even on the part of those in positions of international authority, within and outside this organization, who should know better. The existence of the internal armed conflict and the resulting casualties are bemoaned, and a cessation of hostilities is urged at any price – in seeming inattention to the fundamental fact that it is the armed internal group that is the 'aggressor' and it is the state that is the 'victim'.

Such a blurring of international perceptions in some quarters, as to what the crucial facts are, is distressing, and profoundly disappointing to those, such as we in Sri Lanka, who have struggled and continue to struggle hard to preserve our democratic way of life and the richness of our multi-ethnic, multi-religious, culture in the pluralistic tolerance we were once so blessed to enjoy.

I hope the thoughts I have expressed today on the nature of the affairs of states, and of the affairs of developing states in the main, would show in some measure why a sympathetic, rather than an inquisitorial, style is by far preferable in relation to the affairs of states, as in all human relationships.

The General Assembly, Civil Society and the Imperative of Development

At a more general level, I would like, before I move on from this part of my statement, to refer to two other relevant questions: the role of the General Assembly and the role of civil society in the affairs of the UN. The General Assembly is the only principal organ of the UN in which all member states are represented, and the only principal organ whose terms of reference allow for consideration of any matter within the scope of the Charter.

Yet, there is the perception among some that the centre of gravity in decision-making on questions of major policy importance to the organization appears to have moved away from the General Assembly to an extent unknown in earlier years. Sri Lanka greatly welcomes, therefore, the reaffirmation in paragraph 30 of the Millennium Declaration of 'the central position of the General Assembly as the chief deliberative, policy-making and representative organ of the United Nations, and to enable it to play that role effectively'. The practical manner in which the General Assembly could play that role would, of course, require very careful thought.

The ways in which 'civil society', and the innumerable entities that that expression encompasses, could best contribute to the work of the UN – in terms of data collection, research and analysis and expertise – in a manner that does not prejudice the role of states in the affairs of the UN, will also require most careful examination. Such contributions should be made in a manner that is not partial or partisan, in favour of or against, but rather in a manner that befits an objective and neutral consultant.

Moreover, although civil society within a national context could be, and is, well accommodated into domestic political processes, the manner in which 'civil society' could be internationally accommodated within UN processes still remains a puzzle.

As in all human relationships, so also amongst states, the strong do better than the weak, the rich better than the poor, the developed better than the developing. This is the case most of all when times are hard. The marked decline in official development assistance, and the failure of most of the strong, the rich and the developed to meet their official development assistance pledges, show that for states there is no general safety-net.

If there is one message from the Millennium Summit, and one that is now coming from this Millennium Assembly loud and clear, it is that globalization may be a reality for all but it is no panacea for all – certainly not for the developing world. The benefits of globalization have bypassed much of the developing world. The poorest among us, spanning the continents of Africa, Central America and Asia, have experienced increasing marginalization. There is little opportunity for developing countries to be formative in the shaping of the world economy for the future – in the deliberations that really matter.

Thus, though we leave the past century and the past millennium behind us – and celebrate their passing – more than half of humanity is still haunted by the old, intractable economic and social tragedies that have been with us since the dawn of time: poverty, illiteracy, ill health, hunger, unemployment, the young, uncontrolled urbanization and the growth of mega cities.

Among these, poverty alleviation and poverty elimination remain for most of us in the developing world the highest and, in fact, the only, meaningful priority. Poverty degrades humanity and, in an era of abundance and conspicuous consumption, visible in real time across billions of television screens throughout the world, undermines the very foundations necessary for the growth of humane societies and refined governance.

The developing world needs to be accorded an adequate formative voice in the formulation of a new development chapter for the twenty-first century. Thus we turn to the UN and, in ultimate recourse as it were, to this General Assembly, under whose active supervisory authority there must be a revival of a comprehensive North–South development dialogue – a dialogue that otherwise seems to be fading away.

To tell the countless starving and helpless millions that a free global marketplace will show us the way is, I am sorry to say, simply not enough. Resource deprivation over many generations, and its debilitating consequences on adequate infra-structural growth, has severely damaged the capacity of developing countries to cope with the modern world.

A new development chapter must provide for the catastrophic negative contingencies, be they 'man-made' or otherwise, including such occurrences as the present surge in the price of oil to the highest levels in a decade that now place crushing burdens on the national economies of developing countries struggling desperately to contend with economic realities. They, like Sri Lanka, can only hope and pray that the oil producing countries, which are certainly not insensitive to the plight of the developing world, will find it possible in some way to relieve such pressures in the very near future.

I should also wish at this juncture in my address to say a word about the South Asian Association for Regional Cooperation (SAARC) of the seven states of South Asia – Bangladesh, Bhutan, India, Nepal, Maldives, Pakistan and Sri Lanka – a body which is deeply committed to the advancement of the economic and social well-being of their peoples, numbering now in the region of 1.25 billion, not merely through national endeavour, but through regional and international cooperation. Sri Lanka, as the current Chair of SAARC, is seeking to implement the programme of activities laid down at the 1991 Colombo summit as best it can in difficult circumstances. The people of our region are deeply committed to the goals of SAARC. They continue to interact vigorously on a wide range of professional, cultural, educational and social activities, notwithstanding the temporary setback to high-level political involvement that SAARC has suffered at this time.[6] We in SAARC are confident that it will not be long before our movement is again able to play its full role in the welfare of our peoples.

War-affected Children

I have just returned to New York from the International Conference on War-Affected Children, organized so successfully by the government of Canada and held at Winnipeg.

I cannot conclude my address to the General Assembly this year without making at least a brief reference to the abominable crimes that are being committed against young Tamil children in Sri Lanka by the rebel group known as the Tamil Tigers. They have been, and are, forcibly conscripting even 10-year-old children, boys and girls, for battle against the Sri Lankan Army. Some of these children have been programmed into suicide bombers. They are forced to wear cyanide capsules round their necks and to bite on them to evade capture. This wretched practice continues unabated.

In 1998, at the invitation of my government, the Secretary-General's Special Representative for Children and Armed Conflict, Mr Olara Otunnu, visited Sri Lanka and met some of the Tamil Tiger leaders. They assured him that they would not recruit any person under the age of 17 and would not send into battle any person below 18. A few months ago he stated that since his visit to Sri Lanka there have been continuous reports of the recruitment and use of children by the Tamil Tigers. The assurance they gave him has been totally dishonoured. In a poignant answer to a question by an interviewer, the Special Representative said:

Children who become soldiers lose their innocence. Part of the reason why the fighting groups will tend to reach out to children is because, of course, the adults may become disillusioned, they may be killed off, they may run away, so they reach the children who are less able to defend themselves. But there's a more cynical reason: that children, because they are innocent, can be moulded into the most unquestioning, ruthless tools of warfare, into suicide commandos, into committing the worst atrocities. In other situations, it is ideology – come fight for the homeland, come fight for our ethnic group, come fight for a new society – that may appeal to families and to children. So there are many reasons which facilitate the abuse of children in this way.[7]

I thank the Special Representative for having had the courage to speak out on this important issue. To remain silent in the face of such criminality is to encourage and condone it. It is the duty of all of us who care about the children of the world to rally against the cruelty, brutality and the grievous harm cynically inflicted on them by groups such as the one that abuses them in Sri Lanka.

A few months ago the UNICEF Representative in Sri Lanka told journalists – and I thank him for his statement – that the situation for children in the areas held by the Tamil Tigers had worsened since they gave their assurance to the UN Special Representative. Parents have reported that their children have been recruited. It is a serious problem. He observed that until they (the LTTE) announce to their own people that they have measures to prevent children below 17 years being recruited, we cannot take their promises seriously.[8]

A respected and courageous human rights group in Sri Lanka, consisting mostly of Tamil teachers who used to teach at Jaffna University, have said in a recent report that since last May a fresh child recruitment campaign has been launched by the Tamil Tigers. According to their report, children as young as 10 years are being forcibly conscripted, age being no consideration as long as the child was able to carry a gun. In recent months the international press has focused sharply on the plight of child soldiers in Sri Lanka.

A few days ago Sri Lanka deposited its instrument of ratification of the Optional Protocol on the Involvement of Children in Armed Conflict to the Convention on the Rights of the Child. This Protocol has noted that the Statute of the International Criminal Court makes conscripting, enlisting or using children in combat a war crime in both international and non-international armed conflicts. It holds non-state actors also accountable for such crimes and it calls upon state parties to cooperate in preventing and combating such crimes.

Accordingly, today, in this General Assembly of the United Nations, Sri Lanka calls upon all states to ratify this Protocol, and it calls upon the state parties on whose territory the LTTE has offices and front organizations to take strong punitive action against such establishments, and to declare the LTTE a criminal organization, as the LTTE sustains its criminal activity in respect of the use of child soldiers through funds generated on the territories of other state parties which are obliged to cooperate in terms of the Convention and the Protocol.

The Winnipeg Conference ended yesterday with an impassioned plea to the world to move urgently from words to deeds, to save the hundreds of thousands of children who are abused, maimed, displaced, traumatized and killed by war. In our cruel world if anything should stir the conscience of mankind it is surely the plight of these children. Let it not be said that yet again we have failed – failed to hear and heed the anguished cry of children in distress, children on whom adults have inflicted, and continue to inflict, unspeakable cruelty. No, politics cannot divide us on the issue of child soldiers. Massive funds are not required to save them. What is required is the will and commitment to act of those states which are in a position to act. The Winnipeg appeal is addressed to them. Let us all wholeheartedly support that appeal now so that when the special session of the General Assembly for Follow-up to the World Summit for Children is held here in New York next September, we will be able to adopt practical measures that will finally ensure that children will forever be protected from the ravages of war.[9]

DOCUMENT 8

The Seven Sisters of South Asia: Where are they Going?

Tenth Lal Bahadur Shastri Memorial Lecture,
New Delhi, 11 January 2003

Kadirgamar's interest in international organizations, both global and regional, was reflected in the attention he paid in many speeches and lectures to the role of the South Asian Association for Regional Cooperation (SAARC). He was Chairman of the Council of Ministers in 1998–2001.

SAARC's history, as this lecture amply confirms, has been far from smooth. Following meetings in Colombo in April and August 1981 involving seven countries – Bangladesh, Bhutan, India, Maldives, Nepal, Pakistan and Sri Lanka – this association was established on 8 December 1985 when its Charter was formally adopted by the Heads of State or Government of all seven countries. Attempts within SAARC to establish a free trade area comprising all the members ran into difficulties, due mainly to India–Pakistan tensions. However, SAARC has continued to hold regular meetings, and at the 12th SAARC summit, held in Islamabad in 2004, plans were laid for moves toward a free trade area. Despite this, trade between South Asian countries has remained at a remarkably low level. In April 2007 Afghanistan became the eighth member of the association. Official information about SAARC can be found at: http://www.saarc-sec.org.

This lecture shows not only Kadirgamar's keen interest in international organizations, but also his realistic awareness of the primacy of interest as the key factor in determining states' attitudes to international bodies. This was the tenth in a series of annual lectures to commemorate Lal Bahadur Shastri, the third prime minister of India (1964–6).

*****

Lal Bahadur Shastri rose from humble beginnings to wear the patrician mantle of Jawaharlal Nehru. That alone was an achievement. As I studied his life I noted with awe that Lal Bahadur Shastri – who had immersed himself in political activities as a student during the Raj, spent time in British jails, fought many elections, done strenuous work for his party, held numerous Cabinet portfolios and finally became the prime minister of India, immersed throughout his life in the hurly-burly, the rough and tumble of Indian politics – emerged at the end of the day with his reputation and good name totally intact. That was a superlative achievement.

The writings on Shastriji emphasize one thing about him above all else – his simplicity, unwavering simplicity, from the beginning of his life to its end. He was a man of high principle and sterling integrity. Consider these two manifestations of those qualities. When he married, Lal Bahadur declined to accept anything as a dowry. Under strong pressure from his father-in-law he made a miniscule concession – he accepted only a spinning wheel and a few yards of khadi as a dowry gift! That was in the India of 1928! We can see what manner of man he was at the age of 24. When he was Minister of Railways in 1956 a major railway accident occurred in Madras. Many people lost their lives. Accepting moral responsibility for the disaster, Shastri tendered his resignation to Prime Minister Nehru, who refused to accept it. Shastri insisted, Nehru relented. Speaking in Parliament, where his resignation was hailed as being in the highest traditions of parliamentary democracy, Nehru said:

> I would like to say that it has been ... for long, my good fortune and privilege to have him as a comrade and colleague and no man can wish for a better comrade and better colleague in any undertaking – a man of the highest integrity, loyalty, devoted to ideals, a man of conscience and a man of hard work. We can expect no better. And it is because he is such a man of conscience that he has felt deeply whenever there is any failing in the work entrusted to his charge.[1]

As his political career developed Shastri began to acquire a reputation as a moderator and resolver of disputes. He dealt with the language controversies in Assam and Kerala. In South India he was assigned the task of handling the acute, and potentially explosive, problem of the switch-over to Hindi 15 years after 26 July 1950. In keeping with his promise to the South Indians that justice would be done he steered through Parliament in 1962 the Official Language Bill which provided that even after January 1965 English may be retained, in addition to Hindi, for all official purposes.

Mr Shastri also conducted, on behalf of India, delicate negotiations with other states. The Sirima–Shastri Pact, which bears the names of Prime Minister Sirimavo Bandaranaike of Sri Lanka and Prime Minister Shastri, is well known.[2] He was sent to Nepal to dispel an apprehension that had arisen in that country that India was not paying due respect to Nepal's sovereignty. The visit was widely regarded as 'very useful and fruitful'. Mr Shastri was both a man of war and a man of peace. He was a strong advocate of nonalignment. It fell to his lot to lead India, successfully, in the 1965 war with Pakistan. But he also paved the way for peace between the two countries at the famous Tashkent meeting. There, at the height of his career, only 18 months into his premiership, Lal Bahadur Shastri died, mourned by the whole of India, eulogized by leaders around the world, remembered to this day, 40 years later, by men and women everywhere who yearn to see their political leaders conduct themselves with simplicity, integrity and whole-hearted dedication to the service of the common people. When one surveys the current South Asian political scene one cannot but weep with the silent millions of the sub-continent for the massive absence of men of Shastri's quality. Lal Bahadur Shastri was a lotus that rose from the murky silt and mud of the pond of politics. It seems the giants have gone. In politics, has South Asia become a kingdom of dwarfs?

The Different Agendas of SAARC's Member States

You will notice that the title of this lecture is not 'SAARC: where is it going?' With conscious intent I pose the question 'The seven sisters of South Asia: where are they going?' The nuance is deliberate. It reflects my view that SAARC – the South Asia Association for Regional Cooperation – comprising seven states is a grouping of legal entities. States are devoid of hearts and feelings. They are permanently locked into a pattern of elaborate political and diplomatic manoeuvre which may or may not, at any given point of time or on any particular issue, reflect accurately, or at all, the interests and aspirations of the people at large whom they are supposed to represent. SAARC is state-led, government-driven.

The metaphor of the sisters, on the other hand, conjures up an image of kith and kin, a shared home in our vast sub-continent, and in the language of the Colombo Declaration at the 10th SAARC summit in 1998, 'heirs to a profound common civilizational continuum of great antiquity which constitutes a historical basis for sustaining harmonious relations among the people of the region.' The sisters are mothers. Their children – the peoples of South Asia – are thus, by definition, first cousins. Sisters may suffer estrangement from time to time; more often than not they make up, and family life is resumed. Blood is thicker than water.

During my seven years as the Foreign Minister of Sri Lanka, I had the privilege of a ringside seat at three summits and retreats. I had the special privilege of chairing the Council of Ministers for three and a half years – perhaps the longest tenure of that chair in the history of SAARC – at a time when SAARC was in the doldrums: its very survival at stake. Sri Lanka struggled to keep SAARC afloat. It was a lonely period. I learnt much about SAARC in those years which I intend to share with you today and with all those commentators on the affairs of SAARC from whose writings I have drawn liberally.

The recent rescheduling of the 11th summit which was to have been held in Kathmandu in 2001 and the indefinite postponement of the 12th summit which is scheduled to be held in Islamabad in 2003, have raised, yet again, old questions regarding the future of SAARC.[3] It would be opportune, therefore, in this lecture, to revisit the beginnings. One writer holds the view that SAARC is still at the 'beginning of the beginning'. I do not agree. Much has been accomplished. Certainly, much more remains to be done, but in measuring success and failure the original motivations and expectations of the founders of SAARC must be kept in mind, and in applying a suitable yardstick for measurement the ground realities that differentiate SAARC from other regional organizations – the Association of Southeast Asian Nations (ASEAN) or the European Union (EU), for instance – must not be lost sight of as they are critical to valid judgement.

Let us examine the reasons why the seven states of South Asia formed an association for regional cooperation in 1985, and consider the expectations that event aroused at that time. Although the Charter enumerates a number of worthy regional objectives – promoting the welfare of the peoples of South Asia, accelerating economic growth, strengthening collective self-reliance and mutual trust and understanding, and appreciating one another's problems in the region – each state approached the question of joining the Association from the standpoint of its own national agenda. There is nothing wrong with that. In bilateral and multilateral relationships each nation state strives to secure an advantage; the strong will dictate terms; the weak have to settle for the best available deal.

The evidence shows that when SAARC was under discussion – it took four years to move the concept from the drawing-board in Dhaka to the first officials' meeting in Colombo in 1981 – the other states sought to position themselves advantageously in relation to India, while India had its own regional and geo-political concerns to contend with in deciding whether or not to join the Association.

Pakistan had two obvious concerns – first, the old, haunting fear of India's hegemonistic domination of the region heightened by the prospect that Indian hegemony would be institutionalized through SAARC; second, its ambivalent relationship to South Asia, on the one hand, through geography, and West Asia, on the other, through Islam. Would joining SAARC compromise Pakistan's endeavour to forge closer ties with the Islamic countries to the West of her? Prior to the first SAARC summit Pakistan's President Zia was at pains to stress that Pakistan's participation in the summit would not in any way affect its relations with the Muslim countries, and that it would maintain its national identity at all costs, and continue to play a positive role in the Middle East. In the final analysis Pakistan's decision to join SAARC would, no doubt, have been heavily influenced by the desire not to be isolated regionally. There seems to have been another compulsion – a possible corollary to the theory of Indian hegemony – that might have influenced Pakistan's thinking, namely, that Pakistan's presence in SAARC could, if the need arose, 'deflect the weight of India', in relation to the smaller states of South Asia. Press comments in Pakistan after the first summit stressed the assertion that Bangladesh, Bhutan, Maldives, Nepal and Sri Lanka had very good relations with Pakistan, whereas none of those states had tension-free relations with India. The Pakistan media stated, not surprisingly, that Indo–Pakistan relations were not conducive to regional cooperation. Thus, as a commentator has said, 'just as the blame for the existence of a conflictual relationship was put on India, the onus for improvement in the state of affairs was also put exclusively on New Delhi.'

India also had major concerns. It is well known that India initially suspected that the initiative of President Zia of Bangladesh could have been an American ploy to create, by proxy, a South Asian regional mechanism to counter Soviet influence in the region after its military intervention in Afghanistan. Resistance to outside forces intruding into South Asia has always been a central tenet of India's foreign policy and strategic posture. An allied concern was the theory of 'ganging up': that the neighbours, in pursuit of their own interests, would act in concert against India's interests. I have heard it said – I certainly cannot vouch for the authenticity of the statement – that Prime Minister Indira Gandhi had observed that 'SAARC is a collection of barnacles on the hull of India'. This statement may be apocryphal, but the sentiment it reflects was prevalent at that time, and the echoes of it are still heard in the policy-making chambers of the Indian establishment, albeit with much less resonance now, as it has become clear over the years, on the evidence, that the 'ganging up' theory is insubstantial. However, obviously, India could not reject the establishment of SAARC. It insisted, however, on two basic principles – that 'bilateral and contentious issues shall be excluded from deliberations' and that 'decisions at all levels shall be taken on the basis of unanimity'. As a former Indian Foreign Secretary, Muchkund Dubey, has observed: 'the objective of India was to try to pursue regional cooperation autonomously without allowing it to be subjected to the vicissitudes of bilateral cooperation.' The view that bilateral strains and stresses should not impinge on regional cooperation was articulated by Prime Minister Rajiv Gandhi at the first summit. In my opinion India was right to adopt that approach not only in its own interest but in order to keep the fledgling association intact, especially in its formative years. If India had not taken that attitude SAARC might well have become, right from the beginning, a mere pressure group, a forum for ventilating and seeking redress for bilateral grievances against India and nothing more. Thus, I have no doubt that the injunction against contentious bilateral issues being placed on the formal SAARC agenda saved the organization from early disintegration. In reality, however, given the fractious nature of inter-state relations in the region, then and now, the late prime minister's view must necessarily remain an optimistic exhortation because, inevitably, bilateral stresses and strains have always impinged on the SAARC process, and will continue to do so for the foreseeable future.

But, as the life of SAARC unfolded, SAARC summits have, in fact, come to be regarded as valuable occasions for informal, low-key consultations between the leaders on contentious bilateral matters, outside the formal agenda and away from the spotlight of international publicity. At a SAARC summit arrangements are routinely made for bilateral meetings between the leaders.

The smaller SAARC states also had their own agendas when it came to the establishment of SAARC. Generally, it could be said that they shared a fear and distrust of India. Individually, their capacity to deal with India over bilateral differences or over economic, strategic and security issues was negligible; they knew that, collectively, their prospects of gaining concessions from India were better; they knew that also.

Bhutan saw in SAARC, as a writer has said, an instrument through which it could expand its foreign and economic relations with its neighbours without antagonizing India. Maldives shared this view. In later years Maldives used the SAARC forum to canvass support for the protection and security of small states, and also for their vital environmental concerns.

Landlocked Nepal, which has borders with India on three sides and a fundamental problem of access to the sea, saw the possibility of sharing its immense water resources with regional partners as a way of reducing its overall dependence on India. Since SAARC was dedicated to the principles of sovereign equality, territorial integrity, political independence and mutual benefits, Nepal appears to have assumed that India's alleged support for democracy against its monarchy would be withdrawn, once SAARC came into being, thus ensuring the stability and continuity of the monarchy. At the 5th Non-Aligned Conference held in Colombo in 1976 King Birendra, perhaps shrewdly, had spoken of the desirability of regional cooperation in South Asia well before the idea was formally mooted by Bangladesh. Nepal also proposed that its territory be declared a Zone of Peace. Nepal's enthusiasm for SAARC, and its willingness to host various meetings, culminated in the selection of Kathmandu as the seat of the SAARC Secretariat.

Bangladesh, having failed to internationalize its water problem with India, seems to have seen in a regional mechanism an alternative approach to dealing with India. One writer says that President Zia had his own domestic compulsions for seeking a striking diplomatic success.

Sri Lanka responded positively to SAARC, its earlier flirtation with the possibility of joining ASEAN having come to naught. One problem Sri Lanka did not have was the need to secure the support of its neighbours, in the name of sovereignty, territorial integrity, stability and political independence, to buttress a non-democratic regime. Sri Lanka and India were the only two SAARC states at that time to have thriving democracies. But Sri Lanka's relations with India, when SAARC was being discussed, were under strain because of its perception that certain actions taken by India were exacerbating the ethnic problem in Sri Lanka. India for her part perceived a threat to its security as a result of certain actions by the Jayewardene government such as the proposed handing over of the Trincomalee oil tanks to Coastal Corporation – suspected to have been a US Central Intelligence Agency (CIA) front company – and the expansion of the Voice of America (VOA) facility.[4] This was in Cold War times. The opening of the economy and the invitation to multi-nationals was also perceived as a threat to India's security. Our loosening of links with the Non-Aligned Movement in the eighties was also frowned upon. The question whether India could be trusted dominated Sri Lankan thinking. The lack of trust in India showed in President Jayewardene's approach to SAARC, at the first summit, when he stated that the SAARC states must first trust each other; that India being the largest country could by words and deeds create the confidence among its members so necessary to make a beginning; that India's role was vital. He came back to this point at the 4th SAARC summit in Islamabad where he said: 'the key to progress in SAARC depends on India.' This early line of thought on India's obligations to the rest of the region, emanating from a small SAARC state, was endorsed by India itself, when Mr Gujral, ten years later, outlined his vision for India's relationship with the other SAARC states, in a historic speech, to which I will refer in a while, where he expounded what has come to be known as the 'Gujral doctrine'.

It seems clear that although regional cooperation was the ostensible *raison d'être* of SAARC, the masked agenda of each state, in relation to the others, was the advancement, certainly the protection, of its own national interests in South Asia. In this context SAARC was considered relevant and necessary by its constituent members. It is their opinion that counts. Thus, as I see it, SAARC was primarily intended to be a political instrument designed for managing, through its various regional mechanisms, a dialogue among its members, and by implementing various joint programmes of action in areas of common social, educational, economic, cultural and humanitarian interest to create a degree of stability in inter-state relations that would minimize, by encouraging the habit of constantly working together on a variety of subjects, the risk of disagreements and misunderstandings erupting into conflicts.

If the question is asked whether it is wrong (although in terms of realpolitik nothing could be said to be wrong) for the SAARC states to look to their regional organization to fulfil and protect their individual national interests, my answer would be certainly not – because surely it must be one of the principal aims of regional cooperation to ensure stability in the region and one cannot achieve stability if the interplay of national interests results in a state of chronic disequilibrium.

In my view the questions that should be posed, at this stage in the history of SAARC, are whether SAARC has retained its original political relevance and usefulness to its constituent members as a mechanism for regional cooperation as well as a forum for bilateral consultation; whether the regional social and economic cooperation programmes in which SAARC is engaged are effective; and whether it has acquired additional political relevance and usefulness in the wider international context. These are all mainly questions of fact, and evidence is available on the basis of which answers could be formulated.

On the question of political relevance, given the various national motives that impelled the SAARC states to get together in the first place, there is clear evidence that the states have used the SAARC forum to maintain continuity in their bilateral relations. For instance, the Pakistan News Service reported that at the first summit in Dhaka, Prime Minister Rajiv Gandhi and President Zia of Pakistan met informally and discussed bilateral issues, followed by a visit to India by General Zia.

Prior to the 2nd SAARC summit in Bangalore in 1986 tension was mounting between India and Pakistan in the wake of speculation regarding Indian troop movements on the Western border between the two countries. During the summit the two prime ministers discussed the matter. Prime Minister Junejo of Pakistan visited India after the summit. He stated, and the Pakistan press confirmed, that the discussion in Bangalore had cleared the air and that the reports of unusual troop movements were unfounded. The Pakistan press went on to say that SAARC in the long run may be expected to create a better climate of trust and cooperation between the two countries.

At the same summit President Jayewardene of Sri Lanka and Prime Minister Rajiv Gandhi of India discussed the increasing militancy of the Tamil Tigers (LTTE) in the context of the widely-held belief in Sri Lanka that India was supporting the militants. These discussions led to the dispatch of an Indian Peace Keeping Force to the North and East of Sri Lanka.

After the 4th summit in Islamabad in 1988 Prime Minister Rajiv Gandhi stayed on for a few hours for bilateral talks with Prime Minister Benazir Bhutto. Three agreements were signed, relating to the avoidance of double taxation, the promotion of cultural exchanges and the prohibition of attack on their respective nuclear installations. According to the Pakistan press Prime Minister Gandhi had told Prime Minister Bhutto: 'This is the first agreement since 1972 when your father and my mother signed an agreement in Shimla.' Prime Minister Bhutto is reported to have welcomed the SAARC forum for having made the visit possible and hoped that more such visits would follow.

On the sidelines of SAARC summits Nepal and India have discussed their transit problem, Bangladesh and India their water problem, and

Bhutan and Nepal their refugee problem. A former Foreign Minister of Bhutan has said: 'We threw in our lot with India and India has never harmed us.'

SAARC Meetings 1997–9: Personal Reminiscences

It would be timely, at this stage of the lecture, for me to branch off into some personal reminiscences. They will reinforce my contention that SAARC today retains its political relevance and usefulness. I also raise questions as to whether good personal interactions between SAARC leaders, especially of India and Pakistan, could actually move SAARC forward and improve bilateral relations between its members. I will give you some glimpses of the personal chemistry between SAARC leaders and the mechanics of decision making, at the summit, drawn from my experience of two summits.

1997 Malé Summit

At the 1997 Malé summit Prime Minister Gujral of India and Prime Minister Nawaz Sharif of Pakistan met, I believe, for the first time or after many years.[5] When they embraced each other and broke out immediately into animated Punjabi there was a palpable mood of elation not only among all of us in the SAARC family but among the hardened international journalists and cameramen who had assembled to cover the summit. A number of significant decisions came out of Malé. One was, on the proposal of Pakistan, to establish a Group of Eminent Persons (GEP) to undertake a comprehensive appraisal of SAARC and identify measures to revitalize and enhance the effectiveness of the Association;[6] the second was that, in the interests of promoting overall development, all SAARC projects need not necessarily involve all seven states; the third was, on the proposal of India, that SAARC should move to a Free Trade Area in 2001; the fourth, on the proposal of Sri Lanka, concerned the process of informal political consultations.

With regard to the first, it is well known that the group did produce a comprehensive and stimulating, even controversial, report which merits close study and implementation, whenever possible.

With regard to the second, there was a brief history behind it. The four SAARC states in the north-eastern part of the sub-continent, led by India, had come to an agreement (the Growth Quadrangle) to collaborate on certain projects relevant to their area. Sri Lanka objected not to the concept, which was eminently sound and covered by the Charter, but to the procedure, bypassing Article VII of the Charter, which provides that 'The Standing Committee may set up Action Committees comprising Member States concerned with implementation of projects involving more than two but not all Member States.' Pakistan also lodged an objection; I do not recall on what ground. There was no question of Pakistan, Maldives and Sri Lanka being able to participate in such a geographically distant project but there was no reason why the others could not benefit from a project that was relevant to them. Sri Lanka felt that if the prescribed procedure was bypassed there could be a danger of projects involving only some members of SAARC, leading to the beginning of the disintegration of the Association. Intensive consultations took place at Malé and the agreed formula for solving the problem was expressed in the following words of the Malé Declaration: 'With the objective of enhancing regional solidarity and promoting overall development within SAARC, the Heads of State or Government encouraged, under the provisions of Articles VII and X of the Charter, the development of specific projects relevant to the needs of three or more Member States.'[7] Article X deals with the principle of unanimity in decision making and the non-engagement of contentious bilateral issues.

The third and fourth Malé decisions had an element of drama. At the retreat, where only heads and foreign ministers are present, Prime Minister Gujral said, quite suddenly: 'Excellencies, my country has been creating difficulties for all of you with regard to trade and economic cooperation. Therefore, I propose that we move to a Free Trade Area by 2001.' There was a moment of stunned disbelief. This was unexpected. After all, the South Asia Preferential Trading Arrangement (SAPTA) had come into force only in 1995 and was proceeding slowly in liberalizing intra-regional trade. President Kumaratunga looked at me with a quizzical expression.[8] I said in a whisper: 'Madam, accept it.' She addressed Prime Minister Gujral as follows: 'Excellency, Sri Lanka supports and welcomes your generous proposal.' Seconds later Prime Minister Nawaz Sharif also accepted it. President Gayoom spoke, as often, with caution. He was concerned, and rightly so, that the smaller countries would not be able to keep the pace. It was unanimously agreed that their needs must be respected. The declaration, having noted with satisfaction the entry into force of SAPTA in 1995, 'recognised the importance of achieving a Free Trade Area by the year 2001 and reiterated that steps towards trade liberalization must take into account the special needs of the smaller and Least Developed Countries and that benefits must accrue equitably.'

The fourth decision came equally unexpectedly. President Kumaratunga had long entertained the idea that SAARC had reached a sufficient degree of maturity to warrant engagement in informal political consultations on some of the grave problems that afflict the region without endangering the Charter principle that 'bilateral and contentious issues shall be excluded from the deliberations' – meaning, of course, the formal deliberations. When President Kumaratunga made this proposal

Prime Minister Gujral was visibly taken aback. He began to explain that there were many implications involved and that the matter required study. Then, prudently, he called for a coffee break. When we came back he said, looking directly at President Kumaratunga: 'How can I say no to Your Excellency.' Thus, the words of the Malé Declaration on this point read as follows:

> The Heads of State or Government recalled their commitment to the promotion of mutual trust and understanding and, recognising that the aims of promoting peace, stability and amity and accelerated socio-economic cooperation may best be achieved by fostering good neighbourly relations, relieving tensions and building confidence, agreed that a process of informal political consultations would prove useful in this regard.[9]

This concept was unthinkable some years ago. SAARC has moved a long way from the explicit words of the Charter. Each of the Malé decisions was a significant milestone on the road to effective regional cooperation. An effete organization does not make such decisions.

1998 Colombo Summit

Then came the Colombo summit – the 10th.[10] Nepal, whose turn it was to host the summit after Maldives, gave way to Sri Lanka in order that Sri Lanka would have the honour of hosting the summit in the Golden Jubilee year of its independence. This was the summit that almost never took place. The drama on that occasion was quite deadly. The nuclear tests in May and June 1998 by India and Pakistan shook the region. Indeed, they shook the world. Those who had no faith in SAARC expected a severe disruption of SAARC activities. That did not happen as a result of the tests. The prophets of doom predicted the end of SAARC. That did not happen either.

When the tests occurred the summit, already scheduled for July, was certainly placed in dire jeopardy. Preliminary soundings indicated that the other four states, leaving out India and Pakistan who were not initially consulted, had grave doubts as to whether the summit could be held as scheduled in the poisoned atmosphere that prevailed after the nuclear tests. They were thinking of a postponement. President Kumaratunga, sensing that a fateful moment in the history of SAARC had arrived, decided that we must do everything possible to save the summit. A postponement might have led to a situation where attitudes could harden between India and Pakistan to such an extent that the very existence of SAARC might become imperilled. I must confess Sri Lanka feared that SAARC might actually die, and that it would die in our hands. We decided to propose to the others that the summit should focus on economic matters for the first time. The idea was to move the focus away from confrontation between India and Pakistan by providing a timely forum for the SAARC states to reflect on the lessons to be learnt from the financial difficulties which had then recently engulfed the neighbouring region, South East Asia, indicating that while globalization has many credits, such as enhanced market access and exposure to innovative technologies, it also carries the danger that the contagion of adverse developments elsewhere in the global economic system can spread all too rapidly to other regions. South Asia, furthermore, should realize that a collective approach would be useful in coping with the downside of globalization. The approach of SAARC towards these problems could be twofold. Firstly, it could develop its potential economic strength through SAPTA and SAFTA;[11] and secondly, as a parallel measure to the first, SAARC members could henceforth, to the maximum extent possible, act in concert in multilateral discussions on trade and financial issues.

I was charged by President Kumaratunga with the task of visiting the SAARC capitals with this message in an effort to save the summit. I visited them in alphabetical order as I always did when embarking on a round of formal consultations. In Bangladesh, Prime Minister Sheikh Hasina seemed, initially, to be in favour of a postponement, perhaps because she appeared to be interested in conducting some shuttle diplomacy between India and Pakistan (that is only a surmise), but she soon came round and agreed that the summit on the economic theme should be held as planned. I was unable to visit Bhutan for personal reasons. In India Prime Minister Vajpayee wholeheartedly welcomed both the holding of the summit and the choice of theme, and pledged India's fullest support. A similar reaction came from Prime Minister Koirala of Nepal. And then on to Pakistan. Prime Minister Nawaz Sharif began by insisting at some length that security concerns should take precedence over economic cooperation and that there was no point in discussing the latter while avoiding the former. I said: 'Prime Minister, if you press that line India will not come to the summit. That means the summit will not only have to be postponed but it may never be held. SAARC will die in the hands of Sri Lanka.' His response was swift and unexpected: 'No, no, Minister, don't say that. I cannot let that happen. Please tell President Kumaratunga that I will come and I will give her my full support. In our opening statement I will set out our position relating to India, but at the retreat I will help her.' My last call, by prior arrangement, was on President Gayoom. As the incumbent Chairman he wished to hear the views of the other heads before he made up his own mind. He was hesitant about the wisdom of holding a summit, lest it fell apart, in such a tense atmosphere, but on hearing the reactions of the other heads he agreed to go along with them.

After the nuclear tests, when the very future of SAARC could have been at stake, and while offers were being made by various countries to host a meeting between prime ministers Vajpayee and Nawaz Sharif, both leaders made it clear, and publicly, that, if they were to meet at all, it would be at the forthcoming Colombo summit and nowhere else. To immense global relief they did meet in Colombo in July 1998, just two months after the tests. I remember thinking at that time that when dealing with a family squabble what better place is there for a meeting than the home of one of the other sisters. The invaluable role that SAARC plays in providing a forum for bilateral discussions, especially between India and Pakistan, without any loss of face, at a time when their relations are at a low ebb, was vividly illustrated by the choice of the 10th summit at Colombo for their first meeting after the tests. This event clearly underlined the political relevance and usefulness of SAARC.

When the formal proceedings began Pakistan fired its promised salvo. India's statement was restrained. In the back rooms of the conference, however, the Indian and Pakistani delegations of officials seem to have gone for each other hammer and tongs because the text of the draft declaration which the Standing Committee of Foreign Secretaries sent up to the Council of Ministers was full of what in conference jargon is called square brackets – that is, brackets within which alternative formulations are placed when no agreed text is possible.

When this mangled text came to the Council late on the evening of the second day my assessment of the situation as chairman was that it would be a waste of time for the Council to attempt to remove the square brackets when their officials had deliberately placed them there. Accordingly, I suggested to the Council that we should send up the text, as it was, to the Heads next morning at their retreat for them to deal with the square brackets. This was a highly unusual procedure – bordering on discourtesy to the Heads – but extreme situations call for innovative remedies. The Council agreed and the meeting was terminated in half an hour. Unknown to my colleagues I was, of course, gambling on the assurance that Prime Minister Nawaz Sharif had given me at Islamabad a few weeks earlier – 'at the retreat I will help her.'

Next morning at the retreat all went well. President Kumaratunga handled the meeting with considerable aplomb. Every possible eventuality had been rehearsed. An impressive programme of work emerged including a number of new initiatives to be taken in the areas of poverty eradication; education and literacy through distance learning organized by a forum of vice chancellors of open universities; tourism; communications; science and technology; the environment; youth; children; women and the girl child; health; disabled persons; information; terrorism and drug trafficking; the establishment of a SAARC cultural centre; and so on. Special mention should be made of the decision to start work on a Social Charter for the region. It seemed to me quite remarkable – and it says something for the resilience of SAARC – that barely two months after the nuclear tests, probably the worst flash point in Indo–Pakistan relations, their leaders could participate with their peers in the formulation of such a comprehensive programme of regional activities.

As the retreat drew to a close President Kumaratunga said: 'Excellencies, we are now left with the square brackets in the draft text that was sent to us by the Council. What do we do with them?' Prime Minister Nawaz Sharif immediately said : 'Excellencies, as far as I am concerned we can remove them if Prime Minister Vajpayee agrees.' Mr Vajpayee was reading a document, head down, spectacles on his nose. He looked up – somewhat startled, I think – but he recovered swiftly. He said: 'I also agree.' With those two simple statements the forest of square brackets fell down and the way was cleared for the officials to produce a clean text. Prime Minister Nawaz leant across to me and said 'Minister, if we can't settle a small problem like this how are we ever going to solve Kashmir?' Prime Minister Sharif had certainly delivered on his promise to me. If only an accumulation of small problems solved could lead to the solution of the big one what a happy state of affairs that would be for India and Pakistan, for the region, for the world. But that is only wishful thinking.

The conclusion I draw from these personal experiences is that good chemistry between the leaders, especially of India and Pakistan, and even the smaller states, does have a temporary effect on improving relations, but no more. The road from New Delhi to Islamabad is strewn with the boulders of history. Powerful compulsions and influences, domestic and foreign, unpredictable events, seem to render futile the well-meant attempts of a few individuals, from time to time, to move those boulders. The year 1999 began with a brave bus journey to Lahore which lifted the spirits of the entire sub-continent only to end with the battle in the snows of Kargil which brought the work of SAARC to a near halt for two years. In terms of finding a solution to one of the most complex problems of all time, one cannot reasonably expect a regional organization to achieve in 17 years what the United Nations has failed to achieve in fifty seven; to think otherwise is to condemn SAARC for failing to accomplish a recognized impossibility.

1999 Council of Ministers Meeting at Nuwara Eliya in Sri Lanka

Before I end my personal reminiscences I should mention another episode which also throws light on the workings of SAARC.

The first meeting of the Council of Ministers after the July 1998 summit took place in Sri Lanka in March 1999. The political atmosphere was reasonably good. Prime Minister Vajpayee had journeyed to Lahore; Kargil had not yet occurred. The foreign secretaries it seemed had got off to a good start. They had discussed the Group of Eminent Persons report and had prepared a comprehensive draft of future SAARC activities; but they suddenly hit the rocks when it came to dealing with two seemingly innocuous but terribly contentious issues as far as the Indian and Pakistani bureaucrats were concerned. The contentious issues were whether to include in the final report to be handed over to the foreign ministers references to the Lahore Declaration;[12] and the graduation of the informal dialogue 'process' between member states mentioned in the Malé and Colombo summit declarations to 'operational' procedures. Pakistan was keen on these two items but not India.

Word was trickling out that India and Pakistan had locked horns and were unable to disentangle themselves. I suggested to my two friends, Jaswant Singh of India and Sartaj Aziz of Pakistan, that they might take a stroll in the salubrious woods of the presidential lodge while waiting for the report. They, no doubt, had bilateral issues to discuss. According to a report in a leading Sri Lankan newspaper, the *Sunday Times*: 'By 6 p.m. the foreign secretaries and the officials trooped, almost stormed in from the Grand Hotel across the road.' They gave to the Chairman a single sheet of paper with the significant remark 'this is a bare bones document.' As the newspaper pointed out, this document was the draft that acts as 'the mandate for the Secretary–General' to map out the future activities of SAARC until the next summit. In effect, therefore, the SAARC Secretariat would have had no real work to do in the future; no budget and not even authority to pay the salaries of the Secretariat staff. The Secretary-General who had been appointed to his post only a few months earlier was, understandably, in a panic. The newspaper went on to say:

> A report which had reached comprehensive proportions in three days of substantial work in the Standing Committee had been shrunk, in a fit of pique by the Indian and Pakistan officials, to an inconsequential one-page say nothing, do nothing report that brought the work of SAARC to a grinding halt. Mr Kadirgamar took one look at it and remarked 'we will simply have to improve on this.' ...
>
> Just then with three foreign ministers, foreign secretaries, the Secretary-General of SAARC and other officials standing around, a young lady from the Indian delegation had the temerity if not the inexperience to shoot back at the Chairman of the Council: 'That's your prerogative,' she said.... Prerogative it was for the Foreign Ministers to save SAARC from the foreign secretaries' stubbornness....
>
> One South Asian Minister said the Prime Minister of India and Pakistan may have gone in a bus to Lahore, their officials are still at the bus halt. Mr Kadirgamar, Mr Singh and Mr Aziz then sat down without anyone else and thrashed out appropriate references to the Lahore Declaration and the GEP recommendation, Mr Kadirgamar doing the drafting on the back of an envelope.
>
> The Indian and Pakistani foreign ministers seemed prepared to look beyond their officials. The original parts of the GEP report and the vision for SAARC which had been omitted from the Standing Committee draft were reintroduced. SAARC was salvaged from the brink of virtual collapse....

As one South Asian diplomat observed, 'firm chairmanship had converted a total collapse into a stunning success'. At a final informal meeting of ministers and secretaries before the formal session, the chairman did not mince words. He said the Standing Committee report was a 'disgrace', which would have to be removed from the annals of SAARC. And so it was. The officials were instructed to re-submit their original report together with the paragraphs drafted by the troika of Ministers.[13]

I sought the permission of both my colleagues to deliver a dressing down to their officials in their presence. They agreed. I suspect that both of them, distinguished among many qualities for their sense of humour, rather enjoyed my doing something which both of them might dearly have loved to do but could not have done without destroying the peace of their respective ministries. The newspaper added:

> The formal meeting was then convened and proceeded smoothly. Diplomats observed that for the first time in SAARC history the officials had taken a beating. The next day at the concluding session, the Indian and Pakistani Ministers with their officials by their side seemed to revert to a stronger line on minor drafting points such as the location in the Standing Committee's report of the new paragraphs, should they be at the front of the document, in the middle or at the end, 'as if their officials were breathing down their necks' – a final echo of the earlier battle. The Bangladesh foreign minister wanted a reference to the Dhaka–Calcutta bus route, and with promises to meet in New York everyone left Nuwara Eliya in one piece. SAARC had survived.[14]

Thus concluded the report in the *Sunday Times* of Colombo. The newspaper headline was 'The day SAARC nearly collapsed'. The opening sentence of its report was 'Around 6 p.m. on Wednesday 17 March, up in the central highlands of Nuwara Eliya, SAARC nearly collapsed from a fit of bureaucratic asthma.'

I would add, the leaders of India and Pakistan saved SAARC in July 1998; their officials almost succeeded in destroying it in March 1999. I have often felt that the officials of India and Pakistan sometimes behave as though they are the true keepers of the dogma; that it is their high national duty to restrain their leaders from straying into good sense and reasonableness. I was astonished sometimes at the fanatical devotion to political religiosity displayed by some of these delegations.

SAARC's Regional Social and Economic Cooperation Programmes

A while ago I raised the question whether SAARC has retained its political relevance and usefulness to its constituent numbers as a mechanism for regional cooperation as well as a forum for bilateral consultations. I have offered my answer to that question. I also raised the question whether the regional social and economic cooperation programmes in which SAARC is engaged are effective. I wish to say a few words on that question.

A regional organization which has no independent funding cannot by itself implement regional programmes. It can only provide a series of fora for the exchange of ideas on the various issues of concern to the member states, so that they could learn from each other's experiences in dealing with common problems. This SAARC has done from its inception through technical committees for continuous interaction and cooperation in the fields of agriculture, communications, education, culture and sports, environment and meteorology, health and population activities, prevention of drug trafficking and drug abuse, rural development, science and technology, tourism, transport, and women in development. Some of these committees have performed more efficiently than others. But it cannot be gainsaid that they have all helped to set goals for the region which could be incorporated in national plans.

The Group of Eminent Persons has recommended certain targets to be achieved in the social field. They include reaching a replacement level of population which translates into a birth rate of 21 per thousand before the year 2020; attainment of universal primary education up to the age of 15 before the year 2010; elimination of gender disparities in access to education within the target date of 2010; setting aside 6 per cent of Gross Domestic Product (GDP) for education by the year 2010 (South Asia spends an average of US$ 64 per pupil on public education as compared to an average of US$ 5360 and 21 per cent of Gross National Product (GNP) per capita in the advanced countries); reduction of infant mortality below 50 per thousand live births by the year 2000; attainment of 100 per cent immunization by the year 2000 on targets set by the United Nations Children's Fund (UNICEF) programmes; empowerment of women socially, economically and politically; and poverty alleviation programmes. In this sense there is a permanent social agenda for SAARC. Clearly the implementation of these targets requires national commitments. A failure on the national front cannot be blamed on either the bilateral or regional political environment.

On economic issues it took ten years before SAARC could actually take off with the operationalization of SAPTA in 1995. Progress has been slow and a common complaint is the limited coverage of goods under SAPTA. The smaller member states seem to be convinced that tariff preferences for trade will not bring prosperity unless they are accompanied by investments in their countries to improve their narrow industrial base. Presently, discussions on measures for encouraging intra-SAARC investment and joint ventures are being focused upon, and proposals for a Regional Investment Treaty and a SAARC Arbitration Council have also been initiated. So also with double taxation avoidance. It is the existence of a permanent SAARC forum which allows all these deliberations to take place in a continuous manner. But the plain fact is that intra-SAARC trade is a very small proportion of the member states' trade with the rest of the world – 2 per cent in the 1980s, 4 per cent by the end of the 1990s – compared to Europe's 70 per cent – so that the incentive for a regional treaty is absent, let alone contending with the daunting political problem of obtaining unanimity.

Thus, my answer to the question I posed as to whether SAARC's regional social and economic cooperation programmes are effective is that while on the social side there is promise of continuous engagement and improvement in the quality of the work being done, on the economic side the picture is not very bright and is not likely to improve.

The third question I posed is whether SAARC has acquired additional political relevance and usefulness in the wider international context. Here the evidence points to considerable progress in recent years. In the early days of SAARC India was reluctant to approve of SAARC establishing links with other regional organizations. The situation has changed. Now there is unanimity on the need for SAARC to relate to other regional organizations. Contacts with the European Union began in 1998 and continued in 1999. Contacts with ASEAN have been made but have not proceeded far. On the other hand, in various international fora – the World Trade Organization, the World Intellectual Property Organization, conferences on the environment, natural disaster reduction and social development, and on nuclear questions – the SAARC states have worked together and adopted a unified position. India and Pakistan are divided on issues at home, but they are willing and able to work together abroad with the other SAARC states on issues which unite the developing world.

Prospects

As this lecture nears its close I would like to offer some reflections on the prospects for SAARC, and the South Asian region, in the context of the twenty-first century. Where are the seven sisters going?

As Professor Mansingh has observed, 'technological advances in all fields are forcing the pace of change all over the world into a time scale unfamiliar to most South Asians, where clocks are set to agrarian, not industrial, much less electronic, rhythms.'[15] Technology is unequally distributed across the world. Seventy-nine per cent of Internet users inhabit the developed countries; in India there are only 28 telephones per 1000 people. SAARC states desperately need to invest in education and move relentlessly towards the elimination of class, caste and gender barriers to education if they are to take advantage of the ongoing technological revolution.[16]

We all know that globalization has its advantages and downsides. The process is inexorable. Merely railing at it is not going to help South Asia. What *will* help is the use of globalization forces to improve transport and communications systems – road, rail, air and electronic. Demographic changes, migration and refugee problems which, under its Charter, SAARC is not authorized to discuss, will severely strain the resources of South Asia in the years ahead. 'Floating populations', deepening poverty and easy access to arms can severely destabilize South Asia.

The attitude of the United States in relation to South Asia is going to affect this region considerably. In contrast to its Cold War policies that pitted South Asian states against each other, the US now supports the concept of regional cooperation and is steadily widening and deepening its relations with India.

Against this twenty-first century backdrop what are the possibilities open to SAARC? I agree with Professor Mansingh's analysis of the possibilities. First, the possibility of member states allowing SAARC to 'languish into failure' by neglecting its institutional structure, failing to hold meetings, ceasing to fund the Secretariat, the technical committees and regional centres, not implementing important agreements in the Integrated Plan of Action, the Conventions on Terrorism and Narcotics, and indefinitely postponing a summit. In this scenario the relationship between India and Pakistan is vital. However, I agree in particular with Professor Mansingh's observation:

> Fortunately the voice of those who see the potential of SAARC meetings providing opportunities for quiet diplomacy on high-profile security issues seems to be gaining strength, and the popular demand for expanded regional cooperation is visible in all the member states, so that governments cannot afford to let SAARC fail.[17]

In this lecture I, too, have raised my voice in that cause.

An allied possibility is that without dismantling SAARC – and I have not yet heard or read a reasoned case for that drastic step – India becomes indifferent to it. This is a very real danger if India proceeds alone on a trajectory of economic growth or takes the route of bilateral economic agreements, the Free Trade Agreement between India and Sri Lanka being an example.[18] But in today's world bilateral and regional arrangements are not mutually exclusive, and concentric regional groupings are becoming a common feature of international life. Moreover, I would venture the thought that it would be very much in India's interests to turn SAARC into a viable free trade area and thus make it an engine of economic growth for the region. I would add a further point. If it is perceived that India is deliberately undermining SAARC it would have a very adverse effect on India's standing in the world community, and a very adverse effect on India's prospects of securing a permanent seat in the UN Security Council.

Another possibility is that SAARC could function as an umbrella organization under which some member states acting together, as with the

Growth Quadrangle concept that SAARC has already accepted, or with neighbouring states outside of SAARC, proceed with economic cooperation at a more rapid pace than is possible under SAARC rules of unanimity. The Bangladesh, India, Myanmar, Sri Lanka, Thailand Economic Cooperation grouping (BIMSTEC) established in 1997 is a good example of that possibility.[19] Another example is the Indian Ocean Rim Association for Regional Cooperation (IORARC), an organization to which Bangladesh, India and Sri Lanka belong, along with 16 other states.[20]

Yet another possibility is that SAARC will continue to operate in a modest and unspectacular way slowly carrying on with its programmes of activities in the social field, enabling enhanced people-to-people contacts, increasing intra-regional trade and so on. The trend is certainly against isolation and towards greater cooperation.

The most desirable possibility is for SAARC to grow into a fully functional organization fostering cooperative and even joint action on problems common to the region. For this India is key, for all the obvious reasons that need not be enumerated. If India were to take the lead, since India accounts for about 75 per cent of the land area, population, resources and skills of the region, SAARC could become a regional economic entity of some weight. It is clear that SAARC cannot succeed without India but the other states must help India to participate wholeheartedly.

This is where the Gujral doctrine is important. Shri I. K. Gujral, when he was the Minister of External Affairs of India, delivered a speech at the Royal Institute of International Affairs in London on the 'Foreign Policy Objectives of India's United Front Government'. It was a speech of majestic sweep, elegant and refined and, above all, of almost startling candour.

I spoke earlier of the significant asymmetries of the region – in size, human and material resources, levels of economic and technological development and military power. I spoke of India's huge preponderance. I said that the order of the day has to be the give and take of generosity and matching appreciation; that sort of interaction more than ever requires empowerment by political will.

In that London speech, in a passage of enormous significance for the whole region, Shri Gujral made exactly that commitment of political will on the part of India to mitigate the impact of the asymmetries I referred to earlier. He said:

> The United Front Government's neighbourhood policy now stands on five basic principles: First, with the neighbours like Nepal, Bangladesh, Bhutan, Maldives and Sri Lanka, India does not ask for reciprocity but gives all that it can in good faith and trust. Secondly, no South Asian country will allow its territory to be used against the interest of another country of the region. Thirdly, none will interfere in the internal affairs of another. Fourthly, all South Asians must respect each other's territorial integrity and sovereignty. And finally, they will settle all their disputes through peaceful bilateral negotiations. These

five principles, scrupulously observed, will, I am sure, recast South Asia's regional relationships, including the tormented relationship between India and Pakistan, in a friendly, cooperative mould.[21]

In my Krishna Menon Memorial Centenary Lecture on 'Regional Cooperation and Security: A Sri Lankan view', delivered at Kota, Rajasthan in December 1996, I said this with reference to Shri Gujral's London speech:

> Each of these five propositions is intrinsically sound. Each is wise. Each is capable of implementation. Taken collectively, they constitute a practical and principled foundation for regional cooperation and security. I endorse them without reservation and I express the hope, the fervent hope of all of us in the other five countries of the region, that India and Pakistan will see in these principles the way forward for them on the path of friendship and peace.[22]

In this century SAARC must adopt a number of new initiatives. It must work much more closely with civil society than before. There is a marked international trend towards the decentralization of government, the involvement of the private sector not only in economic but in social and cultural activity, and the empowerment of various interest groups which have a contribution to make towards improving the quality of life of our peoples. Given the lack of consistent political will, bureaucratic lethargy, institutional deficiencies and lack of funds that governments suffer from, there is a great deal that governments cannot, but non-governmental organizations can, do to help the people.

Let me take an example. At the 10th SAARC summit at Colombo in 1998 a decision was taken that SAARC should establish a forum of Vice Chancellors of Open Universities to spearhead the development of distance education in the region. Very little progress has been made. On the other hand, a new non-governmental organization, the South Asia Foundation (SAF), founded by UNESCO Goodwill Ambassador Madanjeet Singh, a retired Indian diplomat, and funded to the extent of millions of dollars through the munificence of his son, a billionaire inventor of a powerful new software, is about to launch a massive distance learning programme at a conference of 21 Vice Chancellors of Open Universities of the region to be held in Colombo next month.[23] This project will link a number of Open Universities and other institutions in the SAARC countries. It will offer a degree course on South Asia studies with subjects that would encompass issues such as sustainable development, women's empowerment, the environment, peace, cooperation and development, renewable energy studies and human rights. Soon this project will reach millions of people in the region, ultimately perhaps hundreds of millions. It will help to bring our young people into the twenty-first century. Other projects already carried out by SAF in various parts of the region include a documentation and information centre in New Delhi, scout and girl guide friendship camps in Bhutan and Maldives, scholarships in journalism, a solar energy project for remote rural areas in India, a project to rehabilitate vulnerable girls in Nepal, assistance to SOS villages in Sri Lanka and so on. The possibilities are almost infinite.

I wish to conclude this lecture with a personal statement of belief. I am optimistic about SAARC. I have always been optimistic about SAARC because to me the establishment of SAARC, the getting together of the seven South Asian nations, was a natural and inevitable process that would have taken place in time. The reason for that optimism is that our cultures are interdependent, deeply common, historically ancient. The links between all seven of us are unfathomable. As ancient as they are, they are deeper than we think. Not only do we look very much alike, we speak languages that have remarkable similarity, our music is common, our culture is common, we are at home wherever we go in this great region of the world. When you have a mass of that kind, a vast number of human beings with enormous potential – potential that is being revealed every day in different areas of life, most recently in the field of information technology – there is surely reason to believe that a bright future awaits our peoples. We are poor but we are full of promise, and when any mass of that kind is full of promise there is hope, there must be hope. Obviously we will meet, periodically, as we have met now, obstacles, difficulties and political problems. That is inevitable in the process of sovereign states trying to work together.

I refer often to Europe after the war. During the past century two savage wars were fought in Europe, wars of the kind that caused countless loss of lives and property and left very deep scars indeed, wounds that many people thought would never heal at all. These wars aroused animosities soaked in blood, if one might put it that way. But what has happened now 50 years after the last war? It is unbelievable. If one had been pessimistic then, one would have said that what has happened now simply could not happen; that France and Germany could never be friends; it is not possible at all. But today the situation is totally different. There has emerged, in that block of countries, an astonishing degree of cohesion among a vast collection of human beings, over 300 million people, with immense resources and immense promise. Historical barriers have been brought down, boundaries are beginning to erode to the point of obliteration and all the time new initiatives are coming up, cultural, legal, technical, scientific, which are inexorably hastening the process of greater cohesion. It is distinctly possible, 25, or even 50 years from now, that there would be a United States of Europe with a common currency, something unthinkable 50 years ago. But those who had *hoped* that would happen, *knew* it would happen. Their reading of the historical situation at that time told them it had to happen. I say the same thing about SAARC. We will overcome the problems that beset us now. There are problems that bedevilled relations among some of us. They are intractable, but not insoluble. There is a vast reservoir of goodwill among all the peoples of our region which in time will propel the member states concerned to get together, to bury their differences, and move SAARC along.

One of the real achievements of SAARC over the past years has been the bonding of our professions, all kinds of professions – doctors, lawyers, accountants, architects, engineers, teachers – all kinds of professions and vocations are working together. It is a natural process for peer groups to collaborate in the pursuit of shared interests. I wish, and hope very much, and I am confident, that they will strengthen the links between them. There are so many natural links between them. There is more and more business being done jointly in the region. Out of this intricate network of contacts strong ties will grow that governments will not be able to ignore. The future of SAARC, I would say, will not lie in the hands of governments. It will be lie in the hands of the people. And it is the people, I am confident, who are going to see to it, who are going to ensure, who are going to insist, that SAARC must be kept alive, functional and positive. It will happen, believe me it will happen. The children of the seven sisters will determine the future of South Asia.

DOCUMENT 9

Flaws in the 2002 Ceasefire Agreement

Speech from the opposition, Parliament,
Colombo, 8 May 2003

Tensions between successive governments of Sri Lanka and parts of the country's large Tamil minority have a long history. In the mid-1970s, a militant organization, the Liberation Tigers of Tamil Eelam (LTTE), was set up. Its military struggle can be said to have begun with its first major attack on a Sri Lanka Army (SLA) unit on 23 July 1983. In the long war that ensued, and with the front lines often changing, the LTTE controlled significant territories in the North and Eastern provinces. These territories constituted some, but by no means all, of the areas in which the Tamil population of Sri Lanka was concentrated. The LTTE advocated secession of a Tamil state from Sri Lanka, but sometimes also indicated that it might be willing to accept a federal or confederal arrangement in which the LTTE-held territories would be largely self-governing.

There were three major negotiated agreements to end the conflict in Sri Lanka, but none of them was lastingly effective in stopping the fighting. Under the terms of the 1987 Indo–Sri Lanka Agreement to Establish Peace and Normalcy in Sri Lanka, there was a major Indian intervention in the areas of conflict by the Indian Peace Keeping Force (IPKF) from 1987 to 1990 – an experience that left India averse to any further military involvement in Sri Lanka's troubles. After five further years of fighting, a ceasefire agreement was signed in January 1995, but it lasted only till April, being followed by a third phase of open armed conflict which lasted till 2002. The 2002 agreement discussed here was the last of these negotiated agreements, and was formally in force for the longest duration.

On 22 February 2002 this Ceasefire Agreement (CFA), negotiated through Norwegian facilitation, was signed, separately, by Prime Minister Ranil Wickremesinghe and LTTE leader Velupillai Prabhakaran.[1] Under its terms Norway agreed to be responsible for monitoring the ceasefire through the Sri Lanka Monitoring Mission (SLMM). There were no maps attached to the CFA, but its Annex B was a list of 17 checkpoints on the 'line of control' of the two parties. (Map 3, indicating where the ceasefire lines were, has been prepared specially for this volume.) The CFA entered into force on 23 February 2002.

Having been defeated in the December 2001 elections, Kadirgamar's party, the People's Alliance (PA), was not in power when the CFA was concluded and implemented. Initially Kadirgamar had extended constructive cooperation in the peace process, which in some respects was a continuation of policies with which he had been associated when the PA government had been in office in 1994–2000. He had cooperated both privately and publicly, including in a speech in parliament on 23 January 2002, while at the same time indicating that the PA would not remain silent if the necessity arose to speak out. As events moved on, the PA became highly critical of an agreement that exposed central problems of many ceasefire agreements in civil wars and other internal conflicts. What sanctions, other than resumption of hostilities, exist to deal with violations of the agreement? Do the parties still have incompatible aims? And can the state still survive in its old form?

The CFA was observed very unevenly, with violations on both sides – the SLMM and other reports indicating that the majority of violations were from the LTTE. The role of the SLMM proved to be difficult and controversial throughout its period of deployment – March 2002 to January 2008. On 3 January 2008 the government of Sri Lanka officially withdrew from the CFA. Subsequently there was a major and controversy-ridden assault on the LTTE strongholds. The LTTE was defeated in battle in May 2009.

Since 2009 criticism of the CFA and SLMM has continued. As a Norwegian report issued in November 2011 stated, some LTTE sympathizers blamed the Norwegians 'for being complicit in a process that weakened the rebel movement'; while among Muslim and Sinhala constituencies there was 'perceived Norwegian appeasement of the LTTE'.[2] *Within Sri Lanka a damning critique was included in the December 2011 report of the Lessons Learnt and Reconciliation Commission.*[3]

In this speech, delivered in May 2003 just 15 months after the CFA entered into force, Kadirgamar demonstrated his notable incisiveness in parliamentary debate and his enduring concern for Sri Lanka's unity and sovereignty. One issue raised towards the end of the speech concerns how the High Security Zones, which were close to the front lines between the belligerents, were being managed under the CFA. Kadirgamar expressed appreciation of the role played by the well-known Indian strategic expert, General Satish Nambiar, in addressing these zones, while at the same time he raised certain questions about Nambiar's work. A note written by General Nambiar in January 2010 is appended as a postscript.

*****

In January 2002 I had the privilege of opening the debate for the opposition on the prime minister's policy statement. On that occasion I said that the opposition would do nothing to disturb the peace process that was just being resumed. The new government must have time to settle in. We have kept that pledge. The prime minister was generous enough, during one of our routine consultations, to say so. I also said that the time will come when the substantive issues will have to be addressed. We reserved our opinion on those issues. That time has come. Hard issues have surfaced. They must be addressed. The opposition owes a duty to the people to raise them and address them.

Our contention is that from the very signing of the Ceasefire Agreement on 22 February 2002, the sovereignty of Sri Lanka has been steadily and visibly eroded to the point where Sri Lanka is in danger of being reduced to a nominal sovereign state. Soon Sri Lanka will be a sovereign shell: the major attributes of a sovereign state – the capacity to govern, to resolve justiciable issues, to enforce the law, to protect its citizens throughout the entirety of its territory – are being drained away by stealth, fractured by assault, and worn down by attrition. This process commenced with, and is being facilitated by, the CFA itself, a structurally flawed document whose imperfections have now been clearly revealed, and are being deeply felt, as the weeks and months go by. The prime minister himself recently said that the CFA is not a perfect document and that if he had striven for perfection there might have been no ceasefire at all. Yes, I agree. But if the prime minister had thought it fit to consult the president about the CFA before it was signed – which did not happen – some of those imperfections could have been removed, and a better balanced document drawn up, not only to serve the interests of the LTTE, but the interests of the nation as a whole. A bi-partisan approach to the problem could have been established at an early stage. However, while the prime minister was prepared to extend his trust and confidence unreservedly to the LTTE, even to the extent of dismantling, with unnecessary alacrity, the security structures that had been erected to protect the city of Colombo – the consequences of which the public are now beginning to understand – his government did not extend an iota of trust and confidence to the Head of State, the Head of Government, the Head of Cabinet and the Commander-in-Chief of the Armed Forces over the so-called peace process.[4] Instead, the government embarked upon a campaign of vituperative abuse against the president and harassment of Opposition supporters which receded only when it became clear that a two-thirds majority in parliament was not forthcoming for certain constitutional amendments.

Eight Flaws in the Agreement

Within a few days of the signing of the CFA, the president outlined in a letter to the prime minister some of the flaws in the Agreement.[5] They were as follows:

One, the question of naval operations. Article 1.2 of the CFA itemizes a number of prohibited military operations, including 'offensive naval operations'. Article 1.3 graciously permits the Sri Lanka Armed Forces to continue 'to perform their legitimate task of safeguarding the sovereignty and territorial integrity of Sri Lanka without engaging in offensive naval operations'.[6] How is the Navy to safeguard the sovereignty and territorial integrity of Sri Lanka if it is prohibited from engaging in offensive operations against the LTTE if required? If a suspicious ship approaches our shores laden with arms, defies challenge and inspection and opens fire on the Navy, and the Navy sinks that ship, is that a prohibited offensive operation? If not, is it a defensive operation? If it is a defensive operation, then what is an offensive operation? If the Navy gives chase in the open seas to an LTTE ship carrying arms, in exercise of the right of hot pursuit, to prevent it from landing those arms on our shores, is that an offensive or defensive operation? Why was this grey area created in the CFA? In the course of a statement made by the prime minister at Vavuniya on 22 February 2002 when he signed the CFA – Mr Prabhakaran having signed it the previous day in the presence of the Norwegian ambassador – he said: 'The Army, Navy and Air Force will have the right to intercept the illegal movement of arms into Sri Lanka.' What does 'intercept' mean? Could there be interception by offensive naval operations, in which case there is a contradiction between the CFA and the prime minister's statement? Why could not the prime minister's oral statement in Vavuniya have been incorporated into the CFA itself? Did the LTTE object? What was the Norwegian position on this issue? The prime minister's statement in Vavuniya being outside the CFA naturally does not bind the LTTE. Did the prime minister seriously believe that the LTTE could be trusted not to smuggle arms by sea into Sri Lanka, so that the meaning of the expression 'offensive naval operations' would never have to be tested?

Two, under Article 3.2 of the CFA if a dispute arises on a question involving the interception of illegal arms, for instance, what is an offensive naval operation? It will be the Head of the Monitoring Mission, a foreign national, who will be 'the final authority regarding interpretation of the Agreement'. Thus, the jurisdiction of the courts of Sri Lanka has been ousted on a question so vital to national security and the protection of the territorial integrity and sovereignty of Sri Lanka.

Three, Articles 1.4, 1.5 and 1.6 of the CFA deal with the drawing up of demarcation lines regarding defence localities in all areas of contention. The parties are required to provide information to the Monitoring Mission about their defence localities. In the event of disagreement between the parties, the demarcation lines will have to be drawn by the Head of the Monitoring Mission who is 'the final authority regarding interpretation of this Agreement'. Article 2.7 refers to the establishment of checkpoints, to facilitate the flow of goods and the movement of civilians, on the 'lines of control'. The 'line of control' is a highly evocative expression in our region and elsewhere in the world where lines of control and demarcation have been a source of confusion, bitterness and tragedy. Inevitably, a line of control becomes a line of division, of separation. This is the first time in the history of post-independence Sri Lanka that a foreign government has been authorized to draw demarcation lines on the soil of Sri Lanka. The submission of such matters to the binding authority of a single individual appointed by a foreign government is wholly inconsistent with the sovereignty of Sri Lanka which is vested in its people and is declared by the Constitution to be inalienable.

Four, the powers and functions which by this Agreement are vested in the Norwegian government travel far beyond the role of a facilitator of the envisaged negotiations towards a political agreement. The Norwegian government has now been cast in the role of a mediator or arbitrator, and the Monitoring Mission has been given the role of a judge, in the resolution of disputes between the parties which is not the basis on which Norwegian assistance was sought in the first place. The nature of the Norwegian government's mandate has changed to such an extent, its role has become so inflated, as to make it incompatible with the sovereign status of Sri Lanka.

Five, in the light of the verified evidence coming in from various LTTE-controlled areas, especially in the East, relating to extortion, intimidation, abduction and harassment of civilians, much of it against members of the Muslim community but extending also to the Tamil and Sinhalese communities in these areas, we surely have to ensure that our people are protected by the strict application of Article 2.1 of the CFA which expressly prohibits such acts. Among the six districts (Jaffna, Mannar, Vavuniya, Trincomalee, Batticaloa and Ampara) in which the Monitoring Mission maintains a presence and local monitoring committees have been established, Kilinochchi and Mullaitivu, which are LTTE-controlled, are not included. This means that if 'hostile acts against the civilian population including such acts as torture, intimidation, abduction, extortion and harassment', referred to in Article 2.1, are committed in these two districts the Monitoring Mission and the local committees cannot intervene to help our citizens who live in these areas. We have thus recognized and legitimized an enclave in those two areas where the government's writ does not run. What does this do to our sovereignty over the entirety of our territory?

Six, what about the plight of children forcibly recruited by the LTTE? This odious practice is continuing. The evidence gathered by the reputable national and international sources is irrefutable and depressing. Sri Lanka has been in the forefront of the international campaign against the conscription of child combatants. There are many treaties and international resolutions on this subject. This is a matter which gravely troubles the conscience of mankind. The LTTE has given to the United Nations, but disregarded in practice, assurances that they will not recruit under-age children. Can we, I ask the House, be so callous, so cynical that in the pursuit of peace we are willing to compromise the rights of these children, to condone the brutal treatment meted out to them and their parents?

Seven, the extensive freedom of movement for 'political work' in government-controlled areas in the North and the East granted to LTTE members under Article 1.13 is not afforded to others (political parties, for instance) who might wish to do 'political work' in LTTE-controlled areas in the North and the East. In a democratic society this is a totally indefensible distinction, violative of the Constitution, between one group of political parties and another. Democratic parties like the EPDP[7] which entered the main stream of national politics many years ago now find themselves at a considerable disadvantage in relation to the LTTE. Disarmed by the CFA they are at the mercy of the LTTE. They have lost a number of their cadres. The government appears to be unconcerned with these terrible violations of the CFA. Is the government unwilling or unable to help the EPDP to protect its cadres? Has the government abdicated its sovereign right, its duty, to bring the culprits to justice even if they be the LTTE?

Eight, this erosion of sovereignty to which I have referred must also be viewed against the backdrop of the significant omission in the Agreement of any reference to any assurance given that negotiations for a political settlement will be commenced by the parties by a fixed date and concluded by an agreed date. Even the apparent suspension of the authority of the state reflected in this document could lead to the accentuation of the movement towards secession on which the Agreement is singularly silent despite the innumerable 'confidence building measures' which have been explicitly stated with great particularity. In his statement to the House in January 2002 the prime minister said: 'After formalising the basic Agreement as regards peace talks, the talks should be held within a definite time frame between the government and the LTTE.' Nearly 15 months have passed. Where is the timeframe? It is nowhere in sight.

Eight Problems with the Naval Provisions of the CFA

The structural flaws in the CFA to which I referred at the opening of my speech are now being dramatically revealed as events unfold on the ground and at sea. The burning issue of the day is the question of the sea. In its so-called initial discussion paper the Head of the Nordic Monitoring Mission made a series of proposals which the opposition parties, in their press release of 25 April, have described as 'preposterous'. One of them was that 'in the spirit of the CFA the government of Sri Lanka, and especially its Navy, should recognize the LTTE Sea Tigers as a de facto naval unit.' Another was that 'the LTTE should be excluded from the law concerning limitations on the horse power of outboard motors.' Yet another was that 'the Sri Lanka Navy and the LTTE Sea Tigers should have specific marked exercise and training areas at sea, designed for navigation training and for live firing exercises as well.'

These propositions can be faulted on a number of grounds:

One, is it 'in the spirit of the CFA' that the LTTE should systematically smuggle arms into the country? If not, why should it be 'in the spirit of the CFA' that the Navy should recognize the LTTE as a de facto naval unit?

Two, the SLMM has cited the *Oxford English Dictionary* meaning of 'de facto' – that is, existing as a fact although it may not be legally accepted as existing – to justify its proposal. A criminal gang may exist as a fact. Does the police force have to 'recognize' it; and having 'recognized' it what is the police force expected to do – ignore it or pursue it and bring it to justice? The plain fact is that the LTTE naval unit is an illegal entity. No country in the world has two navies. To which country does the LTTE's naval unit belong? De facto recognition by a sovereign state of an illegal entity which mounts a challenge to the authority of the state itself is only a whisker away from the achievement of de jure status by that officially recognized illegal entity.

Three, when the CFA was entered into there were no areas marked out at sea for training exercises and live firing by the LTTE and the Navy. The Navy made no such concessions to the LTTE. The preservation of the balance of forces is said to be one of the principal concepts underlying the CFA. If that be so, does not the delimitation of these zones at sea disturb that balance?

Four, in any event, why should a sovereign state hand over to an illegal entity an exclusive zone that derogates from its own sovereignty? The real problem is that the government of the day is by its conduct, by its palpable anxiety to accommodate even the most unreasonable demands of the LTTE, encouraging the LTTE to believe that it is a legal entity with legal rights.

Five, even if the exercise and live firing areas are within our territorial waters, live firing will create serious practical problems. Indian fishing boats habitually enter our territorial waters in large numbers. What would happen if they enter the LTTE zone during live firing practice? There could be a major rupture in our relations with India, especially with Tamil Nadu. The Chief Minister of Tamil Nadu has clearly made known her deep concern that LTTE craft are capturing Indian fishermen. A shooting incident in an LTTE zone recognized by the government of Sri Lanka could have disastrous consequences on our relations with India and Tamil Nadu. Moreover, fishing craft belonging to other countries – China, Japan, South Korea – enter our waters on legitimate business. We must remember what recently happened to a Chinese trawler.[8] If the 'armed criminal gang unknown to Sri Lanka' which is said by the Head of the Monitoring Mission to be prowling our coastal waters enters the LTTE zone, will there be a shoot-out between these two illegal entities? We would then be encouraging gang warfare at sea.

Six, live firing could be with short-range or long-range weapons. The LTTE has 23 mm guns mounted on their naval craft with a range of 6 km. If these guns are fired within the exercise zone, the bullets could go beyond the zone and hit innocent ships fishing or cruising just outside our territorial waters.

Seven, we allow India to use our airspace above our territorial waters. When LTTE live firing is going on, are we to tell the Indian government that our airspace will be closed to them? Would this not be an unfriendly, hostile act towards a neighbour that has proscribed the LTTE?

Eight, when the CFA was entered into, the LTTE was limited to outboard motors of 40 horse power maximum. The Nordic proposal is that they be allowed the use of outboard motors of unlimited capacity. This will allow the LTTE legitimately to acquire inshore craft, gunboats, fast attack craft and offshore patrol craft which are used by blue water navies. During the British colonial period there was only one navy in our region. With the independence of India and Sri Lanka two navies emerged – the Indian and Sri Lankan. Now, is there to be a third navy with a licence to expand at will? Again, I ask the question to which sovereign state does that navy belong?

Our Navy Commander has reacted strongly to the Nordic proposals. He has said: 'The Sea Tiger arm of the LTTE is not a legitimate organization or force to carry weapons and ammunitions at sea according to international laws at sea, and also in the territorial waters of Sri Lanka which are controlled by the Sri Lanka Navy as per 1.7 of the CFA.' At the time the MOU was signed, says the Navy Commander:

> it was very clear that the Sri Lanka Navy was in total control of the sea and is the only legitimate force at sea. Hence, the issue of a de facto force is of no relevance. At the end of peace talks some day even if Federal status is given to the North and East, there will only be one navy and that is the Sri Lanka Navy, therefore excluding the Sea Tigers from the normal law of the country is unacceptable and out of the question.

The Monitors' proposal that the parties' vessels should be marked in accordance with the UN Convention on the Law of the Sea (1982) implies, according to the Navy Commander, that 'LTTE Sea Tigers are on a par with the Sri Lanka Navy which is not so. Therefore, the proposal is totally unacceptable.' As for the proposed confidence building measure that 'the Sri Lanka Navy and the LTTE Sea Tigers should permit observers from the other party on board their vessels while conducting exercises and training', the Navy Commander says, 'the proposal is not possible. Refraining from the violation of the CFA, while at sea off Iranativu on

17 July 2002 and Delft on 6 February 2003, by the LTTE itself would have been a confidence building measure between the parties.' With regard to the Nordic proposal that 'neither the SLN nor the LTTE Sea Tigers should conduct offensive or aggressive operations and movements at sea and that the minimum distance between the parties' vessels should be kept to one nautical mile', the Navy Commander says, 'the Sri Lanka Navy has the right to dominate, and to free movement, at sea because it has to safeguard the sovereignty and territorial integrity of the country and also in conformity with Article 1.3 of the CFA.' With regard to exercise and training areas, the Navy Commander says, 'the territorial waters and the contiguous zone up to the economic zone is under Sri Lanka Navy control. No other party can be allowed to conduct military training at sea since it is against the Constitution and sovereignty of the country and Article 1.3 of the CFA.'

The government, in presenting its response to the SLMM paper, modified the Navy Commander's response in several respects – important among them being the government's willingness to allow the LTTE to conduct training and to exercise within a designated area (which the Navy Commander was opposed to) but without the right to live firing. The SLMM's adjusted proposals return to its initial working paper. It delineates a training and exercise area for the LTTE with live firing rights, and prohibits both the SLN and the LTTE Sea Tigers from 'offensive or aggressive operations and movements at sea'.

The opposition has already made it clear in its press release of 25 April, and now reiterates its position on the floor of the House, that the opposition parties wholeheartedly support the Navy Commander in his opposition to the proposal of the Monitoring Mission with regard to status of the LTTE's Sea Tigers. The opposition has already stated, and now repeats, that it has no confidence in the competence and impartiality of the Monitoring Mission. The opposition proposes that the Monitoring Mission should be re-composed.

Security Zones on Land

I turn now to that other major security question of the day – the High Security Zones. The LTTE wants the Army to withdraw from these zones to accommodate internally displaced persons (IDPs). Major General Fonseka, the Northern Security Forces Commander, supported by the Army Commander, has said in a report last December that while appreciating the urgent need to resettle civilians in these zones, that process should go hand in glove with a de-escalation process agreed between the government and the LTTE; no risks should be taken to weaken the safety environment by making the zones vulnerable; and security can be relaxed only in stages – i.e. disarming the LTTE cadres and decommissioning of LTTE long-range weapons. The Ministry of Defence has confirmed that the 152 Army camps in the Peninsula have been reduced to 88.[9]

The government has hired the services of a retired Indian General, General Nambiar, to advise it on security matters. In his report of last December he has said that SLA commanders in the field, as also at headquarters, appear to be unanimous in the firm conviction that if civilians are allowed unrestricted re-entry in these areas, LTTE cadres would infiltrate, establish their control even if only covertly in the initial stages, and seriously compromise the ability of the Army to conduct operations should the peace process break down. Any vacation of these areas is therefore perceived as dereliction of their responsibility towards the troops and the country's security. Therefore, General Nambiar has proposed that as things stand it would appear that any review of the scope and content of the High Security Zones will only come about if the LTTE deposits its weapons to neutral supervision and initiates measures to withdraw from front-line positions into nominated areas. Such a step would provide a measure of reassurance to the SLA that surprise LTTE attacks may be discounted. Similarly, there would need to be some reassurance that there would be no coercion of civilians and officials by LTTE cadres given access to areas on dismantling of the zones.

General Nambiar in his first report has completely supported General Fonseka's position. Indeed, the last Head of the SLMM also stated, supporting General Fonseka, that during a ceasefire the balance of forces should not be disturbed, that if the Army were to withdraw from the zones it would place the Army at a disadvantage. General Nambiar has also said significantly that there are rumours that in a federal structure the LTTE might be allowed a separate army. He says: 'In my view any such rumour should be scotched at this very stage by the prime minister or minister of defence making it absolutely clear that no matter what constitutional system is finally agreed upon there can be only one Army for the country, namely the Sri Lanka Army.' Those are the words of General Nambiar.

For some mysterious reason the government commissioned General Nambiar to prepare a second report even before the first report had been discussed with the relevant security authorities. I understand that the second report is ready. General Nambiar has returned to Colombo. Between the two reports General Nambiar has been visited more than once by important government personalities. If there are any substantial changes in the second report, serious questions will arise. General Nambiar is not the representative of the government of India. He is a private consultant engaged by our government in his private capacity.[10]

Sri Lanka's Sovereignty

Sri Lanka has become a carnival ground for international players, a sort of hawkers street for foreign experts peddling their wares. Do we really need foreign experts to advise us on how to protect the territorial integrity and sovereignty of the state? Surely, our own service commanders, native to the soil, know best what needs to be done.

What we in the opposition say to these worthy experts – there are many from different nationalities, who come to advise the government – is this: 'Please remember gentlemen, that the Sovereignty of Sri Lanka is precious to us, its citizens, to the Members of this House, to our people. It may be a plaything in the hands of others, to us it is not a marketable commodity; it is not negotiable; it cannot be compromised.' If any of these expert reports make recommendations that impinge on our sovereignty, we of the opposition will be duty bound by the people to denounce such reports whoever the author may be. Remember he who pays the piper calls the tune.

The prime minister in his statement referred to a 'safety net of the international community' and 'a firm expression of views by our friendly countries including the United States, UK, Japan, France and India'. They have certainly made – and with the US and India, in particular, strongly made, statements in support of our territorial integrity and sovereignty. The US has warned the LTTE that it must renounce violence, abandon the notion of a separate state and embrace the concept of a plural society if it is to gain international legitimacy and acceptance. Is it not a great shame that our government has never made a statement of that nature? How does the government expect other countries to uphold our sovereignty when it is shy of doing so itself? But what is this safety net? The prime minister must tell the House what it is. It is important for the House to know. Are there any secret understandings? Will an aircraft carrier come our way if hostilities break out again?

The prime minister has said that in consultation with all parties the government will proceed to develop a 'road map' towards the objective of devolution and that it is open to wide-ranging discussions on many issues – the core issues. We seem to have heard that before. Is it true? If so, it is welcome. The hour is late but not too late to make the process of consultation wider and more inclusive, which it is not at the moment. In the meantime I have to say the opposition is of the view that we are moving inexorably towards the day when Sri Lanka will no longer be a sovereign state.

Postscript: General Satish Nambiar's Work in Sri Lanka in 2002–3

In January 2010 General Satish Nambiar, in an email exchange with Adam Roberts, provided the following information for this book.

*****

I had the privilege of meeting Lakshman Kadirgamar one-on-one for about an hour during my last visit to Sri Lanka in 2003. I recall telling him of being deeply hurt at suggestions made by some of his party members that I was manipulating my report. I also told him that what I was doing was not for remuneration because I had not received a single rupee for the work I did. (Nor have I received any remuneration since.) His disarming response was typical of him: that I should allow for the politics of the situation where the parties will use any means to put the ruling dispensation on the defensive.

I was never 'commissioned' or 'hired' to render advice. Some time in July or August 2002 I was contacted by colleagues in the Indian establishment who informed me that the government of Sri Lanka was looking for a senior retired Indian Army officer to advise them on some aspects of concern. Having conveyed my tentative consent, a meeting with Minister Milinda Moragoda (a close colleague of Prime Minister Wickremesinghe) was arranged. We met in New Delhi in August 2002. He asked me whether I would undertake a trip to Colombo in the first week of September 2002 to meet the prime minister. I did so, and was requested by the prime minister to provide him with some suggestions on 'officer management' in the Sri Lanka Armed Forces. There was no formal commissioning.

I made four visits to Sri Lanka in context of the work I did in an advisory capacity. They were on 1–7 September 2002, 9–14 December 2002, 1–8 February 2003 and the last (to the best of my recollection) at the end of April 2003.

After the first visit, I submitted some preliminary observations on the subject of 'officer management' as desired by Prime Minister Ranil Wickremesinghe. This was followed up with a more detailed set of observations and recommendations in Part One of a report I submitted after my visit in December 2002. In Part Two of that report I made some preliminary observations on the subject of the 'High Security Zones' that Prime Minister Wickremesinghe had requested me to address when I met him in his office on 9 December 2002 soon after arrival in Colombo for the second visit. During that meeting he also requested me to 'give some preliminary thought to measures in the long term for rehabilitation of LTTE cadres and/or their absorption into the armed forces, police, etc'. Part Three of the report contained a couple of paragraphs on this aspect.

In early January 2003, as a consequence of developments at a meeting with LTTE representatives in Bangkok, my involvement in addressing the aspect of the 'High Security Zones' apparently became public. I was requested to undertake a third visit in order to study this specific aspect in greater depth and come up with some detailed recommendations as, in the words of Prime Minister Wickremesinghe 'on this sensitive aspect, it was not possible to analyse objectively within the system'. There was nothing 'mysterious' about this approach, in my view. During the visit in early February 2003, I held detailed discussions with the then defence secretary, the heads of the Army, Navy and the Air Force, commanders in the field in the North and East, senior police and intelligence officials, members of civil society including pro-LTTE Tamil leaders in Jaffna, pro-government Tamil leaders in Colombo, some leading members of the Muslim community, the Bishop of Mannar, etc. I also visited operational areas in the Jaffna, Trincomalee and Batticaloa sectors and had briefings from and discussions with subordinate commanders. I held detailed discussions with the head of the SLMM and his subordinates in the various sectors, the head of ICRC, the head of UNHCR and the then Norwegian ambassador in Colombo. I had very wide-ranging discussions and interaction during the February visit. My report on this visit set out in some considerable detail the points that were made by various interlocutors and my observations and recommendations, including on some operational aspects. The report was well received by the prime minister.

At the request of the prime minister, I visited Colombo in end April 2003. At which time besides thanking me for my efforts, he asked me to provide him with an extract of my report containing only the observations and recommendations on the 'High Security Zones'. This was apparently in order to make that part of the report public (which was done soon thereafter). For obvious reasons my complete report could not have been made public as it contained aspects that were discussed with me confidentially by many interlocutors as also some sensitive operational matters.

I was requested by the prime minister to make another visit to Colombo in mid-May 2003 to personally brief President Chandrika Kumaratunga. In the event, that did not happen as some personal commitments came up, and soon thereafter the talks with the LTTE broke down. I have not been associated with any of the developments in Sri Lanka since, nor have I had any interaction with the political or military leadership in that country.

DOCUMENT 10

Third World Democracy in Action: The Sri Lanka Experience

Brookings Institution, Washington DC, 12 May 2004

This address by Foreign Minister Kadirgamar, given during his visit to Washington DC on 9–13 May 2004, was at an event co-sponsored by the Brookings Institution and the School of Advanced International Studies (SAIS) of Johns Hopkins University.

Of the many issues he tackles, three stand out: first, the operations of democracy in Sri Lanka, one of the few states to maintain a multi-party system in the decades following European decolonization; secondly, the need to find a settlement of Sri Lanka's long-running internal conflict, and the role of outside countries in that process; and thirdly, his view, expressed both clearly and tactfully, that the US-led invasion of Iraq, which had commenced in March 2003, had been a mistake.

This meeting included a Q & A session which is not reproduced here. A short extract from the transcript appears at the end of Chapter 1 in this volume.

*****

Sri Lanka has just come through a parliamentary general election. Other countries are in the process of going through their elections. The result of the Indian election will be known tomorrow. The Philippines election is probably over. I don't know what the result is and, of course, there is the election looming in the United States. This seems to be election season among the democratic countries of the world. The interesting thing about elections in democratic countries is that there is a great deal of commonality irrespective of the size of the country concerned, its power, its wealth, its influence in the world. There are many, many features that are common to the way the democratic system works.

Democracy, it has been said by Winston Churchill, is probably the worst form of government possible, but there isn't a better one. We in the Third World have constantly to assess democracy with all its faults, its difficulties, its drawbacks and its slowness. It does ensure to the ordinary person security, freedom of association, human rights, pluralism and so on. That's on the one hand, with democracy. On the other hand, you have a degree of inefficiency, and particularly in Third World countries, the democratic system is not the most dynamic vehicle for economic reform. Then you have dictatorships, which are often very successful. After all, in

Mussolini's Italy, the trains always ran on time. However, the price you pay for economic success is very often a lack of individual freedom. Now, what does one do between these two concepts?

Within the democratic world itself, I am in no doubt whatsoever that there is simply no substitute for democracy despite all its problems. For one reason, if for no other, and that is that the people of the country do have a genuine possibility of overturning a government, when they feel that the government is no longer responsive to their needs. That is a huge power in the hands of ordinary people. The contrast is obvious. You can have a dictator in power endlessly and there is no possibility of getting him out except by the cold-blooded means of assassination or something of that kind. Sri Lanka clearly falls into the category of countries which believe that democracy is absolutely essential, and there is no substitute for it. We have been free throughout our 56 years of any serious attempt to overthrow the democratic system. *Coups d'état* have not really flourished. Some have been born, but they have died in a few hours.[1] Today, democracy is very firmly rooted indeed. None of us who have been in politics or who have been observers of the political scene for a long time, can visualize a situation in which the ordinary people, the mass of the people, will give up their very cherished right to vote. They guard it, and they use it.

In India, where the numbers are on a staggering scale, we have some 600 million people voting across the sub-continent. The poorest among the poor walk 10 or 15 km to cast their vote. This happens in Sri Lanka, too, although on a much smaller scale. At the recently concluded election, voter turnout was nearly 80 per cent, a turnout that has been pretty average for Sri Lanka over the years.

Electoral Reform – an Urgent Need

We have a multiparty system. We have basically two major parties, and a number of smaller parties. The smaller parties over the years have tended to be delineated on the basis of race or religion, religion to a lesser extent, but certainly you get ethnic parties. More recently we have begun to get used to the idea that coalition politics has come to stay, because the Constitution of Sri Lanka from 1978, the present second Republican Constitution, brought in proportional representation as the means by which members of parliament are elected. The Constitution did away with the first-past-the-post principle, which had the advantage of giving the winning party a large majority. Under that system, governments were elected with two-thirds majorities more than once, but also it denied to smaller parties, and particularly ethnic groups, adequate representation in parliament. So the balance that was struck was proportional representation as against first-past-the-post.

We in politics today, as well as the great majority of our people, have realized after 25 or more years of the present Constitution that the proportional representation system as it stands, is unworkable, unfair and, in fact, wholly preventive of a working majority being assured to the winning party. I do not think this is a good thing. Because whoever wins must have a working majority for its allotted span in office. Moreover, proportional representation is leading to a lot of intra-party fighting.

Candidates for all the parties are probably more concerned about winning a preferential vote. The voter has a right first to vote for the party of his choice, and then he or she can select three people on the party list. Having voted for one party, he cannot cross the party list, and vote for a preferred candidate in another list. So you have a great deal of competition, money being spent, violence being unleashed, by candidates fighting among themselves for preference votes. A candidate will go to a voter's house and say please vote for my party, but don't vote for this man who is Number 3 on the list – from his own party. He is followed half an hour later by somebody else who says vote for my party but don't vote for the other man. All of us are now convinced that this is very unhealthy; very unhealthy, indeed, and I think we are all looking forward to reform.

It is very likely that if reform comes, it would be on lines similar to the German model, with half the parliament elected on the basis of first-past-the-post, and the other half, on a configuration which affords a degree of protection for the minority parties so that their opinions could be reflected on the basis of proportional representation. The need for such reform is very pressing, is very urgent.

Our People, Our Masters

In a democracy, at election time, certainly the people are masters. The people in a democracy, and this happens all over the world, this is one of the commonalities, the people have a habit of fooling their rulers. They lead the rulers to believe that they are going to vote one way and when the vote is published you find that they have done something exactly opposite. I think this is a wonderful weapon that they have in their hands. Because they constantly resort to this weapon and that precious piece of paper which they have in their hand is indeed a very important weapon to remind their rulers that come election time, you are accountable.

The voter says in effect that all the promises you made four years ago or five years ago are going to come home to roost and, believe me, in Sri Lanka as in all the other democracies in the world, which have been practicing democracy for a long time, the voter is very astute. He knows far more than the politician credits him with, and in our country, where literacy is almost at 90 per cent, the average voter is very well informed. Informed about what? He knows what, as far as he is concerned, is best for him or her. He is not interested in the great theories of democracy and politics and philosophy that are put before him from time to time. He knows very well what he wants, what kind of government he wants, what kind of rulers he wants.

That is why it is very necessary for all of us in the democratic community to respect the verdict given by the people in other democratic states. That is very, very important. Anybody who tends to give opinions during election campaigns from outside the country, about whether this party or that is better for the country, is treading on dangerous ground. I will give you two examples of what happened in our election recently.

During the campaign, a senior diplomat from a certain country which I obviously cannot name but from a developed country, a very influential country, said – and this was banner headlines in a newspaper – that he hoped that the people of Sri Lanka would vote for a stable and responsible government. The clear implication being that the people of Sri Lanka might well decide collectively to vote for an irresponsible government. Now this caused very deep offence. The national reaction was who on earth is this man to tell us what responsibility is against irresponsibility. As it happened, we know very well where his preference lay, and the people voted for the government which in his opinion was the irresponsible government. I hope that that kind of person will realize that opinions of that kind are best left unexpressed.

By contrast, Secretary of State Colin Powell wrote to me immediately after our election, congratulating me on my second term in office, actually it's my third term, and he said 'I wish to assure you of full US government support for Sri Lanka's new government. We share common goals for Sri Lanka, lasting peace and prosperity for the country. The US firmly supports the peace process in Sri Lanka and it is my profound desire to work with you and your government as you engage constructively with the Liberation Tigers of Tamil Eelam (LTTE) to reinvigorate the peace process. I hope that you will be able to visit Washington soon' – which is what I am doing at the moment – 'and the United States remains convinced the political solution to the conflict based on democracy, human rights and respect for all ethnic groups within a united Sri Lanka can be achieved. We look forward to this accomplishment.'

This was said after statements made on many occasions during the campaign by the US government making it very clear that they would respect the verdict of the people and work with any government that came to office. To my mind, that is a very clear way, an example of what should be said and what should not be said, and what the correct attitudes are in this kind of question of who should decide what shape a government should take in some other country.

Listen to the Messages

At this last election, as I said, there was a turnout of nearly 80 per cent and the winning party polled 45.6 per cent of the vote. The next largest party in parliament polled 37.83 per cent. Those statistics apart, there were some features which I think I ought to highlight.

Contrary to what many people thought, even Sri Lankans themselves, the election was remarkably peaceful. I say 'remarkably' because in the past, they have not been particularly peaceful. In fact, the contrast between the 2001 parliamentary elections and this one lies very much in this direction. The run up to the election of 2001 was not at all peaceful, and it was massively violent after the election, which was a great setback to the cohabitation process that the people had launched at the 2001 election.

This time it was very clear that the people not only conducted themselves superbly well but they were not going to be stirred and manipulated or manoeuvred into launching violence. They made, in my opinion, a very clear and conscious choice to refrain from violence and, therefore, it made the task of the Police very much easier than it has been in many years. That, in my opinion, and it is opinion of many others, friends all over the world, is a huge victory for democracy, and mark you, this is at a time of turbulence. There is still a war, which is not yet finished. It is in abeyance, but there is violence around us of various kinds. But that kind of violence did not spill over into this election, except that – and it is my duty to say so, but I only mention it and stop at a certain point – there is doubt as to whether the election in the North and the East of Sri Lanka was free and fair. I cannot say more because the matter is presently before the Courts and you will understand that I will have to observe the principle of *sub judice*.

This election sent out certain messages. It is not always possible to read accurately the voices in which the people speak but those who have ears to listen and keep those ears to the ground usually get it right. Quite often the press does not get it right. Very often the ruling party does not get it right at all, and that is the mistake that all ruling parties tend to make, and that is the lesson which people regularly administer to the ruling parties – don't take us for granted. Come polling day, we may have a surprise or two in store for you. They did that this time.

This time, a number of new parties emerged on our political scene, parties which hadn't been in parliament before or hadn't been widely represented before. The most significant of those parties is the party of Buddhist monks. Let me say in parenthesis that Sri Lanka, previously known as

'Ceylon', has been engaged in the democratic process since 1931. We were given universal adult franchise by the British in 1931, long before India. There are reasons behind that, but I can't go into all that now. So women had the vote in 1931, whereas in Switzerland, I believe, women received the right to vote only in 1971. So we have been practising democracy for a long time. Long before we became independent in 1947, we had a State Council, we had a functioning multiparty system for many years before that. So the voting habit has been deeply ingrained. But up to now the electoral process or political forces did not throw up a party of Buddhist monks or monks of any kind.

For in 1956, when there was a kind of social revolution launched by one of the parties, which is today the party, the major party in office, monks played a role certainly in campaigning and so on, and they were influential but never did they seek to enter parliament. In the last parliament, that is between 2001 and 2004, there was one monk who was elected through a Marxist party. But this time, we have a party which has sent nine monks to parliament and they have collectively polled some 500,000 votes, which is big for us. None of them won a seat in his own right but under the proportional representation system if a party polls a certain number of votes then by arithmetical calculation it gets a certain number of seats depending on the district where it gathered those votes. Therefore, although they did not win a single electorate (a 'district', in American parlance), they gathered enough votes to send nine MPs to parliament. Now this is undoubtedly a unique and a very interesting phenomenon in our politics. Nobody knows today how this is going to work out.

The monks have a lot of adjusting to do, not least, on the social side because when they sat in parliament for the first time on 22 April, there was no white cloth provided for them to sit on, which is a traditional courtesy extended to the monks. It was discussed, but the Secretary-General of parliament decided that they had to now accept the fact that they were just MPs like anybody else. On the day of the election of the Speaker, you had a situation where the Secretary-General, a lady, was controlling the proceedings before the Speaker was elected, and they were particularly heated proceedings because a number of ballots had to be cast before the Speaker was found. And you found suddenly this lady Secretary-General telling monks to sit down. Now, in the Buddhist world, you know what that means.

All of us who were observing the scene were obviously speculating in our minds, what does this portend? In one sense it's a huge kind of social revolution. When the monks got up to speak, some of them made statements that were slightly outside the kind of parliamentary acceptance where you have to be a little careful of what you say and you cannot assume that your position is going to guarantee to you respect. I think the monks felt that that was going to be the case. But, of course, they were howled down and that came as a severe blow to them. But, of course, it might well mean that their education is going to be very much quicker than they thought it might be, as far as parliamentary life is concerned. So we have to see how all these things work out, how they take positions on political issues. They entered politics on the basis that they wanted to help to establish a just government. I think they came on the basis they would be tutors and monitors. But in the hurly burly of our politics and indeed anywhere in the world, you cannot carve out a role for yourself. The roles are going to be thrust on you by the forces that prevail at that time. So we will have to watch this carefully and see how this is going to work out.

The JVP gets new role

Then we found that the Janatha Vimukthi Peramuna (JVP), which was a Marxist party with a rather bloody history of insurgencies – there were two of them over the last 30 years – has significant representation in parliament.[2] They first came to parliament in 1994 with one member, and there again on proportional representation, because of the number of votes they polled, although they did not actually win a seat. In 2000, their tally had gone up to 10. In the election of 2001, because that parliament of 2000 collapsed in a year, they went up to 16 and today, in the election of 2004, they have gone up to 39, which when you come to think of it, is a very remarkable progression for a party that was way out on the fringe, and is now in the mainstream.

What this demonstrates is that the people in large numbers – they polled a million or more votes – have decided that their past must be forgotten, and they must be given a chance to prove their worth in a democratic establishment. They are being taken at face value when they say that they are part of the mainstream, and they will soon be tested. They will be put to work. They have four portfolios in this government and are in charge of key ministries – Agriculture, Land, Fisheries and Culture. This covers a vast area of our rural life, and they will have a lot of work to do to prove themselves. I watched their performance very carefully between 1994 and, particularly, between 2000 and 2001, when they had ten seats and after that, 16 seats. I can say very, very clearly, to their credit, that they have very quickly learnt the art of survival in parliament – that is, in terms of rules and procedures.

They have mastered the Standing Orders. They can debate a point on the floor of the House with the best. Their performance in parliament is characterized by solid homework, no unnecessary duplication, and one speaker at a time. They obviously consult each other very carefully and all the evidence of discipline and hard work is there. Whether you like them or not is another matter. They have been put there by the people. They have not been parachuted by any other means. They have earned their votes, and now they are in government. Being in opposition is one thing, being in government is another entirely.

Being in government for the first time they face a different proposition. Most of the other parties have been in and out of government. So there is a residue of institutional experience. The JVP is in government for the first time. I wish to say very, very clearly here in Washington this evening that these JVP parliamentarians, they now have 39 seats, are already showing all the signs of being competent. Their approach to politics and to administration is very sound indeed. A small example just to start with. They are very punctual, and often I have had meetings with them where the other parties did not turn up on time, but they arrived two minutes before time. I have therefore often said to myself I must start with them as a compliment to them, I can't wait for the late comers.

Then, they know what they are about; they are full of ideas, full of plans. Some of them may not be practical; they may not be realistic. They are bringing some of these plans from books and they have to test them with ground realities. But there is dedication, commitment and a great degree of idealism.

We have been saying in Sri Lankan politics for a long time that the two major parties seem to be tired. They have become flabby and they have, to varying extents, been very corrupt and inefficient. The vote this time is a very clear indication from the people at large, for what they are really saying is: a plague on both your houses. Both the major parties have lost, in a sense, one more than the other. But both have lost. The people said clearly, we are giving these people 39 seats, which they did not expect. The best of them did not expect more than 25. As I indicated, this is where the people have this wonderful habit of fooling everybody. They have said, now we are putting you in, and we are putting the two major parties on notice and you are being punished. The JVP is going to be given a chance. So let us see how they perform. I have no doubt whatsoever, if they don't measure up, they in turn will be punished by the very people who put them in office.

That is one of the wonderful things about democracy. I am all in favour of that – the power to throw your rulers out. I remember being asked after the election that you all are really talking of putting everything right and new ideas, new goals, no corruption. And what happens if you don't measure up, and my unhesitating answer was – please throw us out. You must do that. That is your prerogative, you must exercise it. Throw us out as quickly as you can. That is the spirit in which I would like to see Sri Lankan politics developing at this rather critical juncture because there has been a change in the whole line up of parties.

One-issue Agenda

I now come to the Tamil National Alliance (TNA), which is an Alliance of a number of Tamil parties.[3] It is commonly known that they are a proxy of the LTTE. The LTTE did not stand for election. They did not stand at all but they heavily supported this Alliance which has 22 votes in a House of 225. That is a lot of votes and, therefore, the leverage they are going to exercise will be quite considerable. But now, they too, have come into parliament, virtually with a one-issue agenda: self-determination, by whatever name, for the Tamil speaking people in the North and East and, to implement the LTTE's agenda.

When you enter parliament with a one-issue agenda, then you have to be rather careful how you use your voting block. Because, soon they will confront the need to make choices on issues which do not involve the one they are concerned with. There will be a lot of issues on which parties will have their party stand and there will be issues on which all parties are neutral until the issue arises. So, a one-issue-agenda party is going to have to make a number of choices as we go along the road. So we are going to see this development take place as the months go by.

Don't Neglect Basic Needs

Another very key message delivered by the people was something I touched on a moment ago – remember the basic needs of the people. You can have all your fancy economic strategies, all the complicated World Trade Organization (WTO) negotiations, and this that and the other. But remember, we are at the bottom of the heap and ultimately we call the shots. And I think the message delivered this time was if you live in a wishful, fancy world, in a dream world, then you are going to realize that if you neglected our basic needs you are going to be just diced and that I think is what happened. The message is coming through very clearly, whatever you may do on the international front and so on, remember the basic needs of the people in a poor country – that is, the cost of living, unemployment, housing.

Remember, too, that our rural economy is by far the larger section of our economy. More people are engaged in the rural economy than in the urban economy or any other kind of industrialized economy and therefore the message is very clear: you have to do something quickly to uplift the rural economy – that is, small and medium enterprises, agriculture, intermediate technologies that reach out and down to the people, fisheries and all those things.

So we are in for a time when you will find I think, a very conscious shift in policy where we put the rural economy and all its adjuncts at the top of our list. That does not mean that we don't live in the modern world. Obviously it means that you have to cope with globalization, and the WTO, the International Financial Institutions and all that. But we have to get our priorities right and what this government will have to do, very early, and it is bent on doing, whether it succeeds or not only time will tell, is precisely that. Look to the people and give the people a friendly hand.

Towards Peace

I will say a word now about the peace negotiation. Let me just pick out one or two facts. The peace negotiations broke down in about April 2003. It was the LTTE which walked out of the peace negotiations, for one reason or another: one is never sure what the real reason was. It looks as though, at least one of the reasons might well have been that six rounds of negotiations, which the LTTE spokesman at one stage dismissed as a waste of time, obviously in their view did not bring any relief to the ordinary people of the North and the East. I think that this is an incontestable fact. What happened is that there was a mismatch between all the theorizing, all the posturing, the constitutional theories and everything else – and forgetfulness about ordinary people and their basic needs. The LTTE like any organization, be it democratic or not, is ultimately accountable to the people, in the areas in which they live. If they lose the support of their people, even a guerrilla movement cannot function. And they are very sensitive to that I think. Well, they walked out and a year has gone by.

Now it may well be they have realized that if they take themselves out of the loop, then, it is not very likely that they will get the kind of international financial assistance they require, and everybody requires, to begin the huge task of rebuilding an absolutely devastated part of our country – the North and the East – devastated by two decades of war. Rebuilding simply has to be done. While we debate fancy theories on constitutional law and all that, if once again, we all collectively make the mistake of forgetting that there are poor people there, who have to sometimes walk 10 or 15 km to a medical dispensary just to get an aspirin, and medical facilities are woefully absent, schools have been destroyed, wells and sanitation don't exist, we are going to have an even greater accumulation of problems than those we have seen so far. I think the LTTE has probably realized this, and the indications are that they would like to begin the talks again, and put in the forefront the question of rehabilitation and reconstruction.

The vehicle they have chosen for this is a set of proposals which are called the Internal Self-Governing Authority (ISGA) Proposal. These proposals were put forward late last year. The ISGA Proposal contains a number of provisions which on their face, would be very difficult for any government to accept because they are so far-reaching. For instance, there is no reference to parliament in those proposals, no reference to Sri Lanka's Supreme Court. There is a desire to have an unelected Interim Council for a certain number of years giving a dominant role to the LTTE; there is a claim for a 200-mile economic zone on the North and the East coastal area of Sri Lanka, which is two-thirds of the coast. A number of claims like that for a separate Auditor General, separate number of things which add up to possibly, in the view of many, to a blueprint for a future separate state.

Time for Compromise

I think what's going to happen, but I may well be hopelessly wrong, is that these proposals will have to be discussed. They are on the table. There has been some mischief-making about the LTTE reportedly saying: take it or leave it and we are not coming to the table unless you accept these proposals in advance. That is absolutely not so. They have categorically not said that. There is a lot of media mischief being created in certain quarters on that point. So the issue now is, a discussion will take place. Every one of these clauses will have to be argued one by one. And a contrary view will be put. The contrary view is already in the public domain and while all that is going on, it will be a hard long arduous negotiation.

I was saying just today to Secretary of State Powell and Deputy Secretary Richard Armitage that the time has come for horns to be locked. In the wider interest of everybody, one cannot merely skirt issues any longer. It is very necessary to get down to the basics, talk about it, argue about it and see how far you are going to get. Shadow boxing, I think, must stop. It is not helping anybody. If there are tough issues, let us take them head-on. For there are very few issues in the world of politics, international or domestic, which elude solution when they are seriously talked about. Compromise is very much the mechanism that is used internationally and nationally for the solution of problems. So I think negotiations about the ISGA proposal and other matters are going to be approached in that spirit.

The date for restarting talks, to my mind, is a question that will not be answered, even if it is asked. When I am asked that question, my answer is, what does it matter what the date is? Is it not far more important that the parties concerned should be ready, comfortable, have done their homework, and don't waste time shadow boxing when talks resume? It may be better to let a little time elapse. After all, everybody has to gear up again after a year of stoppage. I would say it does not greatly matter when, as long as the interest is maintained, the engagement is maintained.

The Norwegians are back on the scene at the invitation of the new government and they will be facilitators. They will be encouraged to try and make their role a little less high-profile than it was before. Because when a foreigner comes in a high-profile role, we would tend to stir up a lot of resentment among ordinary people who then get very suspicious about what's happening. When they are not told what's happening, they have to make their judgments on photo opportunities, and all that kind of thing. That is not a good state of affairs. So I am hoping that we will learn from the lessons of the past and begin to manage this in a much more low-key manner. Serious, but low-key.

US Consistency

International participation in the peace process is there. It won't go away. But in my view, the internationalization of our process has gone a little bit too far, and there again you are getting a backlash from the people. It was an issue in the election. Pre-election polls showed that clearly there was suspicion and resentment about too many people running around, about what they were actually up to and what are their agendas. These are all legitimate questions in a democracy. So I think, while we greatly appreciate solid support from friends and, in this connection, let me say – not because I am in America, I have said this often in many countries – that the US attitude to the question of what they could do has been characterized by consistency, adherence to a certain set of principles and no departure from those principles in the name of expediency.

The principles they have affirmed frequently is that there can be no solution which does not take into account the territorial integrity, unity and sovereignty of the country. So there is no question of a separate state. Pluralism, human rights and democracy must be built into any solution. The rights and aspirations of all the communities in the country must be accommodated as best as possible. I have no doubt that the government of the US will continue with this constructive and helpful approach.

Governments may change but with major powers like the US there is a degree of consistency and continuity which I know very well. What was reiterated during my meetings with senior officials of this administration was that faces don't really matter. It is the principles and policies and institutional acceptance of a policy that really matters. The message I received from Secretary Powell was that the US government would fully support the government of Sri Lanka that has newly come to office in its endeavours to solve this problem. That is the correct way to look at it, and I have no doubt that that is how it will be looked at.

Confronting Terrorism

I am very much open to questions on any topic you choose. Before that, I do like to say a word on two matters that have been in the air for a long time. One is the question of terrorism. Now Sri Lanka as you all know is a victim country. As far as terrorism is concerned, long before that terrible day 9/11, there was a time when I used to go to the capitals of the world and knock on doors and present my case for some action to be taken by the world community, to help us to combat the terrorism that was unleashed on us, and I would only get polite answers. Everybody was sorry at what was happening, but they did not have laws, they said, to deal with foreign terrorists on their soil. They would commiserate, but do nothing more. There was a tremendous change on the world scene, however, when terrorism became an international phenomenon.

I remember the turning point very, very clearly. It was in 1997 when there was a rash of bombings in Europe, in Paris, in Manchester, in the US, in Japan, and suddenly people realized that terrorism is not somebody else's problem. It is not a problem that you glimpsed through your window when your neighbour's house was burning some distance away and you said, poor man what can I do? I used to say in those days, don't be too complacent because terrorism is on our doorstep today; it will be on your doorstep tomorrow. Looking back I do not want to blow my own trumpet about being prophetically right but inexorably that is what has happened. Terrorism has now become everybody's problem. The moment that happens there is no question about it, everybody has to get together and go to the aid of whoever is in distress at a particular point of time.

In this connection I would like to read you a passage from a speech I made in Warsaw in June 2000, that is a clear year before 9/11. At a ministerial conference on the theme 'Towards a community of democracies', I said:

> A democracy standing alone cannot possibly survive a sustained terrorist onslaught because democracy is vulnerable. It is fundamentally constrained, limited by the demands of democratic practice and tradition. A democracy even at a time of war has to remember the rule of law, the freedom of the press and all those requisites of a practising democracy. How then do we fight? How then do we survive? My plea is a very simple one. . . . Please do not forget that unless the democracies of the world stand together and fight together and always come to the aid of a member in peril, democracy will not survive. A challenge to democracy anywhere in the world is a challenge to democracy everywhere. The great liberal democracies must wake up to the fact that it is their duty to come to the aid of a democracy in peril in practical ways. With moral support yes, words and declarations, yes, but also by a demonstration of political will that sends a message to the terrorists of the world that their days are numbered and there will be no succour, no solace, no safe haven, no place to hide, nowhere to run, for the terrorists of the world when all of us, the democratic states, will stand together and fight together.

That was in June 2000. Today I would not wish to change a single word of that paragraph.

Friends and Admirers

Finally I want to say something about America and the American people. We in the democratic community truly watched with great distress and we truly share the anguish of the American people, when something terrible happens to them, as with 9/11 and even with the events of today. There are many of us all over the world who do not gloat over the failures of American foreign policy and here I can tell you I am speaking as a Foreign Minister of almost nine years. Starting on a third term, I have seen a lot of these things happen, and my own thinking in matters of this kind has developed greatly over the years. Let me therefore refer to a speech I made in New Delhi in August 2003. It was a memorial address in memory of a famous Indian correspondent Prem Bhatia. The Iraq war had started and it had certainly had not got to the stage at which it is today. The speech was a difficult one for me to make. It was on the theme 'The World Order After Iraq', and I was very conscious of the fact that I had been Foreign Minister for seven years, I was out of office, but I was still the Senior Advisor to the President of Sri Lanka on Foreign Affairs. I accepted the challenge of the speech but it gave me a great deal of trouble I can tell you. I knew that I would have to walk on eggshells all the time. But I chose not to duck it. It took me a good month or two to prepare that speech.[4]

I made a rather firm critical analysis of the invasion of Iraq and I came out on the side of saying that US and Britain had made a mistake. But this is what I said about the American people, and I would like to close on that note:

> I wish at this stage to make some observations about America which I believe would command wide acceptance. The people of the USA have countless friends and admirers all over the world. We the people of South Asia must remember that our interactions with the American people have always been friendly. They and their governments harboured no colonial designs against us. They did not stand in the way of our own drive for independence. The society they have built for themselves is a magnet to which others elsewhere are irresistibly drawn.
>
> America has, throughout its history, provided a home for the oppressed in search of refuge. If has been a land of hope and opportunity for those who yearn for a chance of leading a better life, in a country where talent is accommodated and encouraged to flourish, where hard work brings rewards. We must not forget that America has been generous. It has spearheaded astounding progress in every avenue of human endeavour. Her friends would wish to see America remain a strong, confident and benevolent champion of democracy. That is why so many are so disturbed that the image of a fair and just America has been shattered by the events in Iraq.
>
> Notwithstanding those events, the community of democratic states must always remain in dialogue with American governments and the people of America, so that America will never be allowed to feel abandoned, isolated and lonely. When we differ from American policy, our criticisms should be

tempered with understanding. A giant should not be left friendless, bereft of honest counsel, lest it be tempted to use its enormous strength in irrational and harmful ways. India, whose relationship with the US has entered a new phase of warmth and cooperation, has a vital role to play in keeping in touch with America at every level. Hundreds of thousands of South Asians now live and work in America. They profit from, but also contribute greatly to the wealth and prosperity of, that great country. Visceral links have been established between the North American continent and our own sub-continent.

We must not forget that the trauma of September 11 is still fresh in the minds of the American people. They had never before been called upon to face terror in their own homeland – the kind of terror that overshadows our daily lives in South Asia. For them it was a new experience that has coloured their view of the world and brought to them a sense of insecurity that they never experienced before. Being of a trusting nature, safely ensconced in fortress America, the American people for the first time in their history have become distrustful and apprehensive of foreigners in their midst. Their famously open society is now circumscribed by security concerns. In judging the foreign policy motivations of the American government, we must be mindful of the fact that America is a deeply wounded society after September 11. That is why, no doubt, a majority of the people of America, not altogether surprisingly, have supported the war against Iraq. We must therefore be mindful of the context and the national mood in which important governmental decisions came to be made relating to Iraq.

My own country, and whatever government happens to be in office at any particular time, will remain a firm friend of America and its people. We will always look to the interests of America, as much as we can, in our own very small way, when it comes to the security and safety of America and its people.

DOCUMENT 11

The Peaceful Ascendancy of China: A South Asian Perspective

China Institute of International Studies,
Beijing, 28 December 2004

The impressive growth of the Chinese economy from the early 1980s onwards resulted in an extensive public and academic debate about whether China's rise is likely to be peaceful, or will risk the kinds of conflict and war associated with the rise of other major powers in the past. Many, including some of China's Asian neighbours, have indicated concern that China is moving towards an increased capacity for military action abroad, and may seek to use this capacity to achieve military, political or economic objectives.

In a lecture in New Delhi in 1995 Kadirgamar had indicated concern about certain Chinese actions, and had anxiously asked: 'What does an economic superpower do with its economic power once its domestic needs are met?'[1] He concluded that lecture on a pessimistic note with a quotation from Kipling: 'Asia is not going to be civilized after the methods of the West. There is too much Asia and she is too old.'[2]

In the lecture reproduced here, given nine years later when he was visiting Beijing, he places himself firmly in the camp of 'peaceful ascendancy'. This lecture – at an institute associated with the Chinese Ministry for Foreign Affairs – is of particular interest for four reasons: (1) He reveals much about his own early encounter with China in 1954, and his near-death experience in an air crash at Athens in October 1979 when on his way to China. (2) He highlights the long history of good relations between China and Sri Lanka, and also China's extensive aid programme in the country. Unsurprisingly, he does not allude to periods of difficulty – for example, the near-breakdown in relations during Dudley Senanayake's notably anti-communist government of 1965–70, coinciding as it did with the advent of the cultural revolution in China of 1966–76.[3] (3) He mentions human rights only briefly, taking the view that 'China is being unfairly treated in certain quarters.' (4) Informing the whole speech is Kadirgamar's strong belief both in maintaining good relations with Sri Lanka's Asian neighbours, and in the principle of respect for the sovereignty of states.

The Chinese leadership had adopted the concept of 'the development path of China's peaceful rise' from December 2002 onwards. Thereafter the phrase 'peaceful rise', which referred to the whole period from the late 1970s to the mid-twenty-first century, became a party slogan for a time. It was intended to provide commitment and reassurance that China would not seek hegemony, and its rise need not involve the risk of war.

Kadirgamar's use of the particular terms 'peaceful ascendancy' and 'peaceful rise' might now be seen as dated. Starting in April 2004, the phrase was gradually replaced in Chinese official discourse by its even more reassuring near-synonym 'peaceful development'.[4] In light of the rapidly growing capabilities of the People's Liberation Army, the phrase 'peaceful development' has continued to have salience and is frequently used. For example, the 2010 defence white paper affirms that China 'unswervingly takes the road of peaceful development'. It repeats the familiar phrase: 'China will never seek hegemony, nor will it adopt the approach of military expansion now or in the future, no matter how its economy develops.'[5]

Some writers have continued to use the term 'peaceful rise', seeing it as more accurate and less anodyne: in a 2010 article on China's international role, Barry Buzan concluded 'Peaceful rise is an ambitious and difficult aim, but also a worthy and noble one.'[6]

*****

It is a great pleasure and a great privilege for me to stand here today in the auditorium of the China Institute of International Studies to address such a distinguished Chinese audience. From my early childhood I had developed a fascination for China – its culture and history and the beautiful works of art that were produced by successive layers of civilization in China's long history. My interest in China was first aroused by the photographs of Chinese historical sites, ceramics, silk paintings and calligraphy which were available to us even in distant Sri Lanka (then known as Ceylon). In later years the great revolution, the long march, the writings of Chinese political leaders and philosophers became to me, and to many of my generation, a source of deep interest, even inspiration. Throughout the past five decades I have watched with admiration the evolution of China, its political system, its society and economy, through periods of intense pain and trauma, from an effete, fragmented feudal regime to the modern colossus that China is today. It was always my dream to visit China. Allow me, therefore, to commence this address with some personal reminiscences.

My Visits to China

I first set foot on Chinese soil in November 1954. Having completed the first round of my legal studies and sat for the final examination in my own country, before I went to the University of Oxford for further studies, I took a cruise on a ship belonging to the well-known Peninsular and Oriental Line which used to sail from Southampton in the United Kingdom through the Mediterranean and the Suez Canal to Bombay, Colombo, Penang,

Singapore, sometimes Manila or Saigon and on to Hong Kong and Shanghai. I joined the ship in Colombo. The first stop was at Penang where I spent a few days with relations in Malaysia. During that stop I learnt from a Ceylonese newspaper that I had passed the final examination for the admission of lawyers and won the scholarship, worth the then princely sum of four hundred rupees, awarded to the candidate placed first. That award enabled me, through the kindness of an uncle in Malaysia who advanced the equivalent sum of money on promise of repayment, to purchase a ticket on the next cruise liner from Penang to Hong Kong and then to Shanghai. My dream, to visit China, had been realized. I spent only two days in Shanghai, at the famous old Peninsula Hotel. My memories of Shanghai in 1954 were of a somewhat faded city with rather grand old buildings in a state of disrepair. The narrow streets of certain parts of the city conjured up the romantic notions I had always entertained about the mysteries of China.

In April this year, 50 years after my first brief visit to Shanghai, I attended the 60th anniversary meeting of the Economic and Social Council for Asia and the Pacific in Shanghai where ESCAP was born.[7] Visiting foreign ministers were taken on a night cruise on the Huangpu River. I saw a Shanghai that had been totally transformed. The old hotel was there and some of the other old buildings but the landscape on both banks of the river was unrecognizable from the days of my first visit in 1954. Now Shanghai is a forest of skyscrapers and a carnival of lights. The spectacular view of the city through a window on the 56th floor of one of the many new hotels in Shanghai could well be a view of New York. The evidence of China's ascendancy is everywhere. Statistics merely prove what the eye can see.

After 1954, twenty-five years passed before I was able to visit China again. A planned visit in October 1979 ended in tragedy. I was in a team of officials of the World Intellectual Property Organization, a specialized agency of the United Nations, going to China from Geneva to advise the government on the establishment of an intellectual property system. The aircraft crashed while landing at Athens airport and burst into flames, resulting in the death of 15 passengers and compelling the survivors to evacuate the aircraft in a hurry.[8] Since all the escape chutes had collapsed I, being the last to leave the aircraft, had to jump out, sustaining thereby a serious spinal injury which kept me in hospital in Geneva for three months. On recovery I had to decide whether to fly again. I decided to do so, and my first journey was to Beijing in December 1980 – 24 years ago.

I have vivid memories of that month-long stay in Beijing where I and my colleagues conducted workshops on the patent system for officials of the new Patent Office of China. The streets were full of bicycles. They moved slowly, like shoals of fish, parting, and coming together again, as our whale-like Russian-made limousine also drove along slowly through the mass of bicycles to the various places we had to visit for our meetings. Horse-drawn carts full of vegetable produce competed with bicycles for space on the streets. The standard uniform worn by men and women was the black high-necked tunic. However, the ladies were beginning to wear coloured scarves. They looked like flowers in spring. This touch of colour seemed to be a clear manifestation of the end of the cultural revolution and the dawn of the modern era in the history of China. We lived in the Friendship Hotel, a solid, rather drab building with cavernous rooms and an antique heating system that made it a refrigerator in winter.

We met many scholars of an older generation who had been marginalized for decades. Some of them had been severely ill-treated. They had guarded their small libraries through stealth and subterfuge. They cherished the learning they had acquired before the revolution. In coming out into the open at the invitation of the new Chinese regime of Deng Xiao Ping they were extremely cautious, uncertain whether the new economic reforms would take root or whether they would be merely a passing phenomenon. As we began to work with them and acquire their trust and confidence it became evident that the great Chinese tradition of learning was still secure and would be passed on to another generation. The eagerness of the younger cadres to learn new skills was a joy to behold. An intellectual property system, the epitome of capitalism, was by decree of the Chinese government to be established as quickly as possible as one of the major economic reforms. What many other countries in the industrialized world had spent many decades building up, the Chinese wished to establish in a few years. The political will was there. China was in a hurry to modernize, to make up for lost time. That meant that hundreds and thousands of young Chinese officials had to be sent abroad to various countries for training and to learn new languages. I saw this process taking place and I had the privilege of participating in it. I can only describe as astonishing the progress made by these young Chinese in operating an intellectual property system. My own organization engaged a Chinese official for the first time and placed him in the Division of Asia and the Pacific of which I was the head. I visited China many times thereafter, never ceasing to be amazed at the rapid progress being made in establishing the intellectual property system. China had to establish a system of courts to handle the litigation that would inevitably ensue from implementation of the new intellectual property laws. New structures had to be set in place, new ways of thought inculcated. All this was totally alien to the Chinese tradition. But the desire to learn, to experiment, to master the complexities of the new system was evident. We even conducted mock trials in courtroom scenario to familiarize Chinese lawyers with the intricacies of the adversarial system of litigation that prevails in most of the rest of the world. In that month in Beijing in 1980 I witnessed the beginnings of the ascendancy of China.

The Ascendancy of China

In his 1994 book *Diplomacy* Henry Kissinger said:

> Of all the great, and potentially great, powers China is the most ascendant. The United States already is the most powerful, Europe must work to forge greater unity, Russia is a staggering giant, and Japan is wealthy but, so far, timid. China, however, with economic growth rates approaching 10 per cent annually, [and] a strong sense of national cohesion . . . will show the greatest relative increase in stature among the major powers. . . . The Maoist China which emerged [after the revolution] was intent on being an independent great power, but was frustrated by its ideological blinkers. Having put the ideological convulsions behind them, China's reformist leaders have pursued Chinese national interest with skillful tenacity.[9]

The ascendancy of China no longer lies in the realm of prediction. It is now an established fact. With a gross domestic product averaging a steady 9 per cent per year, estimated foreign currency reserves in excess of US$ 400 billion, incoming foreign investment in the region of US$ 40 billion per year, huge infrastructure development programmes in progress and substantial worldwide exports, China has arrived on centre stage as a major economic power with the potential to surpass all others a few decades hence. China is already the world's sixth largest economy and fourth biggest exporter. The US ran a trade deficit with China of US$ 124 billion last year. Thanks to a two-decade old building boom at home, Chinese construction companies now have the skill to compete for contracts abroad – not just in developing countries, but in the US. For example, the China Construction Company will break ground on a US$ 190 million office and retail complex which includes a 220-room Marriott Hotel in New York's Harlem district, and the Shanghai Construction Group will commence a US$ 110 million office building in Flushing, New York State. Last year Chinese construction companies won international contracts worth US$ 17 billion, a 17 per cent increase over 2002. In the same year Chinese firms carried out 17.5 per cent of all construction projects in Asia, 9.5 per cent of the projects in the Middle East and 7.4 per cent of those in Africa.

However, the rapid expansion of the Chinese economy is giving Chinese leaders and planners cause for concern. A number of problem areas have emerged which require to be addressed, chief among them rural poverty, unemployment, inadequate health care, environmental pollution, apart from identified deficiencies in the banking system. Last year the number of people living in extreme poverty (i.e. with incomes of less than US$ 77 per year) rose to just over 3 per cent of the population. It appears that in the countryside housing and electricity are in short supply and roads are often in bad condition. China still ranks just 94th in the UN Human Development Index. As for employment, there may not be enough jobs, especially if the economy is required to slow down, for the 10 million workers a year entering the urban employment market – not to mention the 14 million still laid off from state-owned enterprises, 95 million migrants seeking work and an estimated 150 million surplus labourers in the countryside. In the health care sector the results of a survey recently released by China's Health Ministry underlines the pressing need for reforms. It was found that 36 per cent of patients in cities and 39 per cent in the countryside did not go to see a doctor because they were unable to afford medical treatment; nearly 28 per cent of those admitted to hospital left because of financial difficulties. The cost of medical treatment had increased by 14 per cent annually between 1993 and 2003, a rate far faster than the rise in people's incomes. In the countryside, the cost of an average in-patient treatment is about US$ 270, compared with the average rural income of US$ 315.[10] In the poorer inland areas of central and north-western China, that ratio is even more extreme. Many families are plunged into poverty by illness. China is currently experimenting with pilot rural health insurance schemes under which farmers pay an annual US$ 1.20 which is then matched by local and central governments. Environmental pollution is seen as one of the graver consequences of China's rapid development. The countryside, and with it arable land, is fast diminishing. More and more cities are springing up. The plan is to move 400 million people to the cities in the next 25 years, creating a need for new roads, housing and other infrastructure on a truly massive scale. China now imports grain and also huge quantities of other resources. It is the world's largest consumer of copper, aluminium and cement, and the second biggest importer of oil. It has already become the world's second biggest generator of carbon dioxide emissions and could overtake the US as the biggest source of greenhouse gases in three decades. Coal already supplies 75 per cent of the country's energy needs, and more coal plants are being built, raising the prospect of ever more coal dust and acid rain. As car ownership has been doubling every few years, if per capita ownership were to reach US levels China would have to find room for 600 million cars – more than exist today in the entire world. But despite the scale of the challenges China now faces, all is not gloomy. There seems to be a new public awareness building of the dangers of destroying the resources on which China's long-term health and prosperity depend.

Most importantly, the Chinese leadership is fully aware of the dangers of an over-heated economy and is taking timely remedial measures.

Premier Wen Jiabao issued a sobering warning to the nation early this year. He said that unhealthy banks (China's banks are technically insolvent, according to Standard & Poor's, with bad debts making up 45 per cent of their loans), over-invested industries and an increasingly unwieldy economy posed the biggest challenge to China since the SARS epidemic. He told a press conference at the end of the National People's Congress that the economy had reached 'a critical juncture':

> The deep-seated problems and imbalances in the economy that have accumulated for many years have not been fundamentally resolved. And new problems and imbalances keep cropping up in the process of rapid development, such as excessive investment scale, shortages in energy, transportation capacity and important raw materials, decreasing grain output for quite a number of years, and the obvious trend of rising prices. All these problems must be addressed appropriately and that presents a new and very big test to the government.... If we exercised the right macro-control, we would be able to steer the big ship of the Chinese economy forward in a stable and relatively fast manner. But if we failed to manage the situation well, setbacks to the economy would be inevitable.[11]

Using a colourful analogy in a speech delivered in Europe, the Prime Minister compared himself to 'the driver of a speeding car, trying to avoid an emergency stop. We cannot slam the brakes, we have to press the brakes gently.'[12]

The question the world, particularly other Asian countries, asks themselves is no longer whether China will rise but in what way it will rise, and what level its rise will reach. The core issue seems to be whether China will rise peacefully or whether it will go the way that historically other world or regional powers have gone, namely, expanding their influence and interests by military means. China's relations with its neighbouring countries have markedly improved in recent times and the peripheral environment is relatively stable. The general situation is conducive to China's realization of the strategic goal of building an affluent society through concentration on sustainable economic growth and all-round development of the social sector, thus blazing a trail for a peaceful rise which is diametrically different from the ways other major powers rose in history.

China's Change of Course

After the founding of the Peoples' Republic the issue of national security was for a long time considered the dominant question involving the fundamental national interest of China, making the country unable to concentrate on developing the national economy. This was due to both the objective environment and subjective mistakes. In the 1950s and 1960s China faced military threats and economic blockage from the two superpowers of the time – the US and the Soviet Union. In such a hostile environment

China had to de-emphasize economic construction in favour of enhancing national security. The spread of the ultra 'left' ideology at home and the inappropriate linking of threats emanating from the international situation with domestic political struggles, coupled with the inherent drawback of restraints arising from the planned economy, severely hindered China's economic and social development. However, since the plenary session of the 11th Central Committee of the Communist Party of China priority has been restored to domestic economic construction thus laying the foundation for great achievements on the economic front.[13] It would lack good sense and be totally unnecessary for China to seek military expansion and international hegemony to advance its economic interests. In my view, such a course of action would be inconceivable. As Deng Xiao Ping has said: 'Interventionist military powers cannot be the cornerstone of any peace loving country. National capabilities come out of the broadest possible development of people in the country. The process of development is not purely political. It is a process of all-inclusive reforms, reconstruction and modernization which induces economic growth.'

We know that prevailing perceptions are as important as current reality in assessing an international situation. It is, therefore, necessary to examine some of the perceptions that the rest of the world has of China's ongoing ascendancy.

China's Relations with South Asia

Let me refer to China and South Asia. Long-standing tensions with India were progressively dealt with through a series of consultations preceding Prime Minister Vajpayee's visit to China last June. On that occasion Chinese Premier Wen Jiabao said:

> South Asia is an important part of Asia, and China welcomes equal treatment and peaceful coexistence among South Asian nations. China hopes to see further relaxation of relations between India and Pakistan and supports efforts to ease tensions and safeguard peace between the two countries. China would never seek to push its private interests in South Asian affairs, and the friendly cooperation established among China and South Asian countries would never target any other country. China would continue its role as a constructive player in promoting peace and development in South Asia.

The June 2003 visit of Prime Minister Vajpayee to China with a 40-member business delegation proves that economic ties could be strengthened. Trade between India and China has increased from US$ 338 million in 1992 to nearly US$ 5 billion in 2002. The Declaration on Basic Principles for Bilateral Relationship and Comprehensive Cooperation was signed during this visit as well as ten separate bilateral agreements on education, culture, border trade and quarantine issues. China takes great pains to explain that the improved relationship with India does not in any way affect its long-standing relations with Pakistan. Sikkim is no longer on the Chinese Foreign Ministry's website as an independent country. India accepts Tibet as part of China.

China's relations with other South Asian countries – Bangladesh, Nepal and Sri Lanka – are in good order. South Asian countries have benefited in different ways from China's generous assistance. The bilateral trade volume with Bangladesh in 2003 was US$ 1.2 billion, although imports reached only US$ 32 million. The total trade volume between China and Sri Lanka is currently US$ 330 million. The balance of trade between the two countries has been heavily in favour of China. The unfavourable balance of trade reached a peak level of US$ 247 million in 2003. Pakistan's total imports from China amounted to US$ 575 million and total exports amounted to US$ 228 million. These figures help to underline the close economic links between China and South Asia.

Comparing South Asia taken collectively with China, the average per capita annual income is US$ 440 as against US$ 780, exports are US$ 15.1 billion against US$ 249 billion, imports are US$ 18.3 billion against US$ 217 billion, foreign direct investments are US$ 3.1 billion against US$ 40 billion, and internet users are 5.4 million against 8.9 million. China has evinced interest in establishing a link with the South Asian Association for Regional Cooperation (SAARC). At the SAARC Summit in Malé in 1997 Sri Lanka proposed that SAARC should establish a link with China. The proposal received only a lukewarm response from the other countries. Although the matter could not be pursued at the Colombo Summit of 1998 because relations between Pakistan and India were considerably strained at that time, Sri Lanka informed China bilaterally that in its individual capacity it believed that SAARC should establish a link with China. At the Islamabad Summit in 2004 a statement was read out from the Prime Minister of China wishing the Summit success. Shortly after the Summit the Chinese Ambassador to Nepal made a formal proposal to the Secretary-General of SAARC for establishing a linkage between China and SAARC. The Secretary-General has sought the views of member states on this proposal. The matter will come up at the next summit in Dhaka in January 2005. Subject to the observations of the Secretary-General on the views of other member states, Sri Lanka would consider the proposal with favour.[14]

Sri Lanka and China

Sri Lanka's view of China's place in the modern world is conditioned by many factors. As I move towards the close of this address I would like to bring those factors to your attention.

First, the role of history and the influence of Buddhism. Sri Lanka's earliest contacts with China date back to 206 BC during the Han Dynasty in the reign of Emperor P'ing. Thirteen missions were sent to China by the kings of Sri Lanka, between 13 and 989 AD. In 401 AD, a Chinese monk, Fa Hsien of the Eastern Jin Dynasty, came to Sri Lanka to study the Buddhist scriptures.[15] He wrote a book titled *Accounts of Buddhist Kingdoms*. In 1990, to commemorate the visit of Fa Hsien to Sri Lanka, the Government of China granted three million Yuan to construct the 'Fa Hsien-Mahasen Complex' at one of our ancient archaeological sites. In 428 AD a Sri Lankan king sent a model of the Sacred Tooth Relic shrine to the Chinese emperor. In 527 AD another king sent an ambassador to the Chinese emperor's court. During the Tang Dynasty (618 to 907 AD) several Chinese monks visited Sri Lanka to learn Theravada Buddhism. Fragments of Chinese bowls and coins unearthed in Sri Lanka which were analysed in 1925 show that most of the coins belong to the Tang dynasty. After the eighth century AD two-way missions decreased due to the persecution of Buddhists in China. During the Ming dynasty (1368 to 1644 AD) the island was visited twice by Admiral Cheng Ho.[16] An inscription regarding his visit presently lies in the National Museum in Colombo. One of the greatest emperors of the Southern Kingdoms of China, Liang Wu Ti of the Liang dynasty, was a Buddhist.[17] It is evident that religious contacts played an important role in developing these ancient ties between the peoples of the two countries. The establishment of links with China in those distant times was a significant initiative on the part of the rulers of Sri Lanka, one of the first countries in Asia to undertake such initiatives. It could be said that through Buddhism Sri Lanka made an impact on diplomacy. As the repository of the Theravada doctrine, Sri Lanka attracted pilgrims and scholars from other countries.

Second, prompt recognition of the People's Republic of China. Ceylon regained its independence in 1948 after nearly 450 years of foreign rule. A new chapter in bilateral relations with China was opened with the founding of the People's Republic in October 1949. Soon after the People's Republic was proclaimed, Ceylon ordered the closure of the Kuomintang consulate in Colombo in December 1949. By January 1950, Ceylon had extended diplomatic recognition to the new People's Republic of China.

Third, the historic rubber/rice pact of 1951. In less than one year from the date of the Chinese peoples' liberation, when war broke out on the Korean Peninsula, the fledgling government of China dispatched a million volunteers under Marshal Peng to assist North Korea. The Western bloc and its allies, 17 in all, who fought the Korean War under the UN banner, blocked the export of raw materials and commodities, which in their perception were considered to be strategic, to the newly founded People's Republic of China. Rubber was one such commodity. It was against this backdrop that Ceylon negotiated with China in December 1951, against strong opposition from the West, a barter pact which would facilitate the exchange of Ceylonese rubber for Chinese rice. This historic barter pact was extremely beneficial to both countries given their urgent needs at that time.

The pact had international implications for Sri Lanka. Since rubber was considered a strategic war material by the US, the action of Sri Lanka brought it into conflict with the Hickenlooper Amendment to the US Foreign Assistance Act and caused the US government to stop economic assistance to Sri Lanka.[18] The US government was about to fund the modernization of Colombo airport. It was immediately called off. This was the first punitive action taken by the US against another country for trading with the People's Republic of China. These events took place when China had few friends in the international community, and Sri Lanka had much to lose by offending the economic superpower of that era. At the time the rubber/rice pact was signed Sri Lanka was one of the most prosperous countries in Asia, unlike today. At the time of independence it had sizeable financial reserves and its commodities – tea, rubber and coconut – were doing well in the international markets. The Korean War had boosted rubber exports. China, despite its vast land area and population, was economically in many ways in a worse situation than Sri Lanka. It was an impoverished semi-colonial, semi-feudal society with a weak central administration. The rubber/rice pact was a bold initiative for a small country to have taken in those unsettled times.

Fourth, the early establishment, in 1956, of full diplomatic relations by Prime Minister S. W. R. D. Bandaranaike. It was his vision that enabled China and Sri Lanka to come even closer together in government-to-government and people-to-people relationships.

Fifth, the munificence of China. Chinese Premier Chou En-lai, wishing to commemorate the name of Mr Bandaranaike, gifted to Sri Lanka a huge conference complex dedicated to his memory. This magnificent structure is not only a lasting monument to the memory of one man and his policies; it also symbolizes the warm friendship and cooperation that characterize relations between China and Sri Lanka. The international conference hall enabled Sri Lanka to host the largest gathering of foreign heads of state and government ever held in Sri Lanka – the 5th Non-Aligned Summit Conference in August 1976 at which delegations from more than 100 countries participated. China was represented.

Other gifts from China flowed to Sri Lanka – a massive superior courts complex, a new building to house the central mail room of the Department of Posts, a friendship village, a flood protection scheme, a drinking water project for the North Western and North Central Provinces, hospitals, roads, bridges. A National Performing Arts Centre with massive Chinese financial assistance is on the drawing boards. These are but a few instances of China's enormous generosity to Sri Lanka.

Sixth, the contribution of Madam Sirimavo Bandaranaike, the world's first woman prime minister. She was particularly well known as a friend of China, even among the younger generation. During my first official visit to China as Foreign Minister in 1995, I was walking down a street in a southern Chinese city when a group of youngsters surrounded me and asked me where I came from. When I said Sri Lanka they exclaimed 'Madam Bandaranaike' and inquired about her.

Seventh, the Sino-Indian border dispute. It will be recalled that when the border dispute between China and India erupted into war in October 1962, with China crossing the McMahon Line, it was Madam Bandaranaike, then a novice in international affairs, having been propelled unwillingly into politics three years earlier on the assassination of her husband, who called a conference of six powers in Colombo to settle the dispute. She refrained from naming China the aggressor in order to maintain neutrality as an essential prerequisite for mediation. Her letter of 21 November 1962 to the six powers was copied to China, and at midnight on the same day China declared a ceasefire and withdrawal. Premier Chou En-lai responded to her political initiative by sending her the following message:

> I sincerely admire and thank your Excellency for your repeated efforts to seek a peaceful settlement of the Sino-Indian boundary question. At this moment your Excellency's proposal that the leaders of six friendly Asian African countries meet for discussion on ways to promote reconciliation between India and China is indeed a constructive step.

Madam Bandaranaike was tasked by the six 'Colombo powers' to personally present their proposals to Nehru and Chou En-lai. Ultimately, since no agreement could be reached on the basis for talks, India and China never met directly. However, Sri Lanka had made a noteworthy contribution to the resolution of the dispute.

Eighth, high-level visits, trade and tourism. The visits to each others' countries by Chou En-lai in 1957 and 1964, Madam Bandaranaike in 1961 and 1972, President J. R. Jayewardene in 1984, President Li Xianian in 1986, Premier Li Peng in 1990 and Zhu Rongi in 2001, and President Kumaratunga in 1996 illustrate the high level at which bilateral relations are conducted. Trade and tourism are expanding. The total trade volume increased by 28 per cent between 2002 and 2003. By June 2005 there will be direct flights between Colombo and Beijing. China has granted 'approved destination status' for Chinese tourists to visit Sri Lanka. Cultural contacts have given great pleasure to their respective peoples. Chinese artistes have been acclaimed in Sri Lanka for their exceptional skills. They have been most effective ambassadors of goodwill. China is widely embraced by the people of Sri Lanka as a staunch and genuine friend. On 7 February 2007

China and Sri Lanka will complete five decades of full diplomatic relations. Yet 50 years is but a short period in the interaction between the two countries, which has spanned almost 2000 years.

The question is often asked: Why does Sri Lanka consider its relationship to China so special? What is it that two such disparate countries can have in common? Since a country's foreign policy is designed to protect and advance its own interests, what possible benefit could China derive from its relationship with Sri Lanka? China is a Goliath on the world scene. It is the world's most populous country. It is rich in natural resources. It has enormous influence in world affairs. Sri Lanka is a small island in the Indian Ocean far away from China. As far as Sri Lanka is concerned the benefits it derives from its close relationship with China are obvious. They are tangible. Sri Lanka has been the beneficiary of China's immense generosity. But what can Sri Lanka possibly do for China? First, I believe that the relationship between the two countries which began, as I have said, many, many centuries ago, is based on a secure foundation, the principles of Panchasila.[19] It is based on mutual respect. It is a fact of history that the influence of Buddhism on Chinese thought, culture and civilization has been profound. Therefore, the knowledge that Sri Lanka, from where to a large extent its own Buddhist traditions emanate, also has an old and proud civilization is, I believe, deeply embedded in the psyche of the Chinese people. One can surmise what the scholar pilgrim Fa Hsien must have thought when he came to Sri Lanka in the fifth century AD and saw flourishing in Anuradhapura, its ancient capital, a civilization which he could not have dreamt existed in that distant place. One can imagine what an impact that discovery must have had on the Chinese intelligentsia of his time. When a relationship is based on mutual respect, the size, importance and power of one of the two countries in that relationship does not have a disproportionate influence on the other. Second, Sri Lanka has never been financially dependent on China. The relationship has not suffered from the psychological imbalance that arises from the donor–recipient syndrome. Third, China has never sought to influence the domestic politics of Sri Lanka. Over the years China has proved to be benign and sincere with no ulterior motives for befriending Sri Lanka. She has never tried to dominate, undermine or destabilize Sri Lanka. She has come to our rescue with timely assistance on several occasions when there were threats to Sri Lanka's national security and territorial integrity. And even on those occasions China never tried to strike a quick bargain in a crisis. There have been no strings attached to Chinese aid. When a relationship between two countries is not based on dependence, it is strengthened by the fact that it is based on the mutual recognition of equality. Fourth, Sri Lanka in its own way has been helpful to China. I mentioned the rubber/rice pact of 1951, which was entered into at a time when China was being shunned by powerful members of the international community. In more recent times Sri Lanka has in a modest way been of assistance to China in international fora especially in the field of human rights where Sri Lanka, taking the view that China is being unfairly treated in certain quarters, has been her steadfast ally. It is good for a relationship when both countries are able to contribute something towards sustaining and enhancing it. Fifth, Sri Lanka has remained steadfast and unequivocal in respect of its One China Policy. We believe that Taiwan is an inalienable part of the People's Republic of China – something which the UN has reaffirmed each year. We support China's policy of peaceful reunification and China's efforts to promote cross-straits links for the benefit of the Chinese people and their social and economic development. The so-called pro-independence forces should not be permitted to disrupt these policies and threaten peace in the region.

I have spent time on describing the relationship between China and Sri Lanka because the title of my address requires me to approach the question of the peaceful ascendance of China in recent years from a South Asian perspective. I can speak with conviction and certainty of Sri Lanka's attitude to the situation of China in the world today. That attitude is undoubtedly conditioned by the fact that Sri Lanka and China have built up a warm and trusting relationship over a long period of time. It follows that Sri Lanka wishes China to succeed, and trusts China to exercise responsibly and constructively the enormous power and influence that will necessarily accompany great economic success. Moreover, Sri Lanka being a South Asian country will no doubt, at least to some extent, reflect attitudes to China which also prevail among her neighbours. I cannot presume to speak for them but what I say may find some resonance in their own feelings towards, and assessment of, China as it rises steadily to the position of a major economic power.

LONG MAY THE PEOPLE'S REPUBLIC OF CHINA FLOURISH AND PROSPER!

Notes

Chapter 1 'Dare the Deepening Tide': Lakshman Kadirgamar on the Revolution of our Times

1. Since Kadirgamar's death there have been a number of statements, and articles in the Sri Lankan press, suggesting that he took part in a running relay on 4 February 1948 symbolizing the unity of the peoples of Sri Lanka, and even that he carried a flaming torch and 'lit the lamp of freedom'. The main example is D. B. S. Jeyaraj, 'Kadi: A man destined to achieve glory', *Sunday Leader* (Colombo), 21 Aug. 2005, p. 18. Available at http://www.thesundayleader.lk/archive/20050821/issues.htm. However, I have found no contemporary evidence that there was such a relay in 1948, or indeed that there was a 'lamp of freedom'. There was undoubtedly a relay exactly one year later, reported in *Ceylon Daily News*, 5 Feb. 1949, but, despite extensive searches, I have not found definite proof of Kadirgamar's participation in it.
2. For an account of the symbolic relay in 1952 see A. Arulpiragasam, *A Short Review of the Colombo Exhibition, February 23 to March 22, 1952* (Colombo: Government of Ceylon Press, 1954), p. 12; on Kadirgamar's participation in the 1952 event see also the photograph and caption accompanying S. Piyasena, 'The years of independence', *Ceylon Daily News* (Colombo), 4 Feb. 1978.
3. The Colombo Plan for Co-operative Economic Development in South and South-East Asia, drawn up following a meeting of Commonwealth foreign ministers in Colombo in January 1950, was first published on 28 November 1950. It was a framework rather than a detailed plan. The organization established under it, now called the Colombo Plan for Economic and Social Development in Asia and the Pacific, with a secretariat in Colombo, currently has 26 member states, some of them outside the Commonwealth.
4. Shelton U. Kodikara, *Foreign Policy of Sri Lanka: A Third World Perspective*, 2nd edn. (Delhi: Chanayaka Publications, 1992), p. 4.
5. There have been several major revisions of the Sri Lankan constitution since independence in 1948. An executive presidency, with expanded powers, was introduced by a 1977 amendment to the 1972 constitution. It was confirmed in the 1978 constitution.
6. SinhaRaja Tammita-Delgoda, *The World of Stanley Kirinde* (Colombo: Stamford Lake Pvt. Ltd., 2005).
7. *International Relations in a Globalising World*, the journal of the Bandaranaike Centre for International Studies, Sri Lanka, Sage Publications, New Delhi, ISSN 0972-8864. Only two issues of the journal were produced. The second, dated July–December 2005, had been largely prepared before Kadirgamar's death.
8. Ameen Izzadeen, 'The last night with Kadir', *The Sunday Times* (Colombo), 14 Aug. 2005. Available at http://sundaytimes.lk/050814/news/12.html.
9. For more on the circumstances of the assassination and on the follow-up, see Sinha Ratnatunga's chapter, pp. 56–8.
10. For a full picture of Gandhi's visit to Sri Lanka, see *Collected Works of Mahatma Gandhi*, vol. 40, pp. 353–471. Available at http://www.gandhiserve.org/cwmg/VOL040.PDF.

11. Figures from Department of Census and Statistics, Colombo.
12. Letter from Education Officer, Ceylon High Commission, London, to Mr M. W. Dick, Senior Tutor of Balliol College, Oxford, 24 Nov. 1955. Balliol College archives.
13. In his speech to the UN General Assembly on 23 September 1999 Kadirgamar drew attention to Sri Lanka's proposal on Vesak – the proposal that led to GA Res. 54/115 of 15 Dec. 1999, adopted without a vote.
14. The colleague's recollection is cited in Smriti Daniel, 'Vesak lanterns: a glow of pride at the UN', *Sunday Times* (Colombo), 22 May 2011. Available at http://sundaytimes.lk/110522/News/nws_24.html.
15. L. Kadirgamar, 'The Social Relevance of the Bible for our Times in a Non-Christian Society', The Third Celestine Fernando Memorial Address, Colombo, 9 Oct. 1992, transcript, p. 6. (Kadirgamar papers, Colombo). The Mahabharata is one of the two major Sanskrit epics of ancient India.
16. Fernando Memorial Address, pp. 8–9.
17. Fernando Memorial Address, p. 10. He also referred approvingly to Gandhi on pp. 12–13 and 28.
18. Fernando Memorial Address, pp. 18–19, citing one of the Jataka tales.
19. Figures from Department of Census and Statistics, Colombo.
20. Nira Wickramasinghe, *Sri Lanka in the Modern Age: A History of Contested Identities* (London: Hurst, 2006), pp. 46–8.
21. Wickramasinghe, *Sri Lanka in the Modern Age*, p. 255.
22. Wickramasinghe, *Sri Lanka in the Modern Age*, pp. 28–9.
23. K. M. de Silva, *A History of Sri Lanka* (London: Hurst, 1981), p. 517.
24. Wickramasinghe, *Sri Lanka in the Modern Age*, pp. 272–3.
25. Wickramasinghe, *Sri Lanka in the Modern Age*, p. 185.
26. Wickramasinghe, *Sri Lanka in the Modern Age*, p. 188.
27. Chris Patten's chapter, pp. 61–2.
28. Sinha Ratnatunga's chapter, p. 45.
29. T. J. Barron, 'The Donoughmore Commission and Ceylon's National Identity', *Journal of Commonwealth & Comparative Politics*, XXVI/2 (July 1988), p. 147. See also Tilaka Piyaseeli Meththananda, 'The Donoughmore Commission in Ceylon 1927–1931', DPhil thesis in History, Oxford University, 1974; and de Silva, *A History of Sri Lanka*, pp. 417–22.
30. Kadirgamar, 'Why I Decided to Enter Politics', July 1994, p. 108 above.
31. Prof. W. R. Breckenridge, who was at Trinity at the same time as Kadirgamar and much later became Principal, 'Lakshman Kadirgamar and Trinity', *Daily News* (Colombo), 7 Sept. 2005.
32. Speech at Shaw Wilson Felicitation Dinner at the Taj Samudra Hotel, Colombo, 7 Oct. 2003 (date confirmed in Kadirgamar's diary). Available at http://trinitylk.com/2011/04/speech-by-hon-kadirgamar.
33. Sir Henry Newbolt (1862–1938), 'The Best School of All', *Collected Poems 1897–1907* (London: T. Nelson & Sons, 1910). Available also on the website of Trinity College Kandy: http://www.trinitycollege.lk/College%20Song.html.
34. Sarath Silva's chapter, pp. 37–40.
35. L. Kadirgamar, *Strict Liability in English and Roman-Dutch Law*, BLitt thesis, Oxford University, 1960, 375 pp.
36. Debate of 27 Feb. 1958. Despite his efforts, the motion was defeated by 170 votes to 111. Oxford Union Society's archives in the Oxfordshire Record Office, consulted July 2010.
37. Oxford Union archives in Oxfordshire Record Office.

38. Lalith Athulathmudali, after an academic career as a law teacher, was a Member of Parliament for the United National Party (UNP) from 1977 and held various government offices, including Minister of Trade. In 1990–91 he split from UNP and formed a new party, the Democratic United National Front (DUNF). He was assassinated on 23 April 1993. His role is noted in Sarath Silva's chapter, pp. 38–40; and in Sinha Ratnatunga's chapter, p. 42, where the possibility of the Premadasa government's involvement in his assassination is mentioned.
39. Kadirgamar's recollections of his term as President of the Oxford Union Society at the unveiling ceremony of his portrait there on 18 March 2005, text in *A Portrait at the Oxford Union*, privately published, 2005, pp. 27–31.
40. Solomon West Ridgeway Dias (often called S.W.R.D.) Bandaranaike was shot at his home on 25 September 1959, and died in hospital the following day. As prime minister he had been responsible for the 'Sinhala only' language policy, and he was also criticized for his failure to control anti-Tamil mobs in the May 1958 riots in Sri Lanka.
41. 'Inevitable Failure', report on the Oxford Union debate of 22 Oct. 1959 in *Parson's Pleasure*, issue of late Oct. 1959 (edited by Richard Ingrams and Paul Foot), p. 20. The article's author was 'Tadpole', whose real identity I have not been able to establish. *Parson's Pleasure*, founded by Adrian Berry, was an irregularly appearing and irreverent Oxford student magazine that finally ceased publication in 1961. It was the precursor of the satirical London-based weekly *Private Eye*, founded in 1961. Praise from either journal was very rare.
42. Kadirgamar's speech in Beijing on 28 Dec. 2004, pp. 225–6 above.
43. Sinha Ratnatunga's chapter, p. 41.
44. Francis Deng, Representative of UN Secretary-General, 'Addendum: Profiles in Displacement: Sri Lanka', prepared for UN Commission on Human Rights, UN doc. E/CN.4/1994/44/Add.1 of 25 Jan. 1994, esp. paras 135 and 175.
45. See e.g. the criticisms in 'Country Report – Sri Lanka' in the report issued by the New York-based Freedom House in 2004. Available at http://www.freedomhouse.org/template.cfm?page=140&edition=1&ccrcountry=63&section=50&ccrpage=5.
46. See e.g. *Sri Lanka's Human Rights Crisis* (International Crisis Group (ICG), Asia Report 135, 14 June 2007). Available at http://www.crisisgroup.org/en/publication-type/reports.aspx.
47. See e.g. *Sri Lanka's Judiciary: Politicised Courts, Compromised Rights* (ICG, Asia Report 172, 30 June 2009). Available at http://www.crisisgroup.org/en/publication-type/reports.aspx.
48. See Kadirgamar's support for the HRCSL in speech at the Kotelawala Defence Academy, 19 Mar. 1996, pp. 31–2 above.
49. Winston Churchill MP, House of Commons, 11 Nov. 1947, opposing the Parliament Bill, which he saw as aimed at creating a single-chamber system of government. (Hansard, fifth series, vol. 444, cols. 206–7.) Kadirgamar cited this in his speech in Washington DC on 12 May 2004, p. 207 above.
50. For criticism not only of the internationally assisted peace processes, but also of the ways in which Sri Lanka's constitutional arrangements had fostered ethno-nationalist politics, see Kristian Stokke and Jayadeva Uyangoda (eds.), *Liberal Peace in Question: Politics of State and Market Reform in Sri Lanka* (London: Anthem Press, 2011).
51. Kadirgamar's speech at Brookings Institution, Washington DC, 12 May 2004, p. 208 above.

52. K. M. de Silva, *Reaping the Whirlwind: Ethnic Conflict, Ethnic Politics in Sri Lanka* (New Delhi: Penguin Books India, 1998), p. 33.
53. Kadirgamar, C. V. Guneratne Memorial Lecture, Colombo, 20 June 2001, p. 21 (Kadirgamar papers, Colombo).
54. The Post-Tsunami Operational Management Structure (P-TOMS) agreement, negotiated between the government and the LTTE and aimed at sharing international assistance to Sri Lanka, was signed on 24 June 2005. The JVP had left the coalition on 16 June in protest against the agreement which, they said, would violate the constitution.
55. Kadirgamar's speech at China Institute of International Studies, Beijing, 28 Dec. 2004, p. 235 above.
56. Kadirgamar's speech proposing a toast at a dinner hosted by Myanmar Foreign Minister Ohn Gyaw, between 28 Jan. and 2 Feb. 1996 (Kadirgamar papers, Colombo).
57. See chapter by Shivshankar Menon and Nirupama Rao, pp. 81–6.
58. Barbara Crossette, 'Sri Lanka: in the shadow of the Indian elephant', *World Policy Journal* 19/1 (Mar. 2002), pp. 2 and 5. Available at http://vlex.com/vid/sri-lanka-in-shadow-indian-elephant-54486132# ixzz1NpQ2DlXC.
59. For a critical view of Indian support for the LTTE, see Rohan Gunaratna, *Indian Intervention in Sri Lanka: The Role of India's Intelligence Agencies* (Colombo: South Asian Network on Conflict Research, 1993).
60. The Indo–Sri Lanka Accord, signed in Colombo on 29 July 1987 by the Prime Minister of India, Rajiv Gandhi, and the President of Sri Lanka, J. R. Jayewardene, consisted of the Indo–Sri Lanka Agreement to Establish Peace and Normalcy in Sri Lanka, plus annexed letters. Text published in *International and Comparative Law Quarterly* (London) 37/3, July 1988, pp. 583–7.
61. The names of the IPKF soldiers who died in Sri Lanka in 1987–90 are inscribed in a memorial in Colombo erected c. 2008.
62. Kadirgamar, address on 'Sri Lanka's Foreign and Security Policy', International Institute for Strategic Studies, London, 17 Mar. 2005.
63. J. L. Nehru, 'The Colombo Powers' Peace Efforts', broadcast from Colombo, 2 May 1954. Text in *Jawaharlal Nehru's Speeches*, vol. 3, *March 1953–August 1957* (New Delhi: Government of India, Ministry of Information and Broadcasting, 1958), pp. 251–3.
64. Kadirgamar's speech at Kotelawala Defence Academy, 19 Mar. 1996, p. 112.
65. *The Responsibility to Protect: Report of the International Commission on Intervention and State Sovereignty*, 2 vols. (Ottawa: International Development Research Centre, Dec. 2001). Available at http://web.idrc.ca/en/ev-9436-201-1-DO_TOPIC.html.
66. Kadirgamar, 'The World Order after Iraq', eighth Prem Bhatia Memorial Lecture, New Delhi, 11 Aug. 2003, p. 3 (Kadirgamar papers, Colombo). This lecture was published in *World Affairs: The Journal of International Issues* (New Delhi), July–Sept. 2003. Available at http://www.prembhatiatrust.com/lecture8.htm. Extracts from this lecture can also be found in his talk at the Brookings Institution in May 2004, 'Third World Democracy in Action: The Sri Lanka Experience', pp. 220–1 above.
67. Kadirgamar, 'World Order after Iraq', p. 24.
68. Audrey Kurth Cronin emphasizes the importance of the struggle for legitimacy in her excellent study, *How Terrorism Ends: Understanding the Decline and Demise of Terrorist Campaigns* (Princeton, New Jersey: Princeton University Press, 2009).

69. Kadirgamar, 'Flaws in the Ceasefire Agreement', speech in the Sri Lanka parliament, 8 May 2003, pp. 193–205 above.
70. Chapter by Karl Inderfurth et al., pp. 70, 73–5 and 76–7.
71. de Silva, *Reaping the Whirlwind*, p. 328.
72. Confidential message of US Chargé d'Affaires James F. Entwistle, 18 Aug. 2005, released in 2011 by Wikileaks. Available at http://wikileaksrilanka.blogspot.com/p/sri-lanka-us-cables.html.
73. The EU proscription of the LTTE was renewed by Council Implementing Regulation (EU) no. 83/2011 of 31 Jan. 2011, published in the *Official Journal* of the European Union.
74. On 21 October 2011, the Specialist War Crimes Chamber in The Hague effectively supported the defence's notion that the LTTE was party to a civil war, and not a terrorist organization. However, the five Dutch–Tamil men who were on trial were found guilty of raising money for and supporting an organization on the EU's banned list – a criminal act under Dutch law. Or, to put it differently, the judge considered that the LTTE is not a terrorist group but the fact that the EU thinks that it is one means that Dutch criminal law was being broken. Further information available at http://www.rnw.nl/international-justice/article/tamil-tiger-5-%E2%80%93-a-case-irony-and-disappointment.
75. *LTTE* v. *Council*, General Court of the European Union, Luxembourg, Case T-208/11, action brought on 11 Apr. 2011. Available at http://curia.europa.eu/jcms/jcms/Jo2_7045.
76. News report, 'Peace talks team for Thailand finalized: Government lifts LTTE proscription', *Daily News* (Colombo), 5 Sept. 2002. Available at http://www.dailynews.lk/2002/09/05/new001.html.
77. Kadirgamar's speech at Kotelawala Defence Academy, 19 Mar. 1996, pp. 111–19 above.
78. Crossette, 'Sri Lanka: In the Shadow of the Indian Elephant', p. 7.
79. Defence Secretary Gotabaya Rajapaksa, interview with *Business Today* (Colombo). A news release dated 11 Nov. 2008. Available at http://www.priu.gov.lk/news_update/Current_Affairs/archive.html.
80. See e.g. Sri Lankan army announcement, 22 Jan. 2009, available at the same website.
81. The Vanni is the name given to the mainland area of the Northern Province. It encompasses the whole of Mannar, Mullaitivu and Vavuniya Districts, and most of Killinochi District.
82. *Report of the UN Secretary-General's Panel of Experts on Accountability in Sri Lanka*, 31 Mar. 2011, executive summary, p. 2. The report was released by the UN Secretary-General on 25 Apr. 2011. Available at http://www.un.org/News/dh/infocus/Sri_Lanka/POE_Report_Full.pdf.
83. See e.g. the statement by Prof. G. L. Peiris (Foreign Minister since 2010) in parliament, 3 Apr. 2011.
84. UN doc. SG/SM/13524 of 25 Apr. 2011.
85. Statement of Deputy Minister of Economic Development, Lakshman Yapa Abeywardena, at a cabinet press briefing, Colombo, 26 May 2011. Report of Sri Lanka Broadcasting Corporation, same day.
86. Statement of Mahinda Samarasinghe, Minister of Plantation Industries and the President's Special Envoy on Human Rights, at the 17th Session of the UN Human Rights Council, Geneva, 30 May 2011. Available at http://www.mea.gov.lk/index.php?option=com_content&task=view&id=2795&Itemid=75.

87. *Humanitarian Operation: Factual Analysis July 2006–May 2009* (Colombo: Ministry of Defence, July 2011), p. 1. Available at http://www.defence.lk/news/20110801_Conf.pdf.
88. Statement from UN Secretary-General's office, 12 Sept. 2011. Available at http://www.un.org/apps/sg/sgstats.asp?nid=5506.
89. Joint letter from Amnesty International, Human Rights Watch and International Crisis Group, to LLRC, 14 Oct. 2010, p. 1. See also *When Will They Get Justice? Failures of Sri Lanka's Lessons Learnt and Reconciliation Commission* (London: Amnesty International, 7 Sept. 2011), p. 6. Available at http://www.amnesty.org.
90. *Report of the Commission of Inquiry on Lessons Learnt and Reconciliation* (Colombo, Nov. 2011), p. 145. The report had been submitted to President Rajapaksa on 15 Nov. 2011, and was presented to parliament, and published, on 16 Dec. Report and annexes available at http://www.priu.gov.lk/news_update/Current_Affairs/ca201112/final_report_llrc.htm.
91. *Report of the Commission of Inquiry*, p. 134.
92. *Report of the Commission of Inquiry*, pp. 328 and 329.
93. *Report of Commission of Inquiry*, pp. 335–6.
94. 'Sri Lanka: "counting civilian war deaths"', report posted on 24 Nov. 2011 on BBC website. Available at http://www.bbc.co.uk/news/world-asia-15868038.
95. 'Sri Lanka: Report Fails to Advance Accountability', statement on Human Rights Watch website, 16 Dec. 2011. Available at http://www.hrw.org/news/2011/12/16/sri-lanka-report-fails-advance-accountability.
96. Victoria Nuland, Spokesperson, US State Department, Daily Press Briefing, Washington DC, 19 Dec. 2011. Available at http://www.state.gov/r/pa/prs/dpb/2011/12/178982.htm#SRILANKA.
97. 'Statement on the Report of Sri Lanka's Lessons Learnt and Reconciliation Commission', International Crisis Group, Brussels, 22 Dec. 2011. Available at http://www.crisisgroup.org/en/publication-type/media-releases.aspx.
98. Official Spokesperson, Ministry of External Affairs, India, press briefing, 25 Dec. 2011. Available at http://www.mea.gov.in/mystart.php?id=530318810.
99. 'Promoting Reconciliation and Accountability in Sri Lanka', UN Human Rights Council resolution, Geneva, 22 Mar. 2012. There were 24 votes in favour, 15 against and 8 abstentions.
100. Three critical publications referring to the post-2009 situation are *No War, No Peace: The Denial of Minority Rights and Justice in Sri Lanka* (London: Minority Rights Group International, Jan. 2011). Available at http://www.minorityrights.org/645/reports/reports.html; *Forgotten Prisoners: Sri Lanka uses Anti-terrorism Laws to Detain Thousands* (London: Amnesty International, Mar. 2011). Available at http://www.amnesty.org/en/library/info/ASA37/001/2011/en; and *Out of the Silence: New Evidence of Ongoing Torture in Sri Lanka* (London: Freedom from Torture, Nov. 2011). Available at http://www.freedomfromtorture.org/srilanka-report.

Chapter 3 Lakshman Kadirgamar: The Lawyer Turned Politician

1. The Liberation Tigers of Tamil Eelam (LTTE) claimed to have had what they called their 'historic birth' in 1972 under a different name, and were re-formed in 1976 as the LTTE. They began as militants with the traditional Tamil

minority political parties in the North and launched an armed campaign for a separate state in the North and East of Sri Lanka. The resulting war was ended only with the LTTE defeat in 2009. It is estimated that from 70,000 up to as many as possibly 100,000 people died in the period due to the virtual 'civil war'.
2. The Janatha Vimukthi Peramuna (JVP) founded in 1965 had the aim of being a leading force for socialist revolution in Sri Lanka as a worthy successor to the Trotskyite and Marxist movements there. In 1971 it led a youth rebellion in southern and central Sri Lanka that was swiftly defeated by the security forces at a reported cost of some 15,000 lives. In 1987–9 it led a further revolt, again suppressed by government forces. Several thousand more are reported to have lost their lives in the second JVP uprising. After 1989 it took part in democratic political processes.
3. The United National Party (UNP) was founded in 1946, mainly by amalgamating essentially conservative parties. It was the successor to the Ceylon National Congress that had led the campaign for political independence from the British, which was achieved in February 1948. The party has been in power for a total of 33 years since 1948.
4. The Sri Lanka Freedom Party (SLFP) was formed in 1951 by Solomon West Ridgeway Dias Bandaranaike, an Oxford alumnus, when he broke away from the UNP. He became prime minister in 1956. He was assassinated in September 1959, the first of the political assassinations in independent Sri Lanka. The party has been in power for a total of 28 years and is in office currently (2012).
5. Vijaya Kumaratunga was assassinated on 16 February 1988 in the garden of his house where he lived with his wife Chandrika and their two children. The military wing of the JVP claimed responsibility.
6. *Parliamentary Debates* (Hansard), Sri Lanka Parliament, 25 Aug. 1994.
7. UN General Assembly, *Official Records*, 49th session, 26 Sept. 1994, p. 23.
8. Following the LTTE ambush of 13 soldiers in Jaffna at about 11.30 p.m. on 23 July 1983, anti-Tamil race-riots erupted the next night and for a week thereafter in Colombo and elsewhere in the south of Sri Lanka. An estimated 600 people were killed and many rendered homeless for some time. Thousands left the country in the months and years to follow, especially to the West.
9. Alexander Downer, Lakshman Kadirgamar Memorial Lecture 2008, Colombo, 15 Oct. 2008.
10. Private conversation.
11. Kadirgamar's speech at the unveiling of his portrait at the Oxford Union, 18 Mar. 2005.
12. Letter to Karl Inderfurth, US Assistant Secretary of State for South Asian Affairs, Feb. 1999.
13. Elephant Pass, connecting the Jaffna Peninsula to the mainland, was eventually recaptured by the Sri Lankan Army in January 2009 as part of its major 2008–9 campaign against the LTTE.
14. On 28 February 2001, in a written statement to the House of Commons, the UK Home Secretary, Jack Straw, had recommended adding 21 organizations to the list of proscribed organizations under the Terrorism Act 2000. One of these proscribed organizations was the LTTE.
15. 'World leaders awakened by attacks on US', *The Sunday Times* (Colombo), 16 Sept. 2001. The article was by 'Our Diplomatic Editor'. Available at http://sundaytimes.lk/010916/frontm.html#fLABEL5.

16. President Chandrika Kumaratunga, interview with George Arney, 30 Dec. 1999. Available at http://news.bbc.co.uk/go/em/fr/-/1/hi/world/south_asia/583120.stm; and Report from Susannah Price in Colombo, 1 Feb. 2000. Available at http://news.bbc.co.uk/go/em/fr/-/1/hi/world/south_asia/627281.stm.
17. *Parliamentary Debates* (Hansard), Sri Lanka Parliament, 23 Jan. 2002.
18. In 1997, after several rounds of discussions in both London and Colombo with Kadirgamar, Dr Liam Fox, a front-line Conservative MP, then UK Under Secretary for Foreign and Commonwealth Affairs and later Shadow Defence Secretary and then (from May 2010 to October 2011) Secretary of State for Defence, succeeded in brokering what was to be called 'the Liam Fox Agreement'. Signed on 4 April 1997 by President Chandrika Kumaratunga and opposition leader Ranil Wickremesinghe, it committed the two parties to brief and seek the opinions of each other 'on significant developments relating to the ethnic conflict, both in the strictest confidence; ... the party in opposition will not undermine any discussions or decisions between the party in government and any other party ... aimed at resolving the ethnic conflict, if these discussions and decisions have taken place with the concurrence of the party in opposition; against the background of such concurrence, on election to government, either party will honour all such decisions in full.' It was essentially to ensure that neither the government nor the opposition would torpedo the other's initiative to reach a negotiated settlement with the LTTE for narrow political advantage. Dr Fox's Conservative Party lost that year's general elections in the UK and the agreement itself, however well intentioned, never bore any real fruit as the Sri Lankan government and opposition continued to use the ethnic conflict as a political weapon to knock down the other.
19. *Parliamentary Debates* (Hansard), Sri Lanka Parliament, 23 Jan. 2002.
20. *Parliamentary Debates* (Hansard), Sri Lanka Parliament, 8 May 2003. For the text of this speech, see pp. 193–205 above.
21. Private conversations.
22. LTTE leader V. Prabhakaran's *Mahaveer* day broadcast, 27 Nov. 2005.
23. LTTE Eastern Commander Vinayagamoorthy Muralitharan, alias 'Col. Karuna', in an interview with *The Guardian*, London, 21 Mar. 2009.
24. Private conversations.
25. Kadirgamar, letter to President Chandrika Kumaratunga, 4 Apr. 2004.
26. Mahinda Rajapaksa became prime minister on 6 Apr. 2004, and president on 19 Nov. 2005.
27. Private conversations.
28. President's statement on the assassination of Lakshman Kadirgamar, 13 Aug. 2005.
29. Lakshman Kadirgamar Commemorative Meeting, Colombo, 12 Oct. 2005.
30. Private conversations.
31. *Parliamentary Debates* (Hansard), Sri Lanka Parliament, 23 Sept. 2005.

Chapter 4 A Duty of Service in an Age of Terror

1. Judith M. Brown, *Windows into the Past: Life-Histories and the Historian of South Asia* (Notre Dame, Indiana: University of Notre Dame Press, 2009), chap. 1, 'Colleges, Cohorts, and Dynasties'.
2. Chris Patten, *What Next? Surviving the Twenty-first Century* (London: Allen Lane, 2008), pp. 85–6.

3. Cicero, *Treatise on the Laws*, Book III, in *The Political Works of Marcus Tullius Cicero*, trans. Francis Barham, vol. 2 (London: Edmund Spettigue, 1842), p. 138.
4. Tony Blair, 'Shackled in war on terror', *Sunday Times* (London), 27 May 2007. Blair stepped down as prime minister on 27 June 2007.
5. Tom Bingham, *The Rule of Law* (London: Allen Lane, 2010), p. 136.

Chapter 5 Reflections on a 'Citizen of the World'

1. Madeleine K. Albright, 'State Department List of Terrorist Organizations', signed 2 Oct. 1997 and published in the *Federal Register*, 8 Oct. 1997.
2. Lucien Rajakarunanayake, interview with Kadirgamar, *Business Today* (Colombo), Mar. 1997, p. 20.
3. Interview in *Business Today* (Colombo), Mar. 1997, p. 19.

Chapter 6 A True South Asian

1. Kadirgamar, 'Regional Cooperation and Security: A Sri Lankan View', Krishna Menon Memorial Centenary Lecture, Kota, Rajasthan, 15 Dec. 1996, p. 10.

Document 1 Report to Amnesty International on my Visit to South Vietnam

1. Ngo Dinh Diem was Prime Minister of South Vietnam, 1954–5, and President, 1955–63.
2. Ngo Dinh Nhu, one of Ngo Dinh Diem's brothers, was head of the secret police. His wife, Madame Nhu, a convert to Catholicism, adopted a virulent form of anti-communism. Together they were widely viewed as more powerful than Diem himself.
3. From the context it appears that Kadirgamar meant to say 'seventeen were *Catholics*'.

Document 3 Human Rights and Armed Conflict

1. GA Res. 217 of 10 Dec. 1948, preamble. That resolution did not specifically mandate the formulation of two covenants, but did call for inclusion, within a planned International Covenant on Human Rights, of economic, social and cultural rights.
2. GA Res. 421 of 4 Dec. 1950, section E.
3. Vienna Declaration and Programme of Action, adopted on 25 June 1993 by the World Conference on Human Rights, 14–25 June 1993. Endorsed in GA Res. 48/121 of 20 Dec. 1993.
4. Denise Bindschedler-Robert, cited in ICRC, *Report on Protection of War Victims* (Geneva: ICRC, June 1993), p. 392.
5. The above is a summary of the provisions of common Article 3 of all four 1949 Geneva Conventions. This article, addressing 'armed conflict not of an international character' sets out basic rules applicable even in civil wars.
6. As of June 2012, Sri Lanka is still not a party to 1977 Geneva Protocols I and II on international and non-international armed conflict.

7. 'Profiles in displacement: Sri Lanka', addendum to 'Report of the Representative of the Secretary-General, Mr Francis Deng, submitted pursuant to Commission on Human Rights resolution 1993/95', UN doc. E/CN.4/1994/44/Add.1 of 25 Jan. 1994, para. 67.
8. 'Operation Riviresa' (Operation Sun Rays) was a successful combined military operation by the Sri Lankan Armed Forces in the last three months of 1995 to recapture from the Tamil Tigers the city of Jaffna and the peninsula on which it is situated.
9. The main domestic legislation to which these Sri Lankan presidential directives related was the Prevention of Terrorism (Temporary Provisions) Act no. 48 (1979).
10. Sri Lanka had acceded to the 1984 UN Convention against Torture on 3 January 1994. The Sri Lankan Act giving effect to its provisions was Act No. 22 (1994).
11. The Human Rights Commission of Sri Lanka (HRCSL) was established under the Human Rights Commission Act of 1996. It started its work in 1997 as an independent statutory body to investigate reports of human rights violations. It carried out investigations into cases of torture, disappearances, political killings and other human rights violations in Sri Lanka. At various times, following disagreements among political parties on a range of issues, it suffered shortages of personnel and resources. Its website is http://hrcsl.lk/english. For accounts of its establishment, work and problems see e.g. 'Visit to Sri Lanka', addendum to 'Report of the Special Rapporteur, Mr Bacre Waly Ndiaye, submitted pursuant to Commission on Human Rights resolution 1997/61', UN doc. E/CN.4/1998/68/Add.2 of 12 Mar. 1998, paras 101–10; and Amnesty International, 'The human rights situation in Sri Lanka', submission to the UN Human Rights Council, UN doc. A/HRC/6/NGO/30 of 4 Sept. 2007.

Document 4 The Global Impact of International Terrorism

1. Here Kadirgamar was referring to the truck-bomb attack on the World Trade Centre in New York on 26 February 1993. Six people died. In March 1994 four men were convicted of carrying out the bombing, and in November 1997 two more were convicted.
2. The truck-bomb attack on a federal government building in Oklahoma City was on 19 April 1995. Over 160 people died. In November 1997 those responsible were convicted.
3. This UK official definition of terrorism is in the Prevention of Terrorism (Temporary Provisions) Act 1989, section 20, part 1. The definition has since been superseded by that in the Terrorism Act 2000, which has been further modified in subsequent legislation.
4. Lord Lloyd of Berwick, *Inquiry into Legislation against Terrorism*, Cm 3420, 2 vols. (London: Stationery Office, Oct. 1996).
5. Lord Lloyd of Berwick's notably concise definition of terrorism, modelled on the working definition used by the US Federal Bureau of Investigation, is in his *Inquiry into Legislation*, vol. 1, para. 5.23. It is only 39 words in length. Kadirgamar's two proposed additions would have widened the definition to encompass disruption of vital computer installations and communications; and also added, as possible purposes of terrorism, religious or philosophical objectives.

Subsequently, in section 1 of the UK Terrorism Act 2000, the UK official definition of terrorism was expanded to include disruption of electronic systems; and also to note that the purposes of terrorist action could encompass religious as well as political or ideological causes. In later legislation ethnic causes were added.
6. The attack on the Tokyo underground railway system was on 20 March 1995. Thirteen people were killed, and 50 were severely injured.
7. The terrorist attack on the US base at Dhahran in Saudi Arabia was on 25 June 1996. Nineteen US military personnel were killed.
8. The 22nd G7 summit meeting was held in the Museum of Contemporary Art in Lyon on 27–29 June 1996. It issued the Lyon 'Declaration on Terrorism' on 27 June, just two days after the Dhahran bombing. (In 1997, with the inclusion of Russia, the G7 became the G8.)
9. The International Convention for the Suppression of Terrorist Bombings was adopted by GA Res. 52/164 of 15 December 1997, and entered into force on 23 May 2001.
10. The record of signatures, accessions and ratifications of the International Convention for the Suppression of Terrorist Bombings is available at http://treaties.un.org/pages/Treaties.aspx?id=18&subid=A&lang=en.
11. On 25 January 1998 the Temple of the Tooth in Kandy – perhaps the most sacred shrine in the world for Buddhists – was attacked and severely damaged by suicide bombers. About eight people were killed and 25 injured. There appears to be no doubt that the attack was organized by the LTTE.
12. 'British Tamils fund war in Sri Lanka', *The Times*, London, 23 Oct. 1997, p. 17.
13. This is a reference to GA Res. 49/60 of 9 Dec. 1994, and its annex, Declaration on Measures to Eliminate International Terrorism.
14. 1994 UN Declaration on Measures to Eliminate International Terrorism, paragraph 5(f).
15. Lloyd of Berwick, *Inquiry into Legislation*, para. 12.40. This report was the work of Lord Berwick aided by a team and by an extensive consultative process, not of a 'committee' as such.
16. Lloyd of Berwick, *Inquiry into Legislation*, para. 13.31. The Terrorism Act 2000, section 1, did indeed establish that the act applied to international as well as domestic terrorism. It encompassed actions that were not necessarily threats to UK, and it addressed threats to the public or the government of countries other than the UK.
17. Lloyd of Berwick, *Inquiry into Legislation*, para. 13.32.
18. Lloyd of Berwick, *Inquiry into Legislation*, para. 6.12. This power to proscribe foreign terrorist organizations was in the Terrorism Act 2000, section 3.
19. The UK, having signed the 1997 UN Convention for the Suppression of Terrorist Bombings on 12 January 1998, ratified it on 7 March 2001. In the meantime the UK had also passed the Terrorism Act 2000.

Document 5 The Terrorism Challenge to Democracies

1. The UK legislation containing the prohibition of conspiracy to commit terrorist acts overseas is the Terrorism Act 2000.
2. This is a reference to the G7 summit meeting in Lyon on 27–29 June 1996.
3. The International Convention for the Suppression of the Financing of Terrorism was adopted by GA Res. 54/109 of 9 December 1999, and entered into force on

10 April 2002. Sri Lanka became a party on 8 September 2000, the UK on 7 March 2001, and the US on 26 June 2002. The record of signatures, accessions and ratifications of the convention is available at http://treaties.un.org/pages/Treaties.aspx?id=18&subid=A&lang=en.
4. The Ad Hoc Committee on International Terrorism had been established by the UN General Assembly in GA Res. 51/210 of 17 December 1996. By the end of 2000 it had begun work on a draft comprehensive convention on international terrorism. This proved difficult. On the problems encountered, including in agreeing on a definition of terrorism, see 'Report of the Ad Hoc Committee established by General Assembly resolution 51/210 of 17 December 1996: Fourteenth session (12–16 Apr. 2010)', UN doc. A/65/37 (New York: UN, 2010). Available at http://www.un.org/law/terrorism/index.html.
5. Sri Lanka was one of six countries which signed the International Convention for the Suppression of the Financing of Terrorism on 10 January 2000 – the day on which it was opened for signature.
6. The US placed the LTTE on the list of foreign militant groups under the 1996 US Anti-Terrorism Act on 2 October 1997.
7. SAARC Regional Convention on Suppression of Terrorism, Art. 1(e). The Convention was adopted at Kathmandu on 4 November 1987 by foreign ministers from the seven SAARC member states. Text available at http://www.saarc-sec.org/SAARC-Conventions/63. The Convention entered into force on 22 August 1988 following its ratification by all member states. An Additional Protocol to the Convention, addressing matters relating to the financing of terrorism, was signed at Islamabad in January 2004 and entered into force on 12 January 2006.
8. The case, *Suresh v. Canada (Minister of Citizenship and Immigration)*, concerned a Sri Lankan Tamil, Mr Manickavasagam Suresh, whose deportation from Canada had been ordered in 1997, and who appealed the decision through the Canadian courts. This is an extract from the decision of Canada's Federal Court of Appeal on 18 January 2000. The full text is available at: http://www.haguejusticeportal.net/Docs/NLP/Canada/Suresh_v_Canada_Fed_Court_Appeal_18-01-2000.pdf. (The transcript of Kadirgamar's lecture contained minor errors in the quotation from this source, all rectified here. The only one that affected the meaning was that Mr Suresh was described as the defendant, not the appellant.)
9. Subsequently the case of *Suresh v. Canada (Minister of Citizenship and Immigration)* was considered by the Supreme Court of Canada. The judgment, given 11 Jan. 2002, is available at http://scc.lexum.umontreal.ca/en/2002/2002scc1/2002scc1.html. Mr Suresh was eventually permitted to stay in Canada, but under strict conditions.
10. The PKK is the Kurdish Workers' Party, involved in an insurrection in Turkey. (The transcript of Kadirgamar's lecture referred to 'PPA', but this must have been an error in transcription, as the case in California concerned the LTTE and the PKK.)
11. *Humanitarian Law Project v. Reno*, US Court of Appeals for the Ninth Circuit, decision of 3 Mar. 2000. Available at http://ftp.resource.org/courts.gov/c/F3/205/205.F3d.1130.98-56280.98-56062.html.
12. The quotation as cited by the US Court of Appeals in California is from the US Antiterrorism and Effective Death Penalty Act of 1996.
13. *Humanitarian Law Project v. Reno*, decision of 3 Mar. 2000.

14. The two parties that had been dominant in Sri Lanka were the United National Party (UNP) and the Sri Lanka Freedom Party (SLFP).
15. The relevant legislation in Sri Lanka is Prevention of Terrorism (Temporary Provisions) Act no. 48 (1979). 23 years later, the 2002 'Agreement on a ceasefire between the Government of the Democratic Socialist Republic of Sri Lanka and the Liberation Tigers of Tamil Eelam' would contain the provision (Art. 2.12): 'The Parties agree that search operations and arrests under the Prevention of Terrorism Act shall not take place.'
16. Relevant cases in which the Supreme Court of Sri Lanka struck down particular banning orders under the censorship laws include *Leader Publications Ltd.* v. *Ariya Rubasinghe and Ors.*, 30 June 2000, S.C. (F/R) no. 362/2000. For a critical evaluation see *Global Trends on the Right to Information: A Survey of South Asia* (London: Art. 19 and others, July 2001), para. 4.3.3.
17. The Minister for Industrial Development, C. V. Guneratne, his wife and 20 others were killed in a suicide bombing in Colombo on 7 June 2000.
18. The UNP candidate in the 1994 presidential election, Gamini Dissanayake, was assassinated in Colombo on 24 October 1994.
19. UN Millennium Declaration, GA Res. 55/2 of 8 Sept. 2000, para. 9.
20. SC Res. 1269 of 19 Oct. 1999, on international terrorism.
21. Graça Machel, *Impact of Armed Conflict on Children*, UN doc. A/51/306 of 26 Aug. 1996.
22. From 1998 to 2005 the Special Representative of the UN Secretary-General for Children in Armed Conflict was Mr Olara A. Otunnu.

Document 6 Preventing the Recurrence of Harm to War-affected Children

1. The Children's Charter, enacted in 1992, is the primary Sri Lankan policy document that promotes the rights of the child.
2. The National Child Protection Authority (NCPA) was established in Sri Lanka in 1998 under the Presidential Task Force as an oversight agency for the protection of children against any form of abuse.
3. The UN Committee on the Rights of the Child was established pursuant to Art. 43 of the CRC. Among other things it monitors implementation of the Optional Protocol on Children in Armed Conflict.

Document 7 Address to UN General Assembly

1. General Assembly Millennium Summit, 8 Sept. 2000, UN doc. A/55/PV.7.
2. Kofi Annan, 'Renewing the United Nations: A Programme for Reform – Report of the Secretary-General', UN doc. A/51/950 of 14 July 1997, para. 143.
3. President Bouteflika of Algeria's statement at the conclusion of the UN General Assembly Millennium Summit, 8 Sept. 2000, UN doc. A/55/PV.8, p. 39.
4. 'Financial Havens, Banking Secrecy and Money-Laundering' (Vienna: UN Office for Drug Control and Crime Prevention, 1998). Also published in *Crime Prevention and Criminal Justice Newsletter* (Centre for Social Development and Humanitarian Affairs, Vienna), as a double issue 34 and 35. (In his address Kadirgamar gave the year of this study as 1988. This is incorrect: the mistake has been corrected in this text.)

5. President Bouteflika, statement of 8 Sept. 2000, note 3 above, p. 39.
6. SAARC's activities had been held back by the Kargil War between India and Pakistan in May–July 1999.
7. On the background to Olara Otunnu's statement, see 'Secretary-General's special representative for children and armed conflict condemns attacks on civilians and use of child soldiers: urges International Community to pressure combatants to end practices', UN doc. ST/DPI/PRESS/HR/4388 of 9 Nov. 1998; and *Child Soldiers Global Report 2001*, pp. 401–2. Available at http://www.child-soldiers.org/library/global-reports.
8. On the background to the UNICEF statement, see *Child Soldiers Global Report 2001*, pp. 401–2.
9. The Special Session of the UN General Assembly on Children, originally scheduled for 19–21 September 2001, and postponed on account of the attack on New York on 11 September 2001, was held on 8–10 May 2002. It was convened to review progress since the World Summit for Children in 1990 and re-energize global commitment to children's rights.

Document 8 The Seven Sisters of South Asia: Where are they Going?

1. Jawaharlal Nehru, speaking on the Motion for Adjournment on the Madras Tuticorin Train Disaster, *Lok Sabha Debates*, vol. 9, Fourteenth Session, 26 Nov. 1956, col. 995–6. The train disaster had happened on the morning of 23 November.
2. The Sirima–Shastri Pact between Sri Lanka and India, signed on 30 October 1964, paved the way for the repatriation of some 600,000 people of Indian origin from Sri Lanka to India, with 375,000 being accepted as citizens of Sri Lanka. In 1982 it was abrogated by India.
3. The 11th SAARC summit in Kathmandu had eventually been held on 4–6 January 2002; the 12th was eventually held in Islamabad on 2–6 January 2004.
4. J.R. Jayewardene was Prime Minister of Sri Lanka from 23 July 1977 to 4 February 1978. He was President from 4 February 1978 to 2 January 1989.
5. The 9th SAARC summit was held in Malé, the capital of the Maldives, 12–14 May 1997.
6. This report was published as *SAARC Vision beyond the Year 2000: Report of the SAARC Group of Eminent Persons Established by 9th SAARC Summit* (New Delhi: Shipra Publications, 1999).
7. The Malé Declaration of 14 May 1997, para. 6. Available at http://www.saarc-sec.org/main.php?id=55&t=4.
8. Chandrika Kumaratunga was President of Sri Lanka from 12 Nov. 1994 to 19 Nov. 2005.
9. The 1997 Malé Declaration, para. 8.
10. The 10th SAARC summit was held in Colombo, 29–31 July 1998.
11. The concept of a South Asian Free Trade Area (SAFTA) had been regularly discussed at SAARC summits. An agreement to establish it was reached at the 12th SAARC summit, held at Islamabad on 6 Jan. 2004. It requires ratification by member states.
12. The Lahore Declaration was a bilateral agreement between India and Pakistan signed on 21 February 1999 by Prime Ministers Vajpayee and Sharif.

Notes to pages 184–195　　　　　　　　　　　　　　　　　　　　　　251

13. 'The day SAARC nearly collapsed', *Sunday Times* (Colombo), 21 Mar. 1999. The article was by 'Our Diplomatic Editor'. Available at http://sundaytimes.lk/990321/frontm.html. There are a few minor discrepancies between the text of the article as cited by Kadirgamar (which has been largely followed here) and the text of the article as reproduced on this website. None change the basic facts or meaning.
14. 'The day SAARC nearly collapsed', *Sunday Times* (Colombo), 21 Mar. 1999.
15. Surjit Mansingh, 'Possibilities for SAARC in the twenty-first century in the light of centuries past', in Dipankar Banerjee (ed.), *SAARC in the Twenty-First Century: Towards a Cooperative Future* (New Delhi: India Research Press, for the Regional Centre for Strategic Studies, Colombo, 2002), p. 36.
16. Mansingh, 'Possibilities for SAARC in the twenty-first century', p. 37.
17. Mansingh, 'Possibilities for SAARC in the twenty-first century', p. 28.
18. The India–Sri Lanka Free Trade Agreement (FTA), signed in New Delhi on 28 December 1998, came into force on 1 March 2000.
19. Subsequently, in 2004, Nepal and Bhutan were admitted to the organization. On 31 July 2004, at its first summit, it was agreed that the organization should be known as BIMSTEC or the Bay of Bengal Initiative for Multi-Sectoral Technical and Economic Cooperation.
20. In 2004 Kadirgamar was Chairman of IORARC.
21. Mr Gujral at the Royal Institute of International Affairs (Chatham House), London, 23 Sept. 1996. The speech is reproduced in I. K. Gujral, *A Foreign Policy for India* (New Delhi: Ministry of External Affairs, 1998), pp. 69–81.
22. Kadirgamar, 'Regional Cooperation and Security: A Sri Lankan View', Krishna Menon Memorial Centenary Lecture at Kota, Rajasthan (Kadirgamar papers, Colombo), 15 Dec. 1996, p. 12.
23. See the South Asia Foundation website at http://www.southasiafoundation.org/saf/about_saf.htm.

Document 9 Flaws in the 2002 Ceasefire Agreement

1. The text of the CFA is reprinted in John Gooneratne, *Negotiating with the Tigers (LTTE) (2002–2005): A View from the Second Row* (Pannipitiya, Sri Lanka: Stamford Lake, 2007), pp. 123–34. Available at http://www.priu.gov.lk/news_update/Current_Affairs/ca200202/20020223mou.htm.
2. Gunnar Sørbø et al., *Pawns of Peace: Evaluation of Norwegian Peace Efforts in Sri Lanka, 1997–2009* (Oslo: Norwegian Agency for Development Cooperation, Nov. 2011), pp. 7 and 55. Available at http://www.norad.no/en/tools-and-publications/publications/evaluations/publication?key=386346.
3. *Report of the Commission of Inquiry on Lessons Learnt and Reconciliation* (Colombo), Nov. 2011, pp. 12–30.
4. Under the Sri Lanka Constitution, the president has all of these responsibilities. For President Chandrika Kumaratunga's critical views on the peace process and the government's approach to it, see her interview published in *The Hindu* (New Delhi), 12 Apr. 2003.
5. Letter (9 pages) from President Kumaratunga to Prime Minister Wickremesinghe, 27 Feb. 2002. A summary of the letter, listing in bullet-point form nine areas of concern about the CFA, is available at http://www.priu.gov.lk/Peace_Process.html.

6. The full text of Art. 1.3 of the CFA is: 'The Sri Lankan armed forces shall continue to perform their legitimate task of safeguarding the sovereignty and territorial integrity of Sri Lanka without engaging in offensive operations against the LTTE.'
7. The Eelam People's Democratic Party (EPDP), formed in the late 1980s, has from the early days of its existence proclaimed its opposition to the use of violence and its support for participation in the democratic political mainstream of Sri Lanka. Since 1994 it has been represented in parliament.
8. On 20 March 2003 the Chinese trawler *Fu Yuan Ya 225*, fishing lawfully in Sri Lanka's Exclusive Economic Zone, was attacked, evidently by LTTE naval units. Reports indicated that 17 Chinese crew members died.
9. The Jaffna Peninsula, at the northern tip of Sri Lanka, was the focus of much military action during the conflict.
10. Kadirgamar's allusions here to a second Nambiar report, and the suggestion that Satish Nambiar might be being 'leaned on' to amend his conclusions, require a word of explanation. The text of Nambiar's 2003 report on the resettlement of displaced persons in the High Security Zones set up by the Sri Lanka Defence Forces is in Fernando Austin, *My Belly is White: Reminiscences of a Peacetime Secretary of Defence* (Colombo: Vijitha Yapa Publications, 2008), pp. 793–802. Although the exact date of this report is not stated in that book, it appears that it was in fact handed over to the Sri Lankan government in late April 2003 and was published on 8 or 9 May 2003 – i.e. at about the time of this speech by Kadirgamar. A useful account of Nambiar's work is V. S. Sambandan, 'An Agenda for De-escalation', *Frontline*, New Delhi, vol. 20, no. 11, 24 May–6 June 2003. Available at http://www.frontlineonnet.com/fl2011/fl201100.htm. See also Nambiar's postscript to this chapter.

Document 10 Third World Democracy in Action: The Sri Lanka Experience

1. Here Kadirgamar is evidently referring to an abortive *coup d'état* in January 1962, led by some Roman Catholics and Protestant Christians in reaction to Buddhist agitation for state control. For a brief discussion see K. M. de Silva, *A History of Sri Lanka* (London: Hurst, 1981), p. 528.
2. The JVP (or People's Liberation Front), founded in 1965, had been involved in armed uprisings against the government of Sri Lanka in 1971 and in 1987–9.
3. The Tamil National Alliance (TNA), founded in 2001, won 15 seats in parliament in the elections of December 2001, 22 in April 2004 and 14 in April 2010. Originally supporting the LTTE demand for an independent Tamil state, in 2010 it modified its stance, calling instead for regional self-rule within Sri Lanka.
4. Kadirgamar's 11 Aug. 2003 Prem Bhatia Memorial Lecture. Available at http://www.prembhatiatrust.com/lecture8.htm.

Document 11 The Peaceful Ascendancy of China: A South Asian Perspective

1. 'Asia in the 21st Century', Maulana Abul Kalam Azad Memorial Lecture, New Delhi, 19 Dec. 1995, text, p. 12. (Kadirgamar papers, Colombo.)

2. Rudyard Kipling, 'The Man Who Was', in Kipling, *Life's Handicap: Being Stories of Mine Own People* (1891), pocket edn. (London: Macmillan, 1907), p. 99.
3. Shelton U. Kodikara, *Foreign Policy of Sri Lanka: A Third World Perspective*, 2nd edn. (Delhi: Chanayaka Publications, 1992), pp. 134–9.
4. Bonnie S. Glaser and Evan S. Medeiros, 'The changing ecology of foreign policy-making in China: the ascension and demise of the theory of "peaceful rise"', *China Quarterly* 190 (June 2007), pp. 291–310.
5. *China's National Defense in 2010*, Information Office of the State Council of the People's Republic of China, 31 Mar. 2011, Ch. II. Available at http://www.china.org.cn/government/whitepaper/node_7114675.htm.
6. Barry Buzan, 'China in international society: is "peaceful rise" possible?', *Chinese Journal of International Politics* 3/1 (Spring 2010), pp. 5 and 35. Available at http://cjip.oxfordjournals.org/content/3/1.toc.
7. The UN Economic and Social Commission for Asia and the Pacific (ESCAP) is the regional development arm of the UN for the Asia-Pacific region. It was established at a meeting in Shanghai in 1947.
8. The aircraft mentioned by Kadirgamar was a Swissair DC-8 coming from Geneva, bound for Bombay and Peking. It crashed when landing at Athens-Hellinikon airport on 7 October 1979. It was reported that 14 people died because they were trapped in the centre-aft section of the fuselage, and could not be rescued in the fire; and several passengers were injured during evacuation. The aircraft was written off. Controversies about the causes of the accident and the subsequent cases in the Greek courts are mentioned in several sources, including http://yarchive.net/air/airliners/greek_courts.html.
9. Henry Kissinger, *Diplomacy* (New York: Simon & Schuster, 1994), pp. 829–30.
10. The figure refers to annual income.
11. Wen Jiabao, press conference, Beijing, 14 Mar. 2004. Available at http://www.gov.cn/english/official/2005-07/26/content_17183.htm.
12. At a dinner in London, c. 11 May 2004. Reported at http://news.bbc.co.uk/1/hi/business/3700921.stm.
13. The eleventh Central Committee of the Chinese Communist Party lasted from 1977 to 1982. It held seven plenary sessions in that period. The third of these sessions, held in December 1978, decided to shift the focus of the Party's work to socialist modernization and set a policy of reform and opening up to the outside world.
14. At the 13th SAARC summit in Dhaka on 12–13 November 2005 the member states welcomed the desire of the People's Republic of China and Japan to be associated as observers. Observer status for these and certain other countries was agreed at the 14th SAARC summit in New Delhi on 3–4 April 2007.
15. Fa Hsien's name is also rendered as Fa Xian. In the lecture script Kadirgamar had certain year dates in this paragraph suffixed with 'AC', but to avoid ambiguity they have been rendered here as 'AD'.
16. Cheng Ho lived from 1371 to 1433 AD. His name is also rendered as Zheng He.
17. Emperor Liang Wu Ti (464–549 AD) is also known as Liang Wu Di and as Emperor Wu of Liang.
18. The Hickenlooper Amendment to the 1962 US Foreign Assistance Act was introduced by Bourke B. Hickenlooper, Republican Senator for Iowa. This amendment thus post-dates the events of the early 1950s described by Kadirgamar. The US actions against Sri Lanka were based on the pre-existing US embargo of the People's Republic of China.

19. Panchasila, otherwise known as Panch Sheel, or the five principles of peaceful coexistence. They were enunciated in the preamble to the Sino-Indian Agreement on Trade and Intercourse between Tibet Region of China and India, signed on 29 April 1954: '(1) mutual respect for each other's territorial integrity and sovereignty; (2) mutual non-aggression; (3) mutual non-interference in each other's internal affairs; (4) equality and mutual benefit; and (5) peaceful coexistence.' (*United Nations Treaty Series*, vol. 299, p. 70.) They were incorporated in modified form in a statement of ten principles issued by the April 1955 Asian-African conference at Bandung in Indonesia.

Index

Compiled by Rohan Bolton

Note: *n* following a page number denotes an endnote with relevant number.

9/11 attacks 48, 49, 220

African National Congress (ANC) 26–7
Albright, Madeleine 47, 49, 70, 72
Alexander, Professor Yonah 137, 147, 150
Amarasinghe, Somawansa 56
Amnesty International
  foundation 89
  South Vietnam report 89–105
  and Sri Lanka 66
Anti-Terrorism Act (US/1996) 70, 74, 142
armed forces
  allegations of crimes against civilians 30–34, 111
  duties towards civilians 113–15, 118–19, 146
  education 111, 117
  officer management 204
  Operation Riviresa 116
  weakness 73
arms supplies, to LTTE 73, 74, 147, 196, 199
ASEAN (Association of Southeast Asian Nations) 74
assassinations
  by LTTE 27–8, 39–40, 64, 73–4, 145–6
  and elections 21, 145–6
  Gandhi, Rajiv 27–8, 64, 73–4, 145
  Kadirgamar 6, 35, 40, 57
asylum seekers 128–9, 131, 134
Athulathmudali, Lalith vii 16, 39–40, 42, 48, 239*n*38
Au Ngoc Ho 102
Aung San Suu Kyi 22
Aziz, Sartaj 183

Bandaranaike Centre for International Studies 75–6
  International Relations in a Globalising World (journal) 6, 85, 237*n*7
Bandaranaike, Sirimavo 43, 170, 234
Bandaranaike, S.W.R.D. 16–17, 233, 239*n*40, 243*n*4
Bandung Conference (1955) 24, 254*n*19

Bangladesh 174, 176, 231
Benenson, Peter 89
Berwick report 123–4, 129–31
Bhatia, Prem 220
Bhutan, and SAARC 174, 177
Bhutto, Benazir 176
Bin Laden, Osama 25
Birendra, King of Nepal 174
Blair, Tony 68, 135
Bouteflika, Abdelaziz 160, 162
Brenner, Professor Edgar H. 137, 147
Buddhism
  and Catholics in Vietnam 103–5
  China-Sri Lanka contacts 232, 235
  Hué Buddhist incident 89, 93–5
  Hué Buddhist University 93, 97, 100–102
  and Kadirgamar 10, 11
  in Sri Lanka 71, 211–13, 232, 235
  Temple of the Tooth attack 127, 146, 247*n*11
  UN Vesak Resolution 10
  Vietnamese discrimination 89, 90–91, 92, 93–4
  Vietnamese non-violent campaign 89, 95–9, 100–105
Burma 22
business community 46, 109–110

Cambodia, Pol Pot 135
Can, Ngo Dinh *see* Ngo Dinh Can
Canada
  International Conference on Children 151
  and LTTE 28, 128, 141–2
Cao Van Luan, Fr 91, 93, 101, 102, 103
Catholics, in Vietnam 89, 92, 93, 103–5
Ceasefire Agreement (CFA, 2002) 193–205
  breakdown of peace negotiations 216
  demarcation 'lines of control' 193, 196–7, *map3*
  High Security Zones 201–2, 204–5
  and internally displaced persons 201
  Kadirgamar's criticisms 8, 194–203

Ceasefire Agreement (*continued*)
  Kadirgamar's initial comments 51, 193–4
  lack of timeframe for political negotiations 198
  live firing at sea 199–200
  Nambiar report 202, 204–5, 252n10
  naval operations 195–6, 198–201
  Norway's role 194, 197
  signature 50, 51, 195, 196
  and sovereignty erosion 195–7, 203
  Sri Lanka Monitoring Mission (SLMM) 50, 52, 193, 194, 196–7, 198, 199–201
  violations 52, 194
Ceylon *see* Sri Lanka
Cheng Ho, Admiral 232, 253n16
child soldiers 65, 70, 149–50, 151–2, 154–5, 165–7, 197–8
children
  Child Protection Authority 155, 249n2
  Convention on the Rights of the Child (1989) 114, 155
  education and vocational training 152–3, 154
  International Conference 151, 165, 167
  Optional Protocol on Children in Armed Conflict (2000) 151, 155, 166
  psychological support 154
  SAARC health targets 185
  Sri Lankan government action 154–5
China
  assistance to Sri Lanka 22, 48, 233–4, 235
  car ownership 228
  cultural revolution 226
  diplomatic recognition 232, 233
  economic ascendancy 223, 227–9
  economic problems 229
  employment 228
  environmental pollution 228
  health care 228
  human rights 22, 236
  and India 230–31
  intellectual property system 225–7
  peaceful development 224
  peaceful rise 223–4, 229
  poverty 227–8
  rubber/rice pact with Sri Lanka 232–3, 235–6
  and SAARC 231, 253n14
  Shanghai's transformation 225
  Sino-Indian border dispute 234
  and South Asia 230–31
  and Sri Lanka historical ties 232
  and Sri Lanka relations 231–6
  trawler incident 199, 252n8
Chou En-lai 233, 234
Christianity 10
civil society 152, 163–4, 189
civil war
  Kadirgamar's avoidance of term 29, 111
  see also ethnic conflicts; Sri Lanka conflict (1983–2009)
civilians
  allegations of crimes against 30–34, 111
  casualties 30, 32–3, 66
  duties towards 113–15, 118–19, 146
  LTTE harassment 197
  see also children
Clinton, Hillary 70
Colombo Exhibition 3–4
Colombo Plan for Economic and Social Development 3, 237n3
Commonwealth 49, 52–3
conflicts
  within states 6–7, 159–61
  see also ethnic conflicts; Sri Lanka conflict (1983-2009)
conspiracy law 129, 138
Corbyn, Jeremy 133
corruption 14, 46, 108–9
Crossette, Barbara 29–30
Czech Republic, and Sri Lanka 48

De Saram, John 157
De Silva, H.L. 59
democracy
  cherished and essential 207–8
  coalition politics 208–9
  and collaboration with non-democratic states 8, 22
  and internal state conflict 6–7, 159–61, 163
  Oxford Union debate 16–17
  and sovereignty 22–6
  Sri Lankan tradition of 20, 142–4, 211–12
  and terrorism 20–21, 72, 144–7
  and voter power 209–210
  see also elections
Diem, Ngo Dinh *see* Ngo Dinh Diem
diplomatic service 6, 58
Dissanayake, Gamini (Opposition Leader) 39–40, 146

Index

Donoughmore Commission 14
Downer, Alexander 47
Duong Van Minh, General 99–100

education 152–3, 154, 185, 189
Eelam People's Democratic Party
    (EPDP) 198, 252n7
elections
    1994 42–4, 107
    2001 50, 211
    2004 21, 42–4, 53, 210–215
    2005 66
    and assassinations 21, 145–6
    and bribery 148
    and external interference 210
    reform of proportional representation
        system 20, 208–9
    universal suffrage 13–14, 143
    and violence 211
    voter turnout 144, 211
    and voters' basic needs 209–210,
        215–16
electronic communications, and
    terrorism 124, 127–8, 246–7n5
EPDP (Eelam People's Democratic
    Party) 198, 252n7
ethnic background, Sri Lanka 11–14,
    map1
ethnic conflicts
    1950s 12
    JVP uprisings 17–18, 41, 243n2, 252n2
    see also Sri Lanka conflict (1983–2009)
European Union 28, 63, 64–6, 190,
    241n74
extradition 131–2

Fa Hsien 232, 235
Fonseka, Sarath, Major General 201, 202
Fox, Liam 47, 51, 244n18

Gandhi, Indira 23, 173
Gandhi, Mahatma 9, 10
Gandhi, Rajiv
    assassination 27–8, 64, 73–4, 145
    and Pakistan 176
    and SAARC 173, 176
    and Tamil Tigers 176
Gayoom, Maumoon 178, 180
Geneva Conventions 29, 114–15
globalisation 85, 164, 180
Group of Eminent Persons 177,
    182–3, 185
guerrilla warfare 115

Gujral, Inder Kumar 175, 177, 178, 179,
    188–9
Guneratne, C.V. (Minister of Industrial
    Development) 137, 145–6

Hasina, Sheikh 180
Holterscheidt, Professor 97
Honoré, Tony 16
Hué
    city 92–3
    University 93, 97, 98–9, 100–102
    Vesak incident 89, 93–5
human rights
    China 22, 236
    International Covenant on Civil and
        Political Rights 113, 118
    legal instruments 114
    and Responsibility to Protect 24–5,
        111, 112
    in Sri Lanka 19, 38
Human Rights Commission of Sri
    Lanka (HRCSL) 117–18, 155,
    246n11
Human Rights Task Force (HRTF) 117
Human Rights Watch 33

India
    and China 230–31
    foreign relations 170
    Gujral doctrine 188–9
    High Commissioners 81
    Indian Civil Service 61–2
    Lahore Declaration 183, 250n12
    and LLRC report 33
    LTTE proscription 27, 73–4
    nuclear tests 179
    and Pakistan 170, 172–3, 176, 179–82
    and SAARC 173, 175, 176, 180–82,
        183–4, 187, 188–9
    Sino-Indian border dispute 234
    Sirima–Shastri Pact 170, 250n2
    and Sri Lanka 23, 48, 73, 81, 170, 174–5,
        251n18
    voter numbers 208
India–Sri Lanka Free Trade Agreement
    (1998) 82–3
Indian Ocean Rim Association for
    Regional Cooperation 83
Indian Peace Keeping Force (IPKF) 23,
    48, 64, 176
Indo–Sri Lanka Agreement to Establish
    Peace and Normalcy in Sri Lanka
    (1987) 23, 82, 193

intellectual property 18, 38, 225–7
Internal Self-Governing Authority
    (ISGA) Proposal 216–18
internally displaced persons 19, 116, 201
International Conventions *see* United
    Nations, Conventions
International Covenants *see* United
    Nations, Covenants
International Criminal Court 29, 166
International Crisis Group 33
international humanitarian law *see* laws
    of war
International Labour Organization
    (ILO) 18
*International Relations in a Globalising
    World* (journal) 6, 85, 237n7
Internet, and terrorism 124, 127–8,
    246–7n5
Iraq, US invasion 25, 220–21
ISGA (Internal Self-Governing
    Authority) Proposal 216–18
Israel, assistance to Sri Lanka 48, 73

Jaffna 63–4, 78, 116, 246n8
Jaffna Library 39, 78–9
Japan, terrorist attack 125, 247n6
Jayewardene, J.R. 4, 175, 176, 234,
    250n4
JVP (Janatha Vimukthi Peramuna/
    People's Liberation Front)
  electoral success 21–2, 213–14
  origins 243n2
  respect for Kadirgamar 56
  support for Kadirgamar as prime
    minister 55
  uprisings 17–18, 41, 243n2, 252n2

Kadirgamar, Lakshman
  CAREER
    achievements 4–6, 58–60
    Amnesty report on South Vietnam
      vii, 90–105
    Foreign Minister (1994–2001/2004–5)
      18–19, 38–9, 44–50, 53–8
    ILO consultant 18, 38
    Inner Temple, London 16, 38, 73
    international career postings rejected
      52–3
    international relations contribution
      19–20, 34–5
    law practice 17, 18, 38, 41–2, 73
    Ministry of Media 53, 54
    Opposition (2001–4) 50–53, 194–203
    Parliamentary candidate (1994) 42–4,
      107–110
    possible prime minister 54–5
    President's Counsel 38, 42, 73
    SAARC Council of Ministers
      chairman 171
    UN General Assembly speeches viii,
      45, 61, 75, 157–67
    WIPO Director for Asia and the
      Pacific 18, 38
    WIPO visit to China 225–7
  EDUCATION
    Oxford University, vii, 15–17, 61–2
    President of Oxford Union 16–17,
      37–8, 73, 76
    Trinity College, Kandy 14–15, 37,
      59, 75
    University of Ceylon 15, 37
  PERSONAL
    assassination 6, 35, 40, 57
    Athens air crash 225, 253n8
    and Buddhism 10, 11
    character 40, 58
    citizen of the world 69
    cruise to China 224–5
    debating skills 76
    early fascination with China 224–5
    family background 9, 44
    funeral 11, 40, 58
    hospitality 59, 82, 83
    and Jaffna Library 39, 78–9
    kidney transplant 47–8, 82
    LTTE fatwa 46
    master of English prose vii–viii
    media training 58
    personal relations in official
      conduct 47
    religious scepticism and
      respect 9–11
    running relay 3–4, 237n1–2
    security measures 44, 46, 49, 56–7,
      72, 77
    South Asian identity 81–2
    sporting achievements 15, 37, 75
    Sri Lankan identity 13, 75, 77
  POLITICS
    conflict 'not a civil war' 29, 111
    criticism of Ceasefire Agreement 8,
      194–203
    and ethnic issues 13–14
    and JVP 55, 56
    and laws of war 33–4, 111, 116–19
    and SAARC 62–3, 83, 171–90

Index

Western indifference to terrorism viii, 27, 67, 121, 124–5, 138, 219
Kadirgamar, Rajan (brother) 44
Kadirgamar, Samuel (father) 9, 37
Kadirgamar, Suganthie (wife) 75, 76, 79
Kandy, Temple of the Tooth attack 127, 146, 247*n11*
Kirinde, Stanley 5
Kissinger, Henry, on China 227
Koirala, Girija Prasad 180
Korean War 232–3
Kosovo, NATO intervention 24–5
Kotelawala Defence Academy 111, 117
Kumaratunga, Chandrika
  assassination attempt 145
  background 43
  and Ceasefire Agreement 195
  and China 234
  cohabitation government 50, 65
  and Kadirgamar as future prime minister 54–5
  and Kadirgamar's death 57
  Liam Fox Agreement 244*n18*
  and the LTTE 65, 74
  Millennium Summit message 157–8
  and Ministry of Defence 53
  President 4, 50, 53, 107
  and SAARC 178–9, 179–80, 181–2
Kumaratunga, Vijaya 243*n5*
Kurdish Workers' Party (PKK) 142, 248*n10*

Lahore Declaration 183, 250*n12*
languages
  India 170
  Sri Lanka 12–13
laws of war
  Geneva Conventions 29, 114–15
  international principles 114–15
  Kadirgamar's approach 33–4, 111, 116–19
  Sri Lanka's record 30–34, 116–19
Le Khack Quyen, Dr 94–5, 100–102
Lessons Learnt and Reconciliation Commission (LLRC) 31–3, 194
Li Peng 234
Li Xianian 234
Liang Wu Ti, Emperor 232, 253*n17*
LLRC (Lessons Learnt and Reconciliation Commission) 31–3, 194
LTTE (Liberation Tigers of Tamil Eelam)
  areas of control 193, *map3, map4*
  arms supplies 73, 74, 147, 196, 199
  assassination of Kadirgamar 6, 35, 40, 57
  assassination of Rajiv Gandhi 27–8, 64, 73–4
  assassinations 27–8, 39–40, 64, 73–4, 145–6
  child soldiers 150, 151–2, 154–5, 165–7, 197–8
  Chinese trawler incident 199, 252*n8*
  civilian harassment 197
  defeat 66, 194
  diaspora *see* Tamil diaspora
  fatwa against Kadirgamar 46
  freedom of movement for 'political work' 198
  fund-raising 64, 73, 127–8, 147, 161–2
  and High Security Zones 201–2
  illogicality of a Sri Lanka ban 71
  internal disputes 52
  Internal Self-Governing Authority (ISGA) Proposal 216–18
  international action against *see* proscription (below)
  international isolation 4–5
  and Jaffna 63–4
  Jaffna 'Unceasing Waves' attack 48
  maritime navigation interference 128
  origins and aims 14, 161, 193, 242–3*n1*
  proscription viii, 27–8, 48–9, 70–71, 73–5, 241*n74*
  Sea Tigers 195–6, 198–201
  Sri Lankan deproscription 28
  and Tamil National Alliance (TNA) 215
  Tamil youth insurgency 41
  terrorist atrocities 27, 64, 65, 74, 127, 145–6
  and tsunami aid 56
  and UK 49, 121, 129–34
  see also Ceasefire Agreement (CFA, 2002); Prabhakaran, Velupillai
Luan, Fr *see* Cao Van Luan, Fr

Machel, Graça 150, 151
McKinnon, Don 49, 53
Malaysia, Tamils in 75
Maldives 174, 177–9
Mansingh, Surjit 186, 187
maritime navigation, and LTTE 128
media 144–5, 148–9, 153
Millennium Summit 157–8, 160

Minh, General *see* Duong Van Minh, General
money laundering 131
Moragoda, Milinda 204
Muralitharan, Vinayagamoorthy (Col. Karuna) 52
Myanmar 22

Nambiar, Satish, General 194, 202, 204–5, 252*n10*
NATO, Kosovo intervention 24–5
Nehru, Jawaharlal 24, 170
Nepal 170, 174, 176, 177
Netherlands, LTTE proscription 28, 241*n74*
Ngo Dinh Can 102
Ngo Dinh Diem 89, 90–92, 99, 101, 103, 245*n2*
Ngo Dinh Nhu 91–2, 99, 245*n2*
Ngo Dinh Thuc, Archbishop 93, 101, 104
Nguyen Ding Mau 98–9
Nguyen Van Binh, Archbishop 104
Nhu, Madame 91, 92, 103, 245*n2*
Nhu, Ngo Dinh *see* Ngo Dinh Nhu
Non-Aligned Movement 23–4, 174, 233
Northern Ireland 51, 63, 65, 68
Norway
 and Ceasefire Agreement (2002) 194, 197
 peace negotiations 49–50, 64, 217–18
 see also Sri Lanka Monitoring Mission (SLMM)

Official Language Act (India) 170
Official Language Act (Sri Lanka) 12–13
oil prices 164–5
Olcott, Henry Steel 71
Operation Riviresa 116, 246*n8*
Otunnu, Olara 165–6
Oxford Union Society, Kadirgamar's Presidency 16–17, 37–8, 73, 76
Oxford University 15–17, 61–2

P-TOMS (Post-Tsunami Operational Management Structure) 21, 56, 240*n54*
Pakistan
 assistance to Sri Lanka 48
 and India 170, 172–3, 176, 179–82
 Lahore Declaration 183, 250*n12*
 nuclear tests 179
 and SAARC 172–3, 176, 180–82, 183–4
 and terrorism 25
 trade with China 231
Panchasila principles 235, 254*n19*
Paul VI, Pope 104
peace agreements 29, 193
 Indo–Sri Lanka Agreement (1987) 23, 82, 193
 Liam Fox Agreement 51, 244*n18*
 see also Ceasefire Agreement (CFA, 2002)
peace negotiations
 CFA lack of timeframe for political negotiations 198
 EU support for 64–6
 Internal Self-Governing Authority (ISGA) Proposal 216–18
 and international community 29–30, 203, 218
 Norway's role 49–50, 64, 194, 197, 217–18
People's Alliance (PA) 38, 50, 51, 107, 108–9
People's Liberation Front *see* JVP (Janatha Vimukthi Peramuna/ People's Liberation Front)
Pol Pot 135
post-colonial states 7, 10, 14, 159
Post-Tsunami Operational Management Structure (P-TOMS) 21, 56, 240*n54*
Potomac Institute, International Center for Terrorism Studies 137–8
Powell, Colin 47, 210
Prabhakaran, Velupillai
 assassinations 27–8
 and CFA 52, 193
 crimes against humanity 135
 and European Commissioner's visit 64–6
 inflexibility 64
 and Kadirgamar's assassination 6, 57
Premadasa, Ranasinghe 42, 145
press 144–5, 148–9, 153
Prevention of Terrorism Act (Sri Lanka) 117, 144
Prevention of Terrorism Act (UK) 121, 123, 130
professions 191

Quyen, Dr *see* Le Khack Quyen, Dr

Racial Discrimination, International Convention 114
Rahman, Ziaur (President of Bangladesh) 173, 174

Rajapaksa, Gotabhaya 32
Rajapaksa, Mahinda 21, 52, 55, 66
Ramanathan, Sir Ponnambalam 58
Ratnatunga, Sinha 13
Ratwatte, Anuruddha 48
Ratwatte, Barnes 43
refugees 128–9, 131, 134
regional organizations 7
  see also SAARC (South Asian Association for Regional Cooperation)
Republic of Vietnam see South Vietnam
Responsibility to Protect 24–5, 111, 112
rubber/rice pact, China–Sri Lanka 232–3, 235–6
rule of law 67–8

SAARC (South Asian Association for Regional Cooperation)
  bilateral issues 173–4, 176–7, 181
  and China 231, 253n14
  Colombo Summit (1998) 83, 179–82, 189
  Council of Ministers meeting (1999) 182–4
  economic cooperation 185–6
  establishment 169
  Group of Eminent Persons 177, 182–3, 185
  India's importance 173, 175, 176, 187, 188–9
  informal political consultations 178–9, 183
  Kadirgamar's hopes for 62–3, 83
  Malé Summit (1997) 177–9
  membership 140, 165, 169
  metaphor of the sisters 171
  national interests 172–7, 175–7
  objectives 165, 172, 175
  political relevance 176, 186
  and professions 191
  projects for three or more members 177–8
  prospects 186–91
  regional cooperation 184–6
  social targets 185
  Terrorism Convention 140
  trade agreements 169, 178, 185–6, 250n11
SAFTA (South Asian Free Trade Area) 169, 178, 250n11
SAPTA (South Asia Preferential Trading Arrangement) 178, 185–6
Saudi Arabia, terrorist attack 125, 247n7

security precautions
  Kadirgamar's 44, 46, 49, 56–7, 72, 77
  and terrorism 144, 148–9
Senanayake, Dudley 223
Shanghai 225
Sharif, Nawaz 177, 178, 180–81, 182
Shastri, Lal Bahadur 169–71
Singapore, Tamils in 75
Singh, Jaswant 183
Singh, Madanjeet 189
Singh, Manmohan 62
Sinhalese 11, 45
Sino-Indian border dispute 234
Sirima–Shastri Pact 170, 250n2
South Africa vii, 15–17, 26–7
South Asia 81–5
  and China 230–31
  economic statistics 231
South Asia Foundation 189–90
South Asia Preferential Trading Arrangement (SAPTA) 178, 185–6
South Asian Free Trade Area (SAFTA) 169, 178, 250n11
South Vietnam 89–105
  Buddhist non-violent campaign 89, 95–9, 100–105
  Buddhist Vesak incident 89, 93–5
  Catholic–Buddhist relations 103–5
  Catholics in 89, 92, 93
  coup d'état 89, 90
  crisis background and causes 90–92, 99
  Diem's growing unpopularity 89, 91–2, 101
  discrimination against Buddhism 89, 90–91, 92, 93–4
  Dr Quyen 94–5, 100–102
  fear of communist infiltration 99
  flag regulations 89, 93–4, 102
  Fr Luan 91, 93, 98
  General Minh government 99–100
  Hué Buddhist University 93, 100–102
  press restraint 103
  religious equality 100
  student arrests and torture 97–9
  UN delegation 99
  Viet Cong insurgency 89, 92
  Viet Cong and Vesak incident 94–5
sovereignty 7, 22–6, 158–61, 195–7, 203
Sri Lanka
  Buddhism 71, 211–13, 232, 235
  and China 231–6
  Chinese assistance 22, 48, 233–4, 235
  cohabitation government 50–52, 65

Sri Lanka (*continued*)
  conflicts *see* ethnic conflicts; Sri Lanka conflict (1983–2009)
  constitution 20, 82, 237*n*5
  cultural heritage 83
  democracy 20, 142–4, 211–12
  diplomatic service 6, 58
  economy 49, 83
  education system 143
  ethnic background 11–14, *map1*
  formal title 12
  Freedom Party *see* Sri Lanka Freedom Party (SLFP)
  Human Rights Commission (HRCSL) 117–18, 155, 246*n*11
  human rights record 19, 38
  Human Rights Task Force (HRTF) 117
  illegal immigration 134
  independence 3, 132
  and India 23, 48, 73, 81, 170, 174–5, 251*n*18
  National Security Council 46
  Official Language Act 12–13
  People's Alliance (PA) 38, 50, 51, 107, 108–9
  Prevention of Terrorism Act 117, 144
  provinces and devolution 14, *map2*
  religions 9
  Roman–Dutch law vii, 15–16
  rubber/rice pact with China 232–3, 235–6
  and SAARC 174–5, 177–8, 178–9
  Sirima–Shastri Pact 170, 250*n*2
  SLFP–JVP coalition government 21, 53, 107
  and Soviet intervention in Hungary 24
  and UN membership 23
  United People's Freedom Alliance (UPFA) 21
  and US 71, 77, 78, 210, 218, 233
  violence level 146–7
Sri Lanka conflict (1983–2009)
  allegations of failure to observe laws of war 30–34, 111
  armed forces *see* armed forces
  and arrested persons 117
  causes 14
  and civilians 30–33, 66, 116, 118–19, 146, 197
  final phase 29–34, 66
  four phases 29, 41, 45, 46
  Humanitarian Operation: Factual Analysis (Ministry of Defence) 31

  Indian Peace Keeping Force (IPKF) 23, 48, 64, 176
  and internally displaced persons 19, 116, 201
  and international community 29–30, 203, 218
  Jaffna 'Unceasing Waves' attack 48
  Kadirgamar on possible solution 14, 72
  Lessons Learnt and Reconciliation Commission (LLRC) 31–3, 194
  Liam Fox Agreement 51, 244*n*18
  LTTE defeat 194
  Navy (SLN) 195–6, 198–201
  and 'No Fire Zones' (NFZs) 30, 32
  'not a civil war' 29, 111
  Operation Riviresa 116, 246*n*8
  post-conflict analysis 31–3, 194
  Tamil Tigers *see* LTTE (Liberation Tigers of Tamil Eelam)
  UN *Report of … Panel of Experts on Accountability in Sri Lanka* 30–31
  war within a state 111, 118–19
  see also Ceasefire Agreement (CFA, 2002); LTTE (Liberation Tigers of Tamil Eelam)
Sri Lanka Freedom Party (SLFP)
  1994 election 43–4
  against Kadirgamar as prime minister 54
  background 243*n*4
  coalition partner 21, 53, 107
  foundation 17
  and Liam Fox Agreement 51, 244*n*18
Sri Lanka Monitoring Mission (SLMM) 50, 52, 193, 194, 196–7, 198, 199–201
states
  conflict within 6–7, 159–61
  post-colonial states 7, 10, 14, 159
  regional groupings 7
  sovereignty 7, 22–6, 158–61, 195–7, 203

Taiwan 232, 236
Tam Chau, Venerable Thich 95, 96, 105
Tamil diaspora
  in Canada 141–2
  fund-raising 64, 73, 127–8, 147, 161–2
  moderate and peaceful majority 138
  pressure group 46
  in UK 127, 132
  in US 142
  women's associations 134, 135
Tamil Nadu, India 48, 199

Index 263

Tamil National Alliance (TNA) 215, 252*n*3
Tamil Tigers *see* LTTE (Liberation Tigers of Tamil Eelam)
Tamils 11, 45, 73, 75
Temple of the Tooth attack 127, 146, 247*n*11
terrorism
 9/11 attacks 48, 49, 221
 and asylum seekers 128–9, 131, 134
 Berwick report 123–4, 129–31
 and Bin Laden 25
 biological and chemical 133
 definitions 66, 122–4, 140–41, 246–7*n*5
 and democracy 20–21, 72, 144–7
 and electronic communications 124, 127–8, 246–7*n*5
 and extradition 131–2
 fund-raising activities viii, 127, 128, 130, 131, 147–9, 161–3
 international attacks 125, 139, 219, 247*n*6–7
 Kadirgamar's security precautions 46, 49, 56–7, 72, 77
 laws *see* terrorism laws
 LTTE atrocities 27, 64, 65, 74, 127, 145–6
 media's role against 148–9
 need for international action 26–8, 67, 125, 147–9
 Potomac Institute 137–8
 and rule of law 67–8
 security precautions 144, 148–9
 and sovereignty 7
 in US 48, 49, 122, 221, 246*n*1–2
 war on terror 48, 67
 Western indifference criticized by Kadirgamar 27, 67, 121, 124–5, 138, 219
terrorism laws
 SAARC Regional Convention on Terrorism 140
 Sri Lanka Prevention of Terrorism Act 117, 144
 UK Prevention of Terrorism Act 121, 123, 130
 UK Terrorism Act (2000) 121, 139, 247*n*16
 UN Convention on Suppression of Financing for Terrorist Purposes (1999) 139, 162, 247–8*n*3
 UN Convention for Suppression of Terrorist Bombings (1997) 67, 70, 126–9, 139, 140–41

 UN Security Council Resolution 149
 US Anti-Terrorism Act (1996) 70, 74, 142
Thich Duc Nghiep, Venerable 100, 104–5
Thich Tam Chau, Venerable 95, 96, 105
Thich Thiem Khiet, Venerable 96
Thuc, Archbishop *see* Ngo Dinh Thuc, Archbishop
Tibet 22, 231
Tiruchelvam, Neelan 39–40
Ton-that Chuu 98
torture 7, 117, 246*n*10
Tran Quang Long 98–9
Tran Quang Thuan 97–8
Trinity College 14–15, 37, 59, 75
Truong Van Luong 98–9
tsunami 21, 55, 56, 84, 240*n*54
Tuong Van 95–6
Turkey, Kurdish Workers' Party (PKK) 142, 248*n*10

Ukraine, assistance to Sri Lanka 48
United Kingdom
 conspiracy law 129, 138
 development assistance for Sri Lanka 63–4
 and LTTE 49, 121, 129–34
 money laundering recommendation 131
 Prevention of Terrorism Act 121, 123, 130
 Tamil diaspora 127, 132
 Tamil women's associations 134, 135
 Terrorism Act (2000) 121, 139, 247*n*16
 terrorism law 27
United National Party (UNP) 42, 50, 51, 243*n*3, 244*n*18
United Nations
 and civil society 163–4
 Conventions 114, 139
  against Torture (1984) 117, 246*n*10
  Law of the Sea (1982) 200
  Optional Protocol on Children in Armed Conflict (2000) 151, 155, 166
  Rights of the Child (1989) 114, 155
  Suppression of Financing for Terrorist Purposes (1999) 139, 162, 247–8*n*3
  Suppression of Terrorist Bombings (1997) 67, 70, 126–9, 139, 140–41

United Nations (*continued*)
  Covenants
    Civil and Political Rights 113, 118
    Economic, Social and Cultural Rights 113
  General Assembly 163–4
  Human Rights Commission report on internally displaced persons 19, 116
  and intervention in internal domestic crises 160–61
  and Kadirgamar viii, 45, 61, 75, 157–67
  and LLRC report 33
  Millennium Summit 157–8, 160
  Report of ... Panel of Experts on Accountability in Sri Lanka 30–31
  Secretary-General post and Kadirgamar 52, 53
  Security Council Resolutions
    humanitarian war 25
    terrorism 149
  Special Representative for Children in Armed Conflict 150, 165–6
  and Sri Lanka 8, 23
  UNICEF 166
  Universal Declaration of Human Rights 112–13
  Vesak Resolution 10
  Vietnam delegation 99
United People's Freedom Alliance (UPFA) 21
United States
  9/11 attacks 48, 49, 221
  Anti-Terrorism Act (1996) 70, 74, 142
  and Bin Laden 25
  Chinese construction contracts 227
  Declaration of Independence 71
  and Iraq invasion 25, 220–21
  and Jaffna Library 78–9
  and Kadirgamar 78
  and LLRC report 33
  and LTTE 48–9, 70–71, 74, 139–40, 203
  officials and ambassadors 69
  and South Asia 187
  and Sri Lanka 71, 77, 78, 210, 218, 233
  Tamil diaspora 142
  terrorist bombings 122, 125
  and Vietnam 89
universities, distance learning programme 189

Vajpayee, Atal Bihari 180, 180–81, 182, 230
Van Dinh Hy, Madame 99
Vesak
  South Vietnam incident 89, 93–5
  UN Resolution 10
Vietnam 89, 90
  see also South Vietnam
vocational training, children 153

war on terror 48, 67
Wen Jiabao 229, 230
Wickramasinghe, Nira 11, 12, 13
Wickremesinghe, Ranil
  and Ceasefire Agreement (2002) 51, 59, 193, 195, 203
  and General Nambiar's report 204, 205
  Liam Fox Agreement 244n18
  and peace negotiations 64–6
  Prime Minister of cohabitation government 50–52
Wolff, Professor 97
women, and peace promotion 152
World Conference on Human Rights (1993) 113
World Intellectual Property Organization (WIPO) 18, 38, 225–7

Zheng (Cheng) Ho, Admiral 232, 253n16
Zhu Rongi 234
Zia, President of Bangladesh (Ziaur Rahman) 173, 174
Zia-ul-Haq, Mohammad, President of Pakistan 172, 176